Third Edition # The Iowa Precinct Caucuses: The Making of a Media Event

A BUR OAK BOOK

Third Edition

The Iowa Precinct Caucuses: The Making of a Media Event

Hugh Winebrenner and
Dennis J. Goldford

UNIVERSITY OF IOWA PRESS, IOWA CITY

University of Iowa Press, Iowa City 52242
First and second editions copyright
© 1998 by Iowa State University Press
Updated material for third edition copyright
© 2010 by the University of Iowa Press
www.uiowapress.org
Printed in the United States of America

Portions of this book were previously published as "The Iowa Precinct Caucuses: The Making of a Media Event" in the *Southeastern Political Review* 13 (1985): 99-132; used by permission of *Southeastern Political Review*. Portions of chapter 3 were published as "The Evolution of the Iowa Precinct Caucuses" in the *Annals of Iowa* 46 (Spring 1983): 618-35; used by permission, Iowa State Historical Department. Portions of chapter 7 were published as "Defending Iowa's First-in-the-Nation Status: The 1984 Precinct Caucuses" in the *Annals of Iowa* 48 (1986): 292-303; used by permission, Iowa State Historical Department.

The University of Iowa Press is a member of Green Press Initiative and is committed to preserving natural resources.

Printed on acid-free paper

Library of Congress Cataloging-in-Publication Data
Winebrenner, Hugh, 1937-
The Iowa precinct caucuses: the making of a media event / by Hugh Winebrenner and Dennis J. Goldford.—3rd ed.
p.   cm.—(Bur Oak Book)
Includes bibliographical references and index.
ISBN-13: 978-1-58729-915-5 (pbk.)
ISBN-10: 1-58729-915-1 (pbk.)
ISBN-13: 978-1-58729-954-4 (e-book)
ISBN-10: 1-58729-954-2 (e-book)
1. Presidents—United States—Nomination.   2. Caucus.   3. Mass media—Political aspects—United States.   4. Press and politics—United States.   5. Political parties—Iowa.   6. Iowa—Politics and government.
I. Goldford, Dennis J., 1948-   II. Title.
JK521.W55 2010
324.2777'0152—dc22   2010012548

For my wife and son,
Nancy and Jeffrey Winebrenner

For the women in my life—
Sharon Goldford, and Shannon and Laney Reider

Contents

Preface, ix

Acknowledgments, xi

List of Tables, xiii

1   The Media and American Politics: An Overview, 3

2   Iowa: A Political and Demographic Profile, 11

3   The Iowa Precinct Caucuses: The Decades of Obscurity, 25

4   The 1968 and 1972 Caucuses: The Emergence of a National Event, 35

5   The 1976 Caucuses: The Making of a Front-Runner, 57

6   The 1980 Caucuses: A Media Event Becomes an Institution, 81

7   The 1984 Caucuses: The Kickoff of a Front-Loaded Season, 109

8   The 1988 Caucuses: A Media Extravaganza, 135

9   The 1992 Caucuses: A Favorite Son Emerges, 185

10   The 1996 Caucuses: Back in the Limelight, 201

11   The 2000 Caucuses: More Important than Ever, 253

12   The 2004 Caucuses: Change and Continuity, 283

13   The 2008 Caucuses: From Iowa to the White House, 303

14   Media Event or Local Event? The Caucuses in Perspective, 337

Index, 345

Preface

PEOPLE IN OTHER PARTS of the country are occasionally confused as to Iowa's location on the map, but political reporters in the national press corps have no difficulty pinpointing the state. Although some waggish visitors still refer to Iowa as the state that is "overplowed and overcowed," political observers now recognize Iowa as a weather vane in presidential politics.

In fact, a political accident in the early 1970s propelled Iowa onto the front pages of the nation's newspapers and into the nation's living rooms via prime-time coverage on national news shows. Because Iowa Democrats needed some breathing space in their caucus and convention schedule, they pushed forward the precinct caucuses in 1972. As it turned out, the caucuses became the first presidential nominating event in the nation. Politicos both within and outside Iowa quickly realized the impact of this new status, and along with the national media, they promoted Iowa's caucuses with a vengeance.

This book chronicles the Iowa precinct caucuses—how they began, how they changed, and how they have been manipulated to become a national media event. The caucuses attained their significant position in the presidential electoral process despite the fact that strictly speaking they do not produce meaningful results. The nationally reported "results" are contrived by the Iowa parties to portray a desired picture of the process.

The Iowa precinct caucuses are local party functions that have been manipulated into the position of making or breaking presidential candidacies by the media, the political parties, and the presidential candidates themselves. Essentially, the caucuses have become a media event with an impact on presidential politics totally out of proportion to the reality of their purpose or procedural methods. Thomas E. Patterson and Michael J. Robinson in the 1970s and 1980s were at the forefront of researchers examining the impact of the media on the national electoral process—at the same time that Iowa was gaining national prominence due to its first-in-the-nation status in presidential politics. Drawing heavily on the ongoing relevance of their theories, this work uses Iowa as the premier case study to examine the role of the media in the American electoral process.

The book is divided into fourteen chapters. Chapters 1 through 3 provide historical and demographic information about Iowa, including an analysis of Iowa's political culture. Chapter 4 contrasts the local character of the 1968 caucuses with the 1972 caucuses, which focused a national spotlight on George McGovern as he began his quest for the Democratic presidential nomination. Chapter 5 analyzes how questionable "results" from the Democratic precinct caucuses in 1976 changed the political fortunes of Jimmy Carter from unknown to front-runner. Chapter 6 analyzes the 1980 precinct caucuses as a media event of grand proportions. Republican precinct data reveal that George Bush's emergence as a challenger to Ronald Reagan was based on media perceptions drawn from a preference poll that he may or may not have won. Chapter 7 analyzes the 1984 precinct caucuses and the numerous associated controversies. Chapter 8 examines the 1988 precinct caucuses as a media event that rivals New Hampshire for attention. Chapter 9 chronicles the 1992 precinct caucuses and the absence of national attention due to the favorite son candidacy of Iowa Senator Tom Harkin. Chapter 10 analyzes the 1996 precinct caucuses, their return to national status, and their impact on the presidential nominating race. Chapter 11 details the 2000 caucuses, whose winner, George W. Bush, was the first to reach the White House since Jimmy Carter. Chapter 12 examines the role of the 2004 caucuses in the roller-coaster fortunes of the Howard Dean and John Kerry campaigns. Chapter 13 analyzes the role of the caucuses in sorting out the crowded field in each party and the emergence of the Obama candidacy. Finally, after caucus winners in both 2000 and 2008 successfully reached the White House, Chapter 14 attempts to place the caucuses in some perspective.

In this book, then, we argue that the reporting of the Iowa caucus results is part of the game focus of presidential campaigns. Essentially meaningless caucus outcomes are reported to satisfy the media's needs for "hard data" about the progress of the presidential race, outcomes that have taken on a reality, however manufactured, of their own.

Dr. Goldford is a welcome addition as co-author of the third edition of this book. References to "the author" in chapter 1 and chapters 3 through 10, however, refer only to Hugh Winebrenner.

Acknowledgments

We would like to thank Emeritus Professor Emmett Buell, Jr., of Denison University, who critiqued the new material prepared for the third edition. Any errors that remain are, of course, our own. We also wish to thank the Drake University Center for the Humanities for research support.

List of Tables

4.1   1972 Democratic precinct caucus results

4.2   1972 Democratic county convention results

4.3   1972 Democratic national delegate equivalents compared with national convention delegates

5.1   1975 Jefferson-Jackson Day poll results

5.2   1976 Democratic precaucus campaign activity

5.3   1976 Democratic precinct caucus results

5.4   1976 Democratic precinct caucus results, observing the 15 percent rule

6.1   1980 Candidate precaucus expenditures in Iowa

6.2   1976 and 1980 CBS news stories on Iowa and New Hampshire

6.3   1980 Republican caucus straw-poll results

6.4   1980 Democratic precinct caucus results

7.1   1983 Jefferson-Jackson Day poll results

7.2   1984 candidate precaucus campaign activity and spending

7.3   1980 and 1984 CBS news stories on Iowa and New Hampshire

7.4   1984 Democratic precinct caucus results

8.1   1988 Democratic spending at WHO-TV and KCCI-TV

8.2   1988 *Des Moines Register* Democratic Iowa Polls

8.3   1988 Republican "Cavalcade of Stars" straw-poll results

8.4   1988 Republican spending at WHO-TV and KCCI-TV

8.5   1988 *Des Moines Register* Republican Iowa Polls

8.6   1988 Candidate precaucus campaign activity and spending

8.7   CBS news stories on Iowa and New Hampshire, 1975-76 through 1987-88

8.8   1988 Democratic precinct caucus results

8.9   1988 Republican caucus straw-poll results

8.10   1988 Republican caucus straw-poll results by county

8.11   1988 Network coverage before and after Iowa by number of minutes on evening network news Monday through Friday

9.1   1992 Democratic precinct caucus results

10.1   "Caucus Kickoff '96" straw-poll results

10.2   1996 Republican spending at WHO-TV and KCCI-TV

10.3   1996 *Des Moines Register* Iowa Polls

10.4   1996 Democratic National Committee spending for President
Clinton at WHO-TV and KCCI-TV

10.5   1996 Republican precaucus campaign activity and spending

10.6   CBS news stories on Iowa and New Hampshire, 1975-76
through 1995-96

10.7   1996 Republican caucus straw-poll results

10.8   1996 Republican caucus straw-poll results by county

11.1   1999 Iowa straw poll

11.2   2000 Republican spending at WHO-TV and KCCI-TV

11.3   1999-2000 *Des Moines Register* Republican Iowa Polls

11.4   2000 Republican precinct caucus results

11.5   2000 Democratic spending at WHO-TV and KCCI-TV

11.6   1999-2000 *Des Moines Register* Democratic Iowa Polls

11.7   2000 Precaucus days in Iowa

11.8   2000 Democratic precinct caucus results

12.1   2003 National fund raising

12.2   2004 Democratic spending at WHO-TV and KCCI-TV

12.3   2004 Television ads in the Des Moines viewing area

12.4   2004 Precaucus days in Iowa

12.5   2003-04 *Des Moines Register* Democratic Iowa Polls

12.6   2004 Democratic precinct caucus results

13.1   2007 Iowa straw poll

13.2   2007 *Des Moines Register* Republican Iowa Polls

13.3   2007 *Des Moines Register* Democratic Iowa Polls

13.4   2008 Democratic and Republican spending at KCCI-TV and
WHO-TV

13.5   2008 Precaucus days in Iowa

13.6   2008 Republican precinct caucus results

13.7   2008 Democratic precinct caucus results

Third Edition **The Iowa Precinct Caucuses:**
The Making of a Media Event

Chapter 1 The Media and American Politics: An Overview

BEFORE THE 1970s, studies of elections and voting behavior by political scientists paid relatively little attention to the role of the media in elections in the United States. The landmark study of electoral behavior, *The American Voter* (1960), devoted few pages to the mass media or their impact on election outcomes. Most of the early studies concluded that the media's effects were not of primary importance and focused on party loyalty and attitudes about the issues to explain electoral choice (Patterson 1980, vii).

The growth of television news coverage in the 1960s and increased media interest in the presidential nominating process, particularly in direct primary elections, stimulated research on the role of the media in electoral politics. Although Florida established the direct primary for the selection of national convention delegates in 1904, followed closely by Wisconsin in 1905 (Ranney 1977, 4), the presidential nominating process was dominated by party leaders until recently. The existence of a relatively short primary campaign in less than half of the states did not promote the democratic nature of the process to the extent that early-twentieth-century progressives had hoped. Rather, party leaders, although periodically inconvenienced by primary elections, continued to dominate the nomination of presidential candidates through the caucus and convention system utilized in most states (Crotty and Jackson 1985, 13-18).

In the 1960s the direct primary assumed a more prominent role in the nomination of presidential candidates and began to pose a challenge to the control exercised by party leaders through the caucus and convention system. Several factors contributed to the democratization of the nominating process. Presidential candidates, particularly those who lacked the support of party chieftains in important states, increasingly attempted to demonstrate their voter appeal in primary elections. Although early attempts by Harold Stassen in 1948 and Estes Kefauver in 1952 to gain their parties' nomination via primary elections proved unsuccessful, the increased emphasis on the primaries by presidential candidates contributed to their becoming the dominant component of the nominating process. It was not long before presidential candidates had first to demonstrate their voter appeal in primary elections (Davis 1967, 3-5).

The growth of media coverage, particularly television, was largely responsible for turning presidential primaries into a uniquely American political Olympic contest. Although common now, comprehensive television coverage of the presidential primaries dates only to the 1960s. Television provides a viable, cost-effective alternative to the face-to-face contact between candidates and voters previously considered so important in American political campaigns. Moreover, by providing presidential hopefuls with a means of bypassing the party leadership and appealing directly to ordinary citizens, television focused the nominating process on the candidates themselves rather than on the activities of political party leaders (Davis 1967, 5-9). Austin Ranney concludes that "the advent of television as the principal source of political reality for most Americans has altered the political game profoundly, perhaps more profoundly than all the parties' rules changes and new state and federal laws put together." Furthermore, "it has had an enormous impact on the kinds of persons who become successful politicians and on how they conduct their business" (Ranney 1983, 89).

An additional democratizing factor in the presidential nominating process was the series of party rules changes undertaken by the national Democratic party beginning in 1968 and continuing into the 1980s (Crotty and Jackson 1985, chap. 2). The new rules were designed to increase the impact of citizen participation and to limit the role of party leaders at all levels of the delegate selection process.

The new party rules succeeded in further diminishing the role of party leaders and centering attention on the primary elections. During the period from 1968 to 1980 the presidential primary was very much in vogue, and the number of states selecting national convention delegates by primary elections grew dramatically. (Democratic party primaries increased in number from seventeen to thirty-five and selected 72 percent of the 1980 convention delegates. Republican primaries grew in number from sixteen to thirty-four and selected 76 percent of the 1980 convention delegates [Crotty and Jackson 1985, 63].)

But not everyone viewed the primary movement as a positive development. By 1980 party leaders and elected officials were being excluded in increasing numbers from the national conventions, which now did little more than ratify the results of the primary elections. Dissatisfaction increased to the point that by 1984 the primary election trend had been reversed; only twenty-five states held binding Democratic primaries, compared with thirty-five in 1980, and only thirty conducted Republican presidential primaries, a loss of four states (Crotty and Jackson 1985, 63). According to the *National Journal,* party officials had become increasingly "concerned that the proliferation of primaries was largely responsible for the prolonged, costly, divisive, and media-dominated campaigns and that they further served to undermine organized party control" (1983, 2215). The renewed interest in the caucus and convention system, however, may represent a final effort on the part of state party organizations to save themselves from extinction.

Media-dominated, candidate-centered presidential campaigns have stimulated research into the role of the media in political campaigns. Most studies have concentrated on presidential campaigns, and their areas of research include the media's emphasis on a candidate's "image" (Nimmo and Savage 1976), the media as kingmakers (Graber 1980; Paletz and Entman 1981; Patterson 1980; Ranney 1983), and media influence on the campaign strategies of candidates (Arterton 1984; Barber 1978; Robinson and Sheehan 1983).

Recent studies indicate that the media have replaced political parties as the "main link between presidential candidates and the overwhelming majority of the public" (Paletz and Entman 1981, 32). As a consequence, political parties have become less significant in electoral politics. The modern presidential race is a media campaign, "and campaign managers believe, almost uniformly, that their most efficient means of persuasive communication is these pre-established communications media" (Arterton 1984, 1).

Citizens may be passive consumers of electoral politics and may pay little attention to political parties, but with their televisions playing six to seven hours a day, it is very difficult for average citizens to ignore presidential campaigns. The broadcast media in particular give Americans the opportunity to assess the presidential hopefuls personally, even though they may simply be evaluating their Madison Avenue images. Furthermore, the media seem to have altered the two-step flow of political information, in which information and opinions are transmitted first from elites to attentive publics and from them to citizen voters (Katz and Lazarsfeld 1955). Today the media seem to have assumed the role formerly played by political parties, and the political "reality" consists of the information transmitted from elites to the public by way of the news media.

Research also indicates that the news media play a major role in agenda setting in American electoral politics by determining which candidates the public should take seriously (Robinson and Sheehan 1983, 262-72). Presidential candidates that media correspondents perceive to be viable, serious contenders are portrayed as such and receive extensive coverage. Those whose candidacies are judged to be frivolous or unlikely to succeed find it difficult to gain coverage. The task for presidential hopefuls becomes one of persuading reporters that their candidacies should be taken seriously and covered regularly. Since the 1970s they have often accomplished this by exceeding the media's expectations in polls, primary elections, and caucuses.

The news media, and television in particular, influence the form as well as the content of electoral politics. As a visual medium, television tends to emphasize candidates or, more specifically, images of candidates that they either create or help to develop (Robinson and Sheehan 1983, 269-70). Both Gerald Ford's clumsiness, although he had a strong athletic background, and John F. Kennedy's vigor, although he suffered from back problems that limited his physical activity, are images created and nurtured by the media. In the modern presidential race, style is substance, and since most potential voters cannot experience political campaigns directly, they rely on the media to delimit and interpret the substance of campaigns.

The news media have become increasingly important in American electoral politics in the last thirty years. They have enormous impact on both the content and the form of political campaigns, influencing who chooses to run for the presidency and how they conduct their campaigns. Style and image have become the substance of politics as the broadcast and print media have replaced political parties as the principal linkage between presidential hopefuls and the voters.

This book will examine the media's impact on the Iowa precinct caucuses and the significant role the caucuses have assumed in the presidential nominating process. By highlighting the Iowa caucuses as the first nominating event in the presidential race, the news media have centered national attention on the caucuses and have profoundly affected the process itself. With the enthusiastic cooperation of the officials of the Iowa Democratic and Republican parties, the media have influenced when and how the Iowa caucuses have conducted their business and, in the process, have created a media event. In an article on the media's impact on the presidential nominating process, Michael Robinson coined the term *mediality* to describe "events, developments, or situations to which the media have given importance by emphasizing, expanding, or featuring them in such a way that their real significance has been modified, distorted, or obscured" (Robinson 1981, 191).

The Iowa precinct caucuses provide a dramatic example of media events, or medialities in Robinson's terminology. The media have obscured the basic local functions of the caucuses—selecting delegates to county conventions, generating issues for party platforms, and providing the grass-roots party connections to the citizens—by attributing a meaning to caucuses that does not exist. The media's tendency to interpret Iowa caucus "results" as "hard news" about the progress of the presidential campaign is at best questionable. At worst, media exploitation of the Iowa caucus process (1) disrupts the normal functioning of the local political process, (2) may give a false image of the national political appeal of the candidates involved, and (3) subjects the national electoral process to the influence of a contrived event.

Thomas Patterson provides an interesting explanation of the media's motivation in emphasizing events like the Iowa caucuses. His systematic analysis of the 1976 presidential election suggests that media distortion of the Iowa caucuses stems from a structural bias in the way presidential elections are covered. Patterson's content analysis of news reports of the presidential nominating process provides clear evidence of the media's tendency to exaggerate the "game" aspects of the campaign (Patterson 1980, 22-24). Since media interest centers

Cartoon by Brian Duffy, © 1983, *Des Moines Register*, reprinted by permission

The larger states are unhappy that Iowa and New Hampshire have emerged as kingmakers in the presidential nominating process. Although many states have moved their primary events closer to the beginning of the nominating season, Iowa and New Hampshire continue to deliver knockout blows in the bout for the presidency.

around who is winning and who is losing the game, the candidates' strategies and tactics are emphasized at the expense of the substance of the campaigns: the public problems, the policy debates, and the candidates' leadership qualities. Patterson forcefully argues that the bias in selecting "newsworthy" events has more to do with the interests of the media—conflict, drama, measurable outcomes—than the reality of the campaign. He demonstrates that media bias influences the public's image of presidential campaigns and perhaps their voting behavior.

The reporting of Iowa caucus results is a part of the game focus of presidential campaigns: essentially meaningless caucus outcomes are reported to satisfy the media's need for results or hard news. Further, the media not only report the outcome of the primary games, they also interpret the outcomes for the American public in terms of the expectations that the media themselves often had helped to create (Patterson 1980, 43-48). Much like the handicapper in a horse race, the media assign metaphorical labels—such as favorite, front-runner, long shot, or dark horse—to the presidential candidates and then evaluate their performance in caucuses and primary elections according to the expectations created by the labels. Meeting or exceeding media expectations is crucial to the campaigns of presidential candidates. Since 1972 Iowa has been the first major event in the presidential nominating game, and media expectations and interpretations of caucus outcomes have made Iowa a very important component of the game.

This case study will focus on changes in the Iowa precinct caucuses since 1972 that have been associated with their becoming a media event and will examine the caucuses as part of the presidential nominating game. It will explore the profound impact of the mass media both on the Iowa precinct caucuses and on the presidential nominating system generally. As such, this study is a special case of the broader public problem of setting the public agenda through media initiatives, in this instance the agenda for the presidential nominating process. It is argued that since the media choose to emphasize the outcomes of early nominating events, Iowa plays a major role in setting the presidential nominating agenda, perhaps to the disadvantage of the country.

References

Arterton, F. Christopher. 1984. *Media Politics: The News Strategies of Presidential Campaigns.* Lexington, Mass.: Lexington Books.

Barber, James D., ed. 1978. *Race for the Presidency: The Media and the Nominating Process.* Englewood Cliffs, N.J.: Prentice-Hall.

Campbell, Angus, Philip E. Converse, Warren E. Miller, and Donald E. Stokes. 1960. *The American Voter.* New York: John Wiley and Sons.

Crotty, William. 1984. *American Parties in Decline.* 2d ed. Boston: Little, Brown.

Crotty, William, and John S. Jackson III. 1985. *Presidential Primaries and Nominations.* Washington, D.C.: CQ Press.

Davis, James W. 1967. *Presidential Primaries: Road to the White House.* New York: Thomas Y. Crowell.

Graber, Doris A. 1980. *Mass Media and American Politics.* Washington, D.C.: CQ Press.

Katz, Elihu, and Paul F. Lazarsfeld. 1955. *Personal Influence: The Part Played by People in the Flow of Mass Communications.* New York: Free Press.

National Journal. 1983. *Election '84 Handbook: A Guide to the Candidates, the Issues, and the Voters.* Washington, D.C.: Government Research Corp.

Nimmo, Dan, and Robert L. Savage. 1976. *Candidates and Their Images: Concepts, Methods, and Findings.* Pacific Palisades, Calif.: Goodyear.

Paletz, David L., and Robert M. Entman. 1981. *Media, Power, Politics.* New York: Free Press.

Patterson, Thomas E. 1980. *The Mass Media Election: How Americans Choose Their President.* New York: Praeger.

Ranney, Austin. 1977. *Participation in American Presidential Nominations, 1976.* Washington, D.C.: American Enterprise Institute.

———. 1983. *Channels of Power: The Impact of Television on American Politics.* New York: Basic Books.

Robinson, Michael J. 1981. "The Media in 1980: Was the Message the Message?" In *The American Elections of 1980,* edited by Austin Ranney, 177-211. Washington, D.C.: American Enterprise Institute.

Robinson, Michael J., and Margaret A. Sheehan. 1983. *Over the Wire and on TV: CBS and UPI in Campaign '80.* New York: Russell Sage Foundation.

Wattenberg, Martin P. 1984. *The Decline of American Political Parties, 1952-1980.* Cambridge, Mass.: Harvard University Press.

Chapter 2   Iowa: A Political and Demographic Profile

IS IOWA A GOOD PLACE to start the presidential campaign? Is it a representative state? Party officials in Iowa—and some local and national writers—have asserted that Iowa is a good place to begin the presidential campaign because it is a two-party state whose politics are competitive, clean, and open. Moreover, Iowans are hardworking and fair and take their duties as citizens very seriously. Finally, the state is small enough that less well known and less well financed presidential hopefuls have a chance, through hard work and good organization, to establish themselves as viable candidates. This "legend of Iowa" has gained credibility in many circles even though it developed after the fact; that is, as an attempt to rationalize the role Iowa has assumed in presidential politics.

This chapter examines the political and demographic characteristics of Iowa and shows that although its politics are clean and competitive, Iowa caucus participants are not typical of the national electorate demographically or ideologically. The small-town, agrarian nature of the state and the nature of caucus participants work to the advantage of some candidates and to the disadvantage of others.

In 1968 political scientist Samuel C. Patterson characterized the dominant political style of Iowa as "highly pragmatic, non-programmatic, cautious and moderate" (202). In a later work, Patterson states that Iowa is characterized by its "middleness" (1984, 83). Historian Dorothy Schwieder, who titled her history of the state *Iowa: The Middle Land*, finds in Iowans "a sense of centeredness that connotes balance in both perspective and behavior" (1996, xi). Iowa is located in the geographic middle or center of the nation, and its people are politically, economically, and socially moderate. Unlike its northern neighbors, Wisconsin and Minnesota, Iowa has seldom been in the vanguard of progressive change, but neither has it lagged far behind

Cartoon by Brian Duffy, © 1984, *Des Moines Register*, reprinted by permission

There are certain rituals that all presidential candidates follow in their early campaign visits to Iowa. They spend time with officials of the state parties in Des Moines, and they visit the state capitol, where they often speak to a party caucus of the house of representatives or senate. Perhaps most popular of the Iowa rituals is a visit to a farm, where the candidate is photographed—in new coveralls, boots, and a cap from one of the seed companies—intently gazing into a hog pen.

other states. Within Iowa, particularly in rural areas, politics can be very conservative, but that is balanced by the moderate, and occasionally liberal, politics of urban areas, which include a majority of the state's population.

But how did Iowa politics come to be "highly pragmatic, non-programmatic, cautious and moderate"? Political institutions do not spring full-blown from the minds of philosophers, nor are patterns of political behavior explainable solely on the basis of their internal characteristics. Rather, they are products of the total environment of a society and can be fully understood only in terms of other patterns of rational behavior.

Political culture is that set of learned values, beliefs, and expectations that orient people to the political systems of which they are members. It has its roots in the cumulative historical experience of particular groups. Since values, beliefs, and expectations are learned, political culture is consciously or unconsciously passed on from generation to generation. The political culture influences political practice in a number of ways. It shapes citizens' perceptions and expectations of politics, defines which activities may legitimately be undertaken by government, helps determine the kinds of people who are active in government and politics, and shapes the practices of government. It is, in other words, the conscience and ethics of a political system and its actors (Elazar 1984, 112).

In his book on American federalism, Daniel Elazar examines the impact of political culture in shaping the political structures, functions, and behavior of American states. He classifies Iowa's political culture as "moralistic-individualistic"; that is, the moralistic culture dominates, but there is also a strong individualistic strain (Elazar 1984, 136).

Iowa's Political Culture

To understand the political culture of Iowa, we must first examine Iowans' attitudes toward their state, government, and some issues of the day. Although systematic data are limited, there is sufficient evidence to put forth some generalizations.

Poll data indicate that Iowans consider themselves very patriotic. Responding to the question "How patriotic do you consider yourself—very patriotic, somewhat patriotic, or not patriotic at all?" over

half of the voting-age population (55 percent) said they are very patriotic, 40 percent said they are somewhat patriotic, and only 4 percent
indicated they are not at all patriotic (Iowa Poll: 1996, poll no. 339).
This finding is consistent with earlier Iowa Polls that included the
question about patriotism.

Iowans favor the pro-choice over the pro-life position on the controversial abortion issue (47 percent to 43 percent) (Nov. 2000 Iowa
Poll cited in Beaumont 2005). They oppose same-sex marriages, but
support civil unions for same-sex couples (Feb. 2008 Iowa Poll cited
in Claymore 2008). They favor reinstatement of the death penalty
(Apr. 2005 Iowa Poll cited in Beaumont 2005) and oppose teaching
about homosexuality in the classroom (Iowa Poll: 1995, poll no. 333).
And 76 percent support voluntary prayer in public schools (Iowa Poll:
1995, poll no. 333).

The people of Iowa have positive feelings about their state. They
are particularly proud of the beauty and the bounty of the land. The
rich soil enables Iowa to be a leading producer of corn, soybeans, and
livestock. A commitment to the land, particularly to the family farm,
and to small towns and local financial institutions, and a distrust and
fear of "big cities" (Des Moines and Cedar Rapids, with populations
of over 100,000, are viewed as big cities) are deeply ingrained in the
psyche of Iowans (Iowa Poll: 1986, poll no. 272). A recent Iowa Poll
found that 44 percent of Iowans believe that "in general . . . things
are going in the right direction" in the state, compared with a 20
percent approval rating for the condition of "things in the country
overall" (Feb. 2008 Iowa Poll provided by Iowa Poll staff, Sept. 5,
2008). The percentages are much lower than in previous Iowa Polls,
and undoubtedly reflect the economic and international problems at
the time of the 2008 election.

Patterson has observed that Iowans "have a tendency to be rather
deprecating of their state" (1984, 85). Certainly, many Iowans find it
frustrating that people in the eastern part of the country have difficulty distinguishing among Ohio, Iowa, and Idaho. There is additional
frustration about the stereotyping of Iowa's weather as intemperate
and its people as unsophisticated. The tendency of the eastern press
to portray farms, hogs, and people in bib overalls in their caucus stories probably adds to the homespun image of Iowa and its people. On
the other hand, it would be difficult to demonstrate that Iowans are

more self-deprecating than the citizens of other states.

The positive feelings of Iowa citizens toward their state do not necessarily translate into strong support for the activities and personnel of government. The Iowa political culture fosters the idea of limited government. Private, nongovernment activity is preferred, and government activities and politicians are viewed with some suspicion. Perhaps because they are suspicious of politicians and government activity in general, Iowans have long supported a merit-based state civil service rather than a system of appointments based on political patronage.

The major focus of the Iowa General Assembly at the time of the first edition of this book in 1986 was the reorganization and "downsizing" of state government, which politicians and citizens alike perceived as having grown too large. The general assembly overwhelmingly approved the reorganization plan, which reduced the size of state government, gave the governor more direct control of the executive branch, and reduced government expenses. Almost three times as many Iowans supported as opposed former Governor Terry Branstad's proposal to reorganize state government (49 percent to 18 percent, with 33 percent undecided) (Iowa Poll: 1986, poll no. 272). Interestingly, all of Iowa's 99 counties survived even as the population of many declined dramatically.

At the time of the second edition of this book in 1996 the focus of the general assembly was taxes. Iowa's economy had greatly improved. The general fund had gone from a negative balance of $409 million in fiscal year 1992 to an estimated positive balance of $823 million in 1997. With cash and emergency funds fully funded and a large general fund balance, legislators were in a tax-cutting mood. There was near unanimity on the need to reduce taxes, but Democrats and Republicans disagreed on which taxes to cut and how much to reduce them. With a Republican governor and a GOP majority in both houses of the general assembly, a uniform 10 percent income tax cut and reductions in residential property and inheritance taxes carried the day.

When the Democrats gained control in 2007, education became the focus of the 82nd general assembly. Teacher quality and salaries moved to center stage as the Democrats wrestled with the complex questions associated with accountability and the development of statewide standards to measure student progress. A second major on-going issue is the development of affordable health care for all children in the state and how to fund the expensive endeavor.

Government activity tends to be limited to areas that cannot be undertaken conveniently by private-sector institutions or individual citizens themselves. Beyond the area of public education (which received 59 percent of the appropriations from the general fund in the 2007 fiscal year) and the construction and maintenance of roads and highways, there is little consensus among Iowans as to what properly constitutes a public issue. In recent years the acceptance of the Great Society social welfare programs has declined to 23 percent of the 2007 general fund appropriations. The work ethic and individual self-reliance are still firmly entrenched in the Iowa political culture.

Public service is viewed as the duty of citizens, and this results in part-time, or citizen, politics. Those who serve in elected or appointed political positions generally receive little or no remuneration for their public service. Members of state boards and commissions, city councils, and local boards and commissions, as well as most mayors, are amateur officials who donate their time to the public. Members of the state legislature are also part-time (2009 legislative salaries were $25,000 plus travel and per diem allowances), and most depend on other jobs or professions for some of their income. There continues to be a very strong bias against political office as a full-time endeavor, which in Iowa is seen as synonymous with big government and a loss of citizen control.

Those who pursue public service are expected to serve honestly and in the public interest. In 1992, after a lobbying incident, the general assembly tightened its already strict rules regarding gifts to legislators. The earlier law required lobbyists, legislators, and their employees to report gifts or expenditures in excess of fifteen dollars and prohibited gifts of fifty dollars or more. The new law prohibited gifts in excess of three dollars (Ia. Gen. Assem. 1992, chap. 1228, p. 507).

The political culture, which emphasizes issues and public concerns rather than individual loyalties and partisan friendships, has also influenced the nature of political competition in Iowa. Nonpartisan elections are common at the local government level, and although political parties are well developed in the state, they tend not to be valued for their own sake. Iowans have demonstrated a strong propensity for political independence; at the time of the 2008 caucuses, 38.6 percent of those registered to vote claimed no party identification. Split-ticket voting is widespread, and Iowa has a history of volatility in its support for Republicans and Democrats in elections. Examples are numerous. In 1986 Charles Grassley was the first senator from Iowa to be reelected in twenty years, and in 1990 Tom Harkin was the first Democratic senator to be reelected in over forty years. In 2004 Iowans reelected Senator Grassley and supported President Bush, after four consecutive elections in which the Democratic presidential candidate had carried the state. In 2006 Iowans elected Democrats in three of its five congressional districts after Republicans had controlled at least four of the districts for fourteen consecutive years. Democrats gained control of both houses of the general assembly for the first time since 1996.

At present Iowa has only two major parties, although several minor parties—including the Anti-Monopoly, Greenback, Populist, and Prohibition parties, and recently the Constitution, Green, Libertarian, Reform, and Socialist Workers parties—have qualified as political parties (Ross 1957, 28-29; Iowa Secretary of State, 2009). Neither the existence of minor parties, however, nor the current trend toward nonpartisan elections, large numbers of independent voters, split-ticket voting, and electoral volatility belies the fact that the political party system in Iowa has grown stronger and increasingly competitive in recent years. This fact is largely attributable to increased urbanization and perhaps the increased influence of individualistic elements in the political culture.

Both major parties are organized hierarchically from the local to the state level. To conduct party business, they use a caucus and convention system that does not differ greatly from that found in other states. The local caucuses elect delegates to county conventions, which in turn elect delegates to district and state conventions, where the delegates to the national conventions are selected. Typically, it is the party activists who are the glue that binds this system together, serving as unpaid officials at each level of activity. But in recent presidential campaigns, the publicity associated with the precinct caucuses has drawn many political amateurs into the process.

The system relies on volunteer assistance at all levels, but at the state level in Des Moines, each party has a well-developed organization with a party headquarters and a paid professional staff. The state party organizations play a significant role in fund-raising, the identification and registration of party supporters, the recruitment of candidates, and a variety of campaign activities in election years.

Students of state politics have shown a great interest in two-party competition, which is highly valued in the United States. Although there is disagreement about the impact of inter-party competition on the policy process, and the democratic process itself, Murray S. Stedman, Jr., maintains that "most political scientists who study party systems remain convinced that inter-party competition strongly affects the organization and activities of the parties" (1976, 75). Since the New Deal party realignment of the 1930s, there have been significant changes in the competitive patterns of state party systems, and by the 1990s "a clear majority of the states meet the test of competitiveness" under Austin Ranney's system of classification (Bibby 1996, 54).

Iowa, once classified as "modified one-party Republican" (Ranney 1965, 65), had by the 1990s become a "two-party" state (Bibby 1996, 55). That represents a dramatic change from the earlier Republican dominance in Iowa. During the 82 terms of the general assembly from 1846 through 2008, Republicans controlled the senate 62 times and the house 68, but party politics in Iowa became more competitive in the 1960s, and Democrats were the dominant legislative party in the 1980s and the early 1990s. They controlled the senate for 14 consecutive years until the GOP recaptured the chamber in the 1996 election and maintained a majority in the house for ten consecutive years before losing control to the Republicans in the 1992 election. Republicans dominated in gubernatorial races and controlled the office for 30 years (1968-98). Governor Terry Branstad declared in 1994 that if reelected to a fourth term, he would not run again in 1998. The very popular Robert Ray, who won the support of many Democrats, was governor for 14 years before Branstad. Democrat Tom Vilsack broke the Republican string in 1998, serving two terms, and was succeeded by Democrat Chet Culver in 2006 (Stork and Clingan 1980, 5-8; *Iowa Official Register* 1985-86 through 2007-08). Increased urbanization and industrialization have brought more blue-collar employees into the workforce, and when combined with traditional religious and ethnic bases, they probably account for much of the growth in Democratic strength in Iowa. (Until 1994, Democrats enjoyed a slight registration advantage in every election since statewide registration was started in 1975; then, Republican registrants exceeded Democrats until 2006. At the time of the 2008 caucuses, 31.5 percent were listed as Democrats, 29.9 percent as Republicans, and 38.6 percent as "no party.")

In the 1990s the political mood of Iowa again tilted toward the Republican party. The GOP controlled both houses of the state legislature until the election of 2006 (the Senate was deadlocked at 25 each during the 2005-06 general assembly) when Democrats captured both houses, the governors office, and three of the five seats in the U.S. House of Representatives. Margins were slim in many races, and it appears that Iowa will continue to be a competitive two-party state in the twenty-first century.

Citizen participation (as demonstrated by voter turnout) is associated with political culture (Elazar 1984, 152). Iowans apparently do have a great deal of faith in the efficacy of electoral politics. In 2008, 98.6 percent of the voting-age population was registered to vote, compared with 74.2 percent nationwide (Center for the Study of the American Electorate [CSAE]). Iowa consistently ranks in the top 10 states (7th in 2008) in terms of the percentage of the voting-age population casting votes in presidential elections. In 2008, 69.8 percent of those eligible voted in the presidential election, compared with 63 percent nationally; in 2004 the Iowa and national figures were 69.3 and 60.6 percent; in 2000 they were 61.3 and 54.2 percent (CSAE).

The high levels of voter registration and participation in presidential elections are evidence that Iowans have strong feelings of citizen duty. In indexes of citizen participation, Iowa consistently ranks high among the fifty states, which is further evidence of the strong moralistic influence in the state's political culture.

Iowa's Demographics

A major determinant of political culture is the demographic composition of the population. After growing steadily but undramatically from 1910 to 1980, the population of Iowa declined in the 1980s. There was modest growth in the 1990s, and the 2000 Bureau of the Census figure of 2,926,324 for the Iowa population represents a modest increase from the 1980 figure of 2,913,808 (the 2008 population estimate is 3,002,550). Iowa has declined from the twentieth most

populous state in 1940 to thirtieth in 2000 and will likely lose a congressional seat after the 2010 census (except where noted otherwise,
demographic data are from the United States Bureau of the Census as
organized by the State Data Center of Iowa).

Census data also indicate a continuation of the trend toward urbanization in Iowa, with 61.1 percent of the people residing in urban
areas and 38.9 percent in rural areas. The urban population of Iowa
exceeded the rural population for the first time in 1960. The Census
Bureau definition of an urban area (a population of at least 2500)
is very liberal, however, and Iowa is a state of small communities:
only 467 of the 948 municipalities had populations of more than 500
people in 2000, only 20 had more than 25,000 people, and only 2 had
more than 100,000, including Des Moines, the state's largest city, with
fewer than 200,000 residents (*Iowa Official Register* 2007-08, 305-13).

The Iowa population is becoming increasingly homogenized as national origins grow less distinct. About half of Iowans claimed multiple ancestry or did not specify ancestry in the 2000 census. Still, many
groups in Iowa identify with and retain Old World customs—the Germans in the Amana colonies, the Dutch in Pella and Orange City, the
Czechs in Cedar Rapids, the Norwegians in Decorah, and several small
Amish enclaves are examples. Germans represent the largest ancestral
group, followed by those with an Irish or English background.

The population of Iowa is 93.9 percent white. Blacks constitute only
2.4 percent of the state's population, and two-thirds of Iowa's black
residents live in Des Moines, Waterloo, and Davenport, leaving many
areas of the state with few or no black residents. Hispanics became the
largest racial or ethnic minority group in the state in the early 2000s.

Iowa also has other distinctive demographic characteristics. About
four-fifths of Iowa's population (81 percent) claim to be Christian,
compared with 78 percent of the national population. The Jewish
population is small (less than 1 percent) compared with the national
population (1.7 percent) (Pew Forum on Religion). Roman Catholics,
Lutherans, and Methodists make up the three largest denominations
found in the state, with Methodists strong in most of Iowa's ninety-
nine counties. Women outnumbered men for the first time in Iowa
in the 1950 census (Ross 1957, 6-7) and now represent 50.7 percent
of the population, which is close to the national figure. Finally, Iowa
has an aging population. Young people leaving the state have con-

tributed to a disproportionately large number of citizens aged 65 and over (14.7 percent in Iowa, compared with 12.4 percent nationwide). Iowa's percentage of citizens over 65 was fourth highest among the states in 2005.

The Representativeness of Iowa

The conventional political wisdom portrays Iowans, and particularly Iowa Democrats, as more liberal than partisans in other states. Some national Democrats, including an early critic, former party chair Ron Brown (see Chapter 9), believed that the Iowa caucuses led to the nomination of candidates who are too liberal to win in the general election. As noted in Chapter 8, that was one of the arguments used by those who supported the creation of Super Tuesday.

There is little disagreement that demographically Iowa is representative only of itself and perhaps a few other prairie states. Its small-town nature, small minority population, dependence on agriculture and agribusiness, relatively low crime rates, and above-average literacy rate give Iowa a unique character. Research by political scientists Walter Stone, Alan Abramowitz, and Ronald Rapoport, who have done comparative studies of caucus participants (1989), and by political scientist William G. Mayer, who has examined caucuses as part of the American electoral system and observed caucuses in Maine and Vermont (1996), sheds light on caucus participants but also demonstrates that the question of representativeness is complex and that Iowa's representativeness is not easy to determine.

Basic to the concept of representativeness is the selection of comparison groups. A case can be made for comparing Iowa caucus participants with primary election voters, caucus participants in other states, the Iowa electorate, the national electorate, or any number of groups. Mayer concludes, however, that "no matter which group one uses as a standard of comparison," the demographic traits of caucus participants are "distinctly unrepresentative" (1996, 132). Caucus participants "in both parties are considerably older, wealthier, and better educated than rank-and-file party members" (Mayer 1996, 146). Data collected by Stone in 1984 and Stone and Mayer in 1988 also show that caucus-attenders are more partisan and more ideological than primary or general election voters (Mayer 1996, 134-35; Stone,

Abramowitz, and Rapoport 1989, 29-32).

It certainly comes as no surprise that caucus activists are not representative of the general voting population. As described 50 years ago by social scientist Herbert McClosky, party activists in the United States tend to be more extreme in their political beliefs and positions than their supporters in the voting public (McClosky, Hoffman, and O'Hara 1960, 406-27). Stone and his associates, comparing Iowa caucus participants to those in Michigan and Virginia, find that Iowa Republican and Democratic activists, like their national counterparts, are indeed more conservative/liberal than nonactivist voters in their respective parties, but the high caucus turnout in Iowa has a moderating effect on the activist population. Stone concludes that "if caucus-attenders generally are higher status, more committed to their party, and more ideological than the average citizen, the Iowa caucus-attender is less so" (1989, 45). Stone does not suggest that Iowa is a good "bellwether state," rather the "political context" that results from being first and the relatively large turnout moderate the Iowa caucus-attending population, making it less atypical than in Michigan and Virginia. Presumably, if the campaign began in Virginia or Michigan, the early start would have a similar effect in those states.

That caucus-attenders in general are more ideological does not mean, however, that they support extreme candidates. Party activists might be constrained from voting for candidates perceived too extreme to win. But in 1988, and again in 1996, the ideologically more extreme candidates fared better in caucuses than in primary states. Jesse Jackson and Pat Robertson in 1988, Pat Buchanan in 1996, and Mike Huckabee in 2008 ran much better in caucus states, whereas Michael Dukakis, George Bush, and Bob Dole ran substantially better in primaries (Mayer 1996, 143). It is possible, however, that the supporters did not perceive their candidates as extreme, but saw them as viable contenders. It is also likely that organizational ability rather than ideology played the decisive role in Iowa and other caucus states. It is less daunting to identify and mobilize the 20,000 to 25,000 supporters required to do well in Iowa than to conduct a campaign in a primary state where turnout levels are much higher.

Yet another complicating factor in determining Iowa's representativeness is the role of interest groups in defining the issues of the caucus campaign. The relatively large turnout in the precinct caucuses noted by Stone undoubtedly has a moderating effect in the aggregate, but it is often the small, highly motivated subgroups that set the agenda in Iowa. The Farm Bureau, anti-war and anti-nuclear groups, the right-to-life groups, and others have at times set the tone and/or agenda in the precinct caucuses. The Christian Right has dominated Republican caucus politics in Iowa for the last twenty years. By tailoring their campaigns to one or more of these groups, candidates have done well in Iowa and received a great deal of media attention.

The evidence presented is mixed. Iowa caucus-attenders are atypical demographically and ideologically. They are more partisan and more ideologically extreme than primary and general election voters, but less so than the participants in other caucus states. Extreme candidates have run better in Iowa than in primary states, but their number is limited and their success may have had more to do with the ease of organization in a caucus state than political ideology. Finally, interest groups play an agenda-setting role in the Iowa caucuses, and their narrow agendas skew the issues addressed in the campaign.

Iowa is a small, agriculturally oriented state in the American heartland. The state has no major urban centers, few big labor unions, and a very small minority population. The state is politically competitive and the political arena is fair and open. The people are moralistic, traditional, and moderate but are older and better educated than average. Its political activists are not demographically or ideologically representative of primary voters or the national electorate but are less extreme than caucus participants in other states. The rural, midwestern nature of Iowa has proved advantageous to some candidates and disadvantageous to others, particularly those who did not fit the Iowa mold. Due to the recent dominance of the Christian Right in the Republican caucuses, Iowa has at times misled the nation about the political appeal of Republican candidates (Mike Huckabee, Pat Buchanan, Pat Robertson), but the recent cases of George W. Bush, John Kerry, and Barack Obama have been harbingers of things to come.

References

Beaumont, Thomas. 2005. "2 Issues Muddle Democrat Governor Campaign." *Des Moines Register*, October 2, p. 1B.

Bibby, John F. 1996. *Politics, Parties, and Elections in America*. 3d ed. Chicago: Nelson-Hall Inc.

Center for the Study of the American Electorate. 2008. News Release on Voter Turnout 2008, December 17.

Claymore, Jason. 2008. "Iowans Lean in Favor of Civil Unions." *Des Moines Register,* March 2, p. 1A.

Elazar, Daniel J. 1984. *American Federalism: A View from the States.* 3d ed. New York: Harper and Row.

Federal Election Commission.

Iowa General Assembly. 1992. Acts and Resolutions. Des Moines: State of Iowa.

Iowa Official Register. 1985-2006. Des Moines: State of Iowa.

Iowa Poll: 1982-96. Des Moines: Des Moines Register and Tribune Company.

Iowa Secretary of State. 2009.

Mayer, William G. 1996. "Caucuses: How They Work, What Difference They Make." In *In Pursuit of the White House: How We Choose Our Presidential Nominees,* edited by William G. Mayer, 105-57. Chatham, N.J.: Chatham House.

McClosky, Herbert, Paul J. Hoffman, and Rosemary O'Hara. 1960. "Issue Conflict and Consensus among Party Leaders and Followers." *American Political Science Review* 54: 406-27.

Patterson, Samuel C. 1968. "The Political Cultures of American States." *Journal of Politics* 30: 187-209.

———. 1984. "Iowa." In *The Political Life of the American States,* edited by Alan Rosenthal and Maureen Moakley, 83-98. New York: Praeger.

Pew Forum on Religion and Public Life. 2008. http//religions.pewforum.org.

Ranney, Austin. 1965. "Parties and State Politics." In *Politics in the American States,* edited by Herbert Jacob and Kenneth Vines, 61-99. Boston: Little, Brown.

Ross, Russell M. 1957. *The Government and Administration of Iowa.* New York: Thomas Y. Crowell.

Schwieder, Dorothy. 1996. *Iowa: The Middle Land.* Ames: Iowa State University Press.

State Data Center of Iowa. 2008. Des Moines: State Library of Iowa.

Statistical Abstract of the United States. 1996. Prepared by the Bureau of the Census. Washington, D.C.: Government Printing Office.

Statistical Abstract of the United States. 2007. Prepared by the Bureau of the Census. Washington, D.C.: Government Printing Office.

Stedman, Murray S., Jr. 1976. *State and Local Governments.* Cambridge, Mass.: Winthrop.

Stone, Walter J., Alan I. Abramowitz, and Ronald B. Rapoport. 1989. "How Representative Are the Iowa Caucuses?" In *The Iowa Caucuses and the Presidential Nominating Process,* edited by Peverill Squire, 19-49. Boulder, Colo.: Westview Press.

Stork, Frank J., and Cynthia A. Clingan. 1980. *The Iowa General Assembly: Our Legislative Heritage, 1846-1980.* Des Moines: Iowa Senate.

Chapter 3

The Iowa Precinct Caucuses: The Decades of Obscurity

THE CAUCUS SYSTEM is a product of the Jacksonian democracy of the early 1830s. Until that time, the dominant system for nominating public officials in the United States had been one of caucuses by members of Congress and the state legislatures. The new system began with precinct caucuses that were, theoretically at least, open to all party members. The local caucuses were to elect delegates to county conventions, and from there the system proceeded through district, state, and national conventions, just as today. In practice, however, since it was not regulated by government, the caucus system came to be dominated by party bosses in the latter half of the nineteenth century (Crotty and Jackson 1985, chap. 1). It was not until the Progressive era in the first two decades of the twentieth century that the various state legislatures brought the system under the rule of law.

Developments through 1917

When Iowa joined the Union in 1846, the state's political parties immediately adopted a caucus and convention system. As in other states, charges of manipulation and foul play soon emerged. Emory English, in an article on voting practices in Iowa, outlined a number of common caucus abuses. Cliques or special-interest groups generally dominated party organizations and did their best to limit participation by opposing factions or the general public. Often the times and locations of caucuses were closely guarded secrets, and "snap" caucuses were a favorite device of those "in the know." The knowledgeable would assemble on short notice, elect a slate of delegates to the county convention, and quickly adjourn. When outsiders became aware of caucus times in advance, a caucus might be packed with the supporters of a particular candidate or slate of delegates, or a "competing event" might be organized. English recounts an example of a "competing event" held in northern Iowa, in which "the 'fortunate' burning of an old shed in the outskirts of a small town at exactly the advertised hour ... of the caucus attracted nine-tenths of the people of the village, including members of the volunteer fire department. In the meantime, those in the 'know' assembled at the caucus, ... selected a 'slate' of delegates without opposition and adjourned" (English 1948, 257).

Frequent abuses of the caucus process led to calls for reform, but the Iowa General Assembly was slow to act; the first reform bill was not introduced until 1896. Progressive-era reformers focused on developing a system of primary elections in Iowa rather than on taking the less radical step of revising the caucus and convention system. Three reform bills were introduced and rejected by the Twenty-sixth General Assembly in 1896 (Crossley 1903, 174-75), but in 1898 the Twenty-seventh General Assembly enacted a primary election law for Iowa's counties, although it did not make the primary system compulsory (Ia. Gen. Assem. 1898, chap. 111, p. 59). The first compulsory primary election law passed the Thirtieth General Assembly in 1904, but it applied only to counties with populations in excess of 75,000, and Polk was the only county affected (Ia. Gen. Assem. 1904, chap. 40, p. 29).

In 1907, eleven years of reform efforts in the general assembly culminated in the passage of a statewide primary election law. The law provided for primary elections to nominate candidates for any office filled by direct popular vote in the general election, with the exception of judgeships. It also required that delegates to the county conventions, members of the county central committees, and presidential and vice-presidential electors be nominated by primary election. Finally, it required a preference poll for U.S. senators, who at that time were chosen by the state legislature. Since the 1907 law only affected offices filled by direct popular vote, it did not provide for the nomination of presidential candidates. Moreover, the district and state conventions, not a popular vote, still selected delegates to the national conventions. The 1907 law, however, did represent a major change in Iowa electoral politics, since it opened the previously closed party system to the voters and limited the parties' control over the nominating process (Ia. Gen. Assem. 1907, chap. 51, p. 51).

Although amended several times, the 1907 law remained substantially intact until 1963. Changes in 1913 and 1917 are, however, worthy of examination. In those years Iowa initiated and then abolished a presidential primary. In 1913 the Thirty-fifth General Assembly amended Iowa's primary election law to include the selection of delegates and alternate delegates to the national conventions of all political parties, the selection of national committee members for each party, and a presidential preference poll "for the purpose of ascertaining the sentiment of voters of the state in the respective parties as to candidates for president and vice-president of the United States" (Ia. Gen. Assem. 1913, chap. 111, p. 99).

Iowa held its only presidential primary election on April 10, 1916, with mixed results. None of the major presidential candidates entered the primary (Schier 1980, 58 n. 49), less than one-third of the eligible electorate voted, and the primary election cost the state $122,000 (*Des Moines Register* [hereafter cited as *DMR*] Jan. 30, 1917, 2). Governor George W. Clarke, who in his inaugural address of January 16, 1913, had called for the passage of a presidential preference primary law (Clarke 1913, 19-20), now branded the 1916 presidential preference poll a "farce." In his final biennial message to the general assembly in 1917, he urged the repeal of the entire direct primary law and called for the return to the caucus and convention system of selecting candidates for public office (Clarke 1917, 27).

The Thirty-seventh General Assembly was not willing to abolish the direct primary law in its entirety, but it did agree with Governor Clarke's assessment of the presidential preference primary. A bill to repeal this section unanimously passed both houses in early 1917, and the newly inaugurated governor, William L. Harding, ended Iowa's short flirtation with the presidential primary by signing it into law on February 16, 1917 (Ia. Gen. Assem. 1917, chap. 14, p. 32). Thus, with the one exception in 1916, Iowa has employed the caucus and convention system to select presidential delegates to national conventions.

The Modern Caucus System

The next major modification of the caucus and convention system occurred in 1963, when the general assembly amended Iowa's primary election law and returned the selection of county convention delegates to the precinct caucuses (Ia. Gen. Assem. 1963, chap. 78, p. 117). Two years later, lawmakers also removed the selection of county committee members from electoral politics and provided for their selection at the precinct caucuses (Ia. Gen. Assem. 1965, chap. 89, p. 158). Several factors contributed to these changes, including the high cost of printing separate ballots for each precinct, the low visibility of party offices, and a movement in Iowa for a shorter ballot (Larson 1981). No additional substantive changes in the Iowa primary law occurred after 1965. The current law requires primary elections to nominate candidates for all elective offices below that of president with the exception of judgeships and provides for a caucus and convention system for selecting delegates to the national conventions.

When the general assembly returned Iowa to the caucus and convention system for selecting delegates and committee members, it regulated their conduct. Iowa law provides that "delegates to county conventions of political parties and party committee members shall be elected at precinct caucuses held not later than the fourth Monday in February on each even-numbered year. The date shall be at least eight days earlier than the scheduled date for any meeting, caucus or primary which constitutes the first determining stage of the presidential nominating process in any other state" (Iowa 1985, sec. 43.4). This section of the Iowa Code has been amended several times, most recently in 1983, with the legislative intent to preserve Iowa's first-in-the-nation status (see chap. 6) (Ia. Gen. Assem. 1983, chap. 138, p. 306).

The actual date for precinct caucuses is set by the state central committee of each party, and since 1976 the Republican and Democratic parties have held their caucuses on the same day. The principal motivation for this party cooperation in Iowa is to gain maximum media exposure, and in that they have succeeded. (Tim Hyde, former executive director of the Iowa Republican party, listed two additional reasons for the Republicans' willingness to initiate a common caucus date: to maximize caucus participation through joint announcements and to prevent people from participating in both the Republican and Democratic caucuses [1982].)

The state central committees determine starting times for their caucuses. Iowa law also requires that "the date, time, and place of each precinct caucus of a political party shall be published at least twice ...

not more than thirty days and not less than five days before the date of the caucuses." In addition, the notice must state in substance that each voter affiliated with the specified political party may attend the precinct caucus (Iowa 1985, sec. 43.92). Finally, whenever possible, precinct caucuses are to be held in publicly owned buildings or in places used for holding public meetings (Iowa 1985, sec. 43.93). These requirements are intended to ensure an open and well-publicized caucus process and have succeeded in eliminating most of the earlier abuses. It is still possible to pack a caucus with supporters of a particular candidate or slate of delegates, but greater media coverage and the correspondingly higher salience of the caucuses make the use of this tactic increasingly difficult, especially in presidential election years.

The legislation of 1965 also determined the rules of eligibility for caucus participation. The law requires that caucus participants reside within the precinct and that they be or become eligible electors by the next general election. The law permits seventeen-year-olds who will be eighteen by the time of the general election to participate in the caucuses (Iowa 1985, sec. 43.90).

Since the precinct caucuses are party-sponsored events, the parties may have, and each has, additional requirements for participation. Republicans require that "any person voting at a precinct caucus must be a registered Republican in that precinct," but an eligible "person may register to vote or change party affiliation at the caucus" (Republican Party of Iowa 1996, 5). The Democrats limit participation to those who "support the purposes of the Iowa Democratic Party, and who are registered Democrats, or who register at the time of their request to participate" in the caucuses (Iowa Democratic Party 1996, 1). Although the goal of these requirements is to prevent raiding by the opposition, it is very unlikely that persons willing to "declare" themselves supporters of the party on the evening of the caucus will be prevented from participating by either the Republicans or the Democrats.

Voting procedures within caucuses are at the discretion of each caucus gathering, although the Republican state central committee suggests that votes be taken by secret ballot. Moreover, any questions not covered by state law or party rules are resolved by majority vote of the caucus participants.

The principal concerns of the precinct caucuses are the selection of delegates and the development of issues for the party platform, but the parties differ somewhat in how they conduct caucus business. Both normally elect two precinct committee members to represent their precinct on the county central committee. Each begins the platform-building process by developing and discussing issues, which are then forwarded to the county platform committee. The Democratic caucuses elect members and alternates to serve on the platform committee and the committee on committees, which plan the county conventions. The Republican county committees determine the procedures for filling these positions, and the procedures vary by county.

Iowa as the First Nominating Event

From a position of relative obscurity, the Iowa precinct caucuses moved toward national prominence in 1972, when the Iowa Democratic Party moved its caucus date forward to January 24, making it the first primary event in the nation. The early date for the caucuses is the result of an interesting series of events. The Iowa General Assembly first passed legislation governing the date of precinct caucuses in 1969. The law required that caucuses be held "not later than the second Monday in May in each election year" but did not limit how early they might be held (Ia. Gen. Assem. 1969, chap. 90, p. 124). Prior to 1972 the Iowa political parties tended to hold their precinct caucuses in late March or in April, which fell in the middle of the national primary schedule.

The earlier date was prompted by reforms in the caucus and convention system adopted by the Iowa Democrats between 1968 and 1972. Foremost among the changes was the decision to hold separate district and state conventions and to require proportional representation in the delegate selection process. To facilitate the implementation of the reforms, the Democrats added a clause to their party constitution requiring thirty days between party functions (precinct caucuses, county conventions, congressional district conventions, the state statutory convention, the state presidential convention, and the national convention). Due to the decision to hold the Democratic state convention on May 20—a decision based largely on the availability of a suitable meeting place—the latest possible date for the cau-

Cartoon by Frank Miller, © 1984, *Des Moines Register,* reprinted by permission

The Iowa caucuses were inconspicuous events before 1972. The strictly local functions, held in the middle of the primary and caucus season, were the first step in
the process of selecting delegates to the national conventions. The Iowa parties'
caucus and convention process rarely received national media attention, since
Iowans elect less than 2 percent of the delegates to the parties' respective national
conventions. When the Iowa Democrats chose an earlier date for their caucuses,
the national parties and media quickly took notice.

cuses in 1972 was January 24 (Larson 1983). The January date moved the Iowa Democratic caucuses ahead of the New Hampshire primary election, which was traditionally the nation's first primary event.

The clause in the Democratic party's constitution requiring thirty days between events arose from practical rather than philosophical considerations. The party wanted both to include as many Democrats as possible in the caucus process and to provide delegates to the next set of party functions with good sources of information. Unfortunately, the state party headquarters had severe physical limitations and very poor office equipment, so to complete the paperwork and arrangements required for each level of meetings, a one-month interlude between party functions was necessary. Party leaders maintain that there was no political intent in moving the caucus date forward and confess that they were unaware that the Iowa Democratic caucuses would be the nation's first as a result of the move. It did not take Iowa Democrats long, however, to realize what they had done, and although surprised by the media attention, they set out to capitalize on their new position of prominence (Larson 1983).

References

Clarke, George W. 1913. *Iowa Documents*. Inaugural Address to the Thirty-fifth General Assembly, January 16.

———. 1917. *Iowa Documents*. Biennial Message to the Thirty-seventh General Assembly, January 9.

Crossley, James J. 1903. "The Regulation of Primary Elections by Law." *Iowa Journal of History and Politics* 1: 165-92.

Crotty, William, and John S. Jackson III. 1985. *Presidential Primaries and Nominations*. Washington, D.C.: CQ Press.

Des Moines Register. 1917.

English, Emory H. 1948. "Evolution in Iowa Voting Practices." *Annals of Iowa* 29: 249-89.

Hyde, Tim. 1982. Telephone interview with author, October 8. Hyde was the executive director of the Iowa Republican party from 1980 to 1983.

Iowa. 1985. *Code of Iowa: 1985*.

Iowa Democratic Party. 1980. Precinct Caucus Kit, 1980. Mimeographed.

———. 1984. Precinct Caucus Kit. Mimeographed.

———. 1996. Constitution. Amended 1996.

Iowa General Assembly. 1898-1983. *Acts and Resolutions*. Des Moines: State of Iowa.

Larson, Clifton. 1981. Telephone interview with author, February 23. Larson was the chair of the Iowa Democratic Party from 1970 to 1973.

————. 1983. Telephone interview with author, March 27.

Republican Party of Iowa. 1980. Suggested Procedure for Precinct Caucuses, January 21, 1980. Mimeographed.

————. 1983. Conducting Your Precinct Caucus. Mimeographed.

————. 1996. Constitution. Amended 1996.

Schier, Steven E. 1980. *The Rules of the Game: Democratic National Convention Delegate Selection in Iowa and Wisconsin.* Washington, D.C.: University Press of America.

Chapter 4 The 1968 and 1972 Caucuses: The Emergence of a National Event

THE EARLY DATE for the precinct caucuses was destined to change their character completely. Before 1972 they were strictly local events; attendance was limited and activism was confined to a small band of partisans whose interest allowed them to dominate the meetings by default. A spirited presidential nominating contest, such as the 1952 Eisenhower-Taft race (Clifton 1952, 1), or a controversial issue, like the 1968 anti-war struggle, increased caucus participation, but this went largely unnoticed at the national level. It is not surprising that the local meetings attracted little national media attention, because Iowa Republicans and Democrats held their caucuses in the middle of the presidential nominating process and selected less than 2 percent of the delegates to their respective national conventions. Thus, even though the meetings were open and were regularly covered by the Iowa news media, they were often poorly attended and of little or no national significance.

The 1968 Precinct Caucuses

Before we turn to the events of 1972 that focused national attention on the state, it would be helpful to examine briefly the 1968 precinct caucuses in order to appreciate their purpose and the changes necessary to turn them into a media event. Procedurally, 1968 was a typical year for the caucuses, although the anti-war movement stimulated greater-than-usual participation in the Democratic sessions. Both parties held their 1968 precinct caucuses in March.

The Republican Caucuses

Most of the Republican local meetings in the state's 2484 precincts were held on March 4 (a few were held on the fifth). The opening round in the contest for Iowa's twenty-four delegates to the national convention in Miami centered around the candidacies of former vice-president Richard Nixon and New York Governor Nelson Rockefeller, but there was also interest in some precincts in the possible candidacy of California Governor Ronald Reagan (Mills 1968a).

Generally, the sessions went smoothly and according to traditional procedures. After electing local party officials and considering resolutions that might be appropriate for planks in the county platforms, many caucuses conducted a straw poll; others simply elected delegates to county conventions and forwarded their names to state party headquarters over the next several days (*DMR* Mar. 5, 1968, 1, 6). There was no statewide poll or reporting system, and the state party made no systematic attempt to determine the candidate preferences of the delegates elected to the county conventions. In fact, it was not customary for those seeking to represent the precinct at succeeding levels to declare their presidential loyalties, although there were periodic attempts by candidate organizations to require disclosure (*DMR* Apr. 11, 1968, 4). Even when preferences were known, delegates could change their loyalties, since they were not bound to candidates by law. Thus in 1968 Iowa Republicans had no systematic way to determine which candidates had won, or even to judge with any certainty the number of participants in their caucus process.

Local newspapers, however, attempted to provide information about the candidate preference of caucus participants by covering selected precincts. The *Des Moines Register*, for example, published information about several Polk County meetings, noting that "attendance was spotty," ranging from heavy in some larger precincts to just three persons in a combined caucus of precincts 27, 34, 36, and 37. The paper reported partial results of straw polls taken in Polk County (with Rockefeller favored by 344 participants, Nixon by 321, and Reagan by 64) and listed some of the resolutions passed in the precinct meetings (*DMR* Mar. 5, 1968, 1, 6). The national media paid no attention to the Iowa Republican precinct caucuses.

The local nature of the process and the almost complete absence of systematic information about the candidate preference of caucus participants are further illustrated by a *Register* editorial printed shortly after the meetings, which concluded that "Republican precinct caucuses in Iowa last week showed no clear trend for either of the major presidential prospects. Figures on straw polls (where taken) and elected county delegates who declared themselves (most didn't) are so scattered that nobody can read too much into them" (*DMR* Mar. 12, 1968, 6).

The Democratic Caucuses

The Iowa Democrats held their 1968 precinct caucuses on March 25, their county conventions on April 19, and their combined district and state conventions on May 24 and 25. The Vietnam War was the dominant concern within the Iowa Democratic Party, and, as in the rest of the country, it proved a very divisive issue. The presidential contenders in 1968 were President Lyndon Johnson, whose Vietnam policies led some Iowa Democrats to fear that he could not carry the state in November; Senator Eugene McCarthy, with his potent college cadre of anti-war activists; and Senator Robert Kennedy, who entered the presidential race on March 16, only nine days before the caucuses (Mills 1968b, 1, 3).

Supporters of McCarthy's anti-war campaign spent months organizing at the grass-roots level in an effort to have an impact in Iowa, and in the process they stimulated local interest in the precinct caucuses. The McCarthy campaign attracted many political neophytes into electoral politics in 1968, and large numbers of individuals attended their first precinct caucuses. The presence of large numbers of political amateurs, many of college age, was not greeted warmly by some party regulars, who had grown used to dominating the caucuses. The political newcomers tended to ignore the time-honored tradition of electing established party workers as delegates to county conventions, and "in some counties intense controversy erupted over the tactics used by the McCarthy forces in electing slates of delegates to the county convention" (Schier 1980, 88). It reached the point that the Democratic state chair sent letters to county chairs suggesting that they look into "irregularities" in caucus participation, a thinly veiled recommendation that they check the residences of McCarthy supporters elected as county delegates (Mills 1968d, 1, 3). State Democratic party rules at the time required a six-month residency in the state, sixty days in the county, and ten days in the precinct. They also required that participants be at least twenty-one years old and that they be people who "considered themselves Democrats at the time" of the caucus. The issue quickly died, however, when Governor Harold Hughes announced, "I welcome anybody into the Iowa Democratic Party" (*DMR* Apr. 5, 1968, 11).

As was the case with the Republicans, the Democrats had no formal system to determine and report the presidential preference of caucus participants, and in fact they lacked the ability to ascertain levels of participation throughout the state. Thus local newspaper accounts were based on a limited number of precincts, most selected for reasons of accessibility. Nonetheless, the *Register* quoted Iowa Democratic chairman Clark Rasmussen's estimate that the caucuses attracted perhaps 75,000 people, which the *Register* called the "greatest outpouring of Democrats in such sessions in the state's history" (Mills 1968c, 1).

The *Register* story, whose headline declared, "Foes Capture Large Share of Delegates," concluded that President Lyndon Johnson was in trouble in Iowa. It declared Senator McCarthy the big winner, and his Iowa campaign manager estimated the McCarthy-Kennedy caucus strength at 40 percent (supporters of the two candidates combined forces in a number of precincts to maximize the anti-Johnson effect) (*DMR* Mar. 27, 1968, 6). As with the Republican caucuses, the national news media showed no interest in the Democratic caucuses, which is not surprising, since the campaign for the presidency was well under way and the Iowa Democrats were just beginning their process of electing forty-six delegates to the national convention in Chicago.

On March 31, only six days after the caucuses, President Johnson shocked the country and his supporters in Iowa when, during a speech to the nation on the progress of the Vietnam War, he announced that he would not campaign for reelection. His embarrassing showing in the New Hampshire primary three weeks earlier, where he had shaded McCarthy by 50 to 41 percent, and declining ratings in national public opinion polls were probably the major factors behind Johnson's decision (Weaver 1968, 1). Since the results were not systematically reported and were not reported at all outside Iowa, the Iowa caucuses certainly played little or no role in the decision, but as a result of it, the contest for the presidency in Iowa was wide open (Seplow 1968, 1).

The Impact of the 1968 Caucuses

The 1968 precinct caucuses of both parties demonstrate the grass-roots nature of the process before Iowa became a media event. Small groups of partisans, usually party regulars and a few other highly motivated citizens, came together every two years to begin the caucus and convention process in the state. The meetings frequently were held in private homes, often those of the precinct chair, and the order of business was standard and usually mundane. The participants elected local party officials, representatives on county committees, and delegates to the county convention; circulated nominating petitions for candidates for local, state, and national offices; and discussed issues of concern to the participants and, in presidential years, potential platform issues and approved resolutions concerning them. The normal attendance at precinct caucuses was small, often so limited in rural areas and small towns that it was not possible to elect full slates of delegates to the county conventions or to fill all the elective local party offices. The 1968 Democratic caucuses demonstrated that controversial issues or candidates could stimulate attendance, but given the more reliable information of recent caucuses (Democratic figures for the huge 1984 media event were 75,000), Clark Rasmussen's estimate of a "record" participation in 1968 of perhaps 75,000 was undoubtedly a gross exaggeration.

The 1968 precinct caucuses also show that neither party's procedures were designed to determine winners and losers at the first stage in the multistage Iowa caucus and convention system. There was no systematic attempt to tabulate levels of support for individual presidential candidates. In fact, seldom was the presidential preference of candidates for the position of delegate to the county convention (and succeeding levels) formally announced. Rather, slates of delegates were elected by majority vote, and those elected typically included experienced party workers and elected officials. At no level in the process were formal declarations of candidate support required, and even when expressed, they did not bind the delegates. The first recorded vote for presidential candidates was the first ballot at the national convention. As the newspaper estimates and speculations following the caucuses showed, it was impossible to determine with any precision the level of citizen participation at the local meetings, let alone the level of candidate support among caucus participants and the delegates elected to the county conventions.

Democratic Party Reforms

The 1968 process also demonstrated that although it was local in nature and without national impact, the Iowa caucus and convention system could be spirited and could involve tough political infighting. Just two days after the precinct caucuses, George Mills, a senior political reporter, warned that McCarthy's grass-roots victory "conceivably could be followed by defeats at the state convention" (Mills 1968c, 3), and, indeed, Mills's warning proved prophetic. At the Democratic state convention in May, only five of the forty-six national convention delegates went to McCarthy (*DMR* May 28, 1968, 3).

The explanation for the McCarthy decline between the caucuses and the state convention is all too clear to students of party politics. Forty-two percent of the Iowa delegation to the national convention was elected "at large" at the state convention in 1968, and the remainder were elected as representatives of the state's seven congressional districts. As the caucus and convention process continued, county chairs and other party workers played an ever-increasing role. For example, Mills noted that "a county chairman usually appoints the nominating committee to select a slate of delegates to the state convention," and the county chairs generally did not favor McCarthy (Mills 1968c, 3). Thus the early McCarthy success in the precinct caucuses turned into defeat at the hands of the party pros at the state convention. Reflecting on the loss at the state level, McCarthy's Iowa chair, state senator Harry Beardsley, observed that "essentially we learned that organization is more important than an issue as you move through the party process" (*DMR* May 28, 1968, 3).

Those familiar with the 1968 Democratic National Convention in Chicago will recall that party pros were in control there also. While Mayor Richard J. Daley and the Democratic bosses managed the convention proceedings, the anti-Vietnam War protest movement, which provided the basis for the McCarthy presidential candidacy, was reduced to demonstrating in the streets of Chicago, and they did not fare well there either. Unfortunately for the Democratic party, the American public witnessed from a front-row seat the spectacle of Mayor Daley and the bosses leading their party down the road of political suicide. Television cameras and reporters were everywhere, even in the streets experiencing the tear-gassing with the protesters. The message conveyed by television seemed to be that grass-roots politics was merely an exercise; the real decisions were made by the party pros.

The bad feelings created within the Democratic party by the bitter national convention undoubtedly contributed to the defeat of the party's candidate, Hubert Humphrey, by Vice-President Richard Nixon in the general election. It was not long before calls to reform the party's selection procedures were heard. The party responded by creating the McGovern-Fraser Commission to examine and make recommendations about delegate selection procedures, and the commission's report led to new rules for the 1972 caucus and convention process.

The goal of the new party rules was to expand the influence of the grass-roots levels of the party by limiting the ability of party activists and bosses to work their magic at succeeding levels in the caucus and convention system. The rules replaced the winner-take-all system with one requiring proportional representation at succeeding levels of the delegate selection process. The new guidelines also required that 75 percent of the national convention delegates be chosen at levels no higher than the congressional district convention and called for affirmative action to ensure the inclusion of women, minorities, and young people in state delegations (Crotty and Jackson 1985, chap. 2). Theoretically, under the new rules a strong showing at the precinct caucus level would lead to proportional representation at the county and succeeding levels, and this would prevent a recurrence of McCarthy's 1968 experience of being thwarted by party bosses.

Delegate Selection

The Iowa caucus and convention system does not differ greatly from that found in other states. It begins with precinct caucuses open to all citizens willing to declare themselves supporters of the party whose caucus they attend. Although the precinct caucuses perform several party functions, in presidential years the foremost concern is the election of delegates to county conventions, and Democratic and Republican delegate selection procedures differ significantly. For the Iowa precinct caucuses to become a media event and an integral part of the presidential nominating process, the delegate selection procedures of both parties had to be modified to generate "results" or "outcomes" that would allow the media to determine "winners" and "losers."

Democratic Procedures

In the Democratic party's system of proportional representation, delegates to county conventions are elected in proportion to the level of support for the various presidential candidates in each caucus. There may be, and there usually is, an uncommitted group. Either a candidate preference group or an uncommitted group that includes 15 percent of the total caucus voters is considered viable, meaning that it is eligible to elect delegates to the county convention. If more than 85 percent of those voting at a caucus support one presidential candidate or are uncommitted, they are entitled to elect the entire slate of delegates to the county convention (Iowa Democratic Party 1996).

Delegate selection in Democratic caucuses is a multistage process, with opportunities for bargaining and politicking at each stage. After the chair determines the number of eligible voting members in attendance, caucus participants divide into presidential preference groups. When that stage is completed, the groups are counted for the purpose of determining viability, and preference groups that fail to meet the minimum viability standard have the opportunity to reassociate with other groups. At this point, politicking increases in intensity as viable groups seek to proselytize the "groupless" voters in order to increase the number of county delegates for which they qualify. When all voters are members of a viable candidate preference group or an uncommitted group, the caucus chair again counts the groups and determines the number of delegates to the county convention that each is entitled to elect. The chair informs the county headquarters of the number of delegates committed to each candidate and the number selected as uncommitted, and the final step of delegate selection begins. Delegate selection within groups is often a lively and spirited process that frequently involves speechmaking, bargaining, and vote trading.

As noted, some of the delegates selected are "committed" to support specific candidates at the county convention; others are elected as uncommitted delegates. Committed delegates, however, are not legally bound to support a particular candidate at the county level, nor are delegates from the county to the state convention so bound (Iowa Democratic Party 1980). Similarly, a Hunt Commission recommendation accepted by the Democratic National Committee at its March 26, 1982, meeting called for the abolition of the practice followed in 1980 of binding state delegates at the national convention.

The system of proportional representation made it possible to translate caucus outcomes into "delegate equivalents" at succeeding steps in the process. Since 1972, state Democratic officials have calculated the percentage of weighted county convention delegates (called "state delegate equivalents") won by each of the presidential candidates at the precinct caucuses. They have also projected "national delegate equivalents," that is, the future delegate strength of presidential candidates within the Iowa delegation to the Democratic National Convention (Bender 1983).

The final step in meeting the media's demand for "outcomes" was taken when the Iowa Democratic Party developed a system for compiling caucus results on the evening of the local meetings. In 1972 party officials prepared a list of randomly selected precincts for the purpose of calculating the "state delegate equivalents" and the "national delegate equivalents" each candidate had won (Bender 1983). In 1976 the Democrats established a "caucus returns headquarters" in Des Moines with a telephone reporting system from each of Iowa's ninety-nine counties, and they continue to use this statewide reporting and analysis system.

It is important to keep in mind that all Democratic caucus returns since 1972 have been projections or "delegate equivalents," not raw vote totals. The Iowa Democrats do not tabulate levels of candidate support at the caucuses after the initial division into preference groups, which would be in effect a straw poll. Rather, they count the number of people as reconstituted into viable preference groups. Using the final viable groups, they weight and then project each presidential candidate's strength at the state convention and at the national convention. (The weighting is necessary because each coun- ty sets the size of its convention, and since very small counties may hold large conventions, the weighting brings county delegate totals into proportion with their assigned delegate strength at the state con- vention.) This reporting system undoubtedly proves confusing to some, but the Iowa Democrats believe it provides the most accurate data available (*DMR* Oct. 16, 1983, 2C).

Republican Procedures

The Iowa Republicans' delegate selection process in presidential years is less complex. They normally elect delegates to county conventions on an at-large basis, although individual caucuses determine their own selection procedures, and, should they desire, they may elect del- egates on a proportional basis. A precinct electing six delegates at large would allow each caucus participant to vote for as many as six dele- gates, and the individuals receiving the most votes would be elected regardless of their presidential preference (Republican Party of Iowa 1980). Conceivably, a well-organized candidate organization could pack a caucus and, with a simple majority, control all the delegates elected, a feat that would require the support of 85 percent of the par- ticipants at a Democratic caucus.

Before 1976, Republican caucuses forwarded reports to the state party headquarters in Des Moines that included the names of persons selected to attend county conventions as delegates. The caucus reports did not include the candidate preference of those elected, and it was usually several days after the caucuses before most of the reports arrived in Des Moines (Brown 1983). Since the Republican at-large sys- tem did not lend itself to projecting "delegate equivalents," changes were necessary to provide results. In 1976 the Iowa Republicans initi- ated a presidential preference poll and a system for reporting results to Des Moines on the evening of the caucuses. Beginning modestly, in 1976 sixty-two randomly selected precincts conducted a straw poll, but in 1980 all caucuses did so (Brown 1983). The poll is taken prior to del- egate selection, and there is no requirement that the delegates elected later in the evening reflect the results of the poll. Delegates are not committed or bound to any candidate.

The 1972 Precinct Caucuses

The Iowa Democratic caucuses were scheduled for January 24, making them the nation's first nominating event. The Iowa Republicans had not changed their process, and they scheduled precinct caucuses for April 4. The Iowa Democratic meetings also were the first nominating event to use the reformed party rules that had grown out of the McGovern-Fraser Commission. The heart of the reforms, proportional representation, was designed to limit the influence of the party bosses and open the entire caucus and convention system to the influence of the grass-roots participants. Thus the Iowa Democrats, and some national correspondents, watched closely to see if the caucus process would be affected by the new rules and the early date.

The Democratic Caucuses

Senator George McGovern appears to have been the first presidential candidate to comprehend the potential significance of the early Iowa caucuses. Eager to dispel the conventional wisdom that he could not win the Democratic nomination, McGovern's national staff began putting together an organization in Iowa in the summer of 1971, several months before the other candidates. Through the fall and winter, local volunteers and "border-runners" from McGovern's home state of South Dakota identified McGovern supporters and organized them in preparation for the January caucuses (*Newsweek* Jan. 24, 1972, 15). The grass-roots, McCarthy-style campaign stressed McGovern's lack of ties to special interests and emphasized his desire to win the support of the average citizen of Iowa and the nation. Although he personally campaigned in Iowa for only three days before the caucuses, McGovern explained his major organizational effort in a January 12, 1972, Cedar Rapids speech. "Iowa is terribly important in the presidential nomination," he declared. "It is the first state in the nation where we get any test at all" (Flansburg 1972a, 3).

Senator Edmund Muskie, although slow to organize an Iowa campaign, eventually sent full-time campaigners to supplement his local workers in hopes of demonstrating that his front-runner image was deserved (Miller 1972, 1, 25). Muskie campaign officials had built up the press's expectations about Iowa by claiming that the local caucuses in Iowa and Arizona would demonstrate early strength for their candidate (Hart 1973, 112). The Muskie campaign received a boost shortly before the precinct caucuses when the very powerful and popular Iowa senator Harold Hughes endorsed fellow senator Muskie's presidential candidacy. Hughes, who had previously refused to endorse McGovern, made a joint appearance with Muskie in Des Moines on January 18 and bestowed his blessing on him. The endorsement, which McGovern's campaign manager, Gary Hart, later called "one of the bitterest blows of the campaign" (Hart 1973, 89), was invaluable for Muskie, as it put "virtually all the key figures in the Hughes organization into the Muskie camp" (Risser 1972, 4).

Agents for other candidates made very limited efforts in Iowa in 1972. Supporters of Senator Hubert Humphrey started too late to have any real chance of doing well, and he ultimately urged his supporters to back uncommitted delegates at the precinct caucuses (Miller 1972, 25). Unable to win, Humphrey's only hope was to deny an outright victory to the other candidates, and to pursue that end he came to Iowa on January 24. There was also an unsuccessful "draft Kennedy" campaign early and a late attempt by former senator Eugene McCarthy, who had been so successful in the 1968 Iowa caucuses. In 1972, however, when McCarthy appeared in Des Moines on January 22 the old fervor was missing, and without an organization he was not a viable candidate in Iowa (O'Shea 1972, 4B).

On Monday, January 24, the night of the Democratic precinct caucuses, Iowa was under siege by a fierce winter storm, and in approximately one-fourth of the state's ninety-nine counties the meetings had to be postponed until Tuesday, and in some cases Wednesday. The caucuses were conducted according to the new party rules in the remaining counties, and with a few notable exceptions (such as precinct 70 in Des Moines, where charges of rules violations surfaced), they went quite smoothly (Johnson 1972, 1).

The national news media were present in modest numbers, with approximately thirty to forty reporters on hand to observe the caucuses for the first time, lending credibility to McGovern's earlier observation about the new role Iowa would assume in the presidential nominating process (Hart 1973, 114). Included among the reporters were representatives of the national networks, the wire services, and the

Cartoon by Brian Duffy, © 1983, *Des Moines Register,* reprinted by permission

Iowa is well known for its harsh winters, and on several occasions the weather has
had an impact on the precinct caucuses. In 1972, blizzard conditions forced the
Democrats to postpone their caucuses in a number of counties. The meetings were
eventually held, but in some cases they took place two days after the scheduled
date.

Washington Post and *New York Times* (Schier 1980, 145). The *Des Moines Register,* which is a statewide newspaper widely respected throughout the nation, played up the first-in-the-nation status of the caucuses for several days before and after the meetings.

To accommodate the media need for "hard data," state party officials made an attempt to compile statewide results on the evening of the caucuses, an effort that was complicated by the snowstorm. Using sample precincts, the officials calculated the number of delegates won by the candidates at succeeding levels in the caucus and convention process. They produced two sets of numbers. The first, the set of "national delegate equivalents," was a projection of each candidate's delegate strength at the national convention assuming that delegate loyalties did not change between the caucuses and the national convention, which is a very weak assumption.

The second set of projections, which Democratic officials referred to as "state delegate equivalents," proved confusing to reporters unfamiliar with the complicated reporting system. The confusion is illustrated by the variety of labels used to report the Iowa results. The *New York Times* on January 26 called them "delegates," and although it was not clear, by implication this meant delegates to county conventions; the *Washington Post* that day incorrectly referred to the results as "votes"; and the *Des Moines Register* on January 26 correctly termed the outcomes "state delegate equivalents," and the article explained how they had been derived. The confusion is understandable, since the "state delegate equivalents" were actually weighted county delegates, and to this day few reporters understand the complicated process by which the projections are derived. (In 1984, with literally hundreds of reporters on hand, party officials held press workshops in an attempt to overcome the confusion about the caucus results, but they were not very successful in clarifying the complex process.)

The results produced by the Democratic tally were of dubious validity, but they were nationally reported nonetheless. The results, based on partial returns of sample precincts, are shown in Table 4.1.

Senator McGovern's organizational effort in Iowa paid great dividends. Even though he finished third in the contest for delegates, behind "uncommitted" and Senator Muskie, it was better than most reporters had expected, and as we have come to learn, political reality in the electronic age is determined by the media's perception of polit-

Table 4.1.   1972 Democratic precinct caucus
results

	State delegate equivalents (%)	Projected national delegates
Uncommitted	35.8	18
Muskie	35.5	18
McGovern	22.6	10
Humphrey	1.6	0
McCarthy	1.4	0
Chisholm	1.3	0
Jackson	1.1	0
Others	0.7	0

Source: Data from Apple 1972b, 16.

ical events. The media perception that Muskie was the 1972 Democratic front-runner and that McGovern was an also-ran apparently was based in large part on a January 1972 Gallup poll showing that nationally, 32 percent of the Democrats supported Muskie, while only 3 percent favored McGovern for the party's presidential nomination (Gallup 1972, 4B). Having established who should and who should not be viewed as a serious Democratic presidential contender, the media evaluated the results of the precinct caucuses according to these expectations.

Although national coverage of the 1972 caucuses was sporadic, the media interpretation of the results cast a shadow over the Muskie campaign. The *New York Times* published stories for three consecutive days after the Iowa local meetings on January 25, 26, and 27, and in one, R. W. Apple, Jr., said he thought that Muskie's victory was "clouded by the unexpected strong showing of Senator George McGovern" (1972, 16). A *Washington Post* article stated that the results "gave no new impetus to the Muskie campaign" (Chapman 1972, A4). The stories in both the *Times* and the *Post* noted that Muskie was the winner in Iowa, and in the January 26 article Apple concluded that the Muskie victory "was big enough to insure that politicians across the country would not think that he had stumbled in Iowa." Apple observed, however, that the margin "was not big enough to add much to the bandwagon psychology he has been building" (Apple 1972, 16). Bill Lawrence, reporting on the ABC evening news, viewed the outcome slightly differently. Much to the glee of McGovern's campaign manager, Gary Hart, he reported that "the Muskie bandwagon slid off an icy road in Iowa last night" (Hart 1973, 115).

The reporting of the 1972 Democratic precinct caucuses is consistent with the findings of later research into the media and presidential campaigns, which concludes that "candidates who do better than expected in the race do better than anybody else in attracting coverage" (Robinson and Sheehan 1983, 80). The Iowa coverage emphasized the surprisingly strong showing of McGovern and provided his campaign with access to the media.

The reporting of the 1972 Democratic caucuses was an excellent example of Patterson's "expectations game." Senator Muskie was expected to win in Iowa, and the media had not identified a significant challenger. Senator McGovern fared much better than expected, and "surprised" reporters took note of his campaign. Media interpretation of the 1972 caucus outcomes enhanced the prestige of the Iowa caucuses while providing a tremendous boost to the McGovern presidential campaign.

Projections versus Reality

A theme of this book is that projections based on precinct caucuses are invalid and unreliable indicators of presidential candidate strength in Iowa. They are invalid because no votes are taken anywhere in the process, and delegates selected as loyal to a particular presidential candidate may not actually be supporting that candidate. Supporters of candidates who do not meet the 15 percent threshold for viability, for example, frequently align with any group willing to give them some representation on the delegation to the county convention. Thus the delegate totals for any given candidate may include supporters of other candidates as well.

The fluidity and duration of the caucus and convention system also limit the reliability of projections. The projections of delegate strength for presidential candidates are based on the assumption that campaign conditions will not change between the January 24 precinct caucuses and the state and national conventions held months later. An examination of the political events that occurred in 1972 between the January 24 caucuses and the July 9 Democratic National Convention demonstrates the projections' lack of reliability. The outcomes of ninety-eight of Iowa's ninety-nine county conventions are shown in Table 4.2. The county convention results show that both Muskie and McGovern gained strength as uncommitted delegates began to commit to one of the candidates. Although it does happen that large numbers of delegates remain uncommitted all the way to the national convention, it is not uncommon for their number to dwindle as the campaign progresses.

On March 25 the district conventions, which were held separately from the state meeting for the first time as a result of the new Iowa rules, elected thirty-four of the forty-six delegates to the national convention, with the following loyalties: Muskie 14, McGovern 12, and "uncommitted" 8. Again, the process of winnowing uncommitted delegates continued, and when on April 27, after several primary election reversals, Muskie announced that he was suspending his campaign for the presidency, the race for the Democratic nomination took a new turn in Iowa with the state convention still almost a month away. One Muskie delegate immediately gave his support to McGovern, a few began to look around for another candidate, and the remaining thirteen Muskie delegates decided to stay the course (Flansburg 1972c, 1, 6).

By the time of the Democratic state convention in 1972, there were

Table 4.2.   1972 Democratic county
convention results

	State delegates (%)	Projected national delegates
Muskie	39.3	19
Uncommitted	30.7	14
McGovern	28.2	13
Others	2.2	0

Source: Data from Flansburg 1972b, 1, 8.

significant changes in the presidential campaign. The Muskie campaign was in limbo, and McGovern had emerged as a viable and strong candidate for the nomination. Yet the results reported by the media after the January 24 caucuses included projections of state delegates, numbers that were meaningless by the time of the event for which they were projected.

The state convention selected the remaining ten delegates to the national convention (the two national committee members are unelected delegates, and they favored Muskie). The results were: McGovern 5, Muskie 3, and "uncommitted" 2. Table 4.3 is a comparison of the "national delegate equivalents" projected after the precinct caucuses in January with the expressed candidate preference of national delegates selected at the district and state conventions. The actual national delegate totals demonstrate the lack of reliability of the caucus projections. Whereas the caucus projections had McGovern in third place, he and Muskie were in a dead heat after the state convention. Moreover, the Muskie support was "soft," since he was no longer an active candidate for the presidency.

It is interesting to speculate about how the caucus results might have been reported had the projections more accurately reflected the candidate leanings of the Iowa delegation to the Democratic National Convention. The headlines of the stories in the *Times*, the *Post*, and the *Register* probably would have suggested that McGovern was a surprise big winner and that although in a virtual dead heat, the Muskie campaign had suffered a devastating setback in Iowa. Apple's conclu-

Table 4.3.   1972 Democratic national delegate
equivalents compared with national
convention delegates

	January projection	National delegate preferences
Muskie	18	18
McGovern	10	18
Uncommitted	18	10

Source: National delegate preferences from Flansburg 1972d, 1B.

sion in the *Times* that politicians would not think that Muskie had stumbled might have been replaced by a headline stating, "Political Pros Think Muskie Stumbles Badly in Iowa." New Hampshire would have become even more important to the "faltering" Muskie campaign, and the momentum would have been with McGovern, who might have done even better in New Hampshire as the "big winner" in Iowa. Would Muskie have been knocked out of the race earlier, and if so, would the party pros have been able to convince Hubert Humphrey, or some other mainline Democrat, to make a serious bid for the nomination? Could McGovern have survived an early front-runner status? McGovern might have prevailed anyway, but it is also possible that the reporting of the Iowa media event and its inaccurate projections altered the outcome of the 1972 Democratic nomination.

A final comment about the 1972 Democratic caucuses concerns the implementation of party reforms. The proportional representation procedure was carefully followed at all levels of the caucus and convention system in Iowa, and whereas the state's 1968 national delegates had been appointed (following tradition) by Governor Harold Hughes, the 1972 national delegates were elected, and they included many from the rank and file. Although the party's affirmative action goal was not completely met, over 40 percent of the delegates were women, and other traditionally underrepresented groups were included as well. The only apparent negative side effect of the revised rules was the increased length of the party sessions at every level caused by the proportional representation requirement (Flansburg and O'Shea 1972, 1, 10).

The Republican Caucuses

In 1972 the Iowa Republicans did not hold their caucuses until April 4, and thus they missed out on the national attention attracted by the Democrats. President Richard Nixon was not actively opposed in Iowa, although Ohio Congressman John Ashbrook, who was challenging the president in some states, did receive a few votes in straw polls. There was little controversy, and the meetings received very limited space even in the local press (Johnson and Hansen 1972, 1). The Republican caucuses, whose procedures were unchanged from 1968, received no national attention.

Cartoon by Frank Miller, © 1976, *Des Moines Register,* reprinted by permission

The Iowa precinct caucuses emerged as a weather vane for political pundits after the 1972 presidential race. The *New York Times* and *Washington Post* were among the few national media that covered the 1972 Iowa caucuses. But after missing signs of weakness in the 1972 Muskie campaign, the national media converged on Iowa in 1976 to gather information about the progress of the presidential nominating races.

The Impact of the 1972 Caucuses

The Iowa caucuses alerted the nation that the presidential candidacy of Senator Edmund Muskie was vulnerable. Although the media coverage was modest, significant attention by the news trendsetters—the *New York Times* and the *Washington Post*—and the postcaucus success of the McGovern campaign assured more extensive media attention and a larger role for the Iowa caucuses in succeeding years.

Of greater importance, the 1972 caucuses marked the beginning of a dramatic change in American electoral politics. As the impact of the Iowa caucuses continued to grow in succeeding years, other states would move their primary elections and caucuses to earlier in the presidential nominating season. The traditional four-month primary season beginning in New Hampshire in March and culminating in California in June would be significantly altered. The schedule of primary events would be compressed, and a new front-loaded season emphasizing the nominating processes in Iowa and New Hampshire would develop. The traditionally late primary in California would be of little importance in future years, because presidential nominating races would be decided by the earlier events.

References

Apple, R. W., Jr. 1972. "Muskie Is Victor in Iowa Caucuses." *New York Times,* January 26, p. 16.

Bender, Richard. 1983. Telephone interview with author, March 23. Bender was the director of operations of the Iowa Democratic Party from 1970 to 1975.

Brown, Ralph. 1983. Telephone interview with author, March 16. Brown was the executive director of the Iowa Republican party from 1975 to 1977.

Chapman, William. 1972. "Iowa Caucuses Back Muskie, 33% Undecided." *Washington Post,* January 26, p. A4.

Clifton, C. C. 1952. "Huge Turnout by Republican Voters in D.M." *Des Moines Register,* March 8, p. 1.

Crotty, William, and John S. Jackson III. 1985. *Presidential Primaries and Nominations.* Washington, D.C.: CQ Press.

Des Moines Register. 1952-83.

Flansburg, James. 1972a. "Iowa Swing by McGovern in Demo Bid." *Des Moines Register,* January 13, pp. 1, 3.

———. 1972b. "Democrats Hold County Parleys." *Des Moines Register,* February 28, pp. 1, 8.

———. 1972c. "State Democratic Leader Sees Muskie Out of Race." *Des Moines Register,* April 28, pp. 1, 6.

———. 1972d. "McGovern and Muskie Split." *Des Moines Register,* May 21, p. 1B.

Flansburg, James, and James O'Shea. 1972. "McGovern Gains Strength in 20-Hour State Parley." *Des Moines Register,* May 22, pp. 1, 10.

Gallup, George. 1972. "Muskie Leads Kennedy in Survey of Democrats." *Des Moines Register,* January 23, p. 4B.

Hart, Gary. 1973. *Right from the Start: A Chronicle of the McGovern Campaign.* New York: Quadrangle Books.

Iowa Democratic Party. 1980. Precinct Caucus Kit, 1980. Mimeographed.

———. 1996. Constitution. Amended 1996.

Johnson, Stephen M. 1972. "See Caucus 'Packed' in Precinct 70." *Des Moines Register,* January 27, pp. 1, 7.

Johnson, Stephen M., and Christine Hansen. 1972. "Report Little Controversy at Republican Caucuses." *Des Moines Register,* April 5, pp. 1, 7.

Larson, Clifton. 1981. Telephone interview with author, February 23. Larson was the chair of the Iowa Democratic Party from 1970 to 1973.

Miller, Norman. 1972. "As Iowa Goes ...?" *Wall Street Journal,* January 19, pp. 1, 25.

Mills, George. 1968a. "Iowa G.O.P. in Caucuses." *Des Moines Register,* March 4, p. 9.

———. 1968b. "Add Fire to Already Hot Party Battle." *Des Moines Register,* March 17, pp. 1, 3.

———. 1968c. "Foes Capture Large Share of Delegates." *Des Moines Register,* March 27, pp. 1, 3.

———. 1968d. "Rasmussen Tells of 'Irregularities.'" *Des Moines Register,* April 4, pp. 1, 3.

Newsweek. 1972.

O'Shea, James. 1972. "McCarthy Fans' Fervor Missing." *Des Moines Register,* January 23, p. 4B.

Patterson, Thomas E. 1980. *The Mass Media Election: How Americans Choose Their President.* New York: Praeger.

Republican Party of Iowa. 1980. Suggested Procedure for Precinct Caucuses, January 21, 1980. Mimeographed.

———. 1996. Constitution. Amended 1996.

Risser, James. 1972. "Muskie Wins Support of Senator Hughes." *Des Moines Register,* January 18, pp. 1, 4.

Robinson, Michael J., and Margaret A. Sheehan. 1983. *Over the Wire and on TV: CBS and UPI in Campaign '80.* New York: Russell Sage Foundation.

Schier, Steven E. 1980. *The Rules of the Game: Democratic National Convention Delegate Selection in Iowa and Wisconsin.* Washington, D.C.: University Press of America.

Seplow, Stephen. 1968. "Hughes Says Johnson 'No' Shocks Him." *Des Moines Register,* April 1, pp. 1, 10.

Weaver, Warren. 1968. "McCarthy Gets About 40%, Johnson and Nixon on Top in New Hampshire Voting." *New York Times,* March 13, pp. 1, 33.

Chapter 5 # The 1976 Caucuses:
The Making of a Front-Runner

THE NATIONAL NEWS MEDIA, with notable exceptions, devoted minimal time and space to the 1972 Iowa precinct caucuses. The limited coverage is understandable, given the newness of Iowa as an early source of information about the progress of the presidential campaign, but it also is apparent that the media fell victim to their own expectations about the 1972 presidential nominations. Reporters made up their minds early in 1972 about the likely outcome of the presidential nominating contests. President Nixon would certainly be renominated by the Republicans, and according to Donald R. Matthews, "political pundits nearly to a man had predicted that Senator Ed Muskie of Maine would be the Democratic nominee" (1978, 58).

Thus the Iowa caucuses remained relatively anonymous. Senator McGovern's grass-roots effort went largely unnoticed, receiving minimal coverage by the major newspapers and television networks, whose focus, Jules Witcover has said, "was squarely on Muskie as he collected big-name endorsements en route, nearly everyone thought, to a routine first-ballot nomination" (1977, 200). When Muskie's 1972 presidential campaign collapsed in late April, political reporters found themselves in a very embarrassing position: The man they had already "nominated" was no longer a candidate for the presidency. News reporters badly underestimated the potential of McGovern's grass-roots organizational effort and had failed to discover the signs of weakness in the Muskie campaign. In addition, although the Watergate break-in took place during the campaign, it went undetected when President Nixon escaped the careful eye of the press by conducting a rose-garden campaign. The 1972 mistakes were harmful to the credibility of the reporters who covered presidential nominations, and thus, said Witcover, "in 1976, if there were going to be early signals,

the fourth estate was going to be on the scene en masse to catch them"
(1977, 200).

Precaucus Activity

Meanwhile, the Iowa parties were taking steps to expand the nation's
interest in their caucuses. The Iowa Republicans, who missed out on
the headlines in 1972 by holding their meetings in April, were anxious
to share the limelight with the Democrats. Both parties realized the
desirability for media purposes of a common date. They arranged a
marriage of convenience to hold the 1976 caucuses on January 19, and
they have continued the practice in presidential years. As previously
discussed, the Republicans initiated a straw poll in selected precincts,
and the Democrats developed a statewide system for reporting delegate totals in 1976. Thus the stage was set for a truly national media
event, and Iowa's party leaders were not to be disappointed.

The Democratic Campaign

Jimmy Carter targeted Iowa as a testing ground for his campaign and
spent nearly a year cultivating a following. Virtually unknown outside
the South, Carter endured some very difficult days in the effort to put
together a grass-roots organization in Iowa. In reminiscing about his
first visit to Des Moines in February 1975, Carter recalled a reception
held at a local hotel: "There were Jody and myself and the man and
woman who arranged the reception—and I think there were three
other people" (Schram 1977, 6). Overcoming the embarrassment,
Democratic state chair Tom Whitney suggested to Jody Powell that he
be given a few minutes to make arrangements for a Carter visit to the
courthouse, where he at least shook a few hands and met some Polk
County Democrats (Whitney 1986).

The day before, on February 26, Carter had been the featured speaker at a dinner in Le Mars honoring Marie Jahn, who was retiring after
thirty-eight years as the Plymouth County recorder (Flansburg 1975a,
34). Perhaps the testimonial dinner was not significant enough to
attract a presidential candidate, but Carter was not flooded with invitations in those early Iowa days. After the Le Mars speech Carter campaigned two more days in Iowa, and the extended visit proved well

Cartoon by Frank Miller, © 1979, *Des Moines Register*, reprinted by permission

Jimmy Carter, commonly referred to as "Jimmy Who" in the early stages of the 1976 race for the presidency, used the Iowa caucuses as a springboard to the Democratic nomination. In his early visits to Iowa he spoke to small crowds in obscure places, but his patience and systematic approach to organizing the state paid great dividends when the media interpreted the results of the 1976 meetings as a great victory for Carter.

worth the effort. He received extensive coverage in the *Des Moines Register*—four days of stories—and impressed chief political writer James Flansburg. In a front-page article Flansburg praised Carter's knowledge of the issues and observed that "seldom has a candidate without a fabled name made such a fast and favorable impression on Iowans" (1975b, 1).

Carter, who had earlier decided to make a major effort in New Hampshire and Florida, concluded that he could do well in Iowa, and furthermore, he perceived that he had the opportunity to turn the precinct caucuses into a major media event (Schram 1977, 6). In those early days, the Carter campaign did not have a great deal of competition in Iowa, because, according to Witcover, "other candidates and prospective candidates concentrated most of their pre-election year energies in minor liberal skirmishes in the East or on New Hampshire" (1977, 197). By late August 1975, campaign aide Tim Kraft had persuaded those directing the national effort that he should move full-time into Iowa, and he set out to organize the state. Rather than appoint an Iowa campaign chair and risk being saddled with that person's political image, he put together a group (nineteen or twenty people, depending on whom you read) called the "Iowa Carter for President Steering Committee," which was geographically and ideologically representative and which included some very important Democrats (Schram 1977, 9).

In less than a month, the Kraft effort yielded concrete results in the September 22 "off-year caucuses" held throughout the state. The enterprising Whitney was committed to making the Iowa caucuses a media event, and he had decided that a straw poll might enliven the meetings and draw some media attention. Some 5762 people participated in the poll, and although the results were inconclusive, Carter came in first. He received 9.9 percent of the vote, Sargent Shriver received 8.7 percent, Birch Bayh 8.1, Hubert Humphrey 7.2, Henry Jackson 6.5, Morris Udall 6.1, and Fred Harris 5.7. A total of 45 percent of the participants were uncommitted, and the remaining 3 percent of the votes were broadly scattered (*DMR* Oct. 25, 1975, 1A). The results may have shed little light on the Democratic race, but the poll served to notify reporters that Iowa would provide "an early line on the 1976 contenders," and they were paying close attention when the next poll was held at the Jefferson-Jackson Day dinner in Ames on October 25

(Witcover 1977, 201).

By late October 1975 the field of candidates for the Democratic presidential nomination had grown substantially. In addition to those noted above, Terry Sanford, Lloyd Bentsen, and Milton Shapp were announced candidates, and George Wallace was considered a strong contender for the nomination. These latter four candidates, however, spent little or no time campaigning in Iowa. In fact, prior to the Jefferson-Jackson Day dinner, only Carter, Harris, Shriver, Jackson, and Udall had made major efforts in the state, and the quality of their campaigns was mixed.

Senator Henry Jackson began his caucus effort as early as Carter, but he gained little visibility even though he campaigned frequently in Iowa. By mid-1975 he had withdrawn from the state. Former senator Fred Harris started in Iowa nearly as early as Carter and spent an immense amount of time and effort courting delegates, but he was plagued by limited funds and uneven organization. Sargent Shriver, the 1972 vice-presidential nominee, was also an early starter in Iowa and had hoped to appeal to the heavily Catholic areas of the state, but despite frequent visits, he was unable to persuade local Democratic leaders that his campaign should be taken seriously (Schier 1980, 295-308).

Representative Morris Udall established a presence in Iowa early in 1975, but he targeted few resources for the precinct caucuses. His campaign staff was instead focusing on the New Hampshire primary, which traditionally attracts great media attention as the nation's first primary election. They hoped that success in New Hampshire would be followed by victories in Massachusetts and Wisconsin (Arterton 1978a, 15-17). Senator Birch Bayh announced for the presidency just a few days before the Jefferson-Jackson Day dinner.

This dinner is an important event for Iowa Democrats. It is the major fund-raiser of the year, and it brings large numbers of the faithful together for a huge pep rally. In recent presidential years it has also provided an opportunity to showcase the Iowa Democratic Party. Held in the fall, it is timed perfectly for Democratic presidential candidates to appear and make their case before the partisans most likely to attend the precinct caucuses a few months later. In 1975, for the first time, a large number of the presidential hopefuls attended and spoke at the dinner in Ames.

The Ames gathering, choreographed by state chair Whitney, was political theater at its best. All the presidential candidates were invited, and the affair, according to Jules Witcover, "had all the trappings of a political convention, with booths set up at the back of the arena for each of the hopefuls, and time set aside ... to man the booths, shake hands, and answer questions" (1977, 201). George McGovern, the 1972 Democratic standard-bearer, was the keynote speaker. Seven presidential candidates attended—Bayh, Carter, Harris, Jackson, Sanford, Shriver, and Udall—and they were permitted ten minutes each for speeches, followed by demonstrations of support. All the candidates held beer-and-wine receptions after the dinner activities (Flansburg 1975d, 1A; Flansburg 1975e, 1A, 14A).

The *Des Moines Register*, however, was the key actor at the Jefferson-Jackson Day dinner. The paper, using its own polling organization, arranged a straw poll that Flansburg said "was conducted before the candidates spoke, in an effort to measure organizational effectiveness" (1975f, 1A). Ballots were distributed to the fifty-dollar-a-couple, full-paying guests, but balcony seats were available for two dollars (minus the meal), and Tim Kraft had packed the balcony with Carter supporters, some of whom managed to vote in the poll (Witcover 1977, 201). The results of the poll are shown in Table 5.1.

Carter was judged the big winner in the Jefferson-Jackson Day poll. The *Register* story ran under the headline "Carter Tops Democratic Straw Poll," with the added subtitle, "Other Contenders Trail Far Behind" (Flansburg 1975f, 1A). The *New York Times*, in a story headline of perhaps record length, declared: "Carter Appears to Hold a Solid Lead in Iowa As the Campaign's First Test Approaches." In the *Times* article R. W. Apple noted that Carter "has made dramatic progress while attention was focused on the scramble for liberal primacy among Mr. Udall, Mr. Bayh, Mr. Harris, and Mr. Shriver." Apple concluded that Carter "appears to have taken a surprising but solid lead for Iowa's 47 delegates to the Democratic National Convention next year" (1975, 17L).

The Apple article provided a tremendous boost for Carter because it focused national media attention on his campaign. According to Elizabeth Drew, the Apple story "was itself a political event, prompting other newspaper stories that Carter was doing well in Iowa, and then more news-magazine and television coverage for Carter than might

Table 5.1.   1975 Jefferson-
Jackson Day poll results

	Votes	Percentage of total
Carter	256	23.4
Humphrey	135	12.3
Bayh	112	10.2
Shriver	93	8.5
Udall	77	7.0
Harris	61	5.6
Jackson	56	5.1
Sanford	7	0.6
Wallace	6	0.5
Bentsen	2	0.2
Shapp	2	0.2
Write-ins	47	4.3
Undecided	240	21.9
Total	1094	99.8

Source: Data from Flansburg 1975f,
1A.

otherwise have been his share" (Arterton 1978b, 39). Reporters from
Time and *Newsweek* indicated that their magazines had decided to pay
greater attention to the Iowa caucuses as a result of the Apple story and
one by Jules Witcover in the *Washington Post* (Arterton 1978b, 39).
Others have noted that "the *Times* and, to a lesser degree, the *Post* are
the media's references for subjects to be covered" (Paletz and Entman
1981, 7), and that seems to have been the case with the Iowa caucuses.
The two papers were among the few that had covered the 1972 caucuses extensively, and now they pointed the way in 1976.

After eight months of hard work at the grass-roots level, a victory in
the Jefferson-Jackson Day straw poll, and a story in the *New York Times*,
Carter was now the front-runner in Iowa. He had been judged a viable
candidate by the news media on the basis of very soft evidence: his
apparent organizational skills and his straw-poll successes. Now, how-

Cartoon by Frank Miller, © 1979, *Des Moines Register,* reprinted by permission

The 1976 campaign in Iowa was characterized by straw polls. Democratic leaders discovered that they could increase interest in and attract media attention to a gathering or fund-raiser by holding a well-publicized straw poll. The results of a poll conducted by the *Des Moines Register* at the Jefferson-Jackson Day dinner in 1975 were reported nationally and made Carter the front-runner in Iowa.

ever, a new set of expectations had been created. As the front-runner, Carter would have to win, or at least do very well, in the Iowa caucuses. A campaign worker observed that "if we don't finish first or a close second, ... I'm afraid the press will crucify us. I think I liked it better when we were underdogs" (Hunt 1976, 20).

Udall, who after the campaign referred to the *Register* survey as "that silly poll in Iowa" (Schram 1977, 16), recognized the new reality and altered his strategy to include more time and money for Iowa. He committed ten days in January and approximately $80,000 of his limited campaign funds to the state. An aide justified the investment by the potential for media exposure, observing that the caucuses "will be covered like the first primary always has been in the national press," and he reasoned that "Iowa justifies the expense" (Witcover 1977, 204).

Senator Bayh, who had done surprisingly well in the Jefferson-Jackson Day poll in spite of his late start, also decided to make a major effort to gain support in the precinct caucuses. He was not alone. As the January caucuses approached, presidential hopefuls were so common in Iowa that a State Center couple reported seeing all the Democratic candidates at least twice without ever having driven "more than an hour from their home" (Flansburg 1976a, 16A). With the emphasis on organization and personal contact at the grass-roots level, five of the 1976 Democratic candidates spent more time in Iowa than the combined seven campaign days of the 1972 candidates. Table 5.2 shows the number of campaign days that the most active candidates spent in Iowa. There were also infrequent visits by other candidates, such as Terry Sanford's appearance at the Jefferson-Jackson Day dinner.

A final political event that contributed to media expectations about the upcoming Iowa caucuses occurred one week before the January 19 date of the meetings. The *New York Times* ran a front-page story by R. W. Apple rating the presidential chances of the 1976 Democratic candidates. On the basis of his conversations with political pros in a number of early caucus and primary states, Apple divided the hopefuls into three groups: (1) those "most likely to be selected"—Jackson, Bayh, Carter, and Humphrey; (2) those with "a conceivable chance of being nominated"—Shriver, Harris, and Udall; and finally (3) "those most unlikely to be the nominee"—Bentsen, Shapp, Sanford, Church,

Table 5.2.   1976 Democratic
precaucus campaign activity

	Days in Iowa
Harris	23
Carter	17
Bayh	15
Shriver	13
Udall	12
Jackson	6

Source: Data from Flansburg
1976c, 7A.

Wallace, and Byrd. Apple conceded that "such early calculations are highly speculative" but asserted that media perception of the nominating campaign becomes the all-important reality against which caucus and primary outcomes are judged (Apple 1976a, 1, 19). Political reporters had developed their expectations about the Democratic race for the presidential nomination, and now they awaited the "hard news" that the first caucuses and primaries would provide.

The Republican Campaign

Normally it is the caucuses of the "out party" that provide the excitement, but in 1976 interest in the Republican caucuses increased when Governor Ronald Reagan decided to challenge President Gerald Ford for the nomination. Precaucus media coverage of the Republican meetings was very limited, however, compared to that given the Democrats. Writing about the Republican caucuses shortly before their scheduled date, one reporter explained the disparity this way: "Neither President Ford nor his challenger, Ronald Reagan, has chosen to pay much attention to the Republican caucuses, ... so the press hasn't either" (Hunt 1976, 1). Supporters of the two candidates made some effort to organize in Iowa, but it was a low-visibility campaign.

There was a certain novelty in a challenge to a sitting president, but Reagan had made no secret of his presidential aspirations. Moreover,

Ford was perceived as vulnerable. He had been appointed vice-president by President Nixon when Spiro Agnew resigned under a cloud of scandal, and he succeeded to the presidency when Mr. Nixon resigned as a result of Watergate. Ford had not been elected to either office, and when he pardoned the former president for all Watergate crimes, the conventional wisdom held that Ford's reelection was in jeopardy. Those who reported and those who followed politics were anxious for hard news to confirm or disprove Ford's vulnerability. But President Ford chose not to campaign in Iowa.

Reagan did make a brief appearance in Iowa on the Saturday before the caucuses, when the plane taking him from New Hampshire to California landed in Des Moines to refuel and give the candidate an opportunity to hold an airport rally. About 300 people attended and questioned Reagan about his stands on current political issues, including his proposal to shift many social programs from federal to state jurisdiction (Flansburg 1976b, 5A).

The 1976 Precinct Caucuses

The precinct caucuses operated under a new law passed by the general assembly in 1975. Concerned that participation and democratic processes suffered in overcrowded private homes, the legislature required that precinct caucuses be held in public buildings wherever possible (Ia. Gen. Assem. 1975, chap. 81, p. 162). Since that time, more caucuses have been held in public buildings, but many rural and small-town meetings are still held in private homes.

The Democratic Caucuses

On caucus night the Democrats established a "caucus returns headquarters" at the Des Moines Hilton, with a telephone reporting system from each of Iowa's ninety-nine counties. Party staff were available for analysis, and they provided state delegate equivalents and national delegate equivalents from the precinct caucuses. State chair Tom Whitney, who was rapidly becoming the P. T. Barnum of electoral politics, organized a media-watching event in the grand ballroom of the Hilton. He reasoned that with so many national media dignitaries in attendance, there was money to be made, and he sold tickets to anyone willing to pay ten dollars for the opportunity to watch the reporters in action. Drinks were sold for a dollar, and everyone had a good time watching media stars like Roger Mudd and Herbert Kaplow work (Hollobaugh 1976, 7A). Whitney discovered, however, that it was not always easy to deal with the big egos of the press. The *Los Angeles Times* staff, for example, upon discovering that their seats were in the second row, complained that they should be in the front row with the *New York Times* and the *Washington Post.* The media-watching event made about $4,000 for the party (Whitney 1986).

News reporters contributed to the growth of the Iowa media event by extensively covering the 1976 caucus results as the first hard news in the presidential contest. Most of the major national print and broadcast media sent representatives to cover the process, and the three networks planned live caucus coverage on January 19 (Schier 1980, 316). The networks did not, however, set up temporary studios or move their news anchors to Des Moines, as they would for future presidential caucuses. Party officials estimated that 150 reporters were on hand the day of the caucuses and that each of the three networks had another three dozen people in the state to cover the event (Hunt 1976, 1, 20). "Meet the Press," with four Democratic presidential candidates as guests, originated from Des Moines the week before the caucuses.

The day after the caucuses, the media began interpreting the Iowa results to the nation. The Democratic results are given in Table 5.3. The *New York Times* declared that Carter had "scored an impressive victory in yesterday's Iowa Democratic precinct caucuses" (Apple 1976b, 1). A *Times* story a day later began this way: "Former Gov. Jimmy Carter of Georgia found himself widely regarded today as a major contender for the Democratic nomination." Analyzing the order of finish, R. W. Apple concluded that Bayh "finished a much weaker second than he had expected" and that Udall's poor standing "raised serious questions about his staff's ability to run a national campaign." But perhaps the most novel aspect of the story was the grading of each candidate's performance in the Iowa caucuses: Carter received an A, Harris a B, Bayh a C, Udall and Shriver Ds, and Jackson an "incomplete" (Apple 1976c, 1, 28). The *Wall Street Journal* saw Carter as an impressive winner because of his "convincing two-to-one margin over his nearest rival," while Udall, who "ran a poor fourth in a state where he invested much effort," and Shriver, who "ran a barely visible fifth," were the

Table 5.3.   1976 Democratic precinct caucus
results

	State delegate equivalents (%)	Projected national delegates
Uncommitted	37.2	18
Carter	27.6	13
Bayh	13.2	6
Harris	9.9	5
Udall	6.0	3
Shriver	3.3	2
Jackson	1.1	0
Others	1.8	0

Source: Data provided by the Iowa Democratic Party,
based on 2220 of the 2530 precincts (88%).

big losers (Jan. 21, 1976, 8). Jules Witcover, writing in the *Washington Post,* was more cautious, noting that "Jimmy Carter has gained early momentum in the winnowing out process," although "his victory is far from decisive." Witcover went on to say that "if there were losers," they were Udall and Shriver (1976, A1, A4).

The February 2 editions of *Time, Newsweek,* and *U.S. News and World Report* included major stories about the caucuses. Most of the stories' space in the three magazines was devoted to Carter, and they characterized him as the winner or front-runner, or both. *Time* and *Newsweek,* for example, gave Carter a total of 726 lines of coverage, while Udall, Harris, Bayh, Jackson, and Shriver averaged only 30 lines each (Paletz and Entman 1981, 35). The magazines gave very little space to the other Democrats in any of the articles, although the *Time* story concluded that the Iowa caucuses were "a near disaster for Udall" (Feb. 2, 1976, 17).

Carter had spent January 19 in New York, hoping to turn an anticipated win in Iowa into a media bonanza by being available to the network morning news shows. The networks were indeed interested in Carter, and on the twentieth he appeared on NBC's "Today" show, CBS's "Morning News," and ABC's "AM America" (Schram 1977, 18).

The CBS "Morning News" declared Carter the victor and conducted a rather lengthy interview with him in which he interpreted the impact of the caucuses on his and the other candidates' campaigns. The only other candidate shown during the program was Fred Harris, and he was represented as finishing a poor third (Schier 1980, 336). Carter enjoyed five times as much postcaucus television coverage as any other candidate (Paletz and Entman 1981, 35).

Media reporting of the results of the 1976 Iowa Democratic precinct caucuses was uniform: Carter was the big winner. He met all the expectations of the reporters and captured most of the news space and airtime. Carter was clearly the media front-runner going into the New Hampshire primary election. Many thought that the Bayh and Shriver campaigns had been damaged by their relatively poor showing, but virtually all the media covering the caucuses thought that Iowa had severely hurt Udall. R. W. Apple had even suggested that his campaign was of minor-league quality.

Yet Carter, the media victor, won only 28 percent of the state delegate equivalents, and the largest category of delegates (37%) was the uncommitted group. Further, there would be many changes in support patterns in Iowa between the precinct caucuses and the state convention. Attributing so much importance to the Iowa caucuses is a little like establishing the opening-day winners in the major leagues as the heavy favorites to win the World Series. The difference, of course, is that the media have little impact on the outcome of the baseball season. Furthermore, participation in the caucuses was low in 1976. Party officials estimated that 4 percent (22,000 to 26,000) of the registered Republicans (Roth 1984) and 7 percent (38,500) of the eligible Democrats attended caucuses (Steffen 1984). Caucus attendance figures are very rough estimates by party officials and must be treated carefully. In 1976, for example, Tom Whitney told reporters that 50,000 people had participated in the Democratic caucuses, and that figure was widely reported. Whitney indicated to me that he pulled that figure "off the top of his head" in response to a reporter's question about attendance. The later estimate of 38,500 by party officials is also only an estimate (Steffen 1984). It is little wonder that Michael J. Robinson classified "Carter's media victory in Iowa" as one of the major "medialities" of the 1976 presidential election (1981, 196).

The Validity of the Democratic Results

Less than a week after the precinct caucuses, the staff of the *Des Moines Register* discovered a problem with the 1976 Democratic results. The numbers released to the media by the Iowa Democrats were misleading because the party had not followed its own 15 percent rule in calculating state and national delegates. As indicated in Table 5.3, party officials projected thirteen national delegates for Carter and a total of sixteen for four other candidates—Bayh, Harris, Udall, and Shriver. In analyzing the figures provided by Democratic headquarters, the *Register* found that "Carter was the only candidate to win enough support to guarantee him some Iowa delegates" and that "none of the other candidates [was] close to having enough support to win one single delegate." Although the 15 percent rule was followed in selecting county delegates, state chair Whitney readily conceded that in calculating the state delegate equivalents and projecting beyond, the county party officials ignored the 15 percent rule and instead used a 5 percent threshold. Whitney said this was done so that the "results would be clear-cut and show the rank-and-file sentiment for each of the candidates" (Flansburg 1976d, 1A, 5A). Table 5.4 shows the results of the 1976 Democratic caucuses derived by the *Register* using the 15 percent threshold required by party rules.

The *Register* did not allege that the Iowa Democrats had violated the national Democratic party's 15 percent rule in selecting county delegates. The party did, however, mislead reporters and the nation by ignoring the rule in calculating state and national delegates. Simply stated, the results reported to the media were phony. They did not accurately reflect the delegate selection process that took place on January 19. Official Democratic results completed after all precincts had been tabulated, which were published in the Democrats' 1980 precinct caucus kit, confirm the *Register*'s analysis (p. 2). While Iowa has many laws governing the conduct of precinct caucuses, including laws governing when and where they may be held, and making the manipulation of the outcome of a primary election illegal, no law prohibits the creation and publication of misleading caucus results. (In 1988 the general assembly passed a law governing the reporting of caucus results. See Chapter 8.)

It is very likely that media interpretations of the 1976 Democratic

Table 5.4.   1976 Democratic precinct caucus results,
observing the 15 percent rule

| | State delegate equivalents | | |
	Number	Percentage of total	Projected no. of national delegates
Uncommitted	1070	31.2	39
Carter	940	27.4	8
Bayh	257	7.5	0
Harris	173	5.0	0
Udall	88	2.6	0
Shriver	32	0.9	0
Total	2560	74.6	47

Source: Data from the *Des Moines Register* January 25, 1976, 1A,
5A. The results from 2169 of 2530 precincts (86%) were obtained
from the Iowa Democratic Party. The absence of 14 percent of the
precincts made it impossible to project the other 872 state delegates
(25.4%).

caucuses would have been different had they been given the results
shown in Table 5.4 instead of those in Table 5.3. Carter's victory might
have been seen as even more stunning, and reporters likely would have
held a mass burial for the also-rans who fared so poorly. R. W. Apple's
report card might have been revised to something like this: Carter, A+;
Bayh, D; Harris, D-; Udall and Shriver, F; and Jackson, "incomplete."
Or, and perhaps more likely, the story headline might have read "Iowa
Uncommitted," and neither Carter nor Whitney wanted that interpretation.

It is tempting to go on in this vein, but to do so risks obscuring a
major point of this book: that the Iowa precinct caucuses do not produce meaningful results. Because they represent merely the first stage
in a multistage process, there are no reportable outcomes, and no one
considered that a problem before 1972. The parties contrived results so
that Iowa could become a media event; in 1976 the results were simply
more contrived and deceptive than usual.

The 1976 meetings provide a good example of the problems associated with caucus projections. The media-reported Democratic projection of national delegate equivalents indicated that Carter would control 13 of Iowa's 47 national delegates, Udall 3, other candidates 13, and 18 were uncommitted. As the winnowing process continued during the caucus and primary season, delegate loyalties changed—in some cases several times. The liberal candidates dropped out one by one, and in Iowa their supporters coalesced around Morris Udall. His strength grew steadily, and after the national delegates were elected at the district and state conventions, the candidate totals looked like this: Carter 20, Udall 12, and Harris 2, with 13 uncommitted. On the first and only ballot at the Democratic National Convention in New York City, Iowa gave 25 of its 47 votes to Carter, 20 to Udall, and 1 each to Senator Ted Kennedy and Governor Jerry Brown. The disparity illustrates the danger of projecting outcomes on the basis of the first stage in a multistage process. The media did not report raw vote totals; there were none. They reported phony projections that were never accurate and by the time of the national convention were irrelevant. By that time, however, the caucuses were long forgotten, and there was no demand for accountability for the misleading "results" reported about Iowa.

The Republican Caucuses

The Republicans hoped to stimulate citizen participation and postcaucus media coverage with their new straw poll at some of the meetings. The poll was scheduled for sixty-two randomly selected precincts picked after a survey firm from Shenandoah was consulted to ensure that the methods conformed with standard survey procedures. The precincts chosen for the straw poll were not revealed until the time of the caucuses to prevent packing by supporters of either Governor Reagan or President Ford (*DMR* Jan. 12, 1976, 6A). The goal of the survey was to gain knowledge about the sentiments of those attending Republican caucuses, not to predict delegate totals to county conventions, so there was no weighting of the totals (Brown 1986). Most important, the poll would provide some numbers for the media.

Media coverage of the 1976 Republican caucuses was extensive, but postcaucus stories devoted considerably less space to the Ford-Reagan contest than they did to the Carter victory. The *New York Times* story of January 20, for example, devoted 26 lines to the Republican caucuses and 123 to the Democratic caucuses; the remaining 56 lines explained caucus procedures. The January 21 *Times* article gave 26 lines to the Republican and 357 lines to the Democratic caucuses. The *Times* noted that President Ford had the backing of virtually all Republican party officials but still "barely defeated" Governor Reagan in the straw poll by a vote of 264 to 248 (Apple 1976b, 1). The *Wall Street Journal* said that the straw poll gave Ford a "narrow lead" over Reagan, but it more or less dismissed the poll because it was not an "indicator of how Iowa's delegation will vote at the Republican National Convention" (Jan. 21, 1976, 8). Jules Witcover's caucus story in the *Washington Post* mentioned neither the Republican meetings nor the straw poll (Jan. 21, 1976, A1, A4).

The weekly magazines devoted little space to the Republicans in Iowa. *Time*, in a story that gave 17 lines to the Republican and 130 lines to the Democratic caucuses, interpreted Ford's slim 45 to 43 percent victory in the straw poll as a setback for the president, thus placing Ford on the defensive in his bid for renomination (Feb. 2, 1976, 12, 17). The tone of the other magazines was similar. *Newsweek* thought the president would not find his slim victory in the Iowa straw poll "reassuring" (Feb. 2, 1976, 16), and *U.S. News and World Report* said: "President Gerald Ford may be in trouble" because of his "disappointingly small" margin in the poll (Feb. 2, 1976, 16).

The Republican caucus straw poll seems to have been a red flag for the media. It alerted those who thought that an incumbent president would have little trouble winning renomination against a challenger who was considered too ideological, and it confirmed the suspicion held by others that President Ford was in trouble. The Republican meetings did not receive nearly as much attention as their Democratic counterparts, but that undoubtedly was because their straw poll was unrelated to delegate selection. It was little more than a beauty contest. Iowa Governor Robert Ray put it succinctly: "I don't think our caucuses hold quite the same meaning as the Democrats'" (*DMR* Jan. 20, 1976, 7A).

The 1976 Republican results drawn from the sixty-two sample precincts showed that participants cast 264 votes for Ford and 248 for

Reagan. There were 62 votes categorized as "undecided," and 9 votes were cast for other candidates. Apparently no results were obtained from at least one sample precinct. The *Des Moines Register* reported on January 20 that in a Polk County precinct selected for the survey, Delaware 2, nobody "showed up to unlock the door" (Jan. 20, 1976, 1A). The media interpretation that Reagan was a viable challenger was based on a sixteen-vote plurality among 583 Iowa Republicans. Such a poll may be very slim evidence for that judgment, but it again illustrates the media quest for reportable news about the progress of the campaign.

The Impact of the 1976 Caucuses

The year 1976 was a pivotal one for the Iowa caucuses. The state political parties worked very hard to attract the attention of the presidential candidates and the news media, including observing a common caucus date. The Republicans were disappointed that President Ford and Governor Reagan ignored the state, but the officials did succeed in attracting extensive postcaucus media coverage of their straw poll.

Perhaps no one worked harder to promote the caucuses than Tom Whitney. He initiated straw polls and made sure that the candidates and the media were aware of them and ultimately their outcomes; he provided speaking opportunities for the presidential hopefuls; he created a statewide reporting system and tabulation center so that the caucuses provided hard news; and he even interpreted the results of the 1976 precinct caucuses to make them more interesting and clearcut. With a lot of chutzpah, Whitney turned the caucuses into a media event that attracted to Iowa at least nine presidential candidates and most of the major national print and broadcast media.

The Iowa political parties were very pleased with the result. They had become significant actors in the presidential nominating process, and the impact of the caucuses was far greater than the few votes Iowa controlled at the national conventions. The party leaders and staff were now consulted by presidential hopefuls and were sought after by the national media. The attention focused on the caucuses also served as an excellent party development tool, since potential workers and donors were identified early in the political season.

The new media event was, in fact, good for the people of the state as a whole. Some Iowans tend to suffer from feelings of inferiority about their state. Perhaps too many bad jokes about the cold winters or the tastes of the little old lady from Dubuque had left their mark on the average Iowan's psyche, but the national attention made people feel good about themselves and their state. Reporters sought the political views of everyday people, and the media picture that emerged of a clean, competitive political system gave Iowans some hope that one day people east of the Alleghenies might be able to distinguish between Iowa and Idaho.

The new status of the caucuses was also economically beneficial to the state. No reliable data are available for 1976, but the presidential campaigns rented cars, occupied hotel rooms, dined at restaurants, and spent money in Iowa for various and sundry services. Beyond this, the reporters who followed the campaigns also made their contribution to the state's economy.

The 1976 Iowa caucuses also had a significant impact on the national nominating process. The great boost given the Carter campaign has already been discussed. Carter, unknown nationally before Iowa, became the media front-runner after the caucuses, a fact that was worth untold dollars in free coverage. Carter's national finance director, Joel McCleary, indicated that the campaign had put most of its organizational efforts into Iowa and New Hampshire and "had no structure after Florida; we had planned only for the short haul. After Florida, it was all NBC, CBS, and the *New York Times*" (Arterton 1978a, 6-7).

Iowa was a perfect state for a dark-horse candidate for the presidency. It is a small state whose political culture lends itself to limited-budget personal campaigning. Moreover, the potential of the Iowa caucuses as a media event was relatively unknown in 1976; thus they were of great surprise value to Carter. This would change after 1976 as the Iowa caucuses became nationally known. The Iowa media event would command the attention of presidential candidates in 1980.

In the 1976 presidential race, media attention increasingly focused on the early nominating events, and the media based their expectations for future contests on their outcomes. The game focus of the media led reporters to overemphasize the significance of the early electoral events and to overlook the unrepresentative nature of states like Iowa and New Hampshire. As Morris Udall observed, since the media placed so much emphasis on the early events, presidential candidates had to concentrate more of their efforts and campaign funds on them. The realization also spread among state parties that in order to maximize their influence on the presidential primary process, they would have to hold their primary events early in the season. The front-loading that followed would reach a new high in 1984, when seventeen states scheduled primaries or caucuses in the first twenty-two days of the nominating season (*Congressional Quarterly Weekly Report* [hereafter cited as *CQ*] Dec. 10, 1983, 2605).

The Defense of a Media Event

Not everyone was pleased with the early precinct caucuses and their great impact on the presidential nominating process. Several states, undoubtedly envious of the status afforded Iowa and probably not pleased to see a small farm state that normally supports Republican presidential candidates playing a pivotal role in choosing the Democratic nominee, pressed for changes in party rules governing the Democratic nominating season.

When the legislators in the Iowa General Assembly learned that compression of the primary schedule was a possibility, they reacted to the perceived threat to their now-famous caucuses by enacting legislation that required that precinct caucuses be held no later than the second Monday in February in even-numbered years (Ia. Gen. Assem. 1978, chap. 1042, p. 207). Since national party rules governing primary processes take precedence over state laws, the legislative action was largely symbolic.

Although national party rules that compressed the Democratic nominating season into a thirteen-week period between the second Tuesday in March and the second Tuesday in June were enacted for 1980, Iowa's (and New Hampshire's) position of prominence was preserved by the inclusion of an appeals process for states that had held nominating events earlier in 1976 (Democratic National Committee 1978). The Iowa Democrats requested and received a variance to hold their 1980 precinct caucuses in January, thus successfully parrying the attempt to limit their influence in the presidential nominating process.

References

Apple, R. W. 1975. "Carter Appears to Hold a Solid Lead in Iowa As the Campaign's First Test Approaches." *New York Times,* October 27, p. 17L.

———. 1976a. "Democratic Chiefs Beginning to Rate Presidential Rivals." *New York Times,* January 12, pp. 1, 19.

———. 1976b. "Carter Defeats Bayh by 2-1 in Iowa Vote; Many Uncommitted." *New York Times,* January 20, pp. 1, 20.

———. 1976c. "Carter Is Regarded as Getting Big Gain from Iowa Results." *New York Times,* January 21, pp. 1, 28.

Arterton, F. Christopher. 1978a. "Campaign Organizations Confront the Media-Political Environment." In *Race for the Presidency: The Media and the Nominating Process,* edited by James D. Barber, 3-25. Englewood Cliffs, N.J.: Prentice-Hall.

———. 1978b. "The Media Politics of Presidential Campaigns: A Study of the Carter Nomination Drive." In *Race for the Presidency: The Media and the Nominating Process,* edited by James D. Barber, 26-54. Englewood Cliffs, N.J.: Prentice-Hall.

Brown, Ralph. 1986. Telephone interview with author, April 23. Brown was the executive director of the Iowa Republican party from 1975 to 1977.

Congressional Quarterly Weekly Report. 1983.

Democratic National Committee. 1978. Delegate Selection Rules for the 1980 Democratic National Convention. Mimeographed.

Des Moines Register. 1975 and 1976.

Flansburg, James. 1975a. "Carter Urges Withdrawal of Troops in Far East." *Des Moines Register,* February 27, p. 34.

———. 1975b. "Jimmy Carter: Iowans Find He's No Maddox." *Des Moines Register,* March 2, pp. 1, 6.

———. 1975c. "Democrats to Be Polled on Nominees." *Des Moines Register,* September 22, p. 1A.

———. 1975d. "8 Bring Presidential Campaigns to Iowa." *Des Moines Register,* October 25, p. 1A.

———. 1975e. "McGovern Challenges '76 Hopefuls." *Des Moines Register,* October 26, pp. 1A, 14A.

———. 1975f. "Carter Tops Democratic Straw Poll." *Des Moines Register,* October 27, p. 1A.

———. 1976a. "Campaign '76: Issues Bow to Organization." *Des Moines Register,* January 4, pp. 1A, 16A.

———. 1976b. "Reagan in D.M. to Rally Supporters." *Des Moines Register,* January 18, p. 5A.

———. 1976c. "Parties Set for Caucuses in Iowa Tonight." *Des Moines Register,* January 19, pp. 1A, 7A.

———. 1976d. "Demo Caucus Projections Misleading." *Des Moines Register,* January 25, pp. 1A, 5A.

Hollobaugh, Dix. 1976. "Rubbing Shoulders with the Media at $10 a Head." *Des Moines Register,* January 20, p. 7A.

Hunt, Albert R. 1976. "The Campaigning in Iowa Adds Up to Just About Zero." *Wall Street Journal,* January 15, pp. 1, 20.

Iowa Democratic Party. 1980. Precinct Caucus Kit, 1980. Mimeographed.

Iowa General Assembly. 1975 and 1978. *Acts and Resolutions.* Des Moines: State of Iowa.

Matthews, Donald R. 1978. "Winnowing." In *Race for the Presidency: The Media and the Nominating Process,* edited by James D. Barber, 55-78. Englewood Cliffs, N.J.: Prentice-Hall.

Newsweek. 1976.

Paletz, David L., and Robert M. Entman. 1981. *Media, Power, Politics.* New York: Free Press.

Robinson, Michael J. 1981. "The Media in 1980: Was the Message the Message?" In *The American Elections of 1980,* edited by Austin Ranney, 177-211. Washington, D.C.: American Enterprise Institute.

Roth, Luke. 1984. Telephone interview with author, December 7. Roth was the executive director of the Iowa Republican party from 1983 to 1985.

Schier, Steven E. 1980. *The Rules of the Game: Democratic National Convention Delegate Selection in Iowa and Wisconsin.* Washington, D.C.: University Press of America.

Schram, Martin. 1977. *Running for President 1976: The Carter Campaign.* New York: Stein and Day.

Steffen, J. P. 1984. Interview with author, December 4. Steffen was the caucus chair from 1983 to 1991 and the executive director of the Iowa Democratic Party from 1991 to 1993.

Time. 1976.

U.S. News and World Report. 1976.

Wall Street Journal. 1976.

Whitney, Tom. 1986. Written comments to author, June 5. Whitney was the chair of the Iowa Democratic party from 1973 to 1977.

Witcover, Jules. 1976. "Iowa Victory Gives Carter Momentum." *Washington Post,* January 21, pp. A1, A4.

———. 1977. *Marathon: The Pursuit of the Presidency, 1971-1976.* New York: Viking Press.

Chapter 6

The 1980 Caucuses: A Media Event Becomes an Institution

THE IOWA PRECINCT CAUCUSES were the opening round in the 1980 primary and caucus season. George McGovern's success in 1972 and Jimmy Carter's emergence as the Democratic front-runner in 1976 assured the caucuses of a position of prominence in the presidential nominating game. Iowa now rivaled New Hampshire for media attention, and as Ronald Reagan was to learn, the media expect all candidates to play the game in the early nominating contests. Most of the 1980 candidates realized that Iowa had become a significant part of the presidential race and committed their campaigns to major efforts in the precinct caucuses. George Bush explained his decision to mount a Carter-style campaign in Iowa this way: "The action begins in Iowa. It's where everything starts for everybody" (*Time* Jan. 21, 1980, 28).

Precaucus Activity

The candidates began their organizational efforts well in advance of the 1980 precinct caucuses. Although campaign expenses, particularly media costs, are relatively low in Iowa, media campaigns tend to yield few results. Success in a caucus state is largely dependent on good grass-roots organizing. As one county supervisor put it, "You've got to turn folks out for four hours on the coldest night of the year to fight with their neighbors about politics" (*Newsweek* Nov. 26, 1979, 58). The task is complicated by the dispersion of the population. The state's 2.9 million people are spread throughout ninety-nine counties, with few major population centers. Moreover, organizational efforts at the county level must be targeted to those individuals most likely to attend precinct caucuses. Pinpointing, contacting, and winning the allegiance of Democratic and Republican activists, who represent a small percentage of all registered partisans, require excellent organizational skills.

The successful 1980 Iowa campaigns of Jimmy Carter and George Bush again demonstrated this point. Both spent months putting together their organizations. John Connally and Howard Baker, on the other hand, did little organizing in Iowa and invested heavily in media time in hopes of increasing the caucus participation of their supporters. Their efforts yielded few positive results (*Time* Jan. 21, 1980, 30).

The Republican Campaign

On the basis of much soft evidence, the news media concluded that Ronald Reagan was the early front-runner for the Republican nomination. He was a campaign veteran, was well organized, was strong in the national polls, had a firm base of support within the party, and had access to money (Jones 1981, 73). He was also judged to be the front-runner in Iowa, a position he retained throughout the caucus campaign (*CQ* Jan. 12, 1980, 85). Reagan had worked in Des Moines as a sports announcer for WHO radio in his early professional years, which made him something of a "favorite son" candidate. He had challenged President Ford in 1976, and his strong showing in the Iowa caucus straw poll was the first evidence that Ford was vulnerable. Subsequently, he came very close to wresting the Republican nomination from an incumbent president. In addition, an August 1979 statewide *Des Moines Register* poll indicated strong support for Reagan among the Iowa rank and file. In that poll 48 percent of the respondents favored Reagan, 23 percent Baker, 11 percent Connally, 4 percent Dole, 2 percent Crane, and 1 percent each Anderson, Bush, and "others." Nine percent of the respondents were undecided (Iowa Poll: 1979, poll no. 237B).

As the front-runner, Reagan adopted an early strategy of remaining "above" the campaign. He refused to appear at forums with other Republican candidates, asserting that the debate was with the Democrats, not with members of his own party. Pursuing this strategy in Iowa, his aides developed, at great expense, a significant campaign organization, but the candidate himself campaigned only four times in the state.

George Bush spent the better part of a year campaigning in Iowa.

During that period he made thirty-one visits to the state (Roberts 1984), and one of his sons even resided in Iowa for a time in the fall of 1979. Although the August Iowa Poll indicated that Bush was largely unknown to the rank and file, he spent his time cultivating the support of party activists and local leaders (*CQ* Jan. 12, 1980, 85). These were the people most likely to attend the precinct caucuses, and by January Bush was the best organized of the Republicans. *Time* magazine reported that he had eighteen full-time and eighty part-time workers in the state, had pinpointed the voters most likely to attend the caucuses, and had secured "more endorsements than any of his rivals." The story went on to say that there were "indications that he has strength in the state's more populated areas" (Jan. 21, 1980, 30). Bush needed to do better than expected in Iowa to establish himself as a viable challenger to Reagan.

The other Republican hopefuls—Senator Howard Baker, former Texas governor John Connally, Senator Robert Dole, Congressman Philip Crane, and Congressman John Anderson—conducted Iowa campaigns of varied quality. Connally and Baker made serious efforts but never attained the high levels of organization accomplished by Reagan and Bush. Baker did receive the endorsement of the influential Iowa State Education Association and some late help from Governor Robert Ray, but although helpful, this did not make up for his lack of organization. The Baker and Connally campaigns, characterized by frequent personal visits and large media expenditures as the caucuses neared, were probably better suited for primary elections than precinct caucuses (*Time* Jan. 21, 1980, 30). Dole and Crane failed to develop effective organizations, even though Crane visited Iowa thirty times during the campaign (Roberts 1984), and they never emerged from the ranks of the also-rans. Anderson made little effort in Iowa.

To stimulate interest in their caucuses, the Iowa Republicans employed the tactic used so successfully by the Democrats in 1976: They conducted a presidential preference straw poll at every opportunity. The results of these polls were consistently reported by the *Des Moines Register,* and some found their way into the national media. Bush's organizational efforts began to pay dividends in the form of victories in these polls. In one taken at a May Republican fund-raiser featuring Henry Kissinger, Bush surprised news pundits by outpacing Reagan 40 to 26 percent (Germond and Witcover 1979a, 10A). At an

October 11 Republican fund-raiser in the Second Congressional District, Bush outdistanced the field with 166 votes. His nearest competitor, Connally, with 93 votes, was followed by Crane, with 73 votes, and then Reagan and Baker, who had 44 votes each (Yepsen 1979a, 6A).

It is interesting that these polls of party activists occurred on either side of the August Iowa Poll that showed that only 1 percent of the Iowa Republican rank and file favored Bush. Although largely unknown to most Iowans, Bush was making headway where it counted, among those likely to attend the caucuses. This clearly illustrated the danger of making too much of public opinion polls in a caucus state, since only a small fraction of the partisans attend caucuses. Attempting to extrapolate the preferences of a small group of party activists from a large sample of the rank and file is doomed to failure, and the results can be very misleading. Nonetheless, the results of the August Iowa Poll, and subsequent December and January samplings, were reported nationally, presumably to give the country an indication of the status of the presidential campaign in Iowa.

The most significant Republican event of the fall, and the fifth event to conduct a preference poll, was the October 13 fund-raising dinner in Ames. Reminiscent of the 1975 Democratic Jefferson-Jackson Day dinner, the fifty-dollar-a-plate dinner was held to retire the party's 1978 campaign debt, and all the Republican presidential candidates were invited (Flansburg 1979a, 4A). Nine candidates of varying stature—Anderson, Baker, Bush, Connally, Crane, Dole, California businessman Ben Fernandez, South Dakota Senator Larry Pressler, and perennial candidate Harold Stassen of Minnesota—participated and drew 3500 Iowans to the event (Flansburg, Yepsen, and Pedersen 1979, 1A). The candidates were each permitted eight minutes for speeches and were given "campaign booths" on the floor of the hall. Notably absent was Ronald Reagan, whose official reason for declining the invitation was to avoid fostering disharmony within the party. A more plausible explanation for Reagan's failure to appear was his front-runner status and the desire not to share a platform with the less well-known Republicans (Flansburg, Pedersen, and Yepsen 1979, 1A, 4A).

The Ames fund-raiser was another plus for the Bush candidacy in Iowa. He drew the largest applause during the introduction of candi-

Cartoon by Frank Miller, © 1979, *Des Moines Register,* reprinted by permission

Ronald Reagan was the odds-on favorite to win the Republican presidential nomination in 1980, and he chose to limit his appearances in Iowa and not to appear at campaign functions with other Republican candidates. Reagan's strategy of noninvolvement was resented by Iowans, and they dealt his campaign a setback by supporting George Bush in the Republican caucus poll. After the Iowa defeat, Reagan changed his campaign strategy and began appearing with fellow Republicans.

dates (Flansburg, Yepsen, and Pedersen, 1979, 1A), and he was an easy winner in the straw poll, with 36 percent of the 1454 votes cast. Reagan, with 11 percent of the vote, was a distant fourth behind Connally and Dole, with 15 percent each.

Bush won a sixth straight preference poll two weeks later at a Story County fund-raising event, leading the *Register*'s political reporters to conclude that Reagan's "campaign may be in deep trouble in Iowa" (Flansburg and Yepsen 1979, 1A, 13A). Jack Germond and Jules

Witcover, picking up on the *Register* articles, alerted the nation in a syndicated column that the Reagan strategy of noninvolvement could be hurting his chances in Iowa (1979b, 10A).

Shortly after the Ames dinner the *Register* announced that it would hold a debate for Republican presidential candidates in Des Moines on January 5 and that invitations had been extended to the seven candidates then conducting campaigns in Iowa—Anderson, Baker, Bush, Connally, Crane, Dole, and Reagan. A Democratic debate between Carter and Kennedy was scheduled for January 7, and when all the invited candidates of both parties, except Reagan, accepted the invitations, the television networks decided to provide live coverage of both debates (Graham 1979, 4A).

The late fall was a time of intense campaign activity by the Republican hopefuls in Iowa. The Baker campaign received the endorsement of Iowa teachers and help from Governor Ray, and that helped to compensate for his lack of organization. Connally attempted to keep his campaign visible by purchasing extensive television time. The other candidates, including Reagan, appeared more frequently in the state, and Reagan, at a December 14 fund-raiser in the Fifth Congressional District, claimed party unity as the reason he would not take part in the upcoming *Register* debate (Flansburg 1979b, 16A). Bush continued to make organizational inroads, and a December Iowa Poll found that twice as many people said they had been contacted by Bush as by any other candidate (Iowa Poll: 1979, poll no. 238B).

In Iran, student terrorists seized the U.S. embassy in early November, but this had little immediate impact on the Republican campaign, since the candidates chose not to make the ensuing hostage crisis an issue. Later, however, as the nation rallied around President Carter, Iran had a great effect on the campaign. The president's standing in national public opinion surveys soared, and as it did he became less and less inclined to engage in political dialogue. On December 28, Carter withdrew from the Des Moines presidential debate, announcing that he would not campaign outside Washington for the duration of the hostage crisis. Neither the Republicans nor the press liked the president's decision, and the media let it be known on several occasions (Flansburg 1979c, 1A). The Democratic debate was canceled, and shortly thereafter the networks announced that they no longer planned live television coverage of the Republican debate.

Nevertheless, the Republican debate, minus live TV coverage and Ronald Reagan, went on as scheduled in the Des Moines Civic Center, with six presidential hopefuls, a panel of distinguished journalists, approximately 200 reporters, and over 2000 Iowans in attendance. The candidates, in addition to addressing one another, took turns admonishing Reagan for his absence (Flansburg, Risser, and Graham 1980, 1A, 4A; Pedersen 1980, 1A, 5A). The debate was well received by news reporters, although there was no clear winner, and the *New York Times* called it "surprisingly interesting and revealing" (Jan. 7, 1980, A18). Reporters were uniformly critical of Reagan for failing to participate in the discussion, and so were Iowans; Reagan's share in the Iowa Poll standings plunged from 50 percent in early December to 26 percent the day after the Republican debate (Iowa Poll: 1980, poll no. 238A).

The Democratic Campaign

An incumbent president usually does not have to endure a primary battle, but in 1980 for the second consecutive election a sitting president was challenged for his party's nomination. Ted Kennedy brought his famous name and considerable family to Iowa to contest the Democratic precinct caucuses in 1980, and in the process he assured the Democratic meetings of a great deal of media attention. After suffering a loss to President Carter in the Florida county caucuses in mid-October, the senator downplayed the importance of that event and announced that the Iowa caucuses would be the first "true test" of his challenge to Carter (*DMR* Oct. 14, 1979, 2A). After a late start, he pursued Iowa delegates by personally campaigning in the state for a total of about twenty days, including one six-day stint in January, and by importing his mother, sisters, and many other members of the Kennedy clan to campaign for him (Flansburg 1980a, 1B, 3B).

Carter, on the other hand, did not visit Iowa, because of the Iranian hostage crisis, but he certainly did not ignore the state that had made him the Democratic front-runner in 1976. Rosalynn Carter and Vice-President Mondale were frequent visitors, and a long list of surrogates made their way to Iowa to campaign for the president. In addition, Carter used the traditional advantages of incumbency—international crises, the awarding of grants, and invitations to Washington—to his advantage. In October about 200 Iowans visited the White House for a day of briefings, and it was not uncommon for Iowa Democrats to answer their phones in the months before the precinct caucuses and discover that the caller was the president of the United States. Moreover, Carter understood the nature of organizational politics in a caucus state, and with adequate financial resources, a paid campaign staff of twenty-one people was functioning in Iowa fully nine months before the caucuses (Flansburg and Pedersen 1979, 1A, 5A). He also had the support of the state Democratic establishment—the state chair and most county chairs—and the politically potent Iowa State Education Association (*CQ* Jan. 12, 1980, 84). By the time Kennedy entered the race, Carter was well organized throughout the state.

A third Democratic candidate, Governor Jerry Brown of California, emerged after the *Register* announced the Democratic debate, and he demanded to be included (*DMR* Nov. 12, 1979, 3A). Brown spent a total of six days in Iowa, and in a late November visit he opened a state campaign headquarters in an attempt to persuade the *Register* editorial staff that he intended to mount a serious campaign in the state. The effort was successful, and in early December the *Register* invited Brown to participate in the January 7 Democratic debate (Leavitt 1979, 1A). It is apparent that Brown was only interested in the potential media exposure afforded by the debate, since he did not seriously contest Iowa, and on January 16 he announced his withdrawal from the caucus contests and urged his supporters to run as uncommitted delegates (Flansburg 1980b, 1A).

The Democrats conducted fewer polls in 1979 and 1980 than did the Republicans, primarily because Ted Kennedy did not enter the contest until early November. The first major encounter was a preference poll taken at the November 3 Jefferson-Jackson Day dinner in Ames. A similar poll four years earlier had given the nation the first hint of Carter's organizational strength in Iowa. With the president in self-imposed exile in the White House, the keynote speaker was Vice-President Mondale. Not to be outdone, the Kennedy campaign imported Bobby's widow, Ethel Kennedy, and son Joseph for the event.

Kennedy attempted to persuade the media, however, that he had little chance of doing well in the Ames poll because of his late start in the state and the far superior Carter organization. His position was complicated somewhat by the August Iowa Poll that showed Kennedy holding a commanding 49 percent to 26 percent lead over Carter among the Democratic rank and file (Iowa Poll: 1979, poll no. 237B). It is possible that the August poll raised expectations among Kennedy supporters and the media, since it made Kennedy appear more viable than he was at the time. As of early November, Kennedy had little organization in Iowa, whereas the Carter campaign had been in place for seven months. The Kennedy people were not playing the expectations game with their prediction; they had been out-organized and knew it.

The Jefferson-Jackson Day dinner is normally the big Democratic event of the year, and 1979 was no exception. Some 2800 people paid thirty dollars each to attend the fund-raiser and hear Vice-President Mondale make the case for Carter's reelection, and to have the opportunity to cast a ballot in the straw poll conducted by the Iowa Daily Press Association (Pedersen, Flansburg, and Yepsen 1979, 1A, 12A). The event did not, however, approach the circuslike atmosphere of the 1975 Democratic dinner.

Kennedy was correct in attempting to downplay the Ames straw poll. Carter was the overwhelming winner, with 71 percent of the 2320 participants favoring his candidacy and only 26 percent supporting Kennedy. The margin of victory was so great that Carter aide Bill Romjue felt it necessary to issue his own disclaimer. He contended that Carter was not as strong statewide as indicated by the poll and that the victory margin should not be taken too seriously, given that Kennedy was just starting to organize in Iowa. The media tended to agree with Romjue's assessment and largely discounted the results of the Jefferson-Jackson Day poll (Yepsen 1979b, 3A).

As December approached, Kennedy moved his Iowa campaign into high gear. There was self-imposed pressure to do well in the caucuses since he had dubbed Iowa the first "true test," and now he had to deliver or face a negative media interpretation due to the expectations he had helped to create. He made a strong effort in the final three months before the caucuses, concentrating on the major urban areas, and with the help of organized labor he "created an organization considered to be one of the finest ever seen in Iowa" (CQ Jan. 12, 1980, 84). From an anecdotal standpoint, it is interesting that as Kennedy and his extended family intensified their efforts in Iowa, the senator's poll standing vis-à-vis Jimmy Carter dropped dramatically. The December Iowa Poll showed each commanding the allegiance of 40 percent of the Iowa Democrats. Iran was negating Kennedy's campaign efforts, at least with the rank and file.

Another casualty of the president's soaring popularity in the public opinion polls, as previously noted, was the Democratic presidential debate arranged by the *Des Moines Register*. News organizations all over the country condemned Carter's decision not to participate (*DMR* Jan. 5, 1980, 10A), and James Flansburg asserted that "the Carter record clearly shows that he doesn't debate his political opponents when he believes he's ahead of them" (1979d, 2C). Whatever the reason, the subsequent cancellation of the Democratic debate pulled the plug on live network television coverage for the Republican debate on January 7 and on Brown's Iowa campaign. The action also left Kennedy sparring with a shadow for the support of the Iowa Democrats.

The 1980 Precinct Caucuses

The candidates, and Carter's surrogates, practically lived in Iowa the final week of the campaign. Kennedy, Bush, Connally, Baker, Dole, Crane, and even Reagan attempted by personal contact to win caucus support. It had been a vigorous campaign, and six candidates spent close to the federal limit on their campaigns (Connally, who was not subject to the federal limit, invested heavily in television time and may have outspent each of the other candidates). The figures in Table 6.1 probably understate total campaign spending, as candidates were known to record Iowa expenses elsewhere by renting cars, for example, in bordering states like Nebraska. The institutionalization of the precinct caucuses increased their costs considerably. In 1976 Jimmy Carter had spent less than $100,000 en route to his media victory in Iowa (CQ Dec. 10, 1983, 2601).

Table 6.1.   1980 candidate
precaucus expenditures in Iowa

	Total expenditure
Brown	$ 30,330
Carter	493,067
Kennedy	442,858
Anderson	1233
Baker	480,951
Bush	462,382
Crane	102,844
Dole	227,636
Reagan	466,088

Source: Data are from the Federal
Election Commission report *FEC
Reports on Financial Activity, 1979-80:
Final Report, Presidential Pre-
Nomination Campaigns*, Table A8.
Connally is not included since he did
not accept federal money and there-
fore was not required to file a report.
He also was not bound by the Iowa
spending limit of $489,882.

Media Coverage

Media coverage of the 1980 caucuses was immense. The major national print and broadcast media were represented in Iowa by about 300
reporters and technicians, and unlike 1976, when, to be available for
TV interviews, Jimmy Carter had to be in New York on the night of the
caucuses, the three television networks set up temporary studios in
Iowa. On January 21, the day of the caucuses, NBC's "Today" show and
all three network evening news programs originated from Des Moines
(Hainey 1980, 5A).

   A systematic examination of the election stories aired by the "CBS
Evening News" during a twelve-month period from July 1, 1979,
through June 30, 1980, indicates that coverage of the precinct caucus-

es increased dramatically from 1976 to 1980 and that by 1980 Iowa had replaced New Hampshire as the foremost media event of the presidential nominating season. Robinson and Sheehan had reached the opposite conclusion, that New Hampshire prevailed over Iowa as the most reported nominating event of the presidential campaign (1983, 174-81). Their conclusion was based on an analysis of CBS News and United Press International (UPI) stories, but for only a six-month period from January 1 to June 6, 1980. The Iowa caucuses were held in January in both 1976 and 1980, and by not examining the longer period before the 1980 caucuses analyzed here, Robinson and Sheehan missed many of the Iowa and New Hampshire reports aired by CBS News.

Table 6.2 compares CBS's 1975-76 and 1979-80 coverage of the Iowa precinct caucuses with the New Hampshire primary election coverage for the one-year period from July 1 to June 30. The number of Iowa stories aired by CBS increased from thirteen in 1976 to fifty-four in 1980. The number of New Hampshire primary election stories, on the other hand, declined slightly from forty-four in 1976 to forty in 1980, indicating a proportional increase in Iowa stories rather than a general increase in coverage of the 1980 nominating process. It is apparent that spirited contests in both parties piqued media interest in the precinct caucuses. The early date made Iowa more attractive, at least to

Table 6.2.   1976 and 1980 CBS news stories on Iowa and New Hampshire

	July 1, 1975, to June 30, 1976			July 1, 1979, to June 30, 1980		
	Weekday	Weekend	Total	Weekday	Weekend	Total
Iowa	12	1	13	37	17	54
N.H.	40	4	44	29	11	40

Source: Data are from the *Television News Index and Abstracts*, produced by Vanderbilt University. All evening broadcasts during the two twelve-month periods were reviewed. Stories were counted that related the two events to the national primary race or that described candidates' visits to one of the states. Two or more story headings on the same day were recorded as separate entities. If a story included both Iowa and New Hampshire, it was listed under the tally of both states. Finally, the weekend information is incomplete due to the absence of some weekends from the abstracts.

CBS News, and reporters were willing to ignore the fact that the results produced in Iowa were considerably softer than the "hard news" produced by the New Hampshire primary election.

The early and sustained attention given the 1980 caucuses also stimulated citizen interest, and officials reported record levels of participation throughout the state. The Republican poll indicated that 106,000 persons had participated, and the Democrats estimated that 100,000 people had attended their meetings. The large turnout included many political amateurs attending their first caucus, and some of the usually well-orchestrated events degenerated into rather chaotic affairs. Organizational efforts faltered as meetings spilled over into second and third rooms, and supplies ranging from registration forms to ballots were in short supply (Bullard and Kneeland 1980, 1B).

The large-scale citizen participation produced mixed results. Many meetings elected people who were attending their first caucus to be delegates to county conventions, and others were examples of only symbolic democracy, because citizens unfamiliar with caucus procedures had little impact. An interesting example of the latter occurred in Republican caucus 74 in Des Moines, where 474 people attended and participated in the straw poll, but upon completion of the poll approximately half of those present left, before the real business of delegate selection took place (Bittick 1980).

The Republican Caucuses

The 1980 Republican caucuses shared fully in the media attention previously focused disproportionately on the Democratic meetings. To accommodate the media's need for results, the Iowa Republican party, which does not compile delegate counts, asked all precincts to conduct a preference poll of those in attendance, although the final decision to participate in what Adam Clymer of the *New York Times* called "the biggest straw poll yet" remained with individual caucuses (1980a, 4C). The straw poll was unrelated to delegate selection.

The Reagan camp still expected a victory in Iowa, but the signs were everywhere that a Bush upset was in the making. The string of straw-poll victories indicated a solid Bush organization, and reports had surfaced that he would do well in both the first and second congressional districts (Pedersen and Yepsen 1980, 1A, 3A). Reporters attended

Table 6.3.   1980 Republican caucus
straw-poll results

	Preferences of total votes	Percentage
Bush	33,530	31.6
Reagan	31,348	29.5
Baker	16,216	15.3
Connally	9861	9.3
Crane	7135	6.7
Anderson	4585	4.3
Undecided	1800	1.7
Dole	1576	1.5
Total	106,051	99.9

Source: Data from results provided by the
Republican Party of Iowa. They represent
2389 of 2531 precincts (94.4%). A total of 142
precincts did not hold caucuses, did not conduct the poll, or simply did not report their
results. These results were reported in
Newsweek, Time, and *U.S. News and World
Report.* The other print and broadcast media
reported less complete results that had Bush
leading Reagan by 4 to 6 percentage points.

caucuses to gain a flavor of the process, and most precincts conducted
the straw poll. Table 6.3 reports the outcome of the Republican preference poll. The contest was very close, with George Bush emerging only
2 percentage points ahead of Ronald Reagan.

Although the closeness of the contest was widely reported, it was
secondary to the fact that Bush had won. The media trumpeted his
victory around the nation. Bush's picture was on the cover of
Newsweek, and an accompanying headline declared: "Bush Breaks Out
of the Pack." An eight-page story on the Republican caucuses called
Iowa "the first major test of the 1980 Presidential campaign" and stated that "Bush collected an impressive 31.5 percent of the vote." The
story included twelve pictures of Republican candidates, ten of Bush

and one each of Reagan and Howard Baker, who finished second and third, respectively (*Newsweek* Feb. 4, 1980, 30, 31, 33, 35-38).

The *Washington Post* declared that Bush had "established himself tonight as a serious challenger to Ronald Reagan by running neck-and-neck with the former California governor in the Iowa precinct caucuses" (Peterson 1980, A1). Two days after the caucuses, a *Post* editorial called Bush's win an impressive victory and a "major setback" for Reagan (Jan. 23, 1980, A22).

A *Wall Street Journal* headline read: "Carter and Bush Win 1st Round but Have No Knockdowns Yet." The story went on to explain that Bush had upset Reagan, "whose first name has been front-runner for the past year," and concluded that as a result, Reagan needed a win in New Hampshire to remain a credible contender for the Republican nomination (Perry and Hunt 1980, 1, 37).

The *New York Times* concluded that "Mr. Bush's unexpected comfortable victory and the failures of others suddenly made the Republican race more of a two-man contest," thus reducing the remaining five Republican candidates to the status of also-rans after only one primary event (Clymer 1980c, A1). After two days as part of the George Bush media chorus, the *New York Times* published an editorial entitled "Apples and Oranges in Iowa," in which they placed the Iowa caucuses in perspective. It noted that the caucuses were not a primary election and that Bush's victory was in a straw poll of caucus members held before, and unrelated to, the selection of delegates to county conventions (Jan. 23, 1980, A22). The editorial did little, however, to change the impact of the caucuses: Bush's star rose dramatically after Iowa. A February 1980 CBS News-*New York Times* poll showed that support for Bush among national Republicans had grown from 6 to 24 percent in less than thirty days (Robinson 1981, 203).

It is clear that Bush's win in Iowa was a media victory. He exceeded media expectations and reaped the publicity. Robinson called Bush's "big" victory in Iowa one of the major medialities of the 1980 presidential campaign (1981, 196). Actually, the Bush margin of victory was anything but big—a plurality of just over 2000 out of 106,000 votes—and it was in an essentially meaningless beauty contest conducted for the media. Moreover, Robinson documents that even though the national media elevated Bush to the position of major contender, he never seriously threatened Reagan for the Republican nomination.

(Bush's standing among Republicans after the Iowa caucuses is discussed in Robinson 1981, 203.)

Media events, however, take on a life of their own and affect political campaigns. Iowa forced Reagan to abandon the campaign strategy of ignoring the Republican opposition, and he mounted a full-blown campaign in New Hampshire. Bush may never have seriously threatened Reagan's bid for the Republican nomination, but the media brouhaha generated by the Iowa caucuses gave him sufficient momentum to make him the vice-presidential nominee.

By the time the thirty-seven Republican delegates were finally selected at the district and state conventions in June, Reagan followers were in control and Bush was no longer a candidate for the presidency. He was, however, running hard for the vice-presidential nomination, and in an appearance at the Republican state convention he pledged his support to Ronald Reagan and made a plea for party unity (Flansburg and Yepsen 1980a, 1A, 4A).

The Validity of the Republican Results

The 1980 poll, unlike the 1976 effort, which included only 62 sample precincts, was held on a statewide basis, and with 2531 precincts, the logistics of the endeavor were complex. Party officials set up a tabulation center at the Hotel Ft. Des Moines that included Apple computers and card readers, a bank of telephones, and volunteers staffing the system. Each of the precincts reported by phone directly to Des Moines, and that proved to be the first flaw in the system. Then those receiving the precinct data penciled in the poll results on computer cards and fed them into the card readers, and that was the second weak point of the system. Almost immediately the tabulators fell behind due to the volume of data, then problems developed with the card readers, and one of the computers (indeed, the system in general) was very slow. Reporters, facing deadlines, were angry about the lack of results. Party officials agree that it would have been more practical to have had county party workers collect precinct data and report the numbers to the state tabulation center, thus reducing the Des Moines callers from 2531 to 99, but the idea had been rejected by the state central committee. When the card readers failed to work properly, the system began to come apart (Bonsignoir 1986; Hyde July 3, 1986).

When the system's failure became apparent, one of the party officials supervising the project thought it best to call a press conference to inform the reporters of the fact. The more senior of the two party workers overseeing the counting disagreed, and the job of completing the counting by hand continued into the early-morning hours (Hyde July 3, 1986). During that time it became apparent that some of the totals on the large results board were strange. CBS officials thought the numbers from six counties were too large and favored Bush by too great a margin (Mitofsky 1986). There were also "patterns of error" from the Fifth Congressional District—with more precincts reporting than there were precincts—and at least one party official thought there were some "shenanigans" going on there (Hyde July 3, 1986). At that point, party workers moved the tabulation process from the hotel ballroom to state party headquarters, and with calculators rather than computers, they recounted, or at least spot-checked, all results. Incomplete data from some precincts led to inquiring phone calls and "extrapolations" by those doing the counting. The final results, completed on Tuesday afternoon, showed Bush and Reagan separated by a margin of only 2 percent, rather than the 4 to 6 percent spread reported in the newspapers the day after the caucuses. CBS's tally, based on sample precincts, had it even closer—less than 1 percent separating the two candidates, with Reagan leading—and the network decided the race was too close to call. NBC had projected Bush as the winner (Plissner July 7, 1986).

It is clear from interviews with those present that the 1980 Iowa Republican tabulation system left much to be desired and that the party was unable to complete an accurate and reliable count of the results of its preference poll. Party officials assert that it was simply a case of their first attempt at a statewide reporting system not being up to the job. They are satisfied that they ultimately reported the most accurate figures possible from the available data, and they note that neither the Bush nor the Reagan people protested the results (Hyde July 3, 1986). Still, the candidacy of George Bush was given a tremendous boost by the media perception that he had upset Ronald Reagan in the Iowa precinct caucuses, and it is very troublesome to think that the media perception was based on incomplete and perhaps erroneous results. Bush may well have been the victor in the Iowa Republican straw poll, but even those doing the counting that night admit that we shall never know for sure, because of the problems encountered at the tabulation center.

Newspeople who were aware of the "results problem" were very disturbed that the poll figures they had reported may not have been accurate (Plissner July 7, 1986; Yepsen 1986). When combined with the problems with the 1976 Democratic results, this made two straight caucus seasons in which results given to the news media had been of questionable validity, and the newspeople wanted an independent body to provide caucus results in the future. Various media organizations put pressure on the Iowa Democrats in 1984 to cooperate and to allow the News Election Service to record the candidate preference of those attending caucuses after the first division into preference groups. (This effort is more thoroughly discussed in the next chapter.)

As noted in Chapter 5, there are no laws in Iowa governing the reporting of caucus results. Each party, without independent supervision, has developed a reporting system that purports to represent the outcomes of their respective processes. Reporters, and the nation, are asked to accept the validity, reliability, and honesty of the systems, but without independent judges, this requires an act of faith. The reporting systems are complicated, and with the stakes so high, the possibility of error or fraud in an unregulated process exists. Iowa's political parties should be required to provide independently verified caucus results, or the media should ignore the state and its precinct caucuses. (The legislation passed in 1988, and discussed in Chapter 8, prohibits the reporting of fraudulent results but does not require independent verification.)

The Democratic Caucuses

On January 21 perhaps the most unusual straw poll of the primary season was held in Emmetsburg, a town in northwest Iowa that had become famous for voting for the winning candidate in presidential elections. A local radio station and the town's public works department cooperated to hold the "Cess Poll." KEMB-FM, broadcasting from the city water plant, reported how much the water level dropped in the town's water tower after residents flushed their toilets successively for Carter, Kennedy, and "undecided/don't care." The winner by a two-to-one margin was "undecided/don't care," followed by Carter, with Kennedy a distant third. The station concluded that Kennedy was "in deep water" in Emmetsburg (*DMR* Jan. 22, 1980, 1A).

The Democratic meetings were as lively as their Republican counterparts. A notable difference, however, was in media preparation for the Democratic caucuses. CBS selected ninety precincts and interviewed caucus participants as they arrived for the meetings. On that basis, at 8:51 P.M., before any delegate totals were posted at tabulation headquarters in Des Moines, CBS projected that Carter would defeat Kennedy by "better than 2-1" (Hainey 1980, 5A). (The early projections grew into a controversy in 1984 that is discussed in Chapter 7.)

Ultimately, President Carter outpolled Kennedy by a two-to-one margin in the delegate equivalents, reported in Table 6.4. The media interpretation of the Democratic caucus results was uniform: Carter had won a major victory and Kennedy had been badly damaged. The *New York Times,* for example, declared, "Carter Wins Strong Victory in Iowa" (Clymer 1980b, A1), and a day later stated, "Victory by Carter Staggers Kennedy and Leaves His Campaign in Doubt" (Smith 1980, A17).

The *Washington Post* story said that "President Carter dealt Sen. Edward M. Kennedy a decisive setback tonight" and concluded that

Table 6.4. 1980 Democratic precinct caucus results

	State delegate equivalents (%)
Carter	59.1
Kennedy	31.2
Uncommitted	9.6

Source: Data from results provided by the Iowa Democratic Party, based on 96 percent of the 2531 precincts. In 1980 the national delegate equivalents were downplayed by the party.

the unusually small number of uncommitted delegates also was a setback for Jerry Brown, who had asked his followers to support uncommitted slates in the caucuses. Playing the expectations game, the story concluded that "Carter's landslide was worse than Kennedy expected." Finally, the writer thought that "Carter's victory was a vindication both of his strategy and his national leadership" (Broder 1980, A1, A4).

Whereas the *Post* story credited Iowa with mortally wounding Kennedy and vindicating the policies of President Carter, the *Wall Street Journal,* although it, too, played the expectations game, was considerably more restrained in its interpretation of the outcome of the precinct caucuses. The *Journal* story said that "Carter's overwhelming victory exceeded the White House's fondest hopes," and that Kennedy was "humiliated" because "no Kennedy has ever lost so badly." The *Journal,* however, did refer to the precinct caucuses as the first round of the 1980 primary season, and the story headline stated that there were "No Knockdowns Yet" (Perry and Hunt 1980, 1, 37). The *Christian Science Monitor* presented one of the few balanced and unsensational interpretations of both parties' caucus results in Iowa (Sperling 1980, 1, 10).

The *Newsweek* headline, on the other hand, asked, "Can Kennedy Hang On?" The three-page story used interesting rhetoric to describe the Iowa Democratic outcomes, asserting that the president had made good on his promise to "whip his ass" as he "buried the Senator and the twenty-year legend of Kennedy invincibility." Kennedy, it said, had been "engulfed by a tidal-wave turnout that made the caucuses the moral equivalent of a primary," and the margin of victory had been "big and persuasive enough to propel Carter to within dreaming distance of stitching up his renomination before the winter is out" (*Newsweek* Feb. 4, 1980, 43, 44, 49).

Kennedy did hang on all the way to the Democratic National Convention, but the media interpretation of the Iowa caucuses was very damaging to his campaign. Iowa had demonstrated to the media's satisfaction that Kennedy was not a viable threat to the Carter presidency, and it had proved to be a major step in the battle for the Democratic nomination.

Unlike 1972 and 1976, the two-to-one margin of delegate support for President Carter over Senator Kennedy held throughout the sequence of county, district, and state conventions in Iowa. The Iowa delegation to the 1980 national convention in New York included 31 delegates for Carter, 17 for Kennedy, and 2 uncommitted (Flansburg and Yepsen 1980b, 1A).

The Impact of the 1980 Precinct Caucuses

The precinct caucuses were institutionalized as part of the presidential nominating process in 1980. Iowa came to be well known as an important early nominating event, and as Reagan discovered, the media expected serious candidates to enter the contest. Several presidential hopefuls from both parties made all-out efforts in Iowa, and "surprise campaigns" like those of McGovern in 1972 and Carter in 1976 were no longer possible. The media might find the eventual winner in the precinct caucuses a surprise, but Iowa had become an early source of hard news about the progress of the presidential campaign, and both the candidates and the media were there in large numbers.

Iowa party leaders, businesspeople, and just plain citizens greatly enjoyed and appreciated the notoriety of the Iowa media event. The state's small population had previously limited the influence of the Iowa parties at the national conventions. Now Iowa "made" and "broke" presidential candidacies; the state's parties were significant actors in the presidential nominating game.

Although it is impossible to gain access to reliable figures, the campaigns and those who follow and report on them spent millions of dollars in Iowa in 1980, just as they had in 1976. The capital city of Des Moines and its business community were probably the chief beneficiaries of the financial infusion, and they did their best to support the caucuses. The Des Moines Chamber of Commerce worked hand in hand with the Iowa Republican and Democratic parties to promote the event.

Iowans in general seemed to enjoy the excitement associated with the precinct caucuses. It required little initiative on the part of average citizens to see, hear, and shake hands with presidential candidates, an occurrence that was extremely rare before 1976. There were Iowans who could now brag to their friends and relatives that a presidential candidate had visited or, in the case of Carter in 1976, slept in their homes. Others received telephone calls from the president. In addition, the caucuses and the national attention provided a break in the long, cold Iowa winter.

The 1980 precinct caucuses, like those four years earlier, had a great impact on the presidential race. Ted Kennedy was seriously damaged by the media interpretation that his campaign was in deep trouble after Iowa. Certainly Kennedy helped create the expectations against which reporters evaluated his Iowa showing when he labeled the caucuses the first "true test" of the campaign. Nonetheless, reporters concluded—on the basis of a media event that does not produce meaningful results and a straw poll in Florida—that Kennedy was not a viable challenger to President Carter. In retrospect, Kennedy might have been wiser to concede Iowa as "Carter country," noting the state's 1976 role in making Carter the Democratic front-runner, the excellent Carter organization already in place when he entered the 1980 race, and the special feeling many Iowans held for Carter because of his previous stays in their homes and communities. That strategy might have failed as well, but the media expectations for Kennedy in Iowa might have been lower.

In the case of Ronald Reagan, the opposite was true. He had been judged the front-runner by virtually everyone who engaged in the expectations game, and his decision to remain "above" the Iowa campaign was viewed very negatively by the media. He was uniformly judged the loser in the *Des Moines Register* debate for not participating (Jones 1981, 80). It is likely, based on his 1976 showing and the fact that he carried Iowa in the general election, that if he had just "played the game," Reagan probably would have been the winner in the caucus straw poll. He did not win, however, and the media interpretation of Bush's "big" victory in Iowa created a challenger.

The Iowa precinct caucuses forced Reagan to alter his campaign strategy or face a continued negative press treatment. Reagan indicated in a Los Angeles press conference the day after the caucuses that as a result of Iowa, he would campaign harder in person and would probably begin making joint appearances with other Republican candidates (Clymer 1980c, A1). With the New Hampshire primary election still five weeks away, Reagan had time to recover from the Iowa loss, and he became a very active campaigner in that state. Perhaps the final act in transforming the campaign from a passive to an active state took place when Reagan fired his campaign manager, John Sears, on the eve of the New Hampshire primary (*Newsweek* March 10, 1980, 26-34). Three months later, when addressing the Iowa Republican party's state convention, Reagan credited the later success of his campaign to the changes made as a result of the Iowa loss in January (Flansburg and Yepsen 1980a, 1A).

The 1980 precinct caucuses again demonstrated that the winners and losers in presidential nominating contests are those who exceed or fail to meet the expectations of the unofficial handicappers. Winning by a small margin in the Republican caucus poll can be a "big" victory if unexpected, and losing by a two-to-one margin in the battle for Democratic delegates becomes a knockout blow when the magnitude of the loss exceeds expectations. The essence of the early presidential race in 1980 seems to have been expectations and perceptions, and Iowa played a major role in shaping both.

A Media Event under Fire

Efforts to limit the impact of Iowa and New Hampshire in the nominating process were renewed after the 1980 caucuses and primary elections. The Democratic National Committee (DNC) appointed the Commission on Presidential Nominations (the Hunt Commission) to consider a number of changes in the nominating process. The commission's January 15, 1982, report included a recommendation (proposed rule 10) that the length of the Democratic primary schedule be compressed into a thirteen-week period between the second Tuesday in March and the second Tuesday in June. In deference to Iowa and New Hampshire, the rule granted permanent exemptions from this time frame for the Iowa and New Hampshire nominating events, although both had to be held later in 1984. (Iowa could hold its Democratic caucuses no earlier than fifteen days before the start of the thirteen-week period; and New Hampshire, seven days.) The exception gave Iowa and New Hampshire the opportunity to focus national attention on their primary events as in the past. The recommendations were accepted by the DNC on March 26, 1982, and were made part of the rules of the national party.

Following the DNC decision, a dispute developed between New Hampshire and Vermont over the date of Vermont's Town Meeting Day, which includes a presidential straw poll and which is traditionally held on the first Tuesday in March. In 1984 that fell on March 6, which was the scheduled date for the New Hampshire presidential primary. The DNC-approved thirteen-week "window" did not apply to nonbinding electoral events such as Vermont's. The potential for conflict between the two states apparently had been underestimated by the Hunt Commission. Although the commission members were well aware of the date of the Vermont straw poll, they did not believe it necessary to schedule the New Hampshire primary election earlier than March 6. (For the DNC position on this, see Campbell et al. v. Iowa State Democratic Central Committee 1984.) New Hampshire and the DNC were unsuccessful in resolving the conflict, and the New Hampshire Democrats, not wanting to share the limelight with Vermont on March 6, defied the national party's rules and moved its primary election forward a week to February 28.

Predictably, the decision, which would have narrowed the separation between the New Hampshire primary election and the Iowa caucuses to a single day, was not well received in Iowa. The general assembly reacted to the threat to Iowa's famous caucuses by passing legislation requiring that the precinct caucuses be held at least eight days earlier than any other nominating event (Ia. Gen. Assem. 1983, chap. 138, p. 306).

The Iowa Democratic Party also reacted strongly to the threat. Fearful that the state's impact on the national nominating process would be greatly diminished, the Iowa Democrats discussed changing the date of their 1984 caucuses at a November 19, 1983, meeting of the state central committee. John Law, a former executive director of the Iowa Democratic Party and a member of the Hunt Commission, informed the committee that a commission compromise had led to the new party rules governing the length of the primary and caucus schedule, and it was his understanding that Iowa had been guaranteed an eight-day separation between the New Hampshire and Iowa events. He further argued that if New Hampshire violated party rules by moving its primary election forward and the DNC did not force them back into compliance, Iowa should advance its caucus date to maintain the eight-day separation. Members of the DNC compliance committee in attendance argued against a change in caucus dates and threatened disciplinary action against the Iowa Democratic Party if national party rules were violated. The debate became spirited and sometimes animated before William Sueppel of Iowa City proposed a compromise that ultimately carried by a vote of 20 to 10. The Iowa caucuses would be held on February 20, 1984, unless New Hampshire decided on or before December 10, 1983, to return its primary election to the original March 6 date. If New Hampshire relented, the Iowa caucuses would be held on February 27 as originally scheduled. The deadline passed without action by New Hampshire, and the Iowa Democrats proceeded with plans for a February 20 caucus date in 1984.

The controversy over the decision to change the caucus date did not end on December 10, however. In Iowa three prominent Democrats—Edward Campbell, former state party chair and cochair of the Mondale for President effort in Iowa; Jean Haugland, also a Mondale cochair; and Charles Gifford, a member of the state central committee—filed suit in federal district court to block the change from February 27 to February 20. The plaintiffs requested that "the Court enjoin the State Party from holding statewide caucuses on a date prior to the 27th day of February, 1984, as an earlier date would jeopardize the seating of Iowa delegates at the Democratic National Convention" (Campbell et al. v. Iowa State Democratic Central Committee 1984, 2). In testimony, Mr. Gifford further asserted that "the State Party is obligated to follow the clear dictates of the National Party Rules and that failure to do so may well jeopardize Iowa's first-in-the-nation status in future election years" (p. 10).

In defending the decision to move the caucus date forward, the state party, with presidential candidates Alan Cranston and John Glenn as intervenors, argued that the campaigns of some presidential candidates would suffer irreparable harm due to their large expenditures of time and money in Iowa if the date were not changed to February 20 (Campbell et al. v. Iowa State Democratic Central Committee 1984, 13).

The court ruled in favor of the defendants and let stand the earlier date. In the decision the court agreed that the plaintiffs were entitled to relief but found for the defendants because "the intervenor presidential candidates will suffer a significant harm if the caucuses are not held on February 20, as their previous commitments may be wasted or reduced in effectiveness." The court added that "the individual damages that may be suffered by the plaintiffs are outweighed by the irreparable harm that changing the rules of the presidential nominating process [in Iowa] at this late date may have" (Campbell et al. v. Iowa State Democratic Central Committee 1984, 13).

As the plaintiffs noted, the DNC had threatened sanctions if Iowa moved its caucus date forward, including the possibility of not seating the Iowa delegation selected by the "illegal" caucus process at the Democratic National Convention. Ultimately, the DNC relented, and on May 3, 1984, it agreed to seat both the Iowa and New Hampshire delegations at San Francisco.

References

Bittick, Scott. 1980. Interview with author, January 23. Bittick was a caucus member.

Bonsignoir, Lou. 1986. Telephone interview with author, July 16. Bonsignoir was the organization director of the Iowa Republican party from 1979 to 1980.

Broder, David. 1980. "Kennedy's Challenge Suffers Big Setback." *Washington Post,* January 22, pp. A1, A4.

Bullard, Charles, and Debra Kneeland. 1980. "Ruan, Candidate Fall Short in 'Mighty 74.'" *Des Moines Register,* January 22, p. 1B.

Campbell, Edward, et al. v. Iowa State Democratic Central Committee and David Nagel. 1984. No. 83-115-W, 6 (Southern District of Iowa, January 17).

Clymer, Adam. 1980a. "Candidates and Issues: Caucus Day in Iowa." *Des Moines Register,* January 20, p. 4C.

———. 1980b. "Carter Wins Strong Victory in Iowa As Bush Takes Lead over Reagan." *New York Times,* January 22, pp. A1, A16.

———. 1980c. "Candidates Shifting Tactics." *New York Times,* January 23, pp. A1, A16.

Congressional Quarterly Weekly Report. 1980 and 1983.

Democratic National Committee. 1978. Delegate Selection Rules for the 1980 Democratic National Convention. Mimeographed.

Des Moines Register. 1979 and 1980.

Federal Election Commission. 1981. *FEC Reports on Financial Activity, 1979–80: Final Report, Presidential Pre-Nomination Campaigns.* Washington, D.C.: Federal Election Commission.

Flansburg, James. 1979a. "Ames Dinner Attracts Eight GOP Candidates." *Des Moines Register,* October 13, p. 4A.

———. 1979b. "Reagan: Debate Decision Based on Unity Wish." *Des Moines Register,* December 15, p. 16A.

———. 1979c. "Iowa Forum Is Virtually Ruled Out: President Cites Iran and Afghan Crises." *Des Moines Register,* December 29, pp. 1A, 5A.

———. 1979d. "Carter Is Busy in Iran, but There's a Credibility Gap." *Des Moines*

Register, December 30, p. 2C.

———. 1980a. "Decisive Week for Kennedy Campaign." *Des Moines Register,* January 6, pp. 1B, 3B.

———. 1980b. "Brown Drops from Caucus Race." *Des Moines Register,* January 17, pp. 1A, 9A.

Flansburg, James, and Daniel Pedersen. 1979. "President's Slick Machine." *Des Moines Register,* October 21, pp. 1A, 5A, 6A.

Flansburg, James, Daniel Pedersen, and David Yepsen. 1979. "Dole, Crane Candidacies Seem Doomed: Speculation Arises at Dinner in Ames." *Des Moines Register,* October 15, pp. 1A, 4A.

Flansburg, James, James Risser, and Diane Graham. 1980. "Forum Backs Hostage Policy: but Blames Carter for Crisis." *Des Moines Register,* January 6, pp. 1A, 4A.

Flansburg, James, and David Yepsen. 1979. "Reagan's Iowa Drive Loses Steam." *Des Moines Register,* October 28, pp. 1A, 13A.

———. 1980a. "Reagan: Loss in Iowa Aided My Campaign." *Des Moines Register,* June 8, pp. 1A, 4A.

———. 1980b. "Culver Raps Effort to Bar Anderson." *Des Moines Register,* June 15, pp. 1A, 10A.

Flansburg, James, David Yepsen, and Daniel Pedersen. 1979. "GOP Hopefuls in Iowa." *Des Moines Register,* October 14, pp. 1A, 8A.

Germond, Jack, and Jules Witcover. 1979a. "Stacking Deck for Bush?" *Des Moines Register,* October 1, p. 10A.

———. 1979b. "Reagan Slipping in Iowa, or Just Waiting for the Kill?" *Des Moines Register,* November 12, p. 10A.

Graham, Diane. 1979. "ABC to Cover Both Debates Live from Des Moines." *Des Moines Register,* December 19, p. 4A.

Hainey, Mark. 1980. "In Media Event, Media Are Part of the Event." *Des Moines Register,* January 22, p. 5A.

Hyde, Tim. 1986. Telephone interviews with author, July 3 and 17. Hyde was the executive director of the Iowa Republican party from 1980 to 1983.

Iowa General Assembly. 1983. *Acts and Resolutions.* Des Moines: State of Iowa.

Iowa Poll. 1980 and 1981. Vols. for 1979 and 1980. Des Moines: Des Moines Register and Tribune Company.

Jones, Charles O. 1981. "Nominating Carter's Favorite Opponent: The Republicans in 1980." In *The American Elections of 1980,* edited by Austin Ranney, 61-98. Washington, D.C.: American Enterprise Institute.

Leavitt, Paul. 1979. "Gov. Brown Accepts Bid to D.M. Debate." *Des Moines Register,* December 4, pp. 1A, 7A.

Mitofsky, Warren. 1986. Telephone interview with author, July 9. Mitofsky was the director of the elections and survey unit of CBS News.

Newsweek. 1979 and 1980.

New York Times. 1980.

Pedersen, Daniel. 1980. "Forum Backs Hostage Policy: They Came to Hear, Question, Decide." *Des Moines Register,* January 6, pp. 1A, 5A.

Pedersen, Daniel, James Flansburg, and David Yepsen. 1979. "Mondale Dismayed at White House Anger on Clark Defection." *Des Moines Register,* November 4, pp. 1A, 12A.

Pedersen, Daniel, and David Yepsen. 1980. "Bush Assails Reagan Plan on Welfare." *Des Moines Register,* January 21, pp. 1A, 3A.

Perry, James, and Albert Hunt. 1980. "Carter and Bush Win 1st Round but Have No Knockdowns Yet." *Wall Street Journal,* January 23, pp. 1, 37.

Peterson, Bill. 1980. "Baker Distant Third in the Iowa Caucuses." *Washington Post,* January 22, pp. A1, A5.

Plissner, Martin. 1986. Telephone interviews with author, June 18 and July 7. Plissner is the executive political director of CBS Television.

Roberts, Trish. 1984. Interview with author, February 11. Roberts was a reporter for National Public Television.

Robinson, Michael J. 1981. "The Media in 1980: Was the Message the Message?" In *The American Elections of 1980,* edited by Austin Ranney, 177-211. Washington, D.C.: American Enterprise Institute.

Robinson, Michael J., and Margaret A. Sheehan. 1983. *Over the Wire and on TV: CBS and UPI in Campaign '80.* New York: Russell Sage Foundation.

Smith, Hedrick. 1980. "Reagan Defeated by Bush in Iowa; Carter Deals Kennedy Big Setback: Senator Assesses Campaign." *New York Times,* January 23, pp. A1, A17.

Sperling, Godfrey, Jr. 1980. "Carter, Bush: What Iowa Victories Mean." *Christian Science Monitor,* January 23, pp. 1, 10.

Television News Index and Abstracts. 1975-76 and 1979-80. Nashville, Tenn.: Vanderbilt University.

Time. 1980.

Washington Post. 1980.

Yepsen, David. 1979a. "2nd District Tally Favors Bush, Connally." *Des Moines Register,* October 12, p. 6A.

———. 1979b. "Inconclusive Results Seen in Straw Poll." *Des Moines Register,* November 6, p. 3A.

———. 1986. Telephone interview with author, July 7. Yepsen is the chief political reporter for the *Des Moines Register.*

Chapter 7 The 1984 Caucuses: The Kickoff of a Front-Loaded Season

IN ADDITION TO shortening the presidential primary season, the Hunt Commission proposals had the unintended consequence of contributing to the front-loading of the 1984 primary and caucus calendar. A number of states, anxious to share the influence and attention gained by Iowa and other states that hold early contests and aware that Iowa was now limited in terms of how early it might hold caucuses, moved their electoral events closer to the beginning of the nominating season. Seventeen states scheduled primary elections or caucuses in the first twenty-two days of the 1984 primary period (*CQ* Dec. 10, 1983, 2605).

Other Hunt Commission proposals accepted by the Democratic National Committee gave states greater flexibility in selecting delegates to the national convention. They could hold primary elections, caucuses, or a combination of the two. The greater flexibility and the perceived harmful effects of primary elections on state party organizations led to a resurgence of the caucus and convention system in 1984. Iowa had demonstrated that its early caucus system was an excellent party-building mechanism, and other state parties moved in that direction. Whereas thirty-five states selected 72 percent of the delegates to the 1980 Democratic National Convention by primary election, only twenty-three states (and the District of Columbia and Puerto Rico) used primaries to select 54 percent of the 1984 delegates (Pomper 1985, 9).

Precaucus Activity

Some wondered whether the Iowa precinct caucuses would be lost in the shuffle, with so many states holding early caucuses and primaries in 1984. Others, like Senator John Glenn, thought the front-loading made Iowa and New Hampshire even more important, since successful candidates would get a quick start in what could be a very short race, and there would be very little time to recover from defeats in those states (Yepsen 1983a, 11A). A definitive answer as to the impact of front-loading would not be available until much later, but early signs indicated that presidential candidates were again taking the Iowa caucuses very seriously. A 1982 national magazine article began, "Believe it or not, the 1984 presidential race is already on" in Iowa. The story went on to describe visits by seven Democratic hopefuls seeking support for a nominating event still nearly two years away (*Newsweek* May 24, 1982, 31). It began to appear that the time spent by Iowa Democrats in defending their caucuses' first-in-the-nation status had been well worth the effort.

By 1984 the precinct caucuses had been institutionalized as a significant part of the primary and caucus schedule. The 1980 efforts by Carter, Kennedy, and Bush demonstrated that a strong organization was necessary to compete in the precinct caucuses now that Iowa was a well-publicized event in the presidential nominating process. It would no longer be possible for a candidate to put together an organization quietly and surprise the media, as McGovern had done in 1972 and as Carter had done to a lesser degree in 1976. To do well in Iowa would require a major organizational effort, but with New Hampshire a week later and Super Tuesday and its ten state delegate selection events only three weeks after the caucuses, candidate efforts could not be concentrated in the state, as they had been when several weeks separated Iowa and New Hampshire.

The Democratic Campaign

Visits by Democratic presidential candidates were common in Iowa from 1982 to 1984 as the candidates worked to enlist supporters and develop an organization capable of identifying and turning out potential caucus supporters. Most of the Democratic hopefuls made strong efforts and spent large sums of money and much energy pursuing support from the caucuses, but it was no contest from the start. Minnesota native Walter Mondale was well known in Iowa. On campaign trips to the state, he played on his close ties to Iowa by referring to himself as "Iowa's third senator," or, when criticizing Republican senators Charles Grassley and Roger Jepsen on a visit to Drake University, as "Iowa's only senator."

Mondale opened a Des Moines campaign headquarters in early 1983, and by the end of the year there were twenty-two full-time employees and a large budget, computers, phone banks, district offices, and hundreds of volunteers. His staff's systematic approach to organization building included personally contacting 2500 party activists, canvasing all those who had attended the 1980 Democratic caucuses, and generally attempting to stimulate enthusiasm for the Mondale candidacy (Leavitt 1983, 1B, 6B). He received early support from the United Auto Workers and the Iowa State Education Association. The support of organized groups and endorsements from many prominent Iowa Democrats helped Mondale to develop an organization that was called "clearly superior to others" (CQ Dec. 10, 1983, 2601). Mondale took an early lead in the polls, never relinquished his front-runner status, and entered the final stages of the Iowa campaign with a commanding lead.

Front-runner status, however, is a mixed blessing. It assures high media visibility and easy access to political circles closed to lesser candidates, but it also creates very high expectations. Russell Baker satirically warned Mondale that because he was the expected winner, the press would evaluate his progress more critically:

> Rotten luck ... Mondale, we've made you the front-runner. ... Without a front-runner, we'd have nobody to suffer surprising setbacks in the early stage of the campaign, and without surprising setbacks we would be stuck with a very dull story. We can't get people interested in a bunch of solemn clunks talking about complicated problems of government, Mondale. We've got to have a horse race or nobody's going to watch. It's tough, but somebody's got to make the sacrifice and be the front-runner. ... Say you get only 47 percent of that boondocks vote (in Iowa and New Hampshire). What we'll do is say, well 47 percent may not be disgraceful, but Mondale had been expected to do better, so it looks like he's all washed up. ... We of the press and TV do the expecting. You do the disappointing. That way we work together to give the country an entertaining story (Baker 1983, 12, © 1983, New York Times Co., reprinted by permission).

Not surprisingly, Baker's satirical warning was an accurate prediction of things to come.

Other Democrats also made significant organizational efforts in the state, but with Mondale enjoying a seemingly insurmountable lead, they fought it out for second place and hoped for a stronger-than-predicted finish. Alan Cranston was probably the next best organized of the Democratic candidates, and the fifty-five days and $727,358 that he spent in Iowa in the two years before the 1984 caucuses were among the top figures for both categories. Cranston's message was "peace and jobs," and he made nuclear disarmament the central issue of his campaign. As the campaign progressed, he struggled to overcome the issue of his age and the perception that he was a single-issue candidate. Cranston was well known in Iowa by the time of the caucuses, and he hoped for a second- or third-place finish in the battle for delegates (Yepsen 1984d, 5A).

Gary Hart was one of the first candidates to open an Iowa office, but his was a campaign of fits and starts. His campaign was hindered by several problems, and it took him a long time to develop an effective organization. After the early start, Hart severely damaged his Iowa effort by moving his state coordinator and most of the Iowa staff to Wisconsin to contest a straw poll held there in June 1983. He finished a poor third in the Wisconsin poll and "sent a signal to Iowa Democrats that they weren't being taken very seriously" (Germond and Witcover 1985, 51). The Hart campaign returned after the Wisconsin debacle strapped for funds and minus its Iowa campaign director, who had resigned. With very limited financial resources, Hart adopted a new strategy dubbed the "van caravan." The owner of the van, Steve Lynch of Lawler, drove Hart from small town to small town, particularly in western Iowa. Hart gave speeches and met and talked with anyone likely to participate in or have an impact on the precinct caucuses. The van also served as a mobile press conference room, and reporters and editors from small-town weekly newspapers were invited to interview Hart on the road. Although very taxing of the candidate's time—he spent over sixty days in Iowa—the Hart campaign was consistently front-page news in small-town Iowa (Germond and Witcover 1985, 130-31; Yepsen 1984b, 1M).

Unlike most of the other presidential hopefuls, John Glenn did not have to struggle to develop name recognition in Iowa; the former astronaut drew huge crowds whenever he campaigned in the state. But he had trouble attracting supporters for the caucuses (Yepsen, Healey, and Fuson 1984, 1A). The national press established Glenn as the most viable alternative to Mondale, but he apparently never understood the nature of a caucus organization, because he ran a primary election race in Iowa. He did not employ his large staff—thirty-six full-time employees—or his financial resources effectively, which eventually led to staff shake-ups in both his Iowa and national organizations (Fuson and Healey 1984, 1M; Yepsen 1983b, 4B). The $759,178 his campaign spent in Iowa included heavy expenditures on television, which may work well in a primary election but which generally produces few results in precinct caucuses. (As mentioned earlier, John Connally unsuccessfully employed the same approach in the 1980 caucuses.) It also appears that Glenn misjudged the political climate of Iowa. His "sensible center" message was not well received by likely Democratic caucus participants, who, unlike most Iowans, may lean toward the liberal side of the political spectrum (Yepsen 1984d, 5A).

Reubin Askew's forty-seven campaign days in Iowa were exceeded only by Hart and Cranston, but his attempts to organize the right wing of the party, and particularly the anti-abortion vote, were not appreciated by Iowa Democrats, who had seen that group help defeat Democratic candidates in three recent Iowa general elections (Yepsen 1984c, 15A). Askew eventually ran short of money and canceled last-minute television messages.

Ernest Hollings also came to Iowa early, but after appearing in the state several times in 1982 and 1983, he decided to concentrate his efforts in New Hampshire. Apparently realizing that his chances for success in the caucuses were slim, Hollings decided to allocate his limited resources elsewhere. When Hollings did appear in Iowa in 1984 for forums and debates, he was a press favorite. Unlike those seriously contesting the caucuses, he had little to lose, and his candor and wit were diversions from the more serious campaign rhetoric of the other candidates.

Jesse Jackson tested the Iowa political climate on a quick trip in March 1983 (Germond and Witcover 1985, 68) and decided that a state that required a major organizational effort and included a minority population of less than 2 percent was no place to kick off his presidential campaign.

George McGovern entered the contest late, and although the sentimental favorite of many Iowans, he had difficulty overcoming the perception that he was not a serious candidate (Yepsen 1984d, 5A). He was a familiar sight in Iowa in the later months of the race, campaigning for thirty-seven days in the state. He never really developed a significant organization, but he appeared and performed well in debates and public forums, often playing the role of party sage. In that role he attempted to prevent party divisiveness by keeping the campaign rhetoric directed against Ronald Reagan.

Not only did the campaign begin much earlier in many states in 1984, but also a number of state parties initiated straw polls. By the time of the Iowa Jefferson-Jackson Day dinner in October, five states had already held major straw polls, and their results had been widely reported (Peterson 1983, A3). The media and the candidates took these early indicators very seriously, as shown by Hart's effort in Wisconsin and the national coverage given the results.

The Jefferson-Jackson Day dinner on October 8 was the most successful fund-raising event ever held by the Iowa Democratic Party (Whitney 1986). The event, held in Veterans Auditorium in Des Moines, drew about 6000 people and seven presidential candidates. The speakers list also was large, and eighteen speeches lasting about three hours tested the resolve of those who remained to hear Mondale, the last speaker of the evening. The order of appearance of the presidential hopefuls was determined by draw, and Mondale, having the final word, centered his attack on John Glenn. Glenn had criticized Mondale on a number of occasions as the candidate of special interests, and Mondale chose this opportunity to even the score. He took Glenn to task for a number of his stands on issues, but particularly for his support of President Reagan's 1981 tax cut. Looking directly at Glenn, Mondale thundered that that would have been a good time to stand up to the special interests. Mondale's controversial theme, "I am the only real Democrat," began to emerge during this speech.

Presumably, the thousands seated in the balcony of Veterans Auditorium had each paid ten dollars to witness the party spectacle and participate in the preference poll. (A total of 2600 dinner tickets at forty dollars each and 3600 balcony tickets at ten dollars were sold [Raines 1983, 33].) I do not know how typical my immediate area was, but everyone in the vicinity, including my party of eight, had received complimentary tickets from either the Mondale or Cranston campaigns. Some asserted that Cranston had more tickets than takers for his free passes (Germond and Witcover 1985, 109). The lopsided results of the Associated Press (AP) straw poll shown in Table 7.1 tend to confirm that most of the tickets were purchased by Mondale and Cranston.

The media concluded that the Jefferson-Jackson Day fund-raiser was so obviously stacked by Mondale and Cranston that they discounted the results of the now-famous preference poll. The outcome was widely reported, but most stories downplayed the poll's significance. The *New York Times* reported the results but thought that "by using the straw poll mainly to raise money, the state Democratic Party undermined its legitimacy" (Raines 1983, 33). *Time* magazine's story on the dinner did not mention the poll (Oct. 24, 1983, 28, 29). The irony of the 1983 preference poll is that Mondale and Cranston were too successful in packing the hall. Carter used the same tactic in 1975, but with much less success. Consequently, Carter's more modest victory was widely interpreted as a significant win, while Mondale and Cranston gained little for outdistancing the field in 1983.

Concurrent with the reporting of the Jefferson-Jackson Day poll, and in many cases in the same story, the results of an October Iowa Poll were reported to the nation. That poll, like national Gallup samplings, found the Democratic contest to be a two-person race between

Table 7.1.   1983 Jefferson-Jackson Day poll results

	Preferences	Percentage of total
Mondale	1948	47.0
Cranston	1534	37.0
Glenn	243	5.9
Uncommitted	149	3.6
Hart	146	3.5
McGovern	74	1.8
Askew	35	0.8
Hollings	14	0.3
Total	4143	99.9

Source: Data from the *Des Moines Register,* October 9, 1983, 1A; and Peterson 1983, A3.

Walter Mondale and John Glenn, with those who reported that they "definitely or probably" would attend a precinct caucus divided as follows: Mondale, 46 percent; Glenn, 27; Hart, 7; McGovern, 5; Jackson, 2; Cranston, Askew, and Hollings, 1 percent or less; and "undecided," 10 percent (Iowa Poll: 1983, poll no. 258).

The national media seemed to rely heavily on national and state public opinion polls in developing the two-candidate-race scenario. Critics argued that polls of the general public tend to reflect levels of name recognition, not organized political support, which is so crucial in the early nominating events (*Newsweek* Dec. 12, 1983, 72). The research presented here documents that the Iowa Poll had been a very poor indicator of candidate standing prior to earlier Iowa caucuses, and 1984 would again demonstrate the folly of developing precaucus expectations on the basis of public opinion polls, even when the respondents assure pollsters that they plan to attend the meetings.

Where the 1980 caucus campaign was characterized by dinners and events that conducted preference polls, the 1984 race featured candidate debates and forums. The *Des Moines Register* announced on May 14 that it would sponsor a precaucus debate for Democratic presidential candidates nine months later, on February 11, 1984, at the Des Moines Civic Center. In the months following the *Register*'s announcement, several other organizations scheduled presidential forums, each of which drew several candidates and the media.

On August 13, 1983, a committee known as People Encouraging Arms Control Efforts (PEACE) organized an "Open Forum on Arms Control with the Presidential Candidates" in Des Moines. Five of the six announced Democratic presidential hopefuls—Cranston, Glenn, Hart, Hollings, and Mondale—completed a questionnaire developed by STAR*PAC (Stop the Arms Race Political Action Committee of Iowa) and agreed to appear at the nuclear arms forum. The only candidate not accepting the invitation, Reubin Askew, did not want to be associated with the nuclear freeze movement. (Hollings canceled at the last moment due to the death of his infant granddaughter.) The all-day affair included workshops and a three-hour question-and-answer session for the presidential candidates and was moderated by Iowa Congressman Berkley Bedell. The forum attracted a large audience of about 1800 to 2000 people and national press and television coverage.

The forum was something of a landmark for nuclear freeze groups in Iowa, since it gave the movement legitimacy. A sitting congressman and five presidential candidates were willing to come together and openly compete for the support of Iowa peace groups. The audience was, for the most part, young and liberal, but it also included large numbers of older, middle-class people. It appeared that the young activists of an earlier day were now older but still very opposed to the use of nuclear arms. Senator Cranston, the most outspoken foe of nuclear weapons of the forum participants, attempted to build his campaign in Iowa around the issue.

The ground rules prevented the Democratic participants from criticizing each other, and although they spent time attacking President Reagan's arms control and nuclear policies, the *New York Times* thought the forum "drew out some of the differences, some subtle and some not, between the four candidates who participated" (Gailey 1983, A17). Other columnists were even more enthusiastic about the peace forum. A story by Germond and Witcover called the forum "the single most revealing exercise in the eight months of the campaign for the Democratic presidential nomination" (1983, 8A).

A second forum, sponsored by the Brown and Black Coalition in Des Moines on January 10, 1984, centered on civil rights issues, particularly minority representation in government. Four presidential hopefuls—Cranston, Glenn, Hart, and McGovern—attended, and they agreed on most issues. A panel of minority-community activists questioned the candidates and pressed for specific plans, particularly plans for increasing minority representation in the federal bureaucracy and judiciary. The four assailed Mondale for his absence and called for increased spending for educational programs and a greater role for blacks and Hispanics in government. One of the few areas of disagreement came over government efforts to limit immigration. Glenn favored, and the other three opposed, identification cards for Hispanics (Yepsen, Fuson, and Healey 1984, 1M, 6M).

A third forum, on farm issues, was held in Ames on January 21. Six candidates—Askew, Cranston, Hart, Hollings, McGovern, and Mondale—appeared before a crowd of approximately 1500 people on the Iowa State University campus. Cranston took the only unpopular stand of the day when he proclaimed that the parity index was outdated as a basis for grain prices. The statement drew boos, and one man in the audience stood and proclaimed, "Boy, are you dumb!" The remaining hopefuls, minus Glenn, who was absent because of a previous commitment in the South, played it safe and attempted to blame all of the ills of the farm economy on President Reagan (Yepsen 1984a, 3A).

The grand finale of the forum season was the *Des Moines Register's* debate on February 11 in Des Moines. The *Register* spent months planning and promoting the event, even holding a drawing for the approximately 2500 tickets available to the general public. Eight presidential candidates—Askew, Cranston, Glenn, Hart, Hollings, Jackson, McGovern, and Mondale—participated in the forum, the format of which permitted two-minute opening statements, followed by three rounds of the candidates questioning each other, followed by another round of questions from six panelists, and concluding with a two-minute closing statement by each.

The forum was a media spectacular covered by about 200 reporters representing "every major newspaper, all the networks," and local and regional broadcast systems. CNN provided live television coverage, and the Public Broadcasting Service and C-Span taped and broadcast the event on a delayed basis. Additional live coverage was provided by radio stations throughout the state (Yepsen and Healey 1984, 1A, 11A).

The forum was a time for the candidates to reiterate familiar themes. With the campaign almost two years old, their positions were well developed and were well known to the active Democrats most likely to attend the precinct caucuses. Most seemed to be trying to avoid mistakes before the large audience, but there were notable exceptions. Hollings and Jackson delighted the crowd with their candor and glibness, and McGovern made an impassioned plea to his supporters, asking them not to "throw away your conscience" by supporting a different candidate simply because it was widely believed that he, McGovern, had little chance in 1984. "Reagan bashing" was the most popular activity of the forum, as candidate after candidate attacked the "failed" policies of the administration.

The two and a half hours passed rather quickly, and those in attendance seemed to enjoy being part of the *Register's* forum. It is debatable, however, whether such events have an impact on the caucus process. Perhaps they serve to stimulate interest, which could increase attendance and have an impact on some meetings, but it is unlikely that they alter support patterns significantly.

The media, with their "game" focus, concentrated their efforts on determining who had won or lost the debate. In the four days follow-

Cartoon by Brian Duffy, © 1984, *Des Moines Register,* reprinted by permission

Whereas the 1980 caucus campaign was characterized by dinners and events at which preference polls were conducted, the 1984 Democratic race featured candidate debates and forums. The grand finale of the forum season was a debate sponsored by the *Des Moines Register,* which featured eight presidential candidates. The event attracted an audience of approximately 2500 people and about 200 reporters.

ing the forum, the *Register* analyzed the performance of each of the participants and conducted a statewide poll asking respondents which of the candidates had impressed them favorably or unfavorably in the debate. The newspaper concluded that McGovern had won the debate on the basis of a 40 percent to 4 percent favorable-unfavorable rating among likely caucus participants. Mondale, who apparently just met the writer's expectations, "didn't lose ground" with his 47 percent to

11 percent ranking, but Glenn (16% to 13%) and Hollings (7% to 13%) "were the only candidates who made about as many bad impressions as good" and were judged the losers (Elbert 1984, 1A, 13A; Iowa Poll: 1984, poll no. 261).

The Republican Campaign

President Reagan was seeking reelection in 1984 and without a challenger in Iowa, there was no Republican campaign. The president did not visit the state before the caucuses, and his absence caused at least one negative side effect. The Democratic campaign was identifying supporters and potential campaign workers for the general election struggle, and with no campaign to stimulate interest, the Republicans were unable to match the effort.

The 1984 Precinct Caucuses

The Iowa campaign came to an end, and the soft evidence provided by the polls, debates, and political pundits had been analyzed and reanalyzed. The candidates had made extraordinary efforts in Iowa, and their campaign activity is summarized in Table 7.2. Democratic presidential candidates spent about 300 days in the state, building organizations and engaging in the personal style of campaigning that Iowans have come to expect. Federal financial reports show that Glenn, Cranston, and Mondale reached the federal limit on campaign spending in Iowa, and Hart was not far behind. Again, federal reports understate campaign expenditures. Mondale, for example, had strong labor support, and the unions' "independent expenditures" included phone banks operated by labor volunteers and nineteen local headquarters rented from unions for nominal monthly fees. Also, the rental cars used by the Mondale campaign bore Minnesota license plates. Glenn had a phone bank in St. Louis making Iowa calls, and Cranston stayed in Omaha when campaigning in western Iowa (Yepsen 1984c, 15A). It is evident from the amount of campaign activity in the state that the compressed and front-loaded primary schedule did not minimize the importance of the Iowa caucuses. If anything, the candidates emphasized the caucuses more than in 1980.

Table 7.2.   1984 candidate precaucus
campaign activity and spending

	Days in Iowa	Spending in Iowa
Askew	47	$194,315
Cranston	55	727,358
Glenn	33	759,178
Hart	60	453,503
Hollings	14	11,382
Jackson	2	8953
McGovern	37	52,403
Mondale	34	687,712
Reagan	1	194,821

Source: Spending data are from the Federal
Election Commission report *FEC Reports on
Financial Activity, 1983-84: Final Report, Presidential
Pre-Nomination Campaigns,* Table A9. The Iowa limit
was $684,537. The campaign activity includes 1982,
1983, and 1984. The 1982 data are from the *Iowa
Democratic Party Data Book: 1983-84.* The 1983 and
1984 data were collected from the individual campaigns and are of varying reliability. Most of the
campaigns provided sound information that
included dates and cities visited. The Hart and
Mondale campaigns provided information of lesser
quality. The Hart people, for example, reported that
he was in Iowa only five times in 1984 and on twenty-seven occasions during the three-year period. My
examination of the *Des Moines Register* indicated
that Hart was in the state at least sixty days.

Media Coverage

The media also came to Iowa very early to follow the Democratic candidates. Media coverage waxed and waned between 1982 and 1984,
but on special occasions, such as the "Open Forum on Arms Control
with the Presidential Candidates" in Des Moines on August 13 and the
Des Moines Register's debate on February 11, which was attended by all
eight Democratic presidential candidates, national media attention

focused on Iowa.

In the final days of the caucus campaign, reporters seeking stories searched for "typical Iowans" (those wearing bib overalls were in particular demand) and most of all played the expectations game. Mondale was judged the "clear front-runner" and John Glenn the "primary challenger," even though Glenn never developed an effective campaign organization in Iowa and his campaign showed many signs of weakness. McGovern, Hart, and Cranston made up the second tier. Hollings, Askew, and Jesse Jackson, who did not participate in the caucus race, were given little chance of success.

Media coverage for the caucuses was awesome. The press "filing space" for 1984 was double that of 1980. Over a thousand press credentials were issued by the Iowa Democratic Party to representatives and technicians of approximately 150 U.S. and foreign news organizations. More than thirty television and many radio stations were represented in Iowa; "Meet the Press" and "Face the Nation" originated from Des Moines on the day before the caucuses; and on February 20, the day of the caucuses, the "Today" show and the evening news programs of ABC, CBS, NBC, and CNN originated live from Des Moines (Piatt 1984). In terms of the breadth of coverage, 1984 far exceeded 1980. If input (stories produced) is any indication of output (stories aired or printed), there were probably far more stories aired and printed about the Iowa caucuses at the international and local levels in 1984 than ever before. This was not, however, the case with the CBS television news.

Table 7.3 compares television coverage of the 1980 and 1984 Iowa precinct caucuses and the New Hampshire primary election by CBS's evening and weekend news for one-year periods from July 1, 1979, to June 30, 1980, and from July 1, 1983, to June 30, 1984. The data indicate that there was an overall decline in the number of Iowa and New Hampshire stories aired by CBS in 1984 compared with 1980 and that in 1984 New Hampshire was again the leading early nominations story, after relinquishing that position to Iowa in 1980. A definitive explanation is not possible, but a lengthy discussion with Martin Plissner of CBS produced some tentative thoughts about the reduced coverage (June 18, 1986). In 1980 both parties featured vigorous presidential nominating contests, while in 1984 only the Democrats had a

Table 7.3.   1980 and 1984 CBS news stories on Iowa and New Hampshire

	July 1, 1979, to June 30, 1980			July 1, 1983, to June 30, 1984		
	Weekday	Weekend	Total	Weekday	Weekend	Total
Iowa	37	17	54	8	3	11
N.H.	29	11	40	14	8	22

Source: Data were collected from the *Television News Index and Abstracts,* produced by Vanderbilt University. The criteria for constructing the table are discussed in the source note for Table 6.2.

contest. Simply stated, there was more to cover in 1980. The relatively greater decline in Iowa coverage in 1984 is less easily explained. It is possible that the compressed 1984 schedule had some impact, since Iowa was moved closer to the pack. Iowa was five weeks earlier than New Hampshire in 1980 but only eight days ahead in 1984. Perhaps the fact that Mondale was the overwhelming favorite in the Iowa caucuses diminished media interest. Perhaps New Hampshire received greater coverage because of Hart's perceived success in Iowa.

Turnout for the 1984 precinct caucuses also suffered from lack of interest. Pollsters and party officials predicted a month before the meetings that turnout was likely to be much less than in 1980 (*DMR* Jan. 22, 1984, 2C). Democratic party officials estimated that 75,000 people attended their meetings (approximately 14 percent of the registered Democrats). Again, a definitive explanation is not possible, but Mondale's big early lead and a resulting boredom factor probably contributed to the 25 percent decline in attendance from 1980 (Steffen 1984).

The Democratic Caucuses

In spite of their extensive coverage of the Iowa caucuses, the media had grown wary of the "results" provided by the Iowa political parties. It is well documented that the complex tabulation process confuses many reporters; the *Des Moines Register,* CBS, and other news organizations were aware that the reporting of caucus outcomes was not governed by law and had been manipulated. CBS was very concerned about the validity of caucus results because of its experiences in Iowa in 1976 and 1980 (Plissner July 7, 1986).

These concerns led news organizations to ask the Iowa Democratic Party to provide a breakdown of the candidate preference of those attending the 1984 meetings after the first division into preference groups. In essence, they were asking the party to conduct a straw poll of caucus members and to provide raw vote totals rather than the delegate equivalents reported since 1972. The Iowa Democrats asserted that raw vote totals would misrepresent the caucus process and refused to bow to media demands (*DMR* Oct. 16, 1983, 2C). The media responded to the deadlock by employing the News Election Service (NES), a vote-counting service funded by ABC, CBS, NBC, AP, and UPI, to determine candidate preference totals after the first division into preference groups at the Democratic caucuses. Since the caucus process does not lend itself to tabulating candidate preference, and since the Iowa Democratic Party refused to cooperate, the NES was able to provide preference totals for only 74 percent of the 2495 precincts, and its numbers were of questionable validity due to the dynamic nature of the precinct meetings. Moreover, since the NES did not weight the totals on the basis of county size, the "one person, one vote" principle was badly violated. The presence of two sets of results proved confusing to all.

After months under the media microscope and to the relief of many Iowans, the 8 P.M. time for the February 20 precinct caucuses finally arrived. But it took only twelve minutes for another controversy to erupt. On the basis of a review of sign-in sheets at some caucuses, CBS projected Walter Mondale the Iowa winner at 8:12 P.M. (CST), eighteen minutes before Democratic party rules permitted the delegate selection process to begin (U.S. Congress, House 1984, 12). NBC used polls and NES data to project at 8:18 P.M. that Mondale would be the winner, that John Glenn would not finish second, and that there was a "very good chance" that Gary Hart would be second. ABC withheld its projection that Mondale would win and that Glenn, Hart, and Cranston were "fighting it out for second place" until 8:46 P.M., sixteen minutes after delegate selection began but before any delegate counts were available (U.S. Congress, House 1984, 14).

The Iowa Democrats were very disturbed by the early media projections, and so was Congress. On February 27, 1984, the House Subcommittee on Telecommunications, Consumer Protection, and Finance held a hearing on early election projections, and it centered on the Iowa caucuses. Chairman Tim Wirth, a Democrat from Colorado, informed those present that the hearing was being held "to discuss the civic responsibility of the electronic media and the implications that their methods and their announcements of projected results have on the electoral process" (U.S. Congress, House 1984, 5). The subcommittee received a number of research papers and heard testimony from top media executives and leaders of the Republican and Democratic parties. David Nagle, the Iowa Democratic chair, testified that the state party had evidence that the early projections had found their way into caucuses that were in progress. Nagle warned that "to report the supposed outcome of our process before it even begins ... runs the risk of seriously intruding on the process and damaging the party" (U.S. Congress, House 1984, 78).

The subcommittee continued its hearings, and late in the year, two congressmen—Al Swift, a Democrat from Washington, and William M. Thomas, a Republican from California—formally asked ABC, CBS, and NBC for "a firm, explicit, public, corporate commitment not to use exit poll data to suggest, through interpretation of that data, the probable winner in any state until the polls in that state have closed" (Swift and Thomas 1984).

By early 1985 the three networks had forwarded letters to congressmen Swift and Thomas that stated that in future elections they would not "use exit polling data to project or characterize election results until the polls are closed in [that] state" (Swift and Thomas 1985). In return, the congressmen agreed to begin hearings on uniform hours for voting on election day throughout the United States.

As caucus results began to come in on February 20, the expectations game continued, with the media interpreting the outcomes. The *Des Moines Register*, the *New York Times*, the *Wall Street Journal*, the *Christian Science Monitor*, and *Newsweek* reported NES results; the *Washington Post*, the *St. Louis Post-Dispatch*, *U.S. News and World Report*, and *Time* carried the Democratic party's state delegate equivalent figures; and

Congressional Quarterly reported both. The two sets of numbers are shown in Table 7.4. The official Democratic results showed Mondale, Hart, and "uncommitted" percentages as greater than indicated by the NES outcomes, and the others as less.

The *Newsweek* summary of the Iowa caucuses was representative. It concluded that "Mondale's victory met all expectations" and Glenn's "humiliating fifth-place finish" was a disaster for his campaign. McGovern's third-place finish was "startling," and "the caucuses gave Hart media momentum." Cranston, Askew, and Hollings were declared the big losers along with Glenn. On the basis of the Iowa caucuses, *Newsweek* reduced the field to Mondale, Hart, Jackson, "and maybe Glenn" (March 5, 1984, 22-23).

Mondale was the overwhelming winner in the caucuses, and the press headlines reflected the magnitude of his win. The *Register* said that "Mondale Scores Easy Victory" (Feb. 21, 1A), the *New York Times* reported "Mondale Wins Handily in Iowa" (Raines 1984, A1), and the *Washington Post* headline reported that the "Winner in Iowa Ran Far Ahead of Field" (Peterson and Sawyer 1984, A1). The Mondale perfor-

Table 7.4.   1984 Democratic precinct caucus results

	State delegate equivalents (%)	News Election Service pre-viability results (%)
Mondale	48.9	44.5
Hart	16.5	14.8
McGovern	10.3	12.6
Uncommitted	9.4	7.5
Cranston	7.4	9.0
Glenn	3.5	5.3
Askew	2.5	3.3
Jackson	1.5	2.7
Hollings	0.0	0.3

Source: The state delegate equivalents are the official results of the Iowa Democratic Party and are based on reports from 94 percent of the precincts. The News Election Service results are from 74 percent of the precincts.

mance not only met press expectations, it exceeded them to the point that the *Christian Science Monitor* thought that Mondale had "moved so far ahead of his seven opponents that he could lock up his party's presidential nomination by mid-March" (Dillin 1984, 1).

The big loser in the Iowa caucuses was John Glenn. All of the country's major newspapers emphasized how devastating the results were for his campaign. The *Register* reported that Glenn had "faltered badly" (Feb. 21, 1A); the *New York Times* thought that the Iowa defeat "threatened to cripple his presidential candidacy" (Raines 1984, A1); the *Wall Street Journal* called the Glenn finish a "stunning defeat" (Feb. 21, 1984, 62); the *Christian Science Monitor* thought that Glenn's campaign was in "deep, deep trouble" (Dillin 1984, 1); and the *Washington Post* declared that Glenn had "crash-landed" in Iowa (Peterson and Sawyer 1984, A1).

Unlike the *Christian Science Monitor,* most newspapers and magazines were not ready to concede the nomination to Mondale, and having declared Glenn all but dead, they elevated Hart to the position of main challenger on the basis of his second-place finish in Iowa. The reporting was cautious, because Hart had finished a very distant second in the precinct caucuses, but the *Washington Post* thought that Mondale faced "a new challenge from a strengthened Sen. Gary Hart" (Broder and Balz 1984, A1).

The new reality of the Democratic presidential contest was perhaps best outlined by Germond and Witcover in a story analyzing the impact of Iowa entitled "Iowa Caucuses Change the Candidates' Political-Expectations Game." They opined that "John Glenn has been effectively eliminated as a serious contender to Walter Mondale" because "the political community and press fully expected him to finish second, however distantly. ... Similarly, Gary Hart has been transformed into the sole remaining serious competitor to Mondale, not because he finished second—after all, he ran far behind Mondale—but because he showed so much more strength than the evidence suggested was reasonable to expect" (Germond and Witcover 1984, 8A). It did not take long for Hart to benefit from the perception that he was the last hope to make 1984 a horse race. On the "NBC Nightly News" on February 23, Don Oliver reported that after Iowa, contributions to the Hart campaign had increased from $2,000 a day to $12,000.

Cartoon by Brian Duffy, © 1984, *Des Moines Register,* reprinted by permission

Ronald Reagan was formerly a sports reporter for WHO radio in Des Moines. As the unchallenged Republican incumbent in 1984, he was able to watch the Democrats fight it out in Iowa.

The Republican Caucuses

The Republicans also held precinct caucuses in 1984, but with an incumbent president, there was little campaigning and no media interest in their meetings until President Reagan decided to visit Iowa on February 20, the day of the caucuses. The president appeared in Waterloo and Des Moines in an attempt to increase interest in the Republican caucuses and to steal some of the limelight from the Democrats, who had monopolized media attention in Iowa for several months.

The straw poll initiated in 1976 and continued in 1980 was not conducted in the 1984 Republican caucuses. Republican officials did not think a poll necessary, since the nomination was uncontested. The absence of a poll also assured that if any dissatisfied Republicans attended the caucuses, they would not embarrass President Reagan. Attendance figures for the Republican caucuses could only be very tentative due to the absence of a poll, but it was estimated that 25,000 to 30,000 people participated (Roth 1984).

The Impact of the 1984 Caucuses

Iowans appeared to have grown blasé in 1984 about their now-famous media event. The notoriety associated with the caucuses failed to stimulate the interest in and attendance at the 1984 meetings that it had in 1980. On the other hand, Iowa's political parties and the Des Moines Chamber of Commerce were anything but blasé. The Chamber created a caucus information center in the Des Moines skywalk and promoted the media event. Friendly attendants provided information on anything a visitor or reporter could possibly wish to know about the state and its people. The political parties increased their public relations efforts and were more helpful than ever to the press. The Democrats published a 211-page *Iowa Democratic Party Data Book,* which included everything from previous caucus results and explanations of the process to lists of hotels and motels in counties throughout the state. Everyone worked very hard to accommodate reporters and promote Iowa as a great place to begin the presidential race.

Concerns that the Iowa caucuses might be lost in the shuffle of a front-loaded nomination season proved to be unfounded. In most respects, except possibly the number of television stories aired by CBS, Iowa was a bigger media event than before. Candidate visits to the state were so numerous as to be commonplace. The volume of media coverage and the number of reporters spending time in Iowa also increased substantially. CNN became the fourth national network to set up temporary studios in Des Moines, international reporters were more in evidence, and local broadcast and press people, particularly from the major metropolitan areas, were far more evident than in past caucus seasons.

The compressed primary and caucus schedule maximized the impact of the Iowa caucuses, as John Glenn had predicted. Candidates who fared poorly in the Iowa perceptions game had only eight days to recover before the primary election in New Hampshire, and the task proved too great for most. Alan Cranston, who had spent parts of two years and three-quarters of a million dollars in Iowa, announced on February 29, nine days after the Iowa caucuses and one day after the New Hampshire primary election, that he was no longer a candidate for the presidency. Hollings and Askew withdrew from the race on March 2, McGovern on March 13, and Glenn on March 16. It was indeed a very fast and short race for the majority of candidates in 1984.

But Iowa has gained its reputation as an early indicator in the presidential race not only by exposing weakness. The precinct caucuses also produce "surprise winners"—candidates who do better than expected and as a result gain media momentum. There were few surprises in 1984, other than Glenn's very poor finish. Mondale met media expectations in the caucuses, but with the Glenn candidacy written off by reporters, there was a need for a challenger, and here Hart filled the bill. McGovern was something of a surprise, finishing ahead of the remainder of the second tier, but the media remembered him as the big loser to Nixon in 1972 and thus were unwilling to make too much of his relatively high finish. Hart was a new face, and although he claimed only 16.5 percent of the state delegate equivalents in Iowa, this was enough of a surprise to gain media attention. Hart was still very much a dark horse, but in the eyes of the media he was the only other horse in the race.

The new role brought Hart the media attention he had lacked before Iowa, and when he arrived in New Hampshire, he found a "swollen pack of journalists" willing to trail him everywhere and report his every utterance (*Time* March 5, 1984, 8). Hart and, to a lesser extent, Mondale were the only candidates who benefited from Iowa, and with only eight days separating Iowa and New Hampshire there was no time for the others to recover. Hart went on to win in New Hampshire and in Maine six days later, and for a time at least, he was elevated to the position of front-runner. These successes were made possible by the positive media interpretation of Hart's placing a distant second in the Iowa precinct caucuses.

The Second Defense of a Media Event

Although it has cooperated with its Democratic counterpart, the Iowa Republican party has played a more limited role in defending Iowa's position of prominence. The national Republican party has no rules governing the length of the primary and caucus season, and when Iowa raised the issue at the 1984 Republican National Convention, there was little interest in developing such rules (Paulin 1984). Before 1984 there were no significant threats from other state Republican parties, and in 1984 a change in the Michigan caucus and convention system went largely unnoticed due to the lack of a contest for the Republican presidential nomination. But Michigan had moved its caucus and convention process forward, and the first step in the selection of its 1988 delegates took place on August 5, 1986, when candidates for precinct delegates were selected in the primary election. The move brought presidential hopefuls to the state and attracted some media attention (Germond and Witcover 1986, 4X).

Shortly after the 1984 Democratic National Convention, the now-predictable assault on the date of the Iowa caucuses began anew, but this time from another source. Representative Morris Udall and Senator Dennis DeConcini, both Arizona Democrats, introduced companion bills (H.R. 6054 and S. 2890) to Congress on July 31, 1984. The bills would have required that "Presidential primaries or caucuses be held only during the period beginning on the second Tuesday in March and ending on the second Tuesday in June of the year of the Presidential election." The Task Force on Elections, which had been created by the Committee on House Administration, held a hearing on September 19, 1984, but the bills died in the Ninety-eighth Congress.

Congressman Udall reintroduced identical legislation (H.R. 1380) in the first session of the Ninety-ninth Congress on February 28, 1985. In describing the bill for the House, Udall explained that "it would make two small, but important changes in the way we choose our Presidential nominees. First, the primary season would be limited to a specific period of time, eliminating the disproportionate influence of a few early primary states. Second, a shorter primary season would reduce the amount of campaign spending and relieve some of the 'boredom factor' experienced by many voters" (*Congressional Record* Feb. 28, 1985, E 723).

If judged from a historical perspective, the likelihood of Congressman Udall successfully removing the status of Iowa and New Hampshire as major nominating events was not good; since 1911, none of the approximately 300 bills designed to reform or alter the presidential nominating process has passed Congress (Hyde 1984, 5A).

The national Democratic party did not change the order or length of the 1988 primary season, but it appeared likely that Iowa would have to redefend its first-in-the-nation status in the presidential campaign. Without an incumbent presidential candidate in 1988, both the Republican and Democratic party races would be spirited events. The stakes are so high that in all likelihood other state parties would be tempted to follow the Michigan lead and take aim at the early date of the Iowa caucuses.

References

Baker, Russell. 1983. "Handicappers." *New York Times Magazine,* February 6, p. 12.

Broder, David, and Dan Balz. 1984. "Hart Declares Contest Will Narrow to Two." *Washington Post,* February 22, pp. A1, A12.

Congressional Quarterly Weekly Report. 1983 and 1984.

Congressional Record. 1985.

Des Moines Register. 1983 and 1984.

Dillin, John. 1984. "Iowa Caucuses Reshuffle Field of Democrats." *Christian Science Monitor,* February 22, pp. 1, 28.

Elbert, David. 1984. "Poll Finds McGovern 'Won' Debate." *Des Moines Register,* February 17, pp. 1A, 13A.

Federal Election Commission. 1986. *FEC Reports on Financial Activity, 1983-84: Final Report, Presidential Pre-Nomination Campaigns.* Washington, D.C.: Federal Election Commission.

Fuson, Ken, and James Healey. 1984. "Glenn Replaces National Campaign Director." *Des Moines Register,* January 27, p. 1M.

Gailey, Phil. 1983. "Arms Curb Debate Sets Glenn Apart from Rivals." *New York Times,* August 16, p. A17.

Germond, Jack, and Jules Witcover. 1983. "Peace Forum a Campaign High Spot." *Des Moines Register,* August 17, p. 8A.

———. 1984. "Iowa Caucuses Change the Candidates' Political-Expectations Game ... ." *Des Moines Register,* February 22, p. 8A.

———. 1985. *Wake Us When It's Over.* New York: Macmillan.

———. 1986. "Michigan: Early with Sound and Fury." *Des Moines Register,* June 18, p. 4X.

Hyde, John. 1984. "Bill Would Abolish Early Iowa Caucuses." *Des Moines Register,* September 20, p. 5A.

Iowa Democratic Party Data Book: 1983-84. 1984. Des Moines: Iowa Democratic Party.

Iowa Poll. 1984-87. Vols. for 1983 through 1986. Des Moines: Des Moines Register and Tribune Company.

Leavitt, Paul. 1983. "His Business Is Selling a Political Candidate." *Des Moines Register,* December 4, pp. 1B, 6B.

Newsweek. 1982-84.

Paulin, Tamara. 1984. Telephone interview with author, May 7. Paulin was the organizational director of the Iowa Republican party from 1983 to 1985.

Peterson, Bill. 1983. "Iowa Polls Indicate That Mondale Is Still the Democrat to Beat." *Washington Post,* October 9, p. A3.

Peterson, Bill, and Kathy Sawyer. 1984. "Winner in Iowa Ran Far Ahead of Field." *Washington Post,* February 22, pp. A1, A8.

Piatt, Barry. 1984. Telephone interview with author, March 19. Piatt was the press secretary of the Iowa Democratic Party from 1983 to 1985.

Plissner, Martin. 1986. Telephone interviews with author, June 18 and July 7. Plissner is the executive political director of CBS Television.

Pomper, Gerald. 1985. "The Nominations." In *The Election of 1984: Reports and Interpretations,* edited by Gerald Pomper, 1-34. Chatham, N.J.: Chatham House.

Raines, Howell. 1983. "7 Democrats Visit a Dinner in Iowa." *New York Times,* October 9, p. 33.

———. 1984. "Mondale Wins Handily in Iowa; Tight Race for 2nd As Glenn Trails." *New York Times,* February 21, pp. A1, A20.

Roth, Luke. 1984. Telephone interview with author, December 7. Roth was the executive director of the Iowa Republican party from 1983 to 1985.

St. Louis Post-Dispatch. 1984.

Steffen, J. P. 1984. Interview with author, December 4. Steffen was the caucus chair from 1983 to 1991 and the executive director of the Iowa Democratic Party from 1991 to 1993.

Swift, Al, and William M. Thomas. 1984. Letter to ABC, CBS, and NBC, December 6. Washington, D.C.: U.S. House of Representatives.

———. 1985. Press Conference, Rayburn Office Building, Washington, D.C., January 17.

Television News Index and Abstracts. 1979-80 and 1983-84. Nashville, Tenn.: Vanderbilt University.

Time. 1983 and 1984.

U.S. Congress. House. 1984. *Early Election Projection: The Iowa Experience.* Hearing before the Subcommittee on Telecommunications, Consumer Protection, and Finance of the Committee on Energy and Commerce, February 27. 98th Cong., 2d sess.

U.S. News and World Report. 1984.

Wall Street Journal. 1984.

Whitney, Tom. 1986. Letter to author, June 5. Whitney was the chair of the Iowa Democratic Party from 1973 to 1977.

Yepsen, David. 1983a. "Off to the Races." *Des Moines Register,* May 30, p. 11A.

———. 1983b. "Glenn's New Iowa Director Paints Rosy Picture." *Des Moines Register,* December 4, pp. 4B, 5B.

———. 1984a. "Hart, McGovern Receive Top Marks at Farm Forum." *Des Moines Register,* January 23, p. 3A.

———. 1984b. "Hart Turns On the Heat, Revives His Campaign in Iowa." *Des Moines Register,* January 26, p. 1M.

———. 1984c. "Slipping Past Campaign Spending Limits in Iowa with a Little Help from Outside." *Des Moines Register,* February 6, p. 15A.

———. 1984d. "Caucus Story May Not Be Finished until Fall." *Des Moines Register,* February 19, p. 5A.

Yepsen, David, Ken Fuson, and James R. Healey. 1984. "Four Democrats Flail Reagan over His Rights Record." *Des Moines Register,* January 11, pp. 1M, 6M.

Yepsen, David, and James R. Healey. 1984. "Democratic Rivals to Debate Today at D.M. Civic Center." *Des Moines Register,* February 11, pp. 1A, 11A.

Yepsen, David, James R. Healey, and Ken Fuson. 1984. "Leaders: Glenn May Be Red-Faced Caucus Night." *Des Moines Register,* February 5, pp. 1A, 5A.

Chapter 8 The 1988 Caucuses: A Media Extravaganza

THE 1988 PRECINCT CAUCUSES were the first in which an incumbent president was not seeking reelection since Iowa became a media event in 1972. Competition in both parties assured vigorous nominating contests. The Iowa parties were eager to be a part of campaigns that were expected to be intense, and they went to great lengths to prepare the Iowa playing field for the candidates and the press.

The Republicans hoped to ride the Reagan revolution to another presidential victory. Ronald Reagan had profoundly affected the Republican party and presidential politics. Political scientist Gerald Pomper reminds us that since the New Deal the GOP had been divided into two wings: a moderate-to-liberal eastern faction and a more conservative midwestern faction. But by 1988, "Reagan's victories had completed the transformation of the Republicans to a coherently conservative party with no significant liberal elements. Every aspiring candidate in 1988 claimed to be Reagan's authentic heir and the authentic spokesman of Republican conservatism" (Pomper 1989, 56).

The Reagan era had also diminished the ideological and policy differences between Republicans and Democrats. Massive federal budget deficits limited spending and domestic policy alternatives, and Reagan's cooperation with the Soviet Union meant "there would be no ideological division on foreign policy issues." The parties remained divided, however, on social and lifestyle issues (Pomper 1989, 35).

The Democrats also went into the presidential race with high hopes. The Reagan halo had dimmed somewhat. The 1986 federal elections, in which the Democrats gained control of both houses of Congress; negative publicity about the Iran-Contra arms affair; the failed Supreme Court nomination of Robert Bork; and the stock market crash of October 1987 "all seem to have created a context for a Democratic triumph" in 1988 (Germond and Witcover 1988a, 2882).

Political analyst William Schneider concluded that election indicators such as the Gallup Poll's president's job approval rating, the "misery index" (the sum of the nation's unemployment rate and the inflation rate as measured by the consumer price index), and the "normal" eight-year cycle in American politics pointed to a "close election, with a narrow advantage for the Democratic presidential candidate" (Schneider 1988, 2861).

In Iowa, there were problems in the farm economy. The 1980s were very difficult for agribusinesses as the state experienced one of its worst farm crises. Commodity prices declined sharply, and land values that had grown continuously in the 1970s were in free fall by the mid-eighties. In 1984 alone, farmland prices fell by 20 percent. Almost half of farm families were seriously affected by the crisis, and by 1987 there were 22,000 fewer farms than in 1973. When farmers suffer, agribusinesses and state revenues also suffer (Schwieder 1996, 318). A series of Iowa Polls indicated that President Reagan's popularity had declined along with farm prices (Iowa Poll: 1987, poll nos. 283, 284, 289), and Democrats hoped that some of the blame for the agricultural crisis would fall on Republicans.

The front-loading of the presidential nominating schedule continued in 1988 as more states attempted to increase their influence in the selection process by moving nominating events closer to the beginning of the cycle. A new addition was Super Tuesday, a southern regional primary on March 8 in fourteen southern and border states. The possibility of a southern primary was first discussed in the early 1970s by area Democrats who were interested in promoting candidates "who would address the 'special concerns' of southern voters" and in countering "the liberal activists who were so influential in the Iowa precinct caucuses and the New Hampshire primary" (Germond and Witcover 1989, 41).

Seven nonsouthern states or territories also scheduled caucuses or primaries on March 8, making Super Tuesday a make-or-break day for the candidates still viable after Iowa and New Hampshire. By the closing of the polls on March 8, thirty-four states and territories would have held the caucuses or primary elections of one or both political parties (*National Journal* 1988, 2870).

Although no one was quite sure what the impact of Super Tuesday would be on Iowa and New Hampshire, it was certain that candidates would have to raise more money earlier for television advertising in those media-driven states. The Democratic party's 1988 nominating schedule, though highly compressed, reserved for Iowa and New Hampshire their first-in-the-nation positions. The Republicans' laissez-faire policy, however, provided no such guarantees, and the Michigan, Hawaii, and Kansas Republican parties scheduled caucus and convention events before the date of the Iowa caucuses.

Although Michigan received some media attention, the caucuses in the three states detracted little from the Iowa event, which was now viewed by the candidates and the press as the "official" starting point of the presidential campaign. In a little over a decade, Iowa had become an integral part of what has become a "permanent campaign" for the presidency, and it was difficult to determine exactly when presidential campaigns in Iowa began.

Precaucus Activity

The Democratic Campaign

Presidential hopefuls began testing the political waters very early, and eventually eight candidates declared their intention to pursue the Democratic nomination. A majority of the field pinned their hopes on Iowa and New Hampshire; that is, they hoped to finish strongly enough in these two states to build media momentum for the remainder of the campaign. The strategy successfully used by Jimmy Carter had become the model for recent presidential campaigns. The candidates would struggle to distinguish themselves in a field separated by few major policy differences. Thus the campaign would turn more on style than on substance.

Missouri Congressman Richard Gephardt was the first Democrat to make an exploratory trip to Iowa. He visited with party activists in Cedar Rapids and Iowa City on March 25, 1985, just two months after Ronald Reagan began his second term as president. Although he was the leader of the Democratic Caucus in the House of Representatives, Gephardt was not well known nationally, but 41 percent of the likely Iowa Democratic primary voters had "read or heard about" him by May 1986 (Iowa Poll: 1986, poll no. 276). Gephardt's relatively high name recognition two years before the caucuses was attributable to his residency in neighboring Missouri. To have any chance to win the Democratic nomination, Gephardt had to do very well in Iowa.

Gephardt and his wife, Jane, traveled to Georgia to visit with former president Jimmy Carter, and during the Plains trip Mrs. Carter advised Mrs. Gephardt how to launch a Carter-style presidential campaign: "Go into the small towns in Iowa, just drive in. Go to the local newspaper, and be sure you take a bumper sticker. If they want to take your picture you stand out in front and hold that sticker up. Then go down and introduce yourself to the people on Main Street" (*Newsweek* Nov. 21, 1987, 50).

Gephardt took the Carter advice to heart, spending 148 days in Iowa over the next three years. (Data on candidate visits were collected by the author from the individual campaigns.) He visited each of Iowa's ninety-nine counties, many of them several times, and his mother, Loreen Gephardt, rented an apartment in Des Moines that she and the family used as an Iowa base. By the 1986 midterm election, Gephardt had already spent twenty-nine days in Iowa meeting with party activists and campaigning for state candidates. He was the keynote speaker at the October 1986 Jefferson-Jackson Day dinner in Ames. Gephardt's message of economic populism, spread through his personal visits and some excellent television ads late in the campaign, played well in a state in the depths of a farm crisis.

Gary Hart was well known in Iowa and nationally from his "surprisingly" strong second-place finish in the 1984 Iowa caucuses that gave him the momentum to win in New Hampshire and threaten Vice-President Mondale's nomination. The May 1986 Iowa Poll found Hart was known to 94 percent and favored by 44 percent of the likely Democratic primary voters (Iowa Poll: 1986, poll no. 276). He appeared at a fund-raiser in West Okoboji, Iowa, on August 17, 1985, and put Iowa Democrats on notice that he was interested in a second run for the Democratic nomination. Unlike the lesser-known Democratic hopefuls, Hart was not dependent on an Iowa/New Hampshire strategy. He spent only five days in Iowa before the November 1986 election, but like the others, did build a large Iowa campaign organization.

Hart promoted himself as a visionary and had succeeded in distinguishing himself from the other Democrats in 1984 as a candidate of "new ideas." Although Hart had taken specific and substantive stands on domestic and foreign policy issues in the campaign, Mondale had raised doubts about the depth of Hart's knowledge with the "where's the beef" label, a takeoff on a Wendy's fast-food ad that raised questions about the quantity of beef in their competitors' hamburgers. Hart had begun planning for and pointing toward the 1988 election even before the 1984 race was over. To overcome any doubts that Mondale might have implanted in the public mind about his policy credentials, Hart had written a book on military reform and put forth a number of ideas on arms control, industrial renewal, and international trade competition (*Newsweek* Nov. 21, 1987, 45).

The Reverend Jesse Jackson had also run previously for the Democratic nomination. He finished third in 1984 behind Mondale and Hart after carrying 18 percent of the primary-caucus vote and winning 12 percent of the national convention delegates (*National Journal* 1988, 2880). Like Hart, he was well known nationally and in Iowa, and he was not dependent on an Iowa/New Hampshire strategy to win the nomination. Twenty months before the caucuses, 94 percent of Iowa Democrats had "read or heard about" him, but the downside for Jackson was that only 2 percent "favored" him for the nomination (Iowa Poll: 1986, poll no. 276).

Still, the expectations game worked in Jackson's favor in Iowa. He had won only 1.5 percent of the delegate equivalents in 1984, and it would be surprising if a black candidate did well in a state with a very limited minority population. Jackson made this point frequently, and the media chose to judge him as a black in a white man's race in Iowa. But to move beyond his image as a protest candidate and to prove his electability beyond rank-and-file black voters and liberal whites, Jackson had to expand his "Rainbow Coalition." The farm crisis in Iowa provided an opportunity, and Jackson was the only candidate not to locate his Iowa campaign headquarters in Des Moines. He opened an office in Greenfield, a small farming community southeast of Des Moines, and promoted his message of economic populism. Jackson geared his Iowa campaign to the "little people"—small farmers, those employed in agriculture-related businesses like packing plants, and assembly line workers—and spoke frequently about the evils of corporate mergers. Jackson was one of the few Democrats to differ from the field on the issues. He visited Iowa only once before the 1986 election.

Delaware Senator Joe Biden was another Democratic hopeful who visited Iowa early to explore a run for the nomination. Known for his oratorical skills, he was the featured speaker at the 1985 Jefferson-

Jackson Day dinner held by Iowa Democrats on November 2, and "wowed the assembled party activists with a mixture of self-deprecating wit, audacity and compassion filled phrase-making" (Germond and Witcover 1989, 245).

But, like most of the potential candidates, Biden was not well known to the rank and file. The May Iowa Poll found that only 14 percent of Iowa Democratic primary voters had "read or heard about" Biden and that less than 1 percent favored him for the nomination (Iowa Poll: 1986, poll no. 276). To improve his standing, Biden made frequent visits to Iowa. By the 1986 midterm election he had spent thirteen days in the state speaking at fund-raising events and campaigning for Iowa Democratic candidates for state and national offices. Like Gephardt, Biden placed his hopes for the nomination on an Iowa/New Hampshire strategy.

Former Arizona governor Bruce Babbitt's entrance into the Iowa caucus race was novel. He met privately with Democratic activists in Des Moines on July 18 and 19, 1986, and then he and his family participated in the *Des Moines Register*'s annual "Great Bicycle Ride Across Iowa" (RAGBRAI). The only requirements for participation in the weeklong event are a bicycle and a derriere capable of withstanding six to ten hours a day on a hard bike seat.

RAGBRAI '86 attracted more than 7500 participants, many from outside Iowa, and was a seven-day moving caravan, with daily fun and food provided by the towns along the route. The 1986 route from Council Bluffs on the Missouri River to Muscatine on the Mississippi was 479 miles long. It was a good introduction to Iowa and an opportunity for Babbitt to meet people and to attract some press coverage. Fellow RAGBRAI rider reporter Ken Bode, for example, conducted an interview with Babbitt that aired on the "Today" show the Monday after the bike ride.

For Babbitt, who was unknown and underfunded nationally, everything hinged on Iowa. His campaign staff hoped to exceed expectations in the state and thought that a "close third might be good enough to go into New Hampshire with momentum, just because it's a man-bites-dog story" (Barnes 1988, 2843). But first Babbitt had to become better known in Iowa. Only 24 percent of those surveyed before RAGBRAI knew of him (Iowa Poll: 1986, poll no. 276). He visited Iowa frequently and by the 1986 midterm election had spent nineteen days in the state, with about half of that time devoted to campaigning and fund-raising for Iowa candidates.

Babbitt and his advisers also decided on an early 1987 media effort. They hoped to improve the candidate's name recognition by airing "a costly series of commercials in Iowa in April and May" (Hagstrom and Guskind 1988, 2877). Television advertising had never been used successfully in a caucus campaign, and initiating a $250,000 ad campaign ten months before the February caucuses was ill advised. Babbitt is reported to have said later that the expenditure was "a total waste of money" because few Iowans were paying attention that early in the campaign (Germond and Witcover 1989, 249).

Babbitt became a press favorite for his openness and willingness to take courageous (or naive) stands on complex issues such as the federal budget deficit and international trade. He apparently had not learned from Mondale's 1984 experience that one does not propose tax increases in an election year. His $40 billion deficit reduction package included $20 billion in new taxes (*Wall Street Journal* Dec. 4, 1987, 17D).

Senator Paul Simon of Illinois visited with Democrats in several Iowa cities on a two-day trip to the state in early September 1986. He made two more visits to Iowa before announcing at a press conference on February 25, 1987, that he would not run for president but would support the candidacy of Senator Dale Bumpers. When Bumpers announced that he would not run, however, Simon reconsidered and became a candidate for the Democratic nomination.

Simon, the son of a Lutheran minister, had a political image of honesty and decency, was a fiscal conservative and a social liberal, and was on record as saying that he and his wife, Jeanne, truly enjoyed meeting people and campaigning (Simon 1989, 10). Even though he was from a neighboring state, Simon was not well known in Iowa, and he was favored by only 1 percent of the Democrats in the first *Des Moines Register* poll after his announcement (Iowa Poll: 1987, poll no. 284).

Simon's strategy for gaining the nomination was similar to that of most of the other Democratic candidates in 1988—win in Iowa and "build a strong enough base in New Hampshire so that with the win in Iowa I could either carry New Hampshire or run such a strong second to Dukakis that he would emerge badly damaged as a candidate." From there, victories in Minnesota and South Dakota would provide momentum for Super Tuesday, which would boost him in the later state primaries (Simon 1989, 21).

Governor Michael Dukakis of Massachusetts was a relatively late entrant into the Iowa race. He began a three-day visit to the state on February 4, 1987, and was one of five governors who participated in a National Governors Association task force hearing on "Jobs, Growth and Competitiveness" hosted by Iowa Governor Terry Branstad. In one of the meetings Dukakis made a comment that exposed his lack of farm knowledge and greatly diminished the value of his first Iowa visit. In the context of discussing economic diversification, Dukakis noted that he had encouraged Massachusetts farmers to grow vegetables for urban consumers. He suggested that Iowa farmers who were still struggling to emerge from the 1980s farm crisis should consider diversifying and "try growing apples, blueberries, flowers or Belgian endive." Arkansas Governor Bill Clinton, also in attendance, called Dukakis's ideas "Yuppie agriculture" (*Washington Post* Feb. 15, 1987, A8). The "Belgian endive" faux pas was reported nationally and recounted by others many times during the course of the campaign.

For Dukakis to have a chance in the caucuses, he had to get an organization up and running quickly. He built his early Iowa campaign around the theme that he had been a successful governor, balanced the budget, and cut taxes and that under his leadership Massachusetts had become a high-technology enclave. He offered the "Massachusetts Miracle" as a model for the nation and stressed his successful experience in economic development (*National Journal* 1988, 2880).

Dukakis was widely regarded as a liberal, but "like Carter, stressed 'competence' rather than 'ideology,' and thus had little or nothing to offer segments of the electorate who had once been core New Deal voters" (Burnham 1988, 27). Sampling done for Dukakis in Iowa and New Hampshire found, however, that post–Reagan era voters "were looking for reassurance, for competence and honesty, for character—not for ideological purity" (*Newsweek* Nov. 21, 1987, 43). In joint candidate appearances Dukakis attempted to distinguish himself from the other liberals by stressing his managerial skills honed as a chief executive.

Dukakis also pursued an Iowa/New Hampshire strategy, but his plan was based on the "home state" advantage in neighboring New Hampshire, which relieved some of the pressure in Iowa. But his growing stature nationally also raised expectations for him in Iowa. Still, his campaign staff believed "that a third-place finish in Iowa would not be disastrous because of his strong position in New Hampshire" (Barnes 1988, 2844).

Senator Albert Gore, Jr., of Tennessee was the final Democrat to initiate a caucus campaign. Gore, a relative unknown in Iowa, visited the state on May 4 and 5, 1987, to identify supporters and begin building a campaign organization. The late start would prove a major obstacle, and his later decision to bypass Iowa and New Hampshire and to focus solely on the Super Tuesday primaries in the South probably resulted more from frustration and failure in Iowa than from a comprehensive campaign plan. Nonetheless, Gore had the Super Tuesday primaries as a fallback, and in joint appearances at candidate forums in Iowa, he took relatively conservative positions on issues such as the national defense budget and nuclear disarmament.

Before deciding to bypass Iowa, Gore spent a great deal of time and effort in the state courting potential caucus attenders. From his initial May visit until he ceased active campaigning in Iowa in mid-November, Gore visited the state on thirty occasions, and the staff of twenty in his Des Moines office worked hard to build support for his candidacy. Judged from the perspective of Iowa Polls, Gore had little to show after five months of hard work. In the November 1987 Iowa Poll he stood at 3 percent (Iowa Poll: 1987, poll nos. 284 and 288).

As Gore entered the Iowa race, Gary Hart was fighting for his political life. Hart was accused of having had a weekend rendezvous with a part-time model from Miami. When questioned about earlier allegations of extramarital romances, Hart had challenged the *New York Times* to follow him around if they did not believe his denials. Acting on a phone tip, the *Miami Herald* did just that and found Hart and the woman together in Washington, D.C. The media feeding frenzy that followed drove Hart out of the presidential race (Taylor 1990, 51).

Hart's departure was an opportunity for the remaining candidates who had trailed badly in an Iowa Poll of Democrats completed just before he withdrew. In that survey Hart had the support of 65 percent of Iowa Democrats, followed by Jackson with 9 percent; Gephardt with 7 percent; Dukakis with 3 percent; Babbitt with 2 percent; Biden, Simon, and Gore, with 1 percent each; and "undecided" with 11 percent (Iowa Poll: 1987, poll no. 284).

Brian Duffy of the *Register* captured the moment with a cartoon representing the Democratic field after Hart as "The Seven Dwarfs" singing and marching off to Iowa (*DMR* May 14, 1987, 1). The label caught on immediately and for the next several weeks journalists referred to the Democratic field as "The Seven Dwarfs."

Two months after Hart withdrew from the race, journalists still were attempting to handicap the Seven Dwarfs. One reporter noted that "with the departure of Gary Hart, the field of acknowledged contenders contains not a single giant. Except for the Rev. Jesse Jackson, 'Undecided' has better name recognition" (McLeod 1987, 11).

Dukakis hired several of Hart's Iowa staffers, including Teresa Vilmain, who became his Iowa coordinator. The late starters, Dukakis, Simon, and Gore, found a large new group of "undecided" Democrats on whom to concentrate their campaigns, and the new pool provided opportunities for Babbitt, Gephardt, and Jackson as well (Iowa Poll: 1987, poll no. 286). The candidates all had well-staffed Iowa campaign offices by this time and were positioned to take advantage of their new opportunities.

The Democratic campaign warmed up over the summer, with the candidates spending 130 days in Iowa in June, July, and August. Several debates between candidates took place during this period. In one held at Drake University the last weekend in May, Babbitt and Republican candidate Pete duPont developed a new approach to gain media exposure. The two candidates split the $5,000 cost of a communications satellite hookup, and their staffs called about 700 local television stations to offer them free access to broadcast the debate. Most of the other candidates used this cost-effective method of communication at one time or another in the campaign. Most of the major national newspapers also covered the debate, giving the two underdogs badly needed media exposure (Dionne 1987a, 10).

In another one-on-one debate at Drake University in August, Gephardt and Dukakis discussed trade, national defense, and energy policies. The candidates expressed their differences on the issues, and Dukakis contrasted his managerial experience as an executive with Gephardt's experience as a legislator. Although neither candidate was a clear winner, Dukakis made his point about leadership experience (author's notes from the debate).

The first Iowa forum involving all the Democratic hopefuls was a televised debate in late August at the Iowa State Fair. The debate, called

The Seven Dwarfs.

Cartoon by Brian Duffy, © 1987, *Des Moines Register,* reprinted by permission

Gary Hart's withdrawal from the 1988 contest after allegations of an extramarital affair left a Democratic field composed of candidates with limited national reputations. Although Duffy's cartoon popularized its use, he was not the first to use the term "The Seven Dwarfs" in political print. Richard Benedetto of *USA Today,* for example, referred to Hart and his lesser-known opponents as "Snow White and the Seven Dwarfs" in his May 8, 1987, story reporting that Hart was dropping out of the presidential race.

"The Economics of America" by its sponsors, was held before a packed house that included dozens of reporters. Surprisingly few substantive differences were apparent among the seven candidates, but Gore used the forum to criticize Governor Dukakis repeatedly for, among other things, "speaking in generalities" on the issues. Other candidates joined in the assault, giving the impression they considered Dukakis "to be the current front-runner" (Dillin 1987, 6). Several proposals were put forward to assist farmers still struggling to overcome the agricultural problems of the eighties.

Each candidate was given time for closing remarks at the conclusion of the two-hour State Fair debate. Although reporters did not immediately realize it, Senator Biden's closing speech "borrowed" liberally from a campaign commercial by British Labor leader Neil Kinnock.

One week after the State Fair debate the *Register* published another Iowa Poll. In a year when Democrats had decided not to conduct straw polls at their political events, the Iowa Polls took on added importance, particularly for fund-raising. It had been a little over three months since Gary Hart's departure from the race, and observers were anxious to see which if any of the Seven Dwarfs was emerging from the pack.

The August Iowa Poll was the first of the cycle to report the responses of only those Democrats "likely" to attend a caucus and thus is not comparable to the earlier polls of unscreened Democrats. Although it is difficult to identify for survey purposes the small fraction of Iowans likely to attend the precinct caucuses, this survey was undoubtedly more valid than the earlier five *Register* polls, which included all Democrats. Gephardt was the leader with 18 percent, but it was a closely bunched field, with Dukakis at 14 percent, Simon 13 percent, Biden and Jackson each with 10 percent, Babbitt 9 percent, Gore 2 percent, and "undecided" 18 percent. This poll suggested that no one was breaking out of the pack, but all the candidates except Gore were making progress in their efforts to garner the support of likely Iowa caucus attenders (Iowa Poll: 1987, poll no. 287).

The Iowa Poll results also suggested, as Gephardt had surmised, that Biden would be a significant challenger for the Democratic nomination. *Newsweek* reported that in early August, Gephardt had told aides that "the challenge for me in this race is Joe Biden" (Nov. 21, 1988, 54).

Apparently, John Sasso of the Dukakis campaign agreed. As chair of the Senate Judiciary Committee, Biden was about to gain a great deal of national exposure as he managed the confirmation hearings of President Reagan's controversial Supreme Court nominee, Robert Bork. Sasso saw an opportunity to raise questions about Biden's integrity by exposing Biden's use of Neil Kinnock's words without attribution at the Iowa State Fair debate. He provided a videotape to reporters of the *New York Times*, NBC, and the *Des Moines Register* that juxtaposed the speeches of Biden and Kinnock.

Three weeks after the State Fair debate, the *Times* and the *Register* ran stories about Biden's use of Kinnock's words in his closing speech. Those stories opened the door to other reports of Biden foibles, ranging from using without attribution passages from the speeches of the late Robert Kennedy to plagiarism in law school and embellishing his academic records. On September 23, eleven days after the stories ran in the *Times* and *Register,* Biden abandoned his candidacy (Taylor 1990, 89).

Biden's withdrawal did not end the plagiarism flap. His campaign workers and some reporters did not appreciate Sasso's leaking the videotape. For a time Gephardt's campaign was distracted and perhaps hurt by rumors that his staff was responsible for the video, but it soon came to light that Sasso was the responsible party. He resigned a short time later, and Dukakis "flew to Iowa, where he made a seventeen-city apology tour" and "was booed by angry Biden supporters at several stops" (Taylor 1990, 105).

The remaining six candidates appeared together the weekend following Biden's withdrawal at a STAR*PAC forum on war and peace issues. The 1984 STAR*PAC forum on nuclear arms had made Democratic candidates appear dovish on national security issues, which was used against them by President Reagan in the general election campaign. Gore was the only candidate who differed substantially on the issues, and he used the debate to distinguish himself from the others by taking more hawkish positions on military spending and arms reductions. Gore's tactic was interpreted by the press as an attempt to position himself for the more conservative voters on Super Tuesday (Germond and Witcover 1988a, 2882).

In November, about a month after Biden left the presidential race, the *Register* published another Iowa Poll of "likely" caucus attenders.

Simon now led with 24 percent, followed by Dukakis with 18 percent, Gephardt 14 percent, Jackson 11 percent, Babbitt 8 percent, Gore 3 percent, and "undecided" 22 percent (Iowa Poll: 1987, poll no. 288). Given the context, the poll finding that 42 percent of the respondents considered "personal honesty and integrity" the characteristic most important to them in choosing "a presidential candidate to support at the caucuses" was not surprising. Simon was the first choice of that subgroup.

In the short term Simon benefited more than the others from Biden's withdrawal. Unlike Gephardt and Dukakis, he had not been tarred by the affair and its aftermath. His poll standing improved, and he was encouraged by his campaign's progress in Iowa and New Hampshire (Simon 1989, 23). Several of Biden's staff joined his campaign, but in the long run that was a mixed blessing, as there were difficulties integrating and effectively using the former Biden staffers (Simon 1989, 179-80).

Simon and Dukakis were the first Democrats to purchase TV commercials after Babbitt's ill-advised effort six months earlier. They began running ads at KCCI, the Des Moines CBS affiliate, in November 1987 and were the only Democrats to do so before Christmas. The early spots were biographical and issue-oriented.

Everything seemed to be going Simon's way. Gore gave up on Iowa and concentrated on the Super Tuesday primary states. An Iowa Poll in early December showed Simon pulling away from the reduced Democratic field with a 35 percent share of the "likely" caucus attenders, while the others slumped: Dukakis to 14 percent, Gephardt 11 percent, Jackson 9 percent, Babbitt 8 percent, Gore 3 percent, and "undecided" 20 percent (Iowa Poll: 1987, poll no. 290).

Then Gary Hart reentered the Democratic contest. Hart and his wife, Lee, flew to Concord, New Hampshire, on December 15 and announced that he was again a candidate for the Democratic nomination. The impact on the Iowa campaign was immediate and dramatic. The *Register*'s polling organization was in the middle of its December survey. They continued sampling and completed a two-stage poll: a pre-Hart stage (December 7-14) and a post-Hart stage (December 15-18). The pre-Hart poll discussed above showed Simon surging. The second stage, completed after Hart's New Hampshire announcement, painted a very different picture: Hart was now the leader in the Iowa

Poll with 29 percent, followed by Simon at 18 percent, Dukakis 16 percent, Jackson 9 percent, Gephardt 6 percent, Gore 4 percent, Babbitt 2 percent, and "undecided" 16 percent (Iowa Poll: 1987, poll no. 290).

Certainly, the findings of the second-stage Iowa Poll were suspect (as were the findings of national polls conducted during the period). The sample was quite small, and this was not the best of circumstances under which to conduct a political opinion poll. Hart's reentry into the race dominated the news during the four-day period of the second-stage survey and undoubtedly affected the outcome.

In retrospect, it is difficult to understand how anyone could have taken Hart's renewed candidacy very seriously. When he reentered the race in New Hampshire, Hart admitted, "I don't have a national headquarters or staff. I don't have any money. I don't have pollsters, or consultants or media advisers or political endorsements" (Germond and Witcover 1989, 256). He might have added that he had been humiliated, his reputation sullied, and his credibility largely destroyed by the publicity associated with his extramarital affair.

But Hart's redeclaration of candidacy was news, and for the next three weeks he dominated the airwaves and the front pages. As Senator Simon put it, "Hart's entrance into the race suddenly changed the dynamics of the entire campaign." The media spotlight shifted to Hart, and that affected poll results, fund-raising, and perceptions of who was hot and who was not (Simon 1989, 24).

The Democratic campaign in Iowa intensified in December, and for the first time in the precinct caucuses the candidates used radio and television advertising extensively. Table 8.1 reports precaucus spending for TV advertising in 1987 and 1988 at KCCI and in 1988 at WHO, the NBC affiliate, in Des Moines, Iowa's largest television market. The two stations began compiling summary records of candidate advertising in 1996 to respond to requests from reporters. WHO does not have records for 1987, and neither station has records for spring 1987, when Babbitt ran his early ads. WHO does have some information about the 1984 Democratic caucuses.

The use of television advertising was limited before 1988. (In 1984 Mondale and Cranston had the only recorded purchases at WHO, and they spent $6,390 and $4,665, respectively.) In November 1987, six months after Babbitt's early purchase, Dukakis and Simon began running ads, and Gephardt followed the day after Christmas. Most of the

Table 8.1.   1988 Democratic spending at
WHO-TV and KCCI-TV

	WHO (Jan.–Feb.)	KCCI (Nov.–Feb.)
Gephardt	$31,680	$68,557
Simon	29,055	45,835
Dukakis	27,555	41,836
Babbitt	24,610	19,089
Hart	4540	6900
Jackson	3243	4451
Total	120,683	186,668

Source: Created from records provided by Cheryl
Semerad, director of sales and marketing, WHO, and
Anne Marie Caudron, national sales manager, KCCI.

ads for the 1988 caucus cycle aired after the first of the year. Of the
spending totals in Table 8.1, 81 percent at KCCI and 100 percent at
WHO occurred in the final five weeks leading up to the February 8 caucuses.

Negative advertising, which surfaced in New Hampshire and was
very prevalent in the Bush-Dukakis general election campaign, played
little or no role in the 1988 caucuses. The Iowa ads were biographical
in nature or outlined a candidate's position on one or more issues.

Of the many ads aired in Iowa, Gephardt's Hyundai commercial
was the most memorable and was widely regarded by the campaign
managers as having enhanced Gephardt's position among caucus
attenders. According to William Carrick, Gephardt's campaign manager, his candidate's ad campaign in Iowa began with a bio ad "to tell
people who Dick Gephardt was and what he had done" in Congress
(Runkle 1989, 140). They followed that commercial with the Hyundai
ad, in which Gephardt asserts that if Korean taxes and tariffs were
applied, a $10,000 Chrysler K-car would cost $48,000 in South Korea
and asks how many Americans would buy the comparable Korean
Hyundai car at that price. The purpose of the ad was to show that
Gephardt's trade policy was about fairness, not protectionism, as his
opponents had asserted in some debates (Stengel 1988, 22).

Dukakis's campaign manager, Susan Estrich, believed that "Gephardt's was the only advertising that really made a difference" in Iowa (Runkle 1989, 141). Carrick attributed his candidate's subsequent rise in the Iowa Polls to his television ads and particularly to the Hyundai commercial, which he said "crystallized Gephardt's message on trade and competitiveness" and "was very understandable to the average Democratic caucus attender" (Runkle 1989, 141).

Just how much credit TV advertising deserves for campaign successes is open to debate, but paid media became a factor in the 1988 presidential campaign, and political consultant Ed Rollins asserts that it "became a very, very crucial part of this election cycle and changed the game forever in presidential politics" (Runkle 1989, 161). It certainly began to change the nature of the Iowa precinct caucuses.

January was a month of intense political activity. The Democrats spent 127 days campaigning in Iowa, and by now their campaign staffs had grown substantially. After his plunge in the December Iowa Poll, Gephardt moved his national campaign staff to Iowa, putting all his eggs in the caucus basket. A Gephardt spokesperson claimed "about 100 people" were now on board in Iowa (*DMR* Dec. 24, 1987, 3A). It was no longer possible, however, to obtain reliable figures on the size of Democratic campaign staffs because volunteers were pouring into the state and the numbers changed daily. The Babbitt, Simon, and Dukakis organizations each claimed over 100 paid staff in Iowa.

The *Des Moines Register* held its Democratic presidential debate on January 15 before a full house of about 2700 people and 400 or so reporters at the Des Moines Civic Center. The debate was broadcast live by Public Television in Iowa and in some other parts of the country. It was broadcast nationally on a delayed basis by C-Span, but there was no live network coverage of the event. *Register* editor James Gannon and Illinois Governor James Thompson questioned the seven Democrats. Al Gore, who had not been in Iowa for over two months, returned the day before the debate, and with an entourage that included reporters, he traveled to the city of Independence in northeast Iowa, where he declared his independence from Iowa (Carlson and Norman 1988, 12A).

Anticipation ran high as reporters were anxious to see whether Gary Hart could do something dramatic to improve his chances in Iowa. Many believed that he had to shine if he were to regain momentum in the race. The norm for such forums, however, is that candidates are cautious and stick very closely to their well-developed campaign themes. This event was no exception. It was tame, no fights, and no big winners or losers, with the possible exception of Hart who, "although the equal of his rivals in debate, failed to outshine them," which meant that he was the victim of the high expectations set for him (Dionne 1988, 20).

Ten days after the debate the *Register* released the first of two Iowa Polls conducted during a seventeen-day period in late January and early February, with only five days separating the surveys. The results are shown along with earlier poll outcomes in Table 8.2.

Gephardt, Dukakis, and Simon were in a virtual dead heat in the January poll. Gephardt's lead lengthened in the February survey, which suggests that his organizational efforts and his advertising blitz were successful, as "32 percent of likely Democratic caucus-attenders say they were impressed most by Gephardt's commercials," double the rating of the next highest candidate (Pins 1988, 1). Hart was sinking rapidly, and the second-tier positions of Babbitt and Jackson had changed little from six months earlier.

Table 8.2.   1988 *Des Moines Register* Democratic Iowa Polls

	"Likely" Democratic caucus attenders (%)					
	8-87	11-87	12-87	12-87	1-88	2-88
Hart	—	—	—	29	13	7
Jackson	10	11	9	9	11	9
Gephardt	18	14	11	6	19	25
Babbitt	9	8	8	2	10	9
Dukakis	14	18	14	16	18	15
Biden	10	—	—	—	—	—
Simon	13	24	35	18	17	19
Gore	2	3	3	4	0	1
None/other	24	22	20	16	12	15
Sample size (no.)	316	330	226	201	402	612
Margin of error (%) +/−	5.5	5.4	7	7	4.9	4

The Republican Campaign

Eight Republicans sought their party's nomination for president at some time during the 1988 race, but only five remained active throughout the Iowa campaign. The GOP campaign in Iowa was much smaller in scope than the Democratic campaign: the Republican candidates spent much less time in the state, built much smaller campaign organizations, ran fewer TV commercials, and spent less money on their campaigns.

Vice-President George Bush, seeking the GOP nomination for the second time, was the early favorite. He enjoyed many advantages and had run for the nomination since President Reagan's reelection in 1984. Reporters Germond and Witcover thought that at the onset it was "George Bush against the Field." Bush was well known nationally and in Iowa, where he had edged out Reagan in the preference poll held in the state party's 1980 caucuses (although the results were disputed and unverifiable). He was successful at fund-raising, had a strong staff in place, and enjoyed all the trappings of the vice-presidency. Some of his Iowa supporters from 1980 were still loosely held together by leaders from his 1980 campaign (Germond and Witcover 1989, chap. 5).

Bush had drawbacks as well. The right wing of the Republican party viewed him as nonideological and too moderate in his previous political positions. He was also bedeviled throughout the campaign by the Iran-Contra affair and by questions about how much and when he knew about the arms-for-hostages deal through which President Reagan had obtained the release of the Americans taken hostage in Iran during the Carter administration. Moreover, as Reagan's popularity declined during his second term, particularly in Iowa with the farm crisis, Bush was faced with having to rebuild credibility with farmers and inch away from Reagan's policies while maintaining his loyalty to the president. And finally, it was a mixed blessing to be labeled the odds-on front-runner.

Bush spent little time in Iowa early in the campaign, and his first visit to the state was not among the earliest by Republican hopefuls. He made a two-day trip to Des Moines on November 16 and 17, 1985, but after that did not return to the state until late April 1986, when he attended the Drake Relays and spoke at GOP fund-raising events in Des Moines and Waterloo.

Despite his infrequent visits, Bush was well known to Iowa Republicans, and when the *Register* conducted its first presidential Iowa Poll in May 1986, he was well ahead of the field, with the support of 34 percent of those sampled. Senator Robert Dole was second with 16 percent, followed by former senator Howard Baker, who never became a candidate, with 14 percent, Congressman Jack Kemp with 5 percent, evangelist Pat Robertson 4 percent, General Alexander Haig 3 percent, former senator Paul Laxalt 1 percent, former governor Pete duPont and businessman Donald Rumsfeld less than 1 percent each, and "none/others" 23 percent. The poll of Republicans was not limited to "likely" caucus attenders and probably demonstrated little more than Bush's high level of name recognition in Iowa (Iowa Poll: 1986, poll no. 275).

Senator Robert Dole from Kansas was the other GOP candidate with a national reputation, albeit some of it gained as Gerald Ford's outspoken running mate in 1976. As the minority leader in the Senate, Dole had moderated his earlier image and shown an ability to compromise and get things done. Like Bush, he emphasized his managerial and leadership skills. In Iowa, Dole benefited from representing a neighboring farm state, and although he finished last behind "undecided" in the 1980 GOP caucuses, he had the experience of a previous Iowa campaign. He visited for two days on October 26 and 27, 1985, just before Bush, to raise funds for local candidates and to speak to the Republican Council, a statewide group of party leaders.

Dole was more actively involved in Iowa than Bush, spending eleven days speaking at party and fund-raising events before the 1986 election. In visits he presented himself as a small-town boy of humble beginnings from Russell, Kansas, who had suffered for his country. "I'm one of you" was a frequent refrain when he spoke to Iowans. He also tried to brand Bush as a remnant of the elite eastern establishment (Cook 1988a, 157).

Marion G. (Pat) Robertson, a Southern Baptist minister, founder of the Christian Broadcasting Network (CBN), and host of the CBN program "700 Club," made the earliest exploratory trip of the GOP hopefuls. He was in the state on April 17 and 18, 1985, less than a month after Richard Gephardt's initial visit. Robertson stressed lifestyle issues and hoped to mobilize the Christian Right into a political force, something that had not been done before in Iowa. His first visit and most of his early trips were to support his political organizing arm, the Freedom Council. He participated in their meetings and spoke at fund-raising events as part of his effort to bring evangelical Christians into politics (Kamin 1986, 3M). Steve Scheffler, Robertson's Freedom Council organizer in Iowa, worked at the local level and involved the Christian Right in GOP politics in several counties (Scheffler 1997). Iowa was crucial for Robertson, and it became the focal point of his campaign.

Jack Kemp also visited Iowa early to explore the possibility of a presidential candidacy. In 1985 Kemp may have been better known as a former professional football quarterback than as a sixteen-year member of the House of Representatives. He had, however, become a leading advocate of supply-side economics and had gained national notoriety as the cosponsor of the tax reduction bill that became the basis of Reagan's three-year tax-cutting plan in 1981. In his campaign, Kemp presented himself as "Reagan's true ideological heir" (*National Journal* 1988, 2881).

Kemp's first Iowa visit was on July 4, 1985, and he had spent thirteen days in Iowa raising funds and campaigning for local candidates by the time of the 1986 election. Kemp had a two-fold problem in Iowa: Ronald Reagan and Pat Robertson. First, he was running as a Reaganite, and the President's approval rating was low in Iowa; second, Robertson appealed to conservatives whose support Kemp needed to be successful (Germond and Witcover 1989, 110). Like the candidates of both parties pursuing an Iowa/New Hampshire strategy, Kemp had to do well in the two states to stay alive as a candidate.

Pierre S. (Pete) duPont IV, a former two-term governor of Delaware, was the fifth candidate active in the Iowa GOP race from beginning to end. The duPont family had long been prominent in business and politics, but in previous caucuses, eastern elites had not done well in Iowa.

DuPont was a frequent visitor to Iowa. His first trip was for two days on May 28 and 29, 1985, and he spent fifteen days in Iowa before the 1986 election, more than any other GOP candidate, as he pursued an Iowa/New Hampshire strategy. He had been a moderate governor, but in Iowa he took conservative positions on issues, including controversial proposals to eliminate federal subsidies to farmers and to replace existing welfare programs with jobs programs, both radical positions in 1987 (Dionne 1987a, 10).

Donald Rumsfeld, another early entrant in the GOP race, had served in a variety of posts in the federal government, most recently as secretary of defense in the Ford administration. Now a businessman, he was probably the least well known of the dark-horse candidates when he made an exploratory trip to Iowa on July 22 and 23, 1985. He made other early trips to the state, opened the first Iowa campaign office during a four-day visit in October 1986, and had campaigned eight days in Iowa by the 1986 election.

Rumsfeld had little success in finding a niche in the GOP contest. His business background and positions on issues were appropriately conservative for the post–Reagan era but did not distinguish him from the field. Although Rumsfeld succeeded in gaining the support of a limited number of well-known Iowa GOP activists, he made only two more visits to the state after opening his campaign office. He never exceeded 1 percent support in the Iowa Poll and on April 2, 1987, ten months before the precinct caucuses, announced his withdrawal from the presidential race.

Nearly a year passed after the six GOP candidates initiated Iowa campaigns before Alexander M. Haig, Jr., decided to explore a run for the presidency. Haig had a long and illustrious military career followed by a number of positions in the federal government, including a highly prominent role as Nixon's chief of staff during the Watergate affair. His most recent service was a two-year stint as Reagan's secretary of state, where he is best remembered for his constitutionally incorrect statement that "as of now, I am in control here" after the president was incapacitated in a 1981 assassination attempt (Germond and Witcover 1989, 69).

Haig made a two-day trip to Iowa on October 7 and 8, 1986, to let Republican activists know that he was interested in the GOP nomination. His Iowa campaign never really developed beyond its low-budget beginning, and there was little that resembled a real organization. Haig did show up in the state for a couple of days each month until October 1987, when he more or less dropped out of the Iowa race. His ready-fire-aim approach made him a readily quotable individual but not a very strong presidential candidate.

Former Nevada senator Paul Laxalt was the final candidate to explore a run for the GOP nomination. Laxalt announced the formation of an exploratory committee in late April 1987 and visited Iowa on May 11 for private meetings with party activists. Although Laxalt "portrayed himself as President Reagan's ideological heir and closest friend," he generated little excitement on his infrequent visits to the state. Unable to meet the national $2 million fund-raising goal that he had set for himself, Laxalt announced on August 26 that he was withdrawing from the race (*DMR* Aug. 27, 1987, 3A). His campaign had little or no impact in Iowa.

The early GOP campaign in Iowa was similar to the Democratic race as the candidates spent a good deal of time in the state building organizations and attempting to identify and win over potential supporters. By June 1987, they had campaigned 159 days in Iowa, appearing before small groups and service clubs in the larger cities and the many small towns across the state. Early polls led to the handicapping of the Republican field as "the big two"—Bush and Dole; "the little three"—Kemp, duPont, and Haig; and "the wild card"—Robertson, who was difficult to handicap because no one was sure of the size of his "invisible army" of evangelicals, or whether it existed at all (Iowa Poll: 1986, poll nos. 275 and 282; Iowa Poll: 1987, poll nos. 283 and 284).

The June-August months proved to be something of a summer lull, as the Republican candidates spent only fifty days in Iowa, considerably less than their Democratic counterparts. When in the state, each campaigned as a conservative and Reagan's authentic heir: Kemp attempted with little success to contrast his well-developed conservative credentials with those of Bush, Dole, and duPont, each of whom had more moderate political histories. While there were differences among the candidates on ideology and policy issues, much of the campaign centered on images and personalities, principally those of the "big two." Who was Bush? Was he really the conservative he professed to be? Would he be a strong leader? And always, reporters pressed him about what he knew about the Iran-Contra arms-for-hostages deal. Who was the real Bob Dole—the hatchet man from the 1976 presidential race, or the strong consensus builder who emerged in the Senate; the Kansas boy of modest beginnings or a wealthy Washington insider? Did he have a vision? Did he stand for anything? Could he control his well-known temper when the campaign heated up?

The first Iowa Poll reporting the responses of only those "likely" to attend a caucus was completed in the latter half of August. Because of different survey methodologies, the August poll and the earlier *Register* polls are not comparable. The somewhat surprising outcome was that Bob Dole was leading George Bush in Iowa 32 percent to 29 percent, followed by Kemp with 10 percent, Robertson 7 percent, duPont 5 percent, Haig 4 percent, and "undecided" 12 percent (Iowa Poll: 1987, poll no. 287). Was the poll confirmation of the concern expressed by campaign manager Lee Atwater that Bush's Iowa campaign was not the well-oiled machine professed by his Iowa staff (Germond and Witcover 1989, 103)?

The doubts raised about the viability of the Bush caucus campaign gave added significance to a forum sponsored by the Republican Party of Iowa on September 12 in Ames. The party fund-raiser, called the "Cavalcade of Stars," was held in Hilton Coliseum on the campus of Iowa State University. It was the first time that George Bush agreed to appear on the same platform with the other candidates. A similar Ames fund-raising function in 1979 had provided a boost for the Bush candidacy when he bested Ronald Reagan in a straw poll held at the event.

The party promoted the Cavalcade of Stars as an opportunity for Iowans to see and hear the candidates and was thrilled that five of the six major candidates (Bush, Dole, Robertson, Kemp, and duPont) and two lesser candidates (Kate Heslop and Ben Fernandez) agreed to participate. The draw to the forum was a presidential straw poll, which party officials hoped would encourage attendance and, more important, raise funds to retire the party's substantial debt. Once the major candidates agreed to be part of the forum, there was little doubt it would be covered by the national media and would be used to judge the progress of the campaign (Menke Sept. 21, 1987).

The day began in a festive atmosphere as candidates set up tents in the parking lot outside Hilton Coliseum, served food and beverages, and interacted personally with those attending the event. It was readily apparent to those entering Hilton Coliseum for the evening program that Pat Robertson's "invisible army" had taken form. The center of the hall was packed with Robertson supporters dressed in white campaign T-shirts and hats and sitting in a sea of Robertson balloons and campaign signs. The enthusiastic Robertson crowd was in sharp contrast to the more staid supporters of Bush, Dole, Kemp, and duPont, who were relatively quiet, perhaps shell-shocked by the size

and behavior of Robertson's supporters. The impressive organizational effort was not lost on the reporters in attendance.

The candidates were each permitted fifteen minutes for speeches,
and only Kate Heslop's remarks were not routine. Heslop, who had
sought publicity for her candidacy by walking across Iowa with a pig,
criticized the elected officials (Kemp, Dole, Bush) for not dealing effectively with America's problems. But what the candidates said mattered
little. The boisterous and very visible Robertson crowd dominated the
show (author's notes from the event).

The audience of about 5700 paid twenty-five dollars each to attend,
which entitled them to participate in the party-sponsored straw poll.
Blocks of tickets were available to the campaigns, and each bought
some; the Robertson organization made the largest purchase.
Republican officials were delighted with the turnout and the financial
success of the event (Menke Sept. 21, 1987).

The poll results verified that it was Robertson's night. He finished
ahead of both Dole and the favorite, George Bush, who had been
expected to win because of his presumed superior organization. The
official party count is shown in Table 8.3.

Unfortunately for Vice-President Bush, more than 200 media personnel were registered for the event, and the "surprising" outcome
was reported nationally. The thrust of the stories was Robertson's successful organizational effort and Bush's lackluster performance, which
some thought indicated poor staff work and perhaps a lack of commitment on the part of his supporters.

A front-page headline in the *Washington Post* stated that
"Robertson's Iowa Victory Shocks Rivals," and the accompanying article called Robertson's win in the straw poll "a major embarrassment to
Vice President Bush" in what the writer termed "the first big event of
the fall political season" (Peterson 1987b, A1). The *Los Angeles Times*
said that "Robertson transformed the Saturday night fund-raising
event into a cheering, personal rally for his candidacy, along the way
vanquishing ... Vice President George Bush and Senate GOP leader
Bob Dole" (Balzar 1987, 4). The *New York Times* said that Bush's third-
place finish behind Robertson and Dole "tarnished" the Vice-
President's "image for organizational efficiency" (Dionne 1987b, 1).

But perhaps too much was being made of the straw poll. It was one
thing to attract 1300 supporters to Ames and quite another to turn out

Table 8.3.   1988 Republican "Cavalcade of Stars"
straw-poll results

| | Iowa[a] | | | |
	no.	%	Out of state	Unconfirmed
Robertson	1293	34	69	68
Dole	958	25	13	27
Bush	864	22	31	23
Kemp	520	14	8	26
duPont	160	4	10	6
Heslop	13	0	3	0
Haig	12	0	2	0
Fernandez	8	0	1	0
Others	15	0	1	2
Total[b]	3843	99	138	152

[a]Iowa—able to produce a valid Iowa driver's license (or student picture ID) as well as a ticket; out of state—people with an out-of-state driver's license; unconfirmed—Iowa resident unable to produce an Iowa driver's license.
[b]The total of 4133 ballots cast is considerably less than the perhaps 5700 people who attended. According to Ronda Menke, some were under eighteen, others simply didn't wish to vote, others would not stand in line, and some who did not have their Iowa driver's license refused to vote in the "unconfirmed" poll (Menke Sept. 21, 1987).

several times that many people for the caucuses. *Newsweek* warned, however, not to underestimate the Ames outcome, noting that "the victory in the Iowa straw poll—which involved only 5700 people—was nonetheless achieved with precisely the kind of tactics that could succeed in the important Iowa caucuses in February. Therefore, Bush's third-place finish, behind Robertson and Dole, was an ominous sign for the front runner" (Fineman 1987, 29). The Bush campaign staff must have read the sign, because two days after the Ames event they announced that deputy campaign manager Rich Bond would be spending more time in Iowa.

The Republican campaign picked up again after the Ames poll. The candidates were prominent during the fall months, spending eighty-six days in Iowa from September through December. Bush was in the state fourteen days, which almost equaled his previous visit total, although he still refused to appear with the others in candidate forums. On two occasions in November, Bush was in Iowa at the time of debates (Iowa Homebuilders Association and American Association of Retired Persons) but chose not to participate. The others noted Bush's absence. At the Homebuilders debate, duPont, who claimed to be concerned that the veep was not represented, read Bush quotes from the transcript of an earlier debate in Houston (Fogarty and Hovelson 1987, 4A).

Another Iowa Poll released in mid-November contained good news for Dole and more warning signs for Bush. Dole's share of the poll had increased to 36 percent, and he now led Bush by 6 percentage points. Kemp's support was largely unchanged at 9 percent, followed by Robertson at 8 percent, duPont 5 percent, Haig 2 percent, and "undecided" 10 percent (Iowa Poll: 1987, poll no. 288). Robertson was apparently not benefiting from the Ames straw poll and the ensuing good publicity, or the Iowa Poll was not picking up his support.

As the campaign moved into December, the Republicans also began to air radio and television ads. As previously discussed, this was a break with tradition, as paid media had been used sparingly if at all in previous Iowa caucus races. Earlier campaigns assumed that likely caucus attenders were a very targeted population that could be reached more efficiently and much more reasonably by a strong organization employing telephone banks, direct mailings, and frequent local appearances by the candidates. The only thing that seems to have changed in the equation was the professionalization of political campaigns. With consultants and media advisers commanding big salaries, the Iowa campaigns seem to have been dragged into the modern media campaign era. Table 8.4 shows the spending at two Des Moines television stations. The KCCI data include November and December, the WHO data do not.

Jack Kemp began running television ads in November and Bush aired his first Iowa commercials in December. Dole, duPont, and Robertson waited until January to begin television advertising, and Haig, inactive in Iowa by that time, did not buy TV ads. As with the Democrats, most of the GOP caucus ads aired after the first of the year.

Table 8.4.   1988 Republican spending at
WHO-TV and KCCI-TV

	WHO (Jan.–Feb.)	KCCI (Nov.–Feb.)
Kemp	$17,020	$32,773
Dole	14,450	18,717
Bush	7655	17,074
duPont	12,085	12,692
Robertson	17,110	12,597
Haig	0	0
Total	68,320	93,853

Source: Created from records provided by Cheryl
Semerad, director of sales and marketing, WHO, and
Anne Marie Caudron, national sales manager, KCCI.

Of the Table 8.4 spending totals, 80 percent at KCCI and 100 percent
at WHO ran in January and February. Republican candidates spent
only about half as much on TV commercials as the Democrats.

According to Ed Rollins, "everybody in Iowa ran bio ads," and none
stood out like those used by Dole and Bush in New Hampshire (Runkle
1989, 139). Kemp ran anti-tax ads, a Dole commercial stressed his
small-town Kansas roots. A duPont ad chronicled the dangers of
teenage drug use. Robertson, who was already well known to his hard-
core supporters from his "700 Club" show on the Christian
Broadcasting Network, ran thirty-minute interview shows. Bush highlighted his support of the arms control treaty (Norman 1988a, 1B).
Whereas Gephardt's campaign manager attributed his candidate's rise
in the Iowa Polls to their television ads, particularly the Hyundai commercial, Republican campaign managers made no such claims. Paid
television may not have been a very effective tool in the Republican
caucuses.

In spite of an increasingly intense GOP campaign and the early TV
ads, the December Iowa Poll showed little change in candidate support from the November survey. Dole continued to lead with 37 per-

cent, again followed by Bush with 33 percent, Kemp 9 percent, Robertson 8 percent, duPont 5 percent, Haig less than 1 percent, and "undecided" 8 percent. If Robertson's evangelical followers were on the move, the *Register's* polling arm failed to detect it (Iowa Poll: 1987, poll no. 289).

The *Des Moines Register* held its Republican presidential debate on January 8 before nearly 2700 people and about 400 reporters at the Des Moines Civic Center. The debate was broadcast live in Iowa and some other parts of the country by Public Television and nationally by C-Span on a delayed basis. *Register* editor James Gannon and Colorado Democratic Representative Patricia Schroeder questioned the six Republicans. Al Haig, who had not been in Iowa since late October and who a week earlier had announced that he was shutting down most of his Iowa campaign operation, did participate in the debate (*DMR* Dec. 30, 1987, 3M).

The debate started calmly enough, with Gannon lobbing softballs to Dole, Haig, Kemp, and Robertson, but when he asked Bush about his role in the Iran-Contra affair, the vice-president erupted. Apparently upset by the *Register's* treatment of the subject, Bush went after Gannon and the paper and aggressively defended the administration's handling of the affair. He did not, however, answer the question. After the exchange, Gannon asked duPont whether a man of his wealth could empathize with average Americans, and duPont said he could (author's notes from the event).

Nine days after the debate the *Register* released the first of two Iowa Polls conducted during a twenty-five-day period in late January and early February, with only ten days separating the surveys. The results are shown with earlier poll outcomes in Table 8.5.

With the exception of Dole's growing lead over Bush, levels of support remained remarkably constant over the six-month period, particularly when sampling error is considered.

The 1988 Precinct Caucuses

The date of the precinct caucuses finally arrived. Iowa had experienced a nonstop presidential campaign for the better part of two years,

Table 8.5.   1988 *Des Moines Register* Republican
Iowa Polls

	"Likely" Republican caucus attenders (%)				
	8-87	11-87	12-87	1-88	2-88
Bush	29	30	33	26	23
Dole	32	36	37	41	37
Kemp	10	9	9	8	11
Robertson	7	8	8	11	13
Haig	4	2	0	1	1
duPont	5	5	5	4	7
Undecided	12	10	8	9	8
Sample size (no.)	301	312	300	409	660
Margin of error (%) +/–	5.6	5.5	5.5	4.8	4

and although political activists enjoyed the attention, others were growing weary of the campaign mail, the ever-present TV ads, the endless candidate forums and debates, and most of all, the hundreds of reporters searching the state for the typical Iowa peasant.

The Iowa campaign had started much earlier this cycle. Presidential candidates spent 999 days in the state, and in the final weeks of the campaign they were followed everywhere by a small army of media personnel, including reporters from as far away as Australia and Finland. On some occasions ten presidential hopefuls were in the state on the same day. The campaign time in Iowa and the spending for each candidate are shown in Table 8.6.

Media Coverage

Once again the Iowa campaign had grown dramatically and since the candidates were here more often, the press followed the campaign

Table 8.6.   1988 candidate precaucus campaign activity and spending

	Days in Iowa	Spending in Iowa
Democrats		
Babbitt	118	$651,016
Biden	59	207,029
Dukakis	82	756,411
Gephardt	148	751,157
Gore	32	262,037
Hart	34	207,159
Jackson	63	195,032
LaRouche		312,130
Simon	91	791,257
Others	8	0
Total Democratic	635	4,133,228
Republicans		
Bush	43	774,696
Dole	68	793,228
duPont	92	614,772
Haig	21	39,212
Kemp	79	765,145
Laxalt	6	0
Robertson	41	78,165
Rumsfeld	12	0
Others	2	7724
Total Republican	364	3,768,711
Grand total	999	7,909,663

Source: Spending data are from the Federal Election Commission report *FEC Reports on Financial Activity, 1987–88: Final Report, Presidential Pre-Nomination Campaigns*, Table A9. The Iowa limit was $775,217. As discussed in Chapter 7, the federal reports understate campaign spending in Iowa because the candidates use a variety of means to attribute some of their Iowa expenses to other states. According to officials at the Federal Election Commission, it is almost impossible to audit individual state spending. The FEC has unsuccessfully asked Congress to eliminate state spending limits (Stirton 1997). The campaign activity covers the period from January 20, 1985, through February 8, 1988. Data were collected by the author from the individual campaigns.

more intensely than ever before. The creation in October 1987 of the "Presidential Campaign Hotline," a daily electronic news summary, by Washington, D.C., political consultants Douglas Bailey and Roger Craver made presidential campaign news readily available "to any reporter with a computer and a modem." The hotline gave "special prominence" to campaign news from Iowa and New Hampshire (Klaus and Clift 1987, 83).

By making the "conventional wisdom" available electronically, the hotline would seem to have lessened the need for field research by reporters, who could now cover the candidates without leaving their offices. But in reality, news organizations increased their on-site reporting in 1988 and opened Iowa bureaus much earlier than in the past. To be sure, the press had traveled to Iowa early and often to cover past caucuses. Reporters periodically visited the state for special events or to conduct field research for articles assessing the progress of the race, but they seldom stayed in Iowa for more than a few days at a time before January of the caucus year.

Full-time, on-site coverage began much earlier in the 1988 caucus cycle. The *Los Angeles Times* opened a temporary bureau in Des Moines on August 30, 1987, and assigned a four-person team to cover the campaign from Iowa through the precinct caucuses. Apparently, Iowa was considered hard duty, as team members rotated between Des Moines and Los Angeles, with two reporters reporting from Iowa while the other two enjoyed R&R in California (Balzar 1987a). In the ensuing months, most of the other major print media also based reporters in Des Moines. CNN was the first national TV network to open a Des Moines news bureau on October 12, 1987, with four full-time reporters, and that number increased as the caucuses neared (Greenberg 1987). C-Span followed shortly thereafter, and the big three television networks opened their Des Moines technical facilities in early January.

Iowa became the political news center of the country as the date of the caucuses neared. Reporters visited Des Moines in unprecedented numbers and the national television networks moved major segments of their political units to Iowa (Rhein 1988a, 3TV). About fifty truck-mounted satellite dishes were parked in downtown Des Moines to broadcast news programs and caucus results from Iowa (Elbert 1988,

5B). National and international press coverage was extensive, and on the eve of the February 8 caucuses, the parties estimated that 3000 reporters and technicians were in Iowa covering the precinct caucuses.

Table 8.7 compares television coverage of the Iowa precinct caucuses and the New Hampshire primary election by CBS's evening and weekend news for a one-year period from July 1 to June 30 for four caucus cycles. With presidential nominating contests in both parties, CBS's 1988 coverage of Iowa was extensive. The network aired six times as many stories about the Iowa race as they had in 1983-84, when only the Democrats had a contest, and 28 percent more stories than in 1979-80, when there were nominating races in both parties. With sixteen candidates active at some time during the Iowa campaign and very competitive races in both parties, there was more to cover than in any previous caucus contest.

CBS paid far more attention to the Iowa precinct caucuses than to the New Hampshire primary election in 1987-88. Only eight days separated the two nominating events, and media attention did not shift to New Hampshire until the day after the Iowa caucuses. Germond and Witcover thought that for the first time, "New Hampshire played second fiddle to Iowa," and although "most of the candidates stole some time from Iowa to lay groundwork for the week in New Hampshire, the intensity level didn't come until Iowa was history" (1988b, 10A). Based on CBS news stories, New Hampshire played sec-

Table 8.7.   CBS news stories on Iowa and
New Hampshire, 1975-76 through 1987-88

	July 1 to June 30			
	1975–76	1979–80	1983–84	1987–88
Iowa	13	54	11	69
N.H.	44	40	22	38

Source: Data are from the *Television News Index and Abstracts*, produced by Vanderbilt University. The criteria for constructing the table are discussed in the source note for Table 6.2.

ond fiddle to Iowa in 1979-80 as well, but the five weeks between the two events in 1980 allowed time for a vigorous campaign in New Hampshire after the Iowa caucuses.

The competitive races brought out record numbers of participants in the 1988 caucuses of both parties. Republicans recorded 108,806 votes in their straw poll, and Democrats estimated that 125,000 participated in their caucuses (the News Election Service [NES] counted 87,964 in the 70 percent of precincts they succeeded in tallying). The combined total of about 234,000 (22.9 percent of the registered Republicans and Democrats) substantially exceeded the previous caucus high of 206,000 in 1980. Both parties were delighted with the turnout and the media attention given the 1988 caucuses.

The Democratic Caucuses

The controversy over caucus results discussed in Chapter 7 resurfaced in 1988. The news media, particularly television, had been at odds with the Iowa Democratic Party since the early 1980s over the caucus results. The news organizations again asked the party to help them count the number of caucus attenders supporting each candidate after the first division into preference groups. In essence, they wanted a straw poll comparable to the straw poll being held in the GOP caucuses. Democratic party officials refused once again to cooperate, and the media again turned to NES to gather the caucus results in primary-like form. Without the cooperation of the party, NES had managed to tally only 74 percent of the precincts in 1984, and they would encounter similar difficulties in 1988.

The media's desire for independently verified "first division" or "pre-viability" results from the caucuses has several motives, some more noble than others. CBS's concern about the validity of the Iowa results based on the questionable practices in 1976 and 1980 discussed in Chapter 7 was very legitimate. The Iowa General Assembly responded to that concern in early 1988 by passing legislation making it a "simple misdemeanor" for those reporting caucus results to "willfully" omit, falsify, or fail to perform their duties (Ia. Gen. Assem. 1988, chap. 1001, p. 1).

CBS was also concerned that the reporting of delegate totals would not accurately reflect the strength of the lesser candidates who probably would not reach the 15 percent threshold in many precincts (Oreskes 1988, 14). The Democratic results in Table 8.8 illustrate CBS's point. Gephardt, Simon, and Dukakis were stronger in the party's delegate count, whereas the second-tier candidates came out better in the NES count, where their support was recorded even when it did not reach the 15 percent threshold.

Clearly, the media did not care about unreliable delegate totals, which had little meaning to their viewers. They wanted an indication of how Iowans attending caucuses felt about the candidates after the long campaign. The networks (but not New Hampshire) would be happier if Iowa switched from caucuses to a primary election. In fact, Stan Opotowsky, director of political operations for ABC News, commenting on the networks' efforts through NES to count Democratic caucus

Table 8.8.   1988 Democratic precinct caucus results

	State delegate equivalents (%)	News Election Service pre-viability results	
		no.	%
Gephardt	31.3	24,136	27.4
Simon	26.7	21,403	24.3
Dukakis	22.2	18,041	20.5
Jackson	8.8	9773	11.1
Babbitt	6.1	8049	9.2
Uncommitted	4.5	5251	6.0
Hart	0.3	896	1.0
Others	0.1	223	0.3
Gore	0.0	192	0.2
Total	100.0	87,964	100.0

Source: The state delegate equivalents are the official results of the Iowa Democratic Party from 2464 of 2487 precincts (99%). The News Election Service results are from 1739 of 2487 precincts (70%). The Iowa Democratic Party estimated that 125,000 people participated in their caucuses, which represented 23.2 percent of the 538,939 Democrats registered on February 1, 1988.

attenders before application of the 15 percent rule, reputedly bragged, "We made Iowa into a primary" (*Newsweek* Feb. 1, 1988, 20).

Finally, and perhaps most important to them, the networks want results before their viewers retire for the evening. The Iowa Democratic Party's counting process is too slow for the electronic media who wanted an earlier count and knew NES could provide it.

Without the cooperation of the party, NES managed to obtain pre-viability results from only 70 percent of the Democratic caucuses. The *Register* in an editorial a few days after the caucuses called the NES effort "a botched caucus count" and a "pathetic performance" (Feb. 12, 1988, 14A), but like the television networks and some newspapers, they reported the NES figures rather than the party's official results. The *Wall Street Journal, New York Times, Chicago Tribune, Los Angeles Times,* and other newspapers reported the Democratic delegate equivalents. The *Washington Post* and *Congressional Quarterly* reported both.

Democratic state chair Bonnie Campbell wrote a letter to the *Register* taking it to task for using the NES results rather than the party's official returns and berating NES for the "amateurish way" it performed its tabulation duties (*DMR* Feb. 17, 1988, 11A). Robert W. Flaherty, executive director of NES, responded to the *Register* and Campbell with a letter of his own. He defended NES's performance and contrasted the "full cooperation of the Republican Party staff" to the decision by the Iowa Democratic Party's central committee and Campbell not to cooperate with NES. Flaherty asserted that the party "allowed the word to go forth that they did not want county and precinct officials to cooperate with NES in the pre-viability report" (*DMR* Feb. 26, 1988, 13A). So the "results problem" continued unresolved, with the *Register,* the Democratic party, and NES blaming each other for the problem.

The networks' declaration of winners in the caucuses before any preferences were tallied was a big story in 1984 and had led to congressional hearings. In 1988 the television networks again declared winners shortly after the caucuses began. Using NES entrance poll data, ABC News projected Senator Dole the GOP winner at 7:36 P.M.; NBC followed suit at 7:39 and CBS at 7:42. CBS and ABC projected Congressman Gephardt the Democratic winner at 8:15 and 8:46 P.M., respectively, but NBC waited until much later in the evening. CNN did not project winners until after 10:00 (Rhein 1988b, 7A).

The media interpretations of the Democratic outcome were subdued. R. W. Apple, Jr., of the *New York Times* devoted only 34 lines of his 224-line caucus analysis to the Democratic results and a scant 9 lines to Gephardt, the winner. He concluded that "the state produced no Democratic breakthrough and established no one as a front-runner." In contrast, Apple devoted 157 lines to the second- and third-place finishes of Robertson and Bush, but only 16 lines to the GOP winner, Dole (Apple 1988, B7).

The *Congressional Quarterly*'s analysis also downplayed Gephardt's victory, noting he "finished narrowly ahead of Simon and Dukakis in a state where he emphasized his midwestern roots and invested heavily in time and money." Doubting that Gephardt would receive much of a bounce from Iowa, *CQ* concluded that "Gephardt's showing was neither a surprise—like Gary Hart's second-place showing in 1984—nor decisive—like Jimmy Carter's triumphs over his opposition in 1976 and 1980" (Cook 1988b, p. 290).

The *Wall Street Journal* thought that Pat Robertson's strong showing might "blot out the coverage Mr. Gephardt might otherwise have expected to receive as the Democratic winner" (Rogers and Perry 1988, 66). Indeed it did. Robertson's "stunning" second-place finish ahead of Bush dominated the news after the caucuses, which alternately played up Robertson's strong finish and Bush's weak showing.

And so Gephardt, the Iowa winner, did not receive a media boost for his victory in the caucuses. Bill Carrick, his campaign manager, said, "It would have been nice if someone had told us that Iowa was going to be worth Idaho this time around" (*CQ* 1991, 2418). A narrow win meant little in the expectations game. A big victory might have led to a greater media boost from Iowa, but unfortunately for Gephardt, Pat Robertson finished ahead of the vice-president of the United States in the Republican caucuses the same night. Dukakis, who had run well in a state that generally did not support eastern presidential candidates and where Gephardt and Simon as neighbors had enjoyed home field advantages, was coming into his home territory in New Hampshire, and that made him the Democratic story. Simon received little momentum from his second-place finish in Iowa and was now the man in the middle.

Iowa effectively narrowed the Democratic field to Gephardt, Simon, and Dukakis, with Gore on the sidelines until Super Tuesday and

Jackson sure to reemerge then also. Babbitt, the press favorite, had spent the better part of two years and at least $650,000 in Iowa, and although he gained the respect of many Iowans, he won only 6.1 percent of the delegate equivalents. Jackson expanded his Iowa base in 1988, and his 8.8 percent share of the delegate pool was much greater than the 1.5 percent he had won in 1984. Although Jackson said at a Des Moines press conference before leaving the state that he was pleased with his accomplishments in Iowa, the press saw little that was significant about it, but he would remain in the race to the end (Norman 1988b, 6A). Hart's support in Iowa was minuscule, and he must have wondered whether reentering the race had been a wise thing to do.

In the post-Iowa expectations game, Dukakis had an advantage in neighboring New Hampshire, probably making that primary election a battle for second place. Senator Ted Kennedy, noting the fickleness and impact of the expectations game, joked, "Only eight years ago I finished second in Iowa, and my presidential campaign was finished. This year Mike Dukakis finishes third, and he's on the way to the White House." Few expected that both Gephardt and Simon would survive New Hampshire, which *Time* branded "the Avis primary"— that is, a race between Gephardt and Simon for "the No. 2 try-harder slot" (Feb. 22, 1988, 19).

The Republican Caucuses

The Republicans, who had experienced serious technical difficulties in 1980 with their only other statewide caucus poll, were happy to work with NES to ensure accuracy and to legitimize the caucus count. The GOP caucuses were called to order at 7:00 P.M., and permanent chairs were elected. The first order of business was the presidential preference poll. Speeches for individual candidates were permitted, after which secret ballots were used to conduct the poll. The votes were counted in individual precincts, and a predesignated member phoned in the outcome to the NES system in New York, where the statewide results were tabulated. (Each campaign was encouraged to provide a witness to the phone call, as Robertson supporters had questioned the fairness of the procedure.) An NES printer was located at Republican caucus headquarters at the Marriott Hotel in Des Moines, and as results arrived, they were posted for the hundreds of reporters in attendance (Menke Oct. 9, 1987). Table 8.9 reports the outcome of the Republican preference poll.

When examined on a county basis, Dole's victory was even more impressive. He won in eighty-five of Iowa's ninety-nine counties and came in second in the remaining fourteen counties. Robertson also did well on a statewide basis, finishing among the top three in all but two counties. He won in some heavily Democratic, blue-collar areas, such as Des Moines, Dubuque, Lee, and Wapello counties, but ran well in all areas of the state. Bush, who did not carry a single county, came in second in twenty counties and third in seventy-two counties. Kemp managed a top-three finish in only ten counties and came in behind duPont in fifteen others, a disappointing showing for the conservative icon.

The media interpretations of the results were uniform. Haig and duPont were written off for their poor showings in the caucuses; Kemp was badly damaged by finishing behind Robertson and now had to do well in New Hampshire to survive. Dole was empowered by his impressive win in Iowa, and there were two big surprises: Robertson's strong

Table 8.9.   1988 Republican caucus straw-poll results

	Preferences	Percentage
Dole	40,661	37.4
Robertson	26,761	24.6
Bush	20,194	18.6
Kemp	12,088	11.1
duPont	7999	7.3
No preference	739	0.7
Haig	364	0.3
Total	108,806	100.0

Source: Results are from 2446 of 2487 precincts (98%). The turnout of 108,806 was 22.5 percent of the 482,675 Republicans registered on February 1, 1988.

Table 8.10.   1988 Republican caucus straw-poll results by county

	Counties Won	Counties Second[a]	Counties Third[b]
Dole	85	14	0
Robertson	14	65	18
Bush	0	20	72
Kemp	0	1	9
duPont	0	0	0
Haig	0	0	0

Source: Constructed using News Election Service data reported in the *Des Moines Register* on February 10, 1988, p. 8A.
[a] Bush and Robertson tied for second in Lyon County.
[b] Bush and Kemp tied for third in Wayne County.

second-place showing and Bush's weak third-place finish.

The *Register* said Dole "cruised to an expected victory" while Bush "suffered severe political wounds by running a weak third behind Pat Robertson." The story called the outcome a "stunning defeat" for Bush and concluded that Robertson and Dole "ride out of Iowa on the crest of a wave of momentum," with Bush's nomination "less likely" (Norman and Fogarty 1988, 1A). Dole, like Gephardt, had met the expectations set for him in the Iowa horse race but would receive considerably less attention in postcaucus stories than Bush and Robertson, whose finishes "surprised" the press.

As previously noted, R. W. Apple, Jr., devoted 70 percent of his article to Robertson's "stunning" second-place finish and Bush's "surprisingly feeble showing." Apple concluded that for Bush, "nearly everything now depends upon New Hampshire" (1988, B7). Dole received more attention in other postcaucus coverage.

Robert Shogan of the *Los Angeles Times* lent his perspective. He concluded that the big questions growing out of the results were "whether George Bush can recover from his humiliating third-place finish, whether the winner, Kansas Sen. Bob Dole, can take over Bush's front-runner role and whether former television evangelist Pat Robertson, who finished a surprising second, can match his Iowa success in a broad-based primary" (Shogan 1988, 1).

In the post-Iowa expectations game, Dole fared much better than Gephardt but did not benefit as much as he might have under more favorable circumstances. His margin of victory was impressive and he met or exceeded the expectations set for him, but like Gephardt he was knocked off center stage by Robertson.

Much news space was given to analyzing Bush's poor showing. Several factors probably contributed, among them the depressed farm economy, Dole's status as a neighbor and Senator Grassley's support for him, President Reagan's dip in popularity in the state, the Iran-Contra tar baby, early overconfidence, and organizational problems. Other problems were more directly attributable to the candidate himself. Bush may have been out of touch with Iowans. He never clearly articulated a message in Iowa and he created little excitement for his campaign. He asked for support on the basis of his record and experience, and those reasons did not prove compelling to Iowans.

The *Wall Street Journal* put together an interesting summary of pre- and post-Iowa network coverage of the presidential race. The author, Monica Langley, used data from a New York firm to compare network coverage of the candidates the week before and the week after the Iowa caucuses. The data from the story are reproduced in Table 8.11.

Bush's third-place finish in Iowa dominated the postcaucus network news, receiving as much coverage as all the Democrats combined and almost as much as the other Republican candidates combined. Dole's airtime did not increase, but the positive spin on his campaign did. Robertson enjoyed nearly three times as much post- as pre-Iowa coverage, and most of it was positive. Interestingly, the coverage of Gephardt declined and "a significant portion was negative," with particular attention given to alleged "flip-flops" in his voting record. Simon received twice as much airtime, but it was meager in comparison to the coverage of the Republican first-tier candidates. Dukakis received a great boost of mostly positive coverage. In terms of network attention, the second-tier candidates barely existed after Iowa (Langley 1988, 62).

The media postcaucus analysis focused on the weaknesses of the Bush campaign exposed by Iowa and speculated about Robertson's likely impact in New Hampshire and Super Tuesday states. Table 8.11 shows that Bush and Robertson were the foci of network news stories during the week between Iowa and New Hampshire. Bush, like Reagan

Table 8.11.   Network coverage before and
after Iowa by number of minutes on
evening network news Monday through
Friday

	Week before caucuses	Week after caucuses
George Bush	10:00	24:30
Robert Dole	8:50	9:15
Pat Robertson	5:20	14:10
Jack Kemp	0:20	2:20
Pete duPont	0:15	0:25
Michael Dukakis	2:15	8:10
Richard Gephardt	6:10	4:55
Paul Simon	2:45	5:55
Gary Hart	2:50	0:45
Albert Gore Jr.	—	3:15
Bruce Babbitt	0:35	0:55
Jesse Jackson	0:15	0:40

Source: DWJ Associates Inc.; *Wall Street Journal,*
February 16, 1988, p. 62.
   Reprinted by permission of *Wall Street Journal,* ©
1988 Dow Jones & Company, Inc. All rights reserved
worldwide.

in 1980, was forced to change his campaign strategy after the Iowa
defeat. In New Hampshire he abandoned his imperial candidacy,
mounted a full-blown campaign with frequent personal appearances,
and began aggressively to challenge Dole's campaign positions. Bush
was a big winner in New Hampshire, and three weeks later he carried
sixteen of the seventeen Super Tuesday states. Robertson won one
state and Dole none (Cook 1988c, 640). The Bush candidacy was alive
and well after all, and the Republican campaign was for all intents and
purposes decided a month after the Iowa precinct caucuses.

   With the benefit of hindsight, there was much more to Robertson's
success in Iowa than finishing ahead of Vice-President Bush. He had a
short-term impact on the GOP presidential race, and much of that

impact was due to the way the caucuses were reported. The press had Dole and Robertson on the march after Iowa, and Bush near political death. But after Bush made short shrift of the GOP field, one might have concluded that the Robertson phenomenon was a press creation much like Gary Hart in 1984. Others detected something larger and more enduring. Historian Garry Wills wrote after the caucuses, "A moral alarm clock is going off in America, and not many politicians hear it. Pat Robertson does, and so do more of his fellow citizens than we less godly folk have been willing to admit" (Wills 1988, 27).

Robertson, like Reagan before him, had tapped into a vein of discontent in America, and that vein ran through and beyond the Christian Right. Americans had become disillusioned with the social and moral climate of the country, and Robertson was a harbinger of things to come. He asked the political system to do more than pay lip service to what he saw as the moral decline of the country. His messages about prayer in school, abortion, premarital sex, drugs, homosexuality, pornography, violence, and the breakdown of the family struck responsive chords well beyond the Christian Right.

The Impact of the 1988 Caucuses

Iowa withstood the challenge to its first-in-the-nation status by Michigan, Hawaii, and Kansas, and later by the Super Tuesday states, and emerged stronger than ever in 1988. Iowans were treated to a media event of historic proportions. The candidates and the press devoted far more time to the caucuses than ever before, and in the final weeks of the campaign, media coverage was so extensive as to be oppressive. "Retail" politics came to an end, as ordinary citizens could not get close to the presidential candidates, who were constantly surrounded by journalists. Reporters followed the candidates from one photo opportunity to the next and searched for something unique or different to report.

The Iowa media event changed in other ways as well. The growth of paid television advertising in 1988 began to alter the nature of the caucus campaign. The perceived success of Gephardt's ads in Iowa and the apparent success of negative advertising in New Hampshire the following week assured that Iowans would see and hear more commercials in future caucuses. If the use of paid radio and television increased in Iowa as it had nationally, the retail nature of the Iowa campaign might be lost and with it the rationale for beginning the presidential campaign in a small state.

The media pressure for primary election–like results from Iowa had an impact on the conduct of the meetings. Before Iowa became a media event, the only reportable caucus results were the names of delegates selected to county conventions. Now the GOP caucus poll and the Democratic delegate equivalents were the essence of the meetings. Many people attended caucuses only to express their candidate preferences, remaining long enough to have their "votes" counted before calling it a night. Hundreds of reporters attending caucuses added to the confusion, or in some cases, with the help of TV lights and cameras, created a circuslike atmosphere. The little gatherings of neighbors who deliberated the great issues of the day had been transformed by "votes" and TV cameras. The parties were willing participants in the transformation, adjusting caucus procedures to accommodate the media, with the exception that Iowa Democrats refused to change their reporting of "delegate equivalents."

The impact of the precinct caucuses on the rest of the presidential race was minimal. Gephardt and Dole, who lived in neighboring states, gained only modestly from their "regional" wins in Iowa. Each finished second in New Hampshire, rebounded to win in South Dakota a week later, and then was effectively eliminated by the Super Tuesday primaries. The second-place finishers in Iowa, Simon and Robertson, benefited very little from their "strong" showings in the precinct caucuses. The handicappers had decided that Simon had to finish ahead of Gephardt in New Hampshire, and when he did not, he was effectively eliminated. Robertson finished a distant fourth behind Kemp in New Hampshire, and when he failed to do well in South Carolina and the Super Tuesday states three day later, he too was effectively out of the race.

On the other hand, Bush and Dukakis suffered minimal harm from their third-place finishes in Iowa. Although Bush did change his campaign strategy, his candidacy was very much alive in New Hampshire, contrary to the dire predictions of the media after his "stunning" defeat in Iowa. By the close of the polls on Super Tuesday, little doubt remained that Bush and Dukakis would be their parties' nominees. Both candidates demonstrated the limitations of the Iowa/New

Hampshire strategy followed by Gephardt, Simon, and Robertson. Bush and Dukakis (and to a lesser degree Dole) were prepared organizationally and financially for a campaign beyond Iowa. The others were not.

The Gephardt and Dole victories in the caucuses and the electoral successes of the better-financed Dukakis and Bush campaigns after Iowa call into question part of the "legend of Iowa," namely, the belief that a little-known, modestly financed candidate can mount a Jimmy Carter–style campaign and use the momentum gained from Iowa to go on and win the presidential nomination. Almost all of the Iowa campaigns since 1976, regardless of party, have followed the Carter formula, but the only dark-horse candidate to parlay success in the caucuses to a presidential nomination was Carter himself. The presidential campaign has changed since Carter successfully employed the Iowa/New Hampshire strategy. The compression of the primary and caucus schedule, the addition of Super Tuesday, and the dominance of paid TV have each contributed to the declining influence of Iowa in the presidential race.

Robertson's surprise second-place finish in the GOP caucuses and the media boost that followed highlight other aspects of the reporting of the Iowa media event. Robertson's strong finish was a "surprise" because reporters failed to detect (or take seriously) how well financed and well organized his Iowa campaign was, and because his support did not show up in the public opinion polls conducted in the state. The Iowa Poll, for example, drew its sample of likely caucus attenders from the list of registered Republicans, and many Robertson supporters fell outside the parameters of that population. As previously noted, anyone willing to affiliate on the night of the caucuses may participate in the meetings and in the GOP poll. As a result, the final Iowa Poll understated Robertson's caucus support by almost 50 percent. With so much of the expectations game based on poll outcomes, it is little wonder that the pundits were surprised by Robertson's strong Iowa finish. Unfortunately, reporters compounded their failure to detect Robertson's strength in Iowa by vastly overstating the impact of his second-place finish in the caucuses.

Had the 1988 campaign not started in Iowa, Robertson might never have been a story in the Republican nominating race. His support in Iowa, while well developed in many parts of the state, came disproportionately from the Christian Right, which was a group of modest size in 1988. While Robertson was able to bring out 26,761 supporters for the GOP caucuses (and that was impressive in a small state like Iowa), he was unable to duplicate that success in New Hampshire, South Carolina, or the Super Tuesday states. Robertson was never really a threat to Bush, or Dole for that matter, in the battle for delegates, and his modest levels of support were magnified in Iowa and other early caucus states where his "invisible army" was not overwhelmed by the greater numbers of larger state primary elections. Iowa's small stage was perfect for a Robertson surprise, and the media may have misled the nation about his strength and about Bush's "weaknesses."

Finally, Iowa continued to play the role of winnower. One constant about Iowa's impact on the presidential nominating process is the elimination or mortal wounding of presidential hopefuls who do poorly or fail to meet the expectations of their role. In 1988 several candidates fell into that category. Haig withdrew on February 12, four days after the caucuses. Babbitt and duPont followed suit on March 18, two days after the New Hampshire primary election. Kemp was mortally wounded by finishing behind Robertson in the caucuses. Hart, who had no Iowa organization and much baggage, was not taken very seriously after the caucuses.

References

Apple, R. W., Jr. 1988. "Stunning Result Carries a Grim Message for Bush." *New York Times,* Feb. 9, p. B7.

Balzar, John. 1987a. Interview with author, September 8. Balzar is a reporter for the *Los Angeles Times.*

———. 1987b. "Strong Straw Poll Victory in Iowa Gives Robertson Wild-Card Status in Caucuses." *Los Angeles Times,* September 14, p. 4.

Barnes, James A. 1988. "Campaign Game Plans." In *National Journal Election '88: A Guide to the Candidates, Issues and Voters,* 2842-50. Washington, D.C.: Times Mirror Magazines.

Benedetto, Richard. 1987. "Who's Coming Up As Hart Fades?" *USA Today,* May 8, 6A.

Burnham, Walter Dean. 1988. "The Reagan Heritage." In *The Election of 1988: Reports and Interpretations,* edited by Gerald M. Pomper, 1-32. Chatham, N.J.: Chatham House.

Carlson, John, and Jane Norman. 1988. "Campaign Aide Loses Job over Finance Fuss." *Des Moines Register,* January 15, p. 12A.

Congressional Quarterly. 1991. Special Report: "Iowa." September 7, pp. 2417-19.

Cook, Rhodes. 1988a. "Bush-Dole Nomination Contest Is No Watershed Event for GOP." *Congressional Quarterly,* January 23, pp. 155-57.

———. 1988b. "Iowa's Stars Take a Back Seat in New Hampshire." *Congressional Quarterly,* February 13, pp. 287-90.

———. 1988c. "One Side Is Clearer, the Other Still Murky." *Congressional Quarterly,* March 12, pp. 636-46.

Des Moines Register. 1986-88.

Dillin, John. 1987. "Democratic Hopefuls Grope for Economic Issues in Iowa Debate." *Christian Science Monitor,* August 25, p. 6.

Dionne, E. J., Jr. 1987a. "Underdogs Clash on Issues for '88." *New York Times,* May 30, p. 10.

———. 1987b. "Robertson's Victory in Ballot Shakes Rivals in GOP Race." *New York Times,* September 14, p. 1.

———. 1988. "Hart Joins Debate among Democrats." *New York Times,* January 17, p. 20.

Elbert, David. 1988. "Utilities Ready to Keep Networks Beaming on Caucus Night in D.M." *Des Moines Register,* February 8, p. 5B.

Fineman, Howard. 1987. "The Pat Robertson Effect." *Newsweek,* September 28, p. 29.

Fogarty, Thomas A., and Jack Hovelson. 1987. "Dole, Kemp, duPont in GOP Debate Share New Rhetoric Marks." *Des Moines Register,* November 8, p. 4A.

Germond, Jack W., and Jules Witcover. 1988a. "Still Miles to Go." In *National Journal Election '88: A Guide to the Candidates, Issues and Voters,* 2882-83. Washington, D.C.: Times Mirror Magazines.

———. 1988b. " 'Sudden Death' in New Hampshire." *Des Moines Register,* February 17, p. 10A.

———. 1989. *Whose Broad Stripes and Bright Stars?: The Trivial Pursuit of the Presidency 1988.* New York: Warner Books.

Greenberg, Madeline. 1987. Telephone interview with author, December 17. Greenberg was a CNN reporter.

Hagstrom, Jerry, and Robert Guskind. 1988. "Friendly Advice." In *National Journal Election '88: A Guide to the Candidates, Issues and Voters,* 2877-79. Washington, D.C.: Times Mirror Magazines.

Iowa General Assembly. 1988. *Acts and Resolutions.* Des Moines: State of Iowa.

Iowa Poll. 1986-88. Vols. for 1986 through 1988. Des Moines: Des Moines Register and Tribune Company.

Kamin, Blair. 1986. "Christian TV Founder Backs Helms' CBS Bid." *Des Moines Register,* April 18, p. 3M.

Klaus, Mickey, and Eleanor Clift. 1987. "Fresh Baked Political Wisdom." *Newsweek,* November 2, p. 83.

Langley, Monica. 1988. "In Pre–New Hampshire Flurry, Images Prevail, and TV Coverage May Be Pivotal to Candidates." *Wall Street Journal,* February 16, p. 62.

McLeod, Don. 1987. "Candidates Play the Issues in Iowa Stumping Grounds." *Insight*, July 27, pp. 11-12.

Menke, Ronda. 1987. Telephone interviews with author, September 21 and October 9. Menke was the executive director of the Republican Party of Iowa from 1987 to 1989.

National Journal. 1988. *National Journal Election '88: A Guide to the Candidates, Issues and Voters*. Washington, D.C.: Times Mirror Magazines.

Newsweek. 1987 and 1988.

Norman, Jane. 1988a. "Campaigns Channel Cash into TV Finale." *Des Moines Register*, January 3, p. 1B.

———. 1988b. "Jackson Finds Solace in 4th-place Finish: An Expanded Base of Voters." *Des Moines Register*, February 10, p. 6A.

Norman, Jane, and Thomas A. Fogarty. 1988. " 'Devastating Loss' Seen for the Vice President." *Des Moines Register*, February 9, p. 1A.

Oreskes, Michael. 1988. "Official Says Incomplete Vote in Iowa May Be Misleading." *New York Times*, February 7, p. 14.

Peterson, Bill. 1987. "Robertson's Iowa Victory Shocks Rivals." *Washington Post*, September 14, p. A1.

Pins, Kenneth. 1988. "Gephardt and Dole Lead Caucus Races in Final Poll." *Des Moines Register*, February 7, p. 1.

Pomper, Gerald M. 1989. "The Presidential Nominations." In *The Election of 1988: Reports and Interpretations*, edited by Gerald M. Pomper, 33-71. Chatham, N.J.: Chatham House.

Rhein, Dave. 1988a. "Get Set for Peter, Dan, Tom, Bernie." *Des Moines Register*, January 17, p. 3TV.

———. 1988b. "TV Networks Declare Winners Soon After Caucuses Start." *Des Moines Register*, February 9, p. 7A.

Rogers, David, and James M. Perry. 1988. "Dole Wins Big in Iowa's GOP Caucuses: Tight Democratic Race Led by Gephardt." *Wall Street Journal*, February 9, p. 66.

Runkle, David R., ed. 1989. *Campaign for President: The Managers Look at '88*. Dover, Mass.: Auburn House Publishing Co.

Scheffler, Steve. 1997. Telephone interview with author, February 19. Scheffler is the field director of the Iowa Christian Coalition.

Schneider, William. 1988. "Limiting the Risks." In *National Journal Election '88: A Guide to the Candidates, Issues and Voters*, 2860-62. Washington, D.C.: Times Mirror Magazines.

Schwieder, Dorothy. 1996. *Iowa: The Middle Land*. Ames, Iowa: Iowa State University Press.

Shogan, Robert. 1988. "Iowa Leaves GOP Race in Turmoil." *Los Angeles Times*, February 10, p. 1.

Simon, Paul. 1989. *Winners and Losers: The 1988 Race for the Presidency—One Candidate's Perspective*. New York: Continuum Publishing Co.

Stengel, Richard. 1988. "Pilloried for Pandering." *Time*, February 22, p. 22.

Stirton, Ian. 1997. Telephone interview with author, January 24. Stirton is an employee of the Federal Election Commission.

Taylor, Paul. 1990. *See How They Run: Electing the President in an Age of Mediaocracy.* New York: Alfred A. Knopf.

Television News Index and Abstracts. 1975-76, 1979-80, 1983-84, 1987-88. Nashville, Tenn.: Vanderbilt University.

Time. 1987 and 1988.

Wall Street Journal. 1987.

Washington Post. 1987.

Wills, Garry. 1988. "Robertson and the Reagan Gap." *Time*, February 22, pp. 27-28.

Chapter 9 The 1992 Caucuses: A Favorite Son Emerges

THE CAMPAIGN for the White House had started earlier every presidential cycle. Since the 1970s, candidates for the presidency had faced the prospect of devoting ever longer periods of their lives to the campaign trail. The Iowa campaign began more than two years before the 1988 precinct caucuses, and the candidates of both parties devoted more time and money to Iowa than ever before. Iowa had been institutionalized as the "official" starting point of the "permanent campaign" for the presidency, and its precinct caucus season started earlier, grew larger, and attracted more national attention in every election since 1972.

But things changed in 1992. One year before the scheduled precinct meetings, there was no activity in Iowa and little evidence of a presidential campaign anywhere in the country. *Congressional Quarterly* noted that for the first time since Richard Nixon's election in 1968, "the ides of March has passed in the year preceding the election without at least one officially announced presidential candidate" (Cook 1991a, 764). Four years earlier, seven Republicans and seven Democrats had already campaigned 230 days in Iowa by March 15.

The late start in the 1992 cycle was caused by the Gulf War and the popularity of President George Bush. The threat of armed conflict in the Persian Gulf and the war itself put presidential election politics on hold in the second half of 1990 and the first half of 1991. As the nation learned of Iraq's invasion of Kuwait, and then witnessed the huge American military buildup, the air war, and then the defeat of Saddam Hussein's forces in less than 100 hours, Democratic candidates stayed on the sidelines. The war was only six weeks old when President Bush declared on February 27 that the allies had accomplished their objectives and ordered a halt to hostilities.

Bush had enjoyed sustained popularity in Iowa (Iowa Poll: 1989 and

1990, poll nos. 303 and 307) and with the American public even before the Persian Gulf War, and his rating soared at the time of the conflict. (Gallup Poll approval ratings stayed in the 70 percent range for the first two years of his administration [Cook 1991a, 769].) Following good news about the air war over Iraq in early February, Bush's approval rating reached 82 percent in Iowa (Iowa Poll: 1991, poll no. 312) and 80 percent nationally (Fogarty 1991a, 1A). His national popularity peaked at almost 90 percent in March. In June, three months after the decision to end the fighting and eight months before the 1992 caucuses, Bush's approval rating was still 78 percent in Iowa (Iowa Poll: 1991, poll no. 313) and 75 percent nationally (Fogarty 1991b, 1A).

The president's strong position in the polls and the generally good feeling within the country after the Gulf War led many of the better-known Democrats to forgo a presidential bid in 1992. One by one they decided not to enter or bowed out of the race—Texas Senator Lloyd Bentsen, the 1988 Democratic vice-presidential candidate, New Jersey Senator Bill Bradley, Georgia Senator Sam Nunn, Colorado Congresswoman Patricia Schroeder, former senator and Democratic nominee George McGovern, Congressman Richard Gephardt, West Virginia Senator Jay Rockefeller, Senator Al Gore, Oklahoma Congressman Dave McCurdy, the Reverend Jesse Jackson, and lastly, New York Governor Mario Cuomo on December 20, ninety minutes before the filing deadline for the New Hampshire primary election (Cook 1991f, 3734).

By the time of the Iowa caucuses only Nebraska Senator Bob Kerrey remained from the group of eight individuals listed in a June 1990 Iowa Poll as "people who might seek the Democratic nomination for president in 1992" (Iowa Poll: 1990, poll no. 306). It began to look as if President Bush had frightened off the Democratic first team and would have an easy time of it against whoever emerged.

Another less well-publicized struggle took place in the early 1990s as the Democratic National Committee (DNC) developed its 1992 primary and caucus schedule. Iowa Democrats watched as California legislators considered moving their primary election to the first Tuesday in March from its traditional June date. At an Indianapolis meeting in March 1990, the DNC approved rules changes to the Democratic nominating process that moved the starting date of the primary season forward by one week.

The DNC decision altered the rule that said only Iowa and New Hampshire could hold a caucus or primary election before the second Tuesday in March (*CQ* Apr. 14, 1990, 1148). The change was orchestrated by DNC chair Ron Brown, who told the panel writing the rules, "It is important that a large state crucial to electing a Democratic president weigh in early in the process." Brown's action grew out of the growing perception within the party that the early primary schedule dominated by small states led to the nomination of Democratic candidates who did not fare well in the general election (Cook 1990, 542).

The rules change amounted to an open invitation to California to move its primary from June to March 3. Had that occurred, it would have increased the importance of the California primary and drawn attention away from Iowa and New Hampshire, decreasing their importance as early nominating events. Since California campaigns are media-driven, it might also have changed the dynamic of who chose to enter the presidential sweepstakes. Legislation to move the primary date to March 3 passed both houses of the California legislature but in different forms (*CQ* Apr. 14, 1990, 1148), and a conference committee failed to reconcile the differences. The legislature adjourned in 1991 without taking action, and the California primary remained on the first Tuesday in June. Later, South Dakota decided to hold its caucuses on February 25, which "set off a chain reaction that the DNC was forced to recognize," and New Hampshire and Iowa moved their dates forward a week (Cook 1991b, 2810).

The two states had once again succeeded in preserving their first-in-the-nation positions. (John Roehrick, Iowa Democratic state chair, was never worried that Iowa might lose out to California. He thought it would be difficult for the California legislature to reach a consensus on a new date, and as a member of the national rules committee, Roehrick believed that body would not stop Iowa and New Hampshire from moving their nominating events forward if California changed its primary date. Roehrick also believed that party officials were playing to California because of its importance in the general election. He readily agrees, however, that an early California primary election would have greatly lessened the influence of Iowa and New Hampshire in the presidential nominating process [Roehrick 1997].)

Precaucus Activity

Eventually, Democratic candidates emerged. Former senator Paul Tsongas of Massachusetts made exploratory trips to Iowa in March and April 1991 before announcing his candidacy in Massachusetts, New Hampshire, and Iowa on April 30. Tsongas belonged to a growing group of "neo-liberals" who retained their liberal positions on social issues but wanted to make the Democratic party more sympathetic "to corporate and middle class needs" (Birnbaum 1991, A24). Tsongas had won every election he entered from his first race for city council in 1969 to his U.S. Senate campaign in 1978. He had not sought reelection to the senate in 1984 after doctors discovered cancer of the lymphatic system, but he successfully fought back, enduring chemotherapy and an experimental bone marrow transplant in the process.

On May 1 Tsongas opened an office in Des Moines. The candidate made regular visits to Iowa and spent most of the first two weeks of July in the state getting to know local Democrats. During the summer, Tsongas was the only candidate active in Iowa, but as it became more likely that Iowa Senator Tom Harkin would enter the race, Tsongas began to curtail his efforts in the state. A Tsongas press release on August 26 named a "Midwest Coordinator and Iowa State Director," but for all intents and purposes the Iowa campaign had ended. Tsongas visited Iowa only three times after summer 1991. In December he closed the Iowa campaign office, reopening it for the final days before the caucuses.

Virginia Governor L. Douglas Wilder's one visit to Iowa before he announced his candidacy in Richmond on September 13, 1991, was a two-day trip in June 1990 to campaign for Democratic gubernatorial candidate Don Avenson. His was the earliest visit by a Democrat exploring a presidential run for 1992. Wilder was America's first elected black governor and the "first black since Reconstruction to capture a major statewide office in the South." Like Tsongas, he espoused "neo-liberal" positions. Wilder was fond of saying that "economic development is one of the greatest social equalizers" (Cook 1991c, 3400).

Wilder became a candidate only two days before Harkin. He did not campaign in Iowa and visited the state only twice after his decision to seek the nomination. Wilder was not successful as a fund-raiser and his New Hampshire campaign made little headway. On January 8, less than four months after declaring his candidacy, Wilder was the first Democrat to withdraw from the race (*DMR* Jan. 10, 1992, 4A).

Iowa Senator Tom Harkin declared himself a candidate for the Democratic nomination on September 15. The announcement effectively ended the national importance of the 1992 Iowa precinct caucuses. Harkin launched his candidacy from a farm in Winterset, a few miles from his boyhood home. An unabashed liberal, Harkin took pride in his modest beginnings, his efforts on behalf of the less fortunate, and his close ties to organized labor. He took pleasure in noting that "I've been called a Humphrey Democrat, and to that I say, amen" (Cook 1991d, 3607).

The prospect of a Harkin candidacy had caused Tsongas to forgo an Iowa effort, and it would have the same effect on the other Democratic candidates. Harkin began the abbreviated caucus season as the overwhelming favorite in Iowa, and that was a mixed blessing. He was sure to gain some attention as a "favorite son" candidate in the first-in-the-nation caucuses, but just winning would not be good enough. The pundits expected Harkin to win big, and their task was to define a margin "big enough." *Congressional Quarterly* observed that "Harkin is in a classic no-win situation. A wide margin of victory in his home state is so completely expected that Iowa will be newsworthy only if Harkin loses or wins narrowly" (Cook 1992b, 257).

Two weeks after Harkin announced, Senator Bob Kerrey of Nebraska became the fourth major Democratic candidate to enter the race. He chose a pedestrian mall in Lincoln near the state capitol for his September 30, 1991, announcement of candidacy. Kerrey had won the Medal of Honor in Vietnam and had lost part of his leg in that war. He returned to Nebraska after recuperating from his wounds, embarked upon a successful business career, was elected governor, and while chief executive engaged in a highly publicized romance with actress Debra Winger. Kerrey left the governorship after one term, but soon returned to public life with a victory in a 1988 U.S. Senate race. He was also an unapologetic liberal whose senate voting record, like Harkin's, ranked very high with liberal interest groups. In his senate race, Kerrey had responded "So what?" when his opponent suggested that he would follow the Democratic party line if elected (Cook 1991e, 3651).

Kerrey's only prior activity in Iowa was one day of campaigning for

Democratic candidates in the 1990 election. When he visited Iowa City the day after his Lincoln announcement, Kerrey said he expected to campaign extensively in Iowa (Roos and Fogarty 1991, 2M), but that statement was probably meant for local consumption. His national campaign chair had informed the press in Lincoln the day before that Kerrey would focus on New Hampshire and said that it was not realistic to contest Harkin in his home state (*DMR* Oct. 1, 1991, 7A). Kerrey followed the New Hampshire strategy and appeared in Iowa only once after the Iowa City visit.

Three days after Kerrey, Governor Bill Clinton of Arkansas declared his candidacy at a rally in Little Rock. Clinton had spent his adult life in Arkansas pursuing or serving in public office. He lost his first race for office in 1974, was elected Arkansas attorney general two years later and governor in 1978. He lost his bid for reelection in 1980 but regained the governorship two years later and was reelected three times, most recently to a four-year term in 1990 (Cook 1992a, 60).

Clinton fit between Harkin and Tsongas on the ideological spectrum (for a discussion of the philosophical positions of the 1992 candidates, see Ceaser and Busch 1993, 7). He had "neo-liberal" tendencies and set out to establish a niche as a champion for the American middle class. In his announcement speech he called for a "new covenant" between citizens and their government. Clinton argued that government should create opportunities for its citizens, whose responsibility it was to use them wisely. His proposals included tax breaks for the middle class and reform of the welfare system. He was the only Democratic candidate to support President Bush's use of force in the Persian Gulf (Cook 1992a, 58).

Perhaps the biggest advantage Clinton had was the weakness of his rivals. He effectively became the front-runner after placing second in New Hampshire. Then the primary schedule favored Clinton. Although Super Tuesday was scaled back by about a third from 1988, and a Junior Tuesday primary of several western states was added the week before, there was still a block of southern states voting early in the primary season (Barilleaux and Adkins 1993). Like the other candidates, Clinton conceded Iowa to Harkin. He visited the state only once before becoming a candidate and twice thereafter.

Former California governor Jerry Brown was the final Democrat to enter the race. With his usual flair, Brown began his third run for the presidency from the steps of Independence Hall in Philadelphia on October 21. Brown was the most interesting (or bizarre, depending on your perspective) if not the strongest of the Democratic candidates. Like Clinton, he was a career politician who had spent his adult life seeking or serving in public office. Brown was elected governor in 1974 when Ronald Reagan did not seek a third term. He was reelected in 1978 before losing a senate race to Pete Wilson in 1982. Along the way he ran for the Democratic presidential nomination twice, with his strongest finish a rather distant second to Jimmy Carter in 1976. He was an also-ran in 1980. Known as an unorthodox politician, Brown took varied and sometimes unpopular political positions, and his lifestyle was both free and frugal.

In this campaign Brown promoted finance reform, did not accept contributions larger than $100, advocated abolishing political action committees, and supported term limits for Congress. Few saw his campaign as a serious threat to the others. He had not visited Iowa before but made three trips to the state after becoming a candidate. He did not, however, make an organizational effort in Iowa (Elving 1992).

The Democratic Campaign

The Democratic campaign in Iowa was limited to a substantial effort by Tsongas before Harkin's decision to enter the race, and Harkin's efforts in the final weeks before the caucuses to ensure a respectable turnout for his candidacy. The straw polls and debates were conducted elsewhere, and the candidates and reporters seldom traveled to Iowa. New Hampshire, which had become "the equivalent of a semifinal" after the Iowa caucuses, was again the premier event of the nominating season (Germond and Witcover 1993, 95). After Harkin declared his candidacy, the other five Democrats spent a total of twelve days in Iowa.

The Jefferson-Jackson Day dinner held on November 23 accounted for almost half of the visits. All six Democratic hopefuls attended and spoke at the dinner in Des Moines that had been a major event in previous caucuses. The straw poll at the 1975 dinner had first focused national news on Jimmy Carter's candidacy. But in 1991 the absence of a straw poll, a lack of interest, and a severe fall snowstorm limited attendance (*DMR* Nov. 24, 1991, 1A).

Cartoon by Brian Duffy, © 1992, *Des Moines Register,* reprinted by permission

The Iowa precinct caucuses gained more attention from presidential candidates and the national media every four years until 1992, when Iowa Senator Tom Harkin became a candidate for the Democratic presidential nomination. Much to the chagrin of many Iowans, Harkin's "favorite son" candidacy effectively killed the Iowa caucuses as a national event in 1992.

Harkin's candidacy had a negative impact on central Iowa. There has never been a systematic study of the economic impact of the caucuses, but state economist Harvey Siegelman estimated that the 1988 caucuses generated about $20 million for Iowa, most of it in Des Moines (Chase 1992, 6). The Savery in downtown Des Moines was completely booked for the four weeks prior to the 1988 caucuses, and one television network reserved 125 rooms in the hotel. In 1992 caucus-related business at the Savery was "about 5 percent of what it was in '88" (Brennan 1992, 1A).

Few Democrats were willing to criticize Harkin publicly, but most activists missed the excitement of previous caucuses. The party also suffered revenue losses beyond those of the Jefferson-Jackson Day dinner. An example was the list of party activists and previous caucus attenders that the party makes available to the candidates. The asking price in 1991 was $15,000 but only two copies were sold, one to Kerrey at full price and the other to Brown for $7,500 (Iowa Democratic Party financial reports filed with the Iowa Campaign Finance Disclosure Committee, 1995, 1996). The party also collects donations from those attending caucuses. That effort brought in $92,200 in 1988 but only $29,000 in 1992 (Russett 1997). Ultimately, Senator Harkin raised some money for the party, partly to offset the losses that resulted from his candidacy (Roehrick 1997).

Yet another loser in the diminished caucuses was state chair John Roehrick. His predecessors, David Nagle and Bonnie Campbell, had parlayed their high-profile caucus roles in 1984 and 1988 into the elective offices of congressman and Iowa attorney general, respectively. If Roehrick, who had run against Senator Charles Grassley in 1986, had hoped for a boost for a future campaign, it ended with Harkin's candidacy.

In a June poll, the *Register* asked respondents for their reaction to the loss of the caucus spotlight. The fact that "presidential candidates haven't taken much interest in Iowa this year" was a change "for the better" for 7 percent of Iowans and a change "for the worse" for 37 percent; it did "not make much difference" to 54 percent, and 2 percent were "unsure" (Iowa Poll: 1991, poll no. 313). Anecdotal evidence suggests that most party activists fell into the change "for the worse" category.

The *Register* conducted only two candidate preference polls during the cycle, and Harkin held commanding leads in both, although his percentage share declined between the two polls (Iowa Polls: 1991 and 1992, poll nos. 315 and 316). In late December the *Register* canceled its January presidential debate for lack of candidate interest (*DMR* Dec. 24, 1991, 6M).

The Republican Campaign

President Bush visited Iowa twice and appeared at campaign rallies with Governor Branstad and GOP congressional candidates before the 1990 election, but did not return after the midterm election. Moreover, his very high approval rating began to decline as the economy soured after the Gulf War. At about the time of the caucuses, Bush's approval rating had fallen to 40 percent in Iowa and 39 percent nationally (Fogarty 1992, 1A).

Columnist Pat Buchanan announced his candidacy for the Republican nomination in December and decided to challenge Bush in New Hampshire. He made almost no effort in Iowa.

The Christian Right did not support any candidate in the caucuses. The Iowa Christian Coalition produced an "Iowa Political Handbook 1992" that supplied general political information. The Coalition encouraged people to attend the caucuses and support "pro-family and pro-life" resolutions. According to its leaders, the Iowa Christian Coalition was interested in having an impact on the party platforms (Scheffler 1997). The activities of the Christian Right drew little media attention in Iowa.

The 1992 Precinct Caucuses

Only Senator Harkin, concerned with the need to satisfy media expectations, campaigned in Iowa as the caucuses neared. Party officials estimated that he had captains in about 75 percent of the precincts (Roehrick 1997).

The 1992 candidate activity was in sharp contrast to 1988, when Democrats spent 635 days in Iowa. It was a very limited campaign after Senator Harkin became a candidate, and if attendance at the Jefferson-Jackson Day dinner is subtracted, the five other candidates spent seven days in Iowa during the five months from September 15 to February

10. Only Tsongas campaigned in Iowa extensively, and the great majority of his twenty-seven days in the state were before Harkin entered the race. Brown, Clinton, Kerrey, and Wilder spent five or fewer days in Iowa.

Media Coverage

CBS News aired thirty-one stories on the New Hampshire primary election and only five about the Iowa precinct caucuses in 1992 (*Television News Index and Abstracts* 1991-92). The networks were introspective about the reporting of the 1988 presidential campaign, and Gulf War coverage had taxed their budgets. News president Eric Ober said that CBS hoped to improve its campaign coverage by attempting "to get past the photo opportunities to the issues." He might have added how difficult that was in an era of media consultants. To save money, the four networks experimented with "pool coverage" in New Hampshire, meaning that candidates on the stump were "followed by one network crew instead of four" (Bark 1992, 4TV).

Iowa was not completely ignored on caucus night. An estimated 300 press members and technicians covered the outcome, about one-tenth the number of four years earlier. The networks each planned to cover the results with one reporter and camera crew (Rhein 1991). Only CNN, broadcasting from Harkin's celebration at the Savery Hotel, had live coverage and postcaucus analysis from Iowa.

The Democratic Caucuses

The ongoing debate about the reporting of the Democratic results continued in 1992. The *Register* led a drive to report "pre-viability" results rather than the party's "delegate equivalents" (e.g., Oct. 7, 1991, 12A). State chair John Roehrick was caught between the *Register* and those desiring change in the hope of generating some media interest in a race for second place in the caucuses, on the one hand, and Senator Harkin's desire to retain the traditional counting method, on the other hand. The 15 percent viability requirement would maximize Harkin's delegate strength and limit the delegates for the other candidates who might have some support but not enough to meet the minimum for delegates. There was never any doubt that Harkin would carry the day with the state central committee, and with no competition from NES, the party reported only delegate equivalents (Roehrick 1997). The 1992 caucus results are shown in Table 9.1.

The caucus turnout was approximately twice the attendance at the Iowa State–Colorado basketball game in Ames on the same evening (Hansen 1992). The basketball contest, unlike the caucuses, was televised and may have received only marginally less postgame coverage. The lead story on the Tuesday CBS Evening News was depletion of the earth's ozone layer. Harkin's victory in the Iowa caucuses was reported as part of a story about Tsongas's gains in the New Hampshire opinion polls. NBC led with boxer Mike Tyson's conviction for rape, but about halfway into their evening news aired a lengthy story on Harkin's victory in Iowa. ABC included a small piece on Harkin's victory in Iowa

Table 9.1.   1992 Democratic
precinct caucus results

	State delegate equivalents (%)
Harkin	76.5
Uncommitted	11.9
Tsongas	4.1
Clinton	2.8
Kerrey	2.5
Brown	1.6
Others	0.6
Total	100.0

Source: The state delegate equivalents are the results from 2131 of 2189 precincts (97.4%) as reported in *Congressional Quarterly* on February 15, 1992, p. 371. State party chair John Roehrick estimated that 20,000 to 25,000 people participated, about 4 percent of the 579,875 Democrats registered on February 1, 1992.

before turning to New Hampshire and a story about candidate electability.

The print media gave the caucuses more coverage. Although they were relegated to page 23, two stories in the *New York Times* covered the outcome of the caucuses. They allowed Harkin to set his own expectations—exceeding Jimmy Carter's 59 percent in his 1980 win over Edward Kennedy—but concluded that he, "as expected, overwhelmed his opponents" in the Iowa test. They noted, however, that Harkin "usually ranks near the bottom in popularity in polls in New Hampshire" (Berke 1992).

The *Washington Post* also used the 59 percent figure to evaluate the caucus outcome. Their page 8 story, like that in the *Times*, called his margin of victory "overwhelming" and then downplayed its significance (Walsh 1992). *Congressional Quarterly* also used the term "overwhelming" to describe Harkin's Iowa victory but reported that it was Tsongas, not Harkin, who was advancing in the opinion polls in New Hampshire (Cook 1992c, 371).

Only the *Register* made Harkin's "huge victory" a major front-page story (Feb. 11, 1992). Indeed, as predicted, the caucuses proved to be "a classic no-win situation" for Harkin. His overwhelming victory was big news only in Iowa. Had he lost or not met the expectations of the press, it would have been a national story. Harkin gained no appreciable boost from the victory. He finished fourth in New Hampshire and dropped out of the race on March 9 after finishing poorly in South Carolina.

The Republican Caucuses

The decision not to hold a straw poll generated some controversy regarding the GOP caucuses. The press believed that Iowa Republicans made the decision to protect President Bush from possible embarrassment by challenger Pat Buchanan. *Newsweek,* for example, reported that "critics say" that Iowa Republicans "under pressure from the national committee" decided not to hold a straw poll (Jan. 13, 1992).

Randy Enright, executive director of the state party, said that was not the case. At the August 1991 state central committee meeting, a "call to convention" was written that did not include a straw poll due to the absence of a Republican contest in Iowa. At the December 1991 central committee meeting, the "call to convention" was not amended since Buchanan did not intend to campaign in Iowa. According to Enright, Buchanan never requested a straw poll at the caucuses. The party did not prepare a press package for the 1992 caucuses. The Iowa Republican party headquarters was open caucus night (Enright 1992).

After Iowa, Tsongas had his fifteen minutes of fame when he won in New Hampshire, but after that it was all Clinton. New Hampshire also shocked Bush when Buchanan won 37 percent of the vote, but by mid-March both Bush and Clinton were well on their way to the nominations.

The Impact of the 1992 Caucuses

Senator Harkin's candidacy effectively eliminated any national influence of the Iowa precinct caucuses in 1992. There was concern among Iowa political activists that the early demise of the 1988 caucus winners, Gephardt and Dole, after Iowa, and Harkin's "favorite son" candidacy in 1992 might permanently damage the reputation of the caucuses as an early presidential testing ground and hurt Iowa's chances for retaining its first-in-the-nation status (Roos and Howard 1992, 1A). The fact that some 300 reporters came to Iowa for the uncontested caucuses on February 12 might have eased the fears of party activists. Their concern was put to rest when GOP candidates began visiting the state in 1993, three years before the 1996 presidential election.

The 1992 precinct caucuses gave Harkin a platform from which to launch his presidential bid but did not enhance his candidacy. Although favorite son status virtually assured Harkin a win in Iowa, there was little to be gained from the victory. On the negative side, Harkin was forced to contest Iowa to ensure the expected big win. Although he might have benefited by spending more time and money in New Hampshire, he had no choice. Harkin's big victory in Iowa was barely noticed outside the state and did not give him a boost in New Hampshire. The irony of the 1992 precinct caucuses is that they would have been a national media event only if Harkin had failed to meet expectations. Since he met the expectations of the pundits, Iowa had no impact on the 1992 Democratic race.

References

Barilleaux, Ryan J., and Randall E. Adkins. 1993. "The Nominations: Process and Patterns." In *The Elections of 1992*, edited by Michael Nelson, 21-56. Washington, D.C.: CQ Press.

Bark, Ed. 1992. "Networks Promise to Improve Campaign Coverage." *Des Moines Register*, February 16, p. 4TV.

Berke, Richard L. 1992. "Harkin Dominates State's Caucuses." *New York Times*, February 11, p. A23.

Birnbaum, Jeffrey H. 1991. "For Paul Tsongas, a Miraculous Survival Means an Obligation, 'a Mission' to Seek the Presidency." *Wall Street Journal*, October 15, p. A24.

Brennan, Joe. 1992. "Iowans Feeling Loss of Election Spotlight." *Omaha World Herald*, February 2, p. 1A.

Ceaser, James, and Andrew Busch. 1993. *Upside Down and Inside Out: The 1992 Elections and American Politics.* Lanham, Md.: Rowman & Littlefield.

Chase, Brett. 1992. "Caucuses Not Economic Boost They Once Were." *Business Record*, January 20-26, p. 6.

Congressional Quarterly Weekly Report. 1990. April 14, pp. 1148-49.

Cook, Rhodes. 1990. "Bid to Move Primary to March Draws Wary GOP Response." *Congressional Quarterly*, February 17, p. 542.

———. 1991a. "Late Start for '92 May Signal Trend to Shorter Campaigns." *Congressional Quarterly*, March 23, pp. 764-70.

———. 1991b. "Candidates' Fates Take Shape with Primary Calendar." *Congressional Quarterly*, September 28, pp. 2810-11.

———. 1991c. "Wilder Campaigns on Message of Fiscal Responsibility." *Congressional Quarterly*, November 16, pp. 3400-05.

———. 1991d. " 'American Dream' Personified, Harkin Hits Populist Trail." *Congressional Quarterly*, December 7, pp. 3607-13.

———. 1991e. "Story of Heroism and Romance Fuels Great Expectations." *Congressional Quarterly*, December 14, pp. 3650-55.

———. 1991f. "Cuomo Says 'No' to Candidacy at Last Possible Moment." *Congressional Quarterly*, December 21, pp. 3734-36.

———. 1992a. "Arkansan Travels Well Nationally As Campaign Heads for Test." *Congressional Quarterly*, January 11, pp. 58-65.

———. 1992b. "Iowa Caucuses Lose Limelight As Nominating Season Opens." *Congressional Quarterly*, February 1, pp. 257-58.

———. 1992c. "Tsongas Passes Clinton in N.H.; Harkin Wins in Iowa Caucuses." *Congressional Quarterly*, February 15, pp. 371-72.

Des Moines Register. 1991 and 1992.

Elving, Ronald D. 1992. "Brown Is Unlikely Carrier of a Timely Message." *Congressional Quarterly*, January 18, pp. 126-32.

Enright, Randy. 1992. Telephone interview with author, February 25. Enright was the executive director of the Republican Party of Iowa from 1989 to 1992.

Fogarty, Thomas A. 1991a. "Poll: War Earns Bush Backing of 82% in Iowa." *Des Moines Register,* February 17, p. 1A.

———. 1991b. "Iowans: Bush Ended Iraq War at Right Time." *Des Moines Register,* June 24, p. 1A.

———. 1992. "Bush's Popularity Hits Low in Iowa Poll." *Des Moines Register,* March 3, p. 1A.

Germond, Jack W., and Jules Witcover. 1993. *Mad As Hell.* New York: Warner Books.

Hansen, Marc. 1992. "Caucus or Basketball Game? Survey Shows No Contest." *Des Moines Register,* February 12, p. 3T.

Iowa Campaign Finance Disclosure Committee. 1995 and 1996. Precinct Caucus Candidate Reports, 1995 and 1996.

Iowa Poll. 1989-92. Vols. for 1989 through 1992. Des Moines: Des Moines Register and Tribune Company.

Newsweek. 1992.

Rhein, David. 1991. "Networks Give Iowa Caucuses Cold Shoulder." *Des Moines Register,* January 19, p. 3TV.

Roehrick, John. 1997. Interview with author, March 19. Roehrick was the state chair of the Iowa Democratic Party from 1989 to 1993.

Roos, Jonathan, and Thomas A. Fogarty. 1991. "Kerrey Tells Rally: I Really Don't Expect to Win Iowa." *Des Moines Register,* October 2, p. 2M.

Roos, Jonathan, and Phoebe Wall Howard. 1992. "Caucuses Eyeing Comeback in '96." *Des Moines Register,* February 12, p. 1A.

Russett, Darlene. 1997. Telephone interview with author, March 20. Russett is the comptroller for the Iowa Democratic Party.

Scheffler, Steve. 1997. Telephone interview with author, February 19. Scheffler is the field director of the Iowa Christian Coalition.

Television News Index and Abstracts. 1991-92. Nashville, Tenn.: Vanderbilt University.

Walsh, Edward. 1992. "Harkin Wins Overwhelmingly in Iowa's Precinct Caucuses." *Washington Post,* February 11, p. A8.

Chapter 10 The 1996 Caucuses: Back in the Limelight

REPUBLICANS ENTERED the presidential primary and caucus season with renewed optimism as a result of their dramatic gains in the 1994 congressional elections. Newt Gingrich, the outspoken Speaker of the House of Representatives, had successfully "nationalized" the congressional elections around "The Contract with America." The Republicans gained control of both houses of Congress and had high hopes of reclaiming the White House from President Clinton.

In the 1994 Iowa elections, the Republican margin in the House increased to 64-to-36, a net gain of thirteen seats. Few incumbent Democrats lost, but Republicans won the vast majority of open seats, several in districts where Democrats enjoyed registration edges. Governor Terry Branstad easily won reelection, defeating Democratic Attorney General Bonnie Campbell 58 to 42 percent. The Democrats retained the state senate by a 27-to-23 margin. All five congressional seats went to the Republicans, including Greg Ganske's surprise victory over thirty-six-year Democratic Congressman Neal Smith. (In 1996 Republicans gained control of the Iowa Senate, held the House but by a smaller margin, and lost one U.S. House seat to the Democrats.)

The economic climate in Iowa had changed as well. By the time of the 1996 caucus cycle, the farm crisis had passed and the Iowa economy was stronger. Just before the caucuses, Governor Branstad projected state revenue growth at 4.9 percent in fiscal year 1996 (July 1, 1995 to June 30, 1996) and a year-end balance of over $500 million. (Data are from the governor's 1998/1999 Program and Budget Summary. The year-end balance was actually $657 million for fiscal year 1996 and was estimated to be $823 million for fiscal year 1997 [Tegeler 1997].) Farmers were doing better as crop and land prices rose. Unemployment had fallen to about 3.5 percent.

Although the federal budget and taxes remained a concern, Iowans focused on noneconomic issues. The divorce rate, the number of children born out of wedlock, the breakdown of the traditional family, and violent crime, much of it related to illegal drugs, seemed to be making Iowa a less stable and safe place to live. Also, during the 1980s, state leaders had turned to gambling as a new source of tax revenue, and by the mid-1990s a new industry had developed in the state. The gambling industry now included a state lottery, pari-mutuel betting at horse and dog tracks, and casinos on riverboats and on Native American lands, and in 1995 the state's horse and dog tracks added slot-machine casinos (Schwieder 1996, 320).

The moral and social climate was on the minds of Iowans in the mid-1990s. Social conservatives and the Christian Right had extended their influence, and their spirits were buoyed by successes in the 1988 Republican caucuses and in state and local elections. As they campaigned in Iowa, GOP candidates expounded a social agenda ranging from "family values" and abortion to drugs and crime. This social agenda, which preoccupied most of the nation, would take some of the uniqueness out of the Iowa campaign. The candidates discussed essentially the same social issues in Iowa and New Hampshire.

The media focused on the GOP race since President Clinton was unchallenged for renomination. Republicans did not have rules governing the beginning or the length of the primary and caucus calendar. But the compression started by the Democratic National Committee's decision in 1982 to define a thirteen-week primary and caucus season (with exceptions for Iowa and New Hampshire), and exacerbated by the southern states' decision to hold a "Super Tuesday" primary in 1988, continued. Because most state parties hold their primary events on the same date, Democratic rules influence Republican nominating schedules.

A number of states held nominating events earlier in the 1996 season. Thirty-four states and territories, including many of the largest, held caucuses and primaries by the end of March that selected 1270 of the 1990 delegates to the San Diego convention (63.8%) (*New York Times* Feb. 11, 1996, A25). In addition, many of the states were grouped in regional clusters, so instead of one Super Tuesday, there were multiple primaries every Tuesday in March. It was a far more compressed schedule, and to compete successfully, candidates had to raise huge sums of money, contest Iowa and New Hampshire, and attempt to organize a national campaign at the same time. Doing well early was important, as the first task was to survive Iowa and New Hampshire.

The unanswered question in Iowa was how the outcomes of the 1988 and 1992 caucuses would affect the 1996 event. The candidates and media had invested heavily in contesting and covering the 1988 precinct caucuses, but Bob Dole and Dick Gephardt, the winners, had faded rapidly thereafter. And George Bush and Michael Dukakis, the eventual nominees, were third-place finishers in Iowa, raising doubts about the value of the state as a predictor. Tom Harkin's favorite son candidacy ended the state's influence in the 1992 nominating process.

On the Democratic side, would President Clinton pay any attention to Iowa during the caucus season? Unchallenged incumbent presidents had campaigned little in Iowa during previous caucuses. President Reagan in 1984, for example, did not visit Iowa until the day of the caucuses for appearances in Waterloo and Des Moines. In the most recent cycle, President Bush did not visit after the 1990 election.

It did not take long, however, to determine that the candidates were treating Iowa's February 12 caucuses as the "official" kickoff of the primary and caucus season. They started coming to the state within months after President Clinton's inauguration in 1993. (Some candidates, Gramm for example, had made periodic visits to Iowa for years; I do not discuss visits that took place before January 20, 1993— Clinton's inauguration.)

The Iowa GOP was prepared to make as much out of the caucuses as possible, both in terms of publicity and income for the state party. The Greater Des Moines Chamber of Commerce and the Iowa Department of Economic Development entered into a cooperative effort to use the caucuses to promote Iowa. Eventually, two public relations firms, CMF&Z and Schreurs & Associates, were hired to manage the 1996 caucus project and to promote stories about economic development opportunities in Iowa. They hoped to dispel Iowa's limited image as an agricultural state and promote Iowa as a place for business development and growth. The Iowa Democrats, though playing a secondary role, would also attempt to make the most of the caucus opportunity.

Precaucus Activity

The Republican Campaign

An *Atlantic Monthly* article by David Frum titled "The Elite Primary" is an interesting essay about the real "first-in-the-nation" contest, which Frum asserts "is a shadowy national competition to raise money, sign up prominent supporters, and impress the media in the year preceding the election year" (1995, p. 24). In two research papers, Emmett Buell, Jr., examines systematically the concept of an elite or "invisible primary," first described by Arthur Hadley in 1976. Buell collected data on fund-raising, early standing in the national polls, success in straw polls, and television news coverage of the candidates to demonstrate that an extended "invisible primary" between presidential campaigns winnows out many presidential aspirants before a single vote is cast in a caucus or primary election (1996a).

Buell asserts that this invisible primary winnowed out former secretary of education and "drug czar" William Bennett, former congressman and defense secretary Dick Cheney, former congressman and secretary of housing and urban development Jack Kemp, former vice-president Dan Quayle, and other Republican aspirants in the "run-up" to the 1996 caucuses and primary elections. The explanations for their decisions not to run support Buell's thesis that "a candidate who fails to raise serious money, rise in the polls, and get his candidacy reported by the national news media is much less likely to win the nomination" (Buell 1996b, 7). Both Kemp and Quayle cited the need to raise $20 million for the front-loaded presidential contest when they announced their decisions not to run. Quayle added "family-related" reasons for not running (Seib 1995a, A10).

Quayle had visited Des Moines on February 6, 1995, three days before his announcement that he would not be a candidate. In meetings with party activists he had found little support or discovered that activists who might have supported him had already taken sides. A Gramm supporter who met with Quayle during the visit said that he and his conservative friends liked Quayle but thought he was "too damaged from his vice-presidential days to overcome the many negative images he carried" (Robinson 1995).

On June 24, 1994, the Republican Party of Iowa held a "Star-

Spangled Preview" in Des Moines in conjunction with their state convention the next day. Party leaders, hoping to raise funds and stimulate interest in the 1996 presidential caucuses, included a straw poll as part of the event. Tickets cost twenty-five dollars and according to party officials, over 1800 were sold.

The program began at 7:30 P.M. with Governor Branstad welcoming the audience before live television coverage by C-SPAN. The seven featured guests—Lamar Alexander, Pat Buchanan, Dick Cheney, Phil Gramm, Thomas Kean, Lynn Martin, and Arlen Specter—each spoke for about ten minutes. Party chair Richard Schwarm announced the poll results to a sparse crowd of reporters and a few lingering participants at about 10:15. The 1349 votes were cast as follows: Bob Dole 356, Lamar Alexander 205, Phil Gramm 200, Jack Kemp 156, Dick Cheney 130, Dan Quayle 81, Pat Buchanan 69, William Bennett 59, Lynn Martin 20, Colin Powell 13, James Baker 9, Howard Baker 8, Robert Dornan 6, Arlen Specter 6, John Engler 5, Newt Gingrich 5, Tommy Thompson 3, William Weld 3, Thomas Kean 2, Christine Whitman 2, Pete du Pont 1, Pete Wilson 1, and "none of the above" 8 (1 vote was apparently missed, as the numbers add up to 1348). The *Washington Post* made a tongue-in-cheek declaration that "it's official—the Republicans have a front-runner, sort of, for the party's 1996 presidential nomination" (Walsh 1994, A6).

The frequent visits of Republican presidential hopefuls that followed indicated that Iowa would be important and that a traditional caucus race would be waged in the state. Several potential candidates helped raise funds and campaigned extensively for Iowa candidates in the off-year election (by the November 1994 election, GOP candidates had spent seventy days in Iowa). Three showed up immediately after the election—Dole and Gramm to gloat, and Specter to "explore" a run for the presidential nomination.

Although the "invisible primary" eliminated several well-known Republicans, the field grew and at one time or another during the campaign eleven individuals were candidates for the Republican nomination. The 1996 Iowa race began as "Bob Dole versus the field." Much like Walter Mondale in 1984, Dole portrayed himself as Iowa's third senator. He was a well-respected neighbor, enjoying high name recognition among the party faithful and strong support among

Iowa's elected officials. Dole used his Kansas background to claim a special understanding of Iowans, farm issues, and agribusiness. He had won the 1988 Iowa Republican caucus, visited the state frequently, was well financed, and enjoyed an early organizational edge in Iowa. Political pundits concluded that Iowa was "Dole's state to lose and that his main competition comes from the standard he set in 1988," when he won 37 percent of the caucus vote (*CQ* Aug. 19, 1995, 2496). There were, however, nagging questions about his age and the lack of passion in his businesslike campaign.

With good reason for optimism, Dole made his first postinaugural campaign visit to Iowa on April 17, 1993. He opened a temporary office funded by his political action committee around June 1, 1994, a one-person operation in Des Moines that worked to maintain a Dole presence by arranging appearances with local GOP candidates. By the time of the November 1994 election, Dole had campaigned ten days in the state and had established himself as the Iowa front-runner largely on the basis of his winning performance in the 1988 caucuses.

Dole closed the campaign office after the first of the year but reopened it as the "Dole for President" office with a staff of six on May 1, 1995 (Gibbs June 16, 1995). Dole conducted a "traditional Iowa campaign"; that is, he followed the caucus campaign plan developed by Jimmy Carter in 1976 that had become the blueprint for presidential campaigns in Iowa. Dole initiated his Iowa campaign early, built a statewide organization, began identifying potential caucus supporters, and spent many days campaigning in the state.

By mid-July Dole had campaigned eighteen days in Iowa, his staff had grown to eight, and the office was running a large field operation and preparing for the straw poll at the Ames "Caucus Kickoff '96" on August 19. The 1987 Ames event had alerted the nation to Pat Robertson's strength in Iowa, and the Dole team believed that political pundits would use the 1995 poll to make an early assessment of the relative strength of the candidates in Iowa. The staff planned to use the Ames poll as a dry run for turning out their caucus supporters and thought they had prepared well to accomplish their goal of winning the poll (Gibbs July 25, 1995).

Senator Phil Gramm of Texas was another early entrant in the caucus campaign. He first visited Iowa during the 1996 cycle on April 14, 1993. Many of the Iowa and national press thought Gramm was Dole's principal challenger in Iowa and perhaps in the country. Gramm was in Iowa often and, like Dole, campaigned for candidates in the off-year election. By the November election, he had spent fifteen days in the state. Gramm worked hard to establish his credentials among likely caucus attenders, particularly the more conservative elements of the party. He was a fiscal conservative, and he reminded Iowans frequently of the Gramm/Rudman/Hollings Bill. Like most of the candidates in Iowa, he took conservative stands on abortion, illegal immigration, affirmative action, and crime, and spoke out against gun control. Gramm's mannerisms and heavy southern drawl probably did not help him in the Midwest and Iowa. He targeted straw polls everywhere and won six of the eleven, but although he received some national media attention, it was not always positive (Buell 1996b, table 4).

Bob Haus, a Dole supporter in 1988, opened a temporary Gramm office in his home on December 15, 1994. The campaign operated with volunteer help until Gramm's candidacy announcement on February 24; two paid field staffers were added shortly thereafter, and a campaign headquarters opened in Des Moines on April 6 (Haus July 17, 1995). The staff grew to six by mid-June and eleven by late July. Haus and his staff worked diligently to put together a statewide organization and, like Dole, they ran a traditional caucus campaign with frequent visits by the candidate. By mid-July Gramm had spent thirty-one days campaigning in Iowa. He too hoped for a large turnout of supporters at the August Ames straw poll. Haus believed that Gramm was in a "solid second position in Iowa" and hoped to do "very well" in the Ames straw poll (Haus July 25, 1995).

Lamar Alexander was the third early candidate to visit Iowa. His first Iowa trip, on May 8, 1993, came a few weeks after the initial Gramm and Dole visits. Even though he had spent many years in the federal government—first as a summer intern in Robert F. Kennedy's Justice Department, later in Senator Howard Baker's senate office, then as a junior aide in the Nixon White House, and finally, after serving as governor of Tennessee and president of the University of Tennessee, as secretary of education for President Bush from 1991 to 1993—Alexander attempted to exploit the anti-Washington feeling that was emerging in Iowa and around the country in 1993-94 by claiming to be a Washington outsider running against a field composed primarily of Beltway insiders (Seib 1995b, A1).

Alexander was relatively unknown in Iowa. He persuaded Dick Redman, a longtime Iowa GOP activist, to lead his campaign in the state. When Alexander began campaigning in Iowa in 1993, he and Redman made their way around the state, meeting party activists. Those early sojourns were solitary affairs with little fanfare and no media coverage (Redman 1996). But Alexander campaigned frequently in Iowa and by the 1994 election had spent twenty-two days in the state. He attempted to position himself as a younger alternative to Bob Dole and worked hard to establish his conservative credentials in a year when almost everyone in the field claimed to be a conservative.

Alexander was the first to open a permanent Iowa campaign headquarters. Five employees were on the job in the Des Moines office on February 1, 1995, almost a month before Alexander's formal announcement of candidacy on February 28 in his hometown of Maryville, Tennessee. Alexander also conducted a "traditional Iowa campaign." Although he had already spent twenty-eight days in the state by May 8, 1995, Alexander was not satisfied with his low levels of name recognition in Iowa and decided to buy summer television ads to increase Iowans' awareness of his candidacy (Humeston June 19, 1995). Babbitt had tried the same strategy in 1987 with little success. Alexander's attempt suffered a similar fate, as most Iowans paid little attention to politics and political ads during the 1995 summer months.

Alexander faced an uphill struggle in competing with Buchanan, Gramm, and Alan Keyes, who had better-established conservative credentials, for the support of social and Christian conservatives in Iowa. He began the campaign with a "cut their pay and send them home" message, but the GOP's sweep of Congress in 1994 made that argument inappropriate, and he never replaced it with a winning theme. As the campaign progressed, Alexander was able to persuade some that he was a younger alternative to Dole, but he failed to clearly define a niche for himself among Iowa caucus attenders.

Pat Buchanan, TV commentator, former speechwriter for presidents Nixon and Ford, and communications director for President Reagan, had bypassed Iowa during his 1992 challenge to President George Bush. He visited Iowa on June 24 and 25, 1994, to explore another run for the GOP nomination. After participating in the "Star-Spangled Preview" and visiting with Republicans attending the state convention, Buchanan did not return to the state until he announced his candidacy for the nomination in New Hampshire and Iowa on March 20, 1995.

Known as an uncompromising and sometimes strident champion of conservative ideas, Buchanan geared his campaign to the social conservatives and the Christian Right in Iowa with a social agenda that he claimed was the most conservative of all the candidates. Buchanan was against abortion, illegal immigration, affirmative action, international trade agreements, and criminal behavior, and he portrayed himself as "a crusader in a 'cultural war' against lewdness and violence in the media, in music and in museums that 'welcome exhibits that mock our patriotism and our faith'" (*DMR* Mar. 21, 1995, 5A). For good measure, he played to the sense of economic insecurity felt by some Americans with his attacks on the "New World Order," the North American Free Trade Agreement (NAFTA), the General Agreement on Tariffs and Trade (GATT), and the Mexican economic bailout (Klein 1995, 45). His message of social conservatism and economic populism gained Buchanan good crowds and press attention in Iowa. Although Dole was his foil, Buchanan's struggle for the hearts and minds of the most conservative of Iowans was with Gramm and Keyes.

Once in the race, Buchanan campaigned frequently in Iowa. He hired his first Iowa staff (one full-time and two part-time workers) in May and opened a campaign office in Des Moines on June 12, 1995. By mid-July, Buchanan had campaigned eighteen days in the state, although his state headquarters continued to be a modest operation with two full-time and several part-time and volunteer staff (Roepke 1995).

Social conservatives in the state welcomed Buchanan and attended his campaign events in large numbers. They were more vocal and passionate about the candidate than the supporters of the other candidates, with the possible exception of Keyes. With a modest budget and staff, Buchanan had the ability "to live off the land." His campaign in Iowa relied heavily on volunteers, conservative groups, and free radio and TV. Buchanan was readily available for interviews with local radio stations and conducted as many as two dozen in a day (Roepke 1996).

Senator Arlen Specter of Pennsylvania tended to alienate social conservatives in Iowa. His pro-choice position on abortion and support for affirmative action programs made him the oddball in the Iowa campaign. It is likely that early on, Specter thought he was the one moderate who might emerge in a contest dominated by competing conservatives. But his campaign made little progress, and his positions on the issues consistently led to confrontations with the more conservative elements of the party.

Specter first visited Iowa on April 2, 1994, to meet with local GOP activists, and he returned to the state on three other occasions before the November election. He announced his candidacy for the Republican nomination in Washington, D.C., on March 30, 1995, and six weeks later opened an Iowa office in Des Moines. He hired a part-time office manager and a full-time Iowa coordinator. No additional employees were added during the campaign.

Specter described himself as a "pro-choice centrist" and expressed his commitment to the "big tent" concept of the Republican party. He worried that the party had become narrow, with the far right exerting too much influence, which he thought hurt the party's chances for recapturing the presidency in 1996 (Wall Howard 1994, 5M). He attracted the support of some of Iowa's leading GOP moderates, but in the year of the conservative, they were few and far between.

At forums beginning with the "Star-Spangled Preview" in June 1994, he bantered with members of the audiences, and those who opposed his views booed him. He seemed to relish these encounters, but they won him little support. Although he had appeared in Iowa eighteen days by mid-July, his Iowa organization was modest. As the campaign progressed, Specter found it increasingly difficult to raise funds as his Iowa campaign made few inroads. It was not surprising that Specter ended his campaign early with an announcement on CNN's "Larry King Live" show on November 21 that he was "suspending" his candidacy.

Senator Richard Lugar of Indiana may have been too nice a person to run for president. He was courteous, seldom if ever spoke ill of the other GOP candidates, and conducted his campaign on a high plane. He entered the caucus contest relatively late, making his first visit to Iowa on April 1, 1995. Lugar opted for a slightly different campaign approach in Iowa. He hired Jeanette Schmett and Mike Day, co-owners of the public relations firm JS/Day & Associates in Des Moines, to manage his Iowa precinct caucus effort. They opened a Des Moines headquarters around May 1, 1995, two months after Lugar had unofficially announced his candidacy on "Larry King Live." Richard Schwarm, former GOP state chair, served as Iowa campaign chair.

The Iowa office was a modest operation staffed by Schmett and Day, who were not experienced political operatives, and a secretary, with volunteers helping out in the evenings. Lugar struggled in Iowa to establish his conservative credentials and to find a niche for his campaign. His underfunded, limited organization experienced little success. Lugar was not able to compete with Dole, Gramm, and Alexander in Iowa. But by mid-July, Lugar had campaigned sixteen days in the state, and Day believed the campaign was making inroads with middle-of-the-road GOP voters. They hoped to do well in the Ames poll even though Day indicated their budget for the event was quite modest (Day 1995).

Maurice (Morry) Taylor, president and chief executive officer of Titan Wheel International, Inc., of Quincy, Illinois, was a man with a mission. He hoped to persuade voters that government could and should be run like a business, and that he, a successful businessperson, was just the person to lead such a renaissance. Taylor's campaign was self-financed and unorthodox. He hired a staff and opened a national campaign headquarters in late April 1995 in the third-floor offices of his Titan Tire Co. on Des Moines' east side.

National campaign manager Bill Kenyon led a "traditional Iowa campaign" but used unorthodox methods to try to connect Taylor to a constituency. Taylor as a dark-horse candidate was willing to take chances that other candidates were not. The campaign leased six thirty-foot Airstream recreational vehicles with red, white, and blue "Morry Taylor for President" logos on each and drove them in a long caravan from town to town (and later to New Hampshire and other states). They went to great lengths to get Taylor into the news. For example, when Speaker of the House Newt Gingrich spoke at a $100-a-plate breakfast for Congressman Greg Ganske at the Des Moines Marriott Hotel in July, the six Taylor vehicles circled and then parked around the Marriott in an attempt to gain national attention and to impress those attending the breakfast. His staff enjoyed the freedom Taylor gave them to innovate and to have fun running a presidential campaign (Stanhope Dec. 12, 1995).

Taylor, an outspoken and colorful business executive, believed that he had a message about running government in a businesslike fashion and thought that he was the only candidate who understood budget numbers and could read a balance sheet (Stanhope Dec. 12, 1995). He also was very skeptical about government regulation and before his candidacy had engaged in a running battle with the Environmental Protection Agency.

Alan Keyes, a Harvard Ph.D., nationally syndicated radio talk show host in Baltimore, and former ambassador to the United Nations Economic and Social Council, also ran an unorthodox campaign for the nomination. Keyes had little money and few professional staffers, but with volunteers and a passion matched only by Buchanan, he became a conservative force in the Iowa precinct caucuses. Keyes visited Iowa for the first time on June 4, 1995. He was represented in Iowa by volunteer Chris Hurley, a Fayette homemaker, until a Des Moines office staffed by volunteers was opened in early August 1995. It was November before a paid staffer was working in the Des Moines office. A second Keyes staffer spent some time in Iowa (Jackson 1995).

Few thought a black candidate could do well in a state with a limited minority population, but Keyes was a powerful speaker with a message of family and God that resonated well with conservatives and particularly with the Christian Right in Iowa. Every Keyes speech sounded like a sermon, and the message varied little from audience to audience: the breakdown of the two-parent family had weakened the moral and social fabric of America, and there was an overriding need to get government and its policies out of family life so that people might once again become self-reliant and strong. He was against abortion, gay rights, and affirmative action. As the campaign progressed, Keyes was hurt by the perception that he could not win the nomination, and ultimately by Buchanan, who some thought was a more viable candidate (Hurley 1996).

California Congressman Bob Dornan declared his candidacy for the GOP nomination at the National Law Enforcement Officers Memorial in Washington, D.C., on April 13, 1995. An outspoken conservative "renowned in Congress for his impassioned attacks on President Clinton, abortion, and homosexuality," Dornan stated that he sought the presidency to stop "the moral decay that is rotting the heart and soul of our country" (*DMR* Apr. 14, 1995, 3A). Dornan was not a significant force in Iowa. He spent only six days in the state and was not an active campaigner, but at candidate forums and other gatherings, he berated Senator Tom Harkin and President Bill Clinton at every opportunity.

California Governor Pete Wilson made a short, three-month run for the GOP nomination in Iowa. Wilson and his wife, Gayle, dedicated an Iowa campaign office in Des Moines on June 19, 1995, with much fanfare. With a small group of supporters and a rather large contingent of California press, Wilson portrayed himself as an experienced executive and "can do" candidate who as president would make things happen. Wilson's effectiveness as a speaker was hampered by a vocal cord problem that reduced his voice to a whisper. The governor announced his Iowa leadership team, but it was very short on well-known Iowa Republicans (author's notes from the event).

Wilson's fellow Californians Ronald Reagan in 1980, Jerry Brown in 1980 and 1992, and Alan Cranston in 1984 had not fared well in the Iowa caucuses, and Wilson would suffer a similar fate. Wilson got a late start in a state process that traditionally requires a strong organization and a great deal of candidate time. As a conservative in the year of the conservative, he did not have a message that distinguished him from the pack. As a sitting governor tied to his own budget battles in California, he had little time to spend in Iowa, and his late-starting, weakly organized Iowa campaign made little headway. Wilson's six visits to Iowa included ten days in the state during his three-month campaign. With mounting campaign debts, he terminated his Iowa campaign on September 11, and eighteen days later was the first formally declared candidate to drop out of the GOP race (*Newsweek* Oct. 9, 1995, 40).

On September 22, 1995, shortly after Wilson's departure, magazine publisher Malcolm (Steve) Forbes, Jr., held a news conference in Washington, D.C., to announce that he was entering the race for the Republican presidential nomination. A *Newsweek* article reported that "supply-side economics thinkers" led by Jude Wanniski approached Forbes and urged him to seek the GOP nomination after former congressman Jack Kemp and Massachusetts Governor William Weld, who were sympathetic to their ideas, "decided not to run." After initial reservations, Forbes warmed to the idea of a campaign based on the supply-side ideals of "low taxes" and "hard money" (Fineman 1995, 47).

Forbes said that he would conduct a self-financed, multimillion-dollar campaign with tax reform as the centerpiece. He vowed to replace "the 7-million-word federal tax code with a flat 17 percent income tax rate" and to "tie the nation's currency to the gold standard to insure stability" (Powell 1995, 5A). He visited Iowa four days later and reiterated his call for a flat tax and a return to the gold standard. Fully two months after Wilson ended his Iowa campaign and a week before Specter would suspend his efforts, Forbes was present for the November 15 grand opening of his Des Moines campaign headquarters.

It is doubtful that anyone foresaw the impact that Forbes would have on the presidential race. Judged on the basis of traditional Iowa precinct caucus campaigns, Forbes's candidacy was a long shot because of his late entry into the contest. With little time and a very modest organization, Forbes embarked on a radio and TV campaign of a magnitude not witnessed before in the state. His media campaign affected the strategies of the other candidates and dramatically altered the 1996 presidential campaign in Iowa.

As the campaign developed, the candidates and their staffs, the press, party officials, and political pundits engaged in the time-honored practice of handicapping the presidential race. In Iowa, the horse race receives great attention. Political pundits use several indicators to gauge the odds, including the perceived strength of the candidates' Iowa campaign organizations, levels of attendance at candidate appearances in the state and the reactions of those attending, fundraising success, scientific polls, and straw polls held at political events. Scientific polls and straw polls tend to receive the most attention.

The *Register*'s Iowa Poll under the direction of Sharon Pilmer conducted four surveys of likely 1996 GOP precinct caucus attenders over a ten-month period, and the results were widely reported. Participants randomly selected from the statewide list of registered Republicans were interviewed by phone. A screening question asked respondents whether they were "very likely," "fairly likely," "just somewhat likely," or "not at all likely" to attend a caucus, and the interviews were continued only with respondents "very" or "fairly likely" to attend. According to Pilmer, 7760 names were used to get to the final 628 respondents in the fourth poll (Feb. 12, 1996).

The first Iowa Poll was conducted May 6-10, 1995, perhaps too early for a reliable test of candidate strength. Although Dole, Gramm, and Alexander had been visiting for two years, most of the candidates were not very well known in Iowa, and the results bear that out. The percentages of support registered for each candidate in the sample were:

Dole 57, Gramm 11, Buchanan 6, Alexander 2, Wilson 2, Thompson 2, Keyes 1, Lugar 1, Dornan 1, Specter 1, and "undecided" 16. Dole's overwhelming five-to-one lead in the early caucus race probably indicated little more than that he was the only GOP candidate with broad name recognition in Iowa, despite the fact that the other early starters, Gramm and Alexander, had campaigned twenty-three and twenty-eight days, respectively, in the state. Gramm could take some comfort from being the only other candidate to achieve double figures in the poll (Iowa Poll: 1995, poll no. 334).

In the expectations game, however, the survey results provided additional evidence that Dole was the candidate to beat in Iowa. The poll also made the campaign more difficult for Dole by raising expectations to very high levels. The senator had won 37 percent of the 1988 GOP caucus vote in a six-person field. As the other 1996 candidates became better known in Iowa, meeting or exceeding his 1988 margin of victory in a field that was half again as large would be difficult.

"Caucus Kickoff '96," called the Iowa "Presidential Straw Poll" by C-Span in its live telecast, was a party fund-raiser held at Hilton Coliseum in Ames on August 19, 1995. The Republican Party of Iowa put a great deal of time and effort into making Caucus Kickoff '96 the premier political event of the summer. The essence of the event was a straw poll, and ten presidential candidates and a sizable contingent of national political reporters attended. The Ames poll known as the "Cavalcade of Stars" in 1987 had received national attention when evangelist Pat Robertson and Senator Bob Dole both finished ahead of the front-runner, Vice-President George Bush. The outcome may have signaled the increasing influence of the Christian Right in Iowa, and when Bush finished third in the 1988 caucuses behind Dole and Robertson, it became likely that future party-sponsored straw polls would draw presidential candidates and receive national attention.

For the Iowa GOP, however, the Ames straw poll was first and foremost a fund-raiser, and they hoped for a large turnout at the event. Unlike 1987, when the party had reported the votes of Iowans and non-Iowans (there were few) separately, anyone willing to purchase a twenty-five-dollar ticket was eligible to vote in the Caucus Kickoff '96 straw poll. The decision to include non-Iowans in the vote was criticized before and after the event by the candidates and the press reporting the story. But party finance assistant Kathleen Masteller made no apologies for the wide-open poll, stating that "this is a fund-raiser and I don't care who buys or how many seats they buy" (Masteller 1995).

The party offered each of the ten candidates a block of 100 of the 1000 seats on the floor of the coliseum at twenty-five dollars each. Only Dole (thirty-four) and Dornan (zero) did not purchase their full allotment of floor tickets (Kennedy 1995). Most of the campaigns admitted to buying their allotment, but an Alexander aide reported that more tickets had been purchased by "Nashville," although he did not know how many (Humeston Aug. 23, 1995). The Taylor campaign bought 1000 additional tickets to draw supporters to Ames (Stanhope Aug. 23, 1995). Party officials reported that they sold about 14,000 tickets to the fund-raiser, approximately 11,000 people attended, 10,598 people voted in the straw poll, and the event raised about $350,000, making it the most successful fund-raiser ever held by the party (Kennedy 1995).

Story County provided fifty voting machines for the event. Ticket holders were able to vote before and after the candidate speeches. Two volunteers at each booth punched the tickets of those who voted and marked their hands as well. There was some voting fraud, mostly by campaign workers, according to Republican state chair Brian Kennedy, but he did not think it widespread or significant (Kennedy 1995).

The day was carnival-like. Before the straw poll and evening speeches, the presidential candidates held picnics or "open houses" in tents outside Hilton Coliseum. The evening activities drew a large, enthusiastic crowd that was dominated by socially conservative people (Kennedy 1995).

The evening opened with the singing of "The Star-Spangled Banner" and then an invocation by Marilyn Quayle, wife of former vice-president Dan Quayle. GOP state chair Brian Kennedy introduced the many Republican notables. The celebrity introductions were followed by a dramatic, spotlighted introduction of the nine GOP presidential candidates (Dornan was late and missed the introduction) and Dan Quayle, who gave a fifteen-minute speech and served as master of ceremonies. Candidates were each allowed twelve minutes to speak, and the order was Dole, Wilson, Lugar, Gramm, Keyes, Buchanan, Specter, Taylor, Alexander, and Dornan. (Governor Branstad and New Hampshire Governor Steve Merrill each spoke briefly after Keyes.)

The speeches of Buchanan, Gramm, and Keyes received enthusiastic responses from the crowd, but the other candidates repeated themes often heard by those who followed the Iowa campaign. Senator Dole said that the "sea of silence" that followed parts of his speech was "a little scary" (Harwood 1995, A10). Senator Specter was booed by a segment of the crowd when he was introduced, and the boos continued during his speech when he discussed his controversial pro-choice stand on abortion and the need for the GOP to be a "big tent" party. The crowd included large numbers of social conservatives who were sympathetic to Gramm, Buchanan, and Keyes but unsympathetic to pro-choice positions and the concept of the GOP as an umbrella party.

Specter seemed to relish the encounter with the crowd. He also denounced the straw poll because participation was not limited to Iowans. Large numbers of non-Iowans had been bused and flown into Iowa for the event. In the context of sniping at President Clinton, Specter said "at a time when integrity and character give us a great advantage, I question the wisdom of having an Iowa straw poll which is not for Iowans. At a time when there's an enormous challenge, that money is too important in politics, I don't think the Iowa straw poll [ought to] be for sale, and I don't think you [ought to] buy this straw poll" (author's TV tape of the event).

It was already a long evening when state chair Kennedy announced there would be an additional forty-five minutes for voting, although only a very small portion of the original crowd remained by this time. At the four-hour and twenty-four minute mark, or one hour and eighteen minutes after the vote break began, Kennedy returned to the podium in the almost empty hall to announce the straw poll results that are reported in Table 10.1.

The results of "Caucus Kickoff '96" were reported and analyzed by the national press for the next three days. "Dole Takes Hit in 'Important' Early Iowa Poll" was the story headline in the *Christian Science Monitor* (Shillinger 1995, 1). The *New York Times* called the results "an unmistakable disappointment for Mr. Dole," who "had been considered the overwhelming favorite in the poll" (Berke 1995, A1). A *Wall Street Journal* editorial raised questions about the support for Senator Dole. After the obligatory disclaimer that "too much can be made of the results," the editorial opines that the poll results "were a wake up call" for Dole, who is from "nearby Kansas" and enjoys "universal name ID" in Iowa. The editorial continued, "Mr. Dole has clearly won the primary held by the Beltway elites, but out in the heartland

Table 10.1.   "Caucus Kickoff '96"
straw-poll results

	Votes	Percentage of total votes
Dole	2582	24.4
Gramm	2582	24.4
Buchanan	1922	18.1
Alexander	1156	10.9
Keyes	804	7.6
Taylor	803	7.6
Lugar	466	4.4
Wilson	129	1.2
Dornan	87	0.8
Specter	67	0.6
Total	10,958	100.0

Source: Republican Party of Iowa.

his support doesn't seem either deeply committed or enthusiastic" (Aug. 22, 1995, A10).

While the preponderance of the lines written about the Ames straw poll were about Senator Dole and his surprisingly poor showing, the *Christian Science Monitor* thought Phil Gramm "scored an upset in the most important straw poll of the pre-season presidential campaign" and was the chief beneficiary of Dole's misfortune because he tied for first place with Dole (Shillinger 1995, 1). The *Washington Post* thought that Gramm's strong showing gave him an advantage over Buchanan in their struggle for "the mantle of leading conservative alternative" to Bob Dole (Taylor 1995, A10).

All the Ames stories discounted the results to a degree because non-Iowans participated in the poll. A *Time* magazine story said "of course the ballot was phony" because non-Iowans participated, but thought it "was still a test of organizational strength" (Kramer 1995, 34). A *New York Times* editorial concluded that "straw polls are not reliable gauges of anything durable" and noted that Dole was still well ahead in the polls (Aug. 22, 1995, A14). Nonetheless, the Ames poll took on a life of its own, and the fallout affected the Iowa contest.

The Dole organization made personnel changes. The Iowa campaign manager was demoted to director of field operations, and long-time GOP activist Darrell Kearney became the manager of the Iowa campaign. Kearney, who had been a leader in Kemp's Iowa campaign in 1988 and was a leading Kemp supporter until Kemp opted out of the 1996 race, took a leave of absence from his job to devote himself full-time to the Dole campaign. He indicated that the Ames outcome was indeed a wake-up call for Dole supporters and the Iowa and national campaign staffs as well. The campaign staff renewed its efforts at the local level with the goal of finding leaders in every precinct. They also hoped to bring the candidate to Iowa more frequently. Kearney thought that the Ames vote might lower expectations for Dole in Iowa, but that may have been wishful thinking (Kearney 1995).

Less than a month after the Ames straw poll, the *Register* published a second Iowa Poll. The survey of likely caucus attenders completed between September 9 and 13, 1995, showed Senator Dole falling from a five-to-one lead in the first Iowa Poll to a two-to-one lead over his nearest competitor, Senator Gramm, whose support had grown by fifty percent. The results were: Dole 40 percent, Gramm 18, Buchanan and Alexander 7 each, Wilson 4, Keyes 3, Lugar 2, Taylor 2, and Dornan and Specter 1 each, with 15 percent undecided (Iowa Poll: 1995, poll no. 335). The *Register* story analyzing the poll noted Dole's continuing lead in the caucus race "despite a sharp decline in support during the summer" and concluded that "the new poll shows the race has changed substantially." There was some good news in the poll for Dole: he was the only candidate viewed in "overwhelmingly positive terms" by likely caucus attenders (Fogarty 1995a, 1A).

The earlier Iowa Poll had asked those expressing a preference for Dole, "Would you say your mind is made up to support Dole, or could you be persuaded to support another candidate?" Only 28 percent said their minds were "made up." By the time of the second Iowa Poll, candidates had campaigned 267 days in Iowa, compared with 107 days at the time of the first survey. As the other candidates appeared frequently in the state and Iowans became familiar with their campaign themes and positions on the issues, Bob Dole was no longer the only recognizable name in the GOP field.

Senator Dole was suffering the fate of front-runners noted in Chapter 7 as the media and the other campaigns focused on him. Dole was put under a microscope and his long congressional career was examined and discussed in meetings all over Iowa. A *Time* magazine article cautioned us to "remember Republican history. As the real voting draws nearer, the front runner invariably loses some market share, and the electorate expresses its dissatisfaction with the field, and then the front runner captures the prize anyway" (Kramer 1995, 34).

The prediction eventually proved true, but Dole had some very difficult times in Iowa. If, as the old adage suggests, bad luck runs in threes, then Steve Forbes's entry into the GOP presidential race shortly after the Ames straw poll and the second Iowa Poll was the third piece of bad news for Dole. The Forbes campaign, self-financed and therefore not subject to federal spending limits, began running ads on television and radio in Iowa that outlined his message of "hope, growth, and opportunity," and used a lot of airtime to attack Dole.

But first, the presidential campaign in Iowa and the nation was interrupted by "Powellmania." The press covered General Colin Powell extensively, and from mid-September until mid-November he was a familiar figure in the print media and on television and radio news programs as he used the promotion of his new book to explore a run for the GOP presidential nomination. Until Powell ended "weeks of speculation that he might become a Republican candidate" by announcing on November 8 that he would not run "for president or any elective office next year," he effectively froze the GOP presidential campaign in Iowa (Seib 1995c, 1A).

Powell was interesting from several perspectives: his exceptional military career, his perceived integrity during a time when the integrity of many public officials was questioned, and probably foremost, his status as an African-American Republican whose political views were largely unknown. *Newsweek* ran five multipage stories on Powell during the period, and he was featured on their cover for a second time after he announced that he would not enter the presidential race. The O. J. Simpson murder trial dominated the news during the month of October, or Powell might have been covered even more extensively.

As the press focused on Powell, the Iowa campaigns of the other candidates received little national attention. Unable to compete for attention with Powell's "book tour," the Simpson murder trial, and the war in Bosnia, candidates built their local organizations and with local media coverage stumped the state in search of supporters. The press characterized the Iowa campaign as "frozen," and some likely caucus attenders may have remained uncommitted to await the Powell decision.

Powell's decision not to run was good news for the other candidates. National polls had Powell leading President Clinton "in head-to-head tests," challenging Senator Dole for the lead in the Republican nominating race (*CQ* Nov. 11, 1995, 3471), and relegating the remainder of the field to single-digit also-rans (*DMR* Nov. 9, 1995, 3A). After a short period of press speculation about Powell's decision and about how the remaining candidates might be affected by it, his withdrawal and the conclusion of live CNN coverage of the Simpson trial allowed the national press more time to cover the GOP race.

Two aspects of the fall 1995 GOP campaign in Iowa stand out: the contest for the support of members of the Christian Right, and the Forbes media campaign and his subsequent rise in the polls. Nationally, the Christian Right was a growing movement, with 1.4 million members at the time of the 1994 elections. They had become "a 'dominant' force in eighteen state Republican parties and a 'substantial' force in thirteen more" (Oldfield 1996, 254). Although a substantial force at the grass roots, the Christian Right was still "a minority movement within the party and the nation" (Oldfield 1996, 255).

Pat Robertson had demonstrated in 1988 that a well-organized group of modest size could successfully compete for attention and support in the Iowa precinct caucuses. Previously not active in Iowa politics, the Christian Right had an alternative form of organization in the churches of its members. Their nontraditional approach was largely unrecognized by the parties and the media, and traditional polling techniques had failed to detect the high level of activity by Robertson supporters. The Iowa Christian Coalition founded in 1989 was an outgrowth of the Robertson effort in Iowa (Scheffler 1996).

By the time of the 1996 caucus cycle, the Christian Right was well established in Iowa Republican politics. About half of the members of the central committee were identified with the Christian Right (Kennedy 1996). The four Iowa Polls conducted in the precaucus period found that 31 to 41 percent of the likely caucus attenders described themselves as "born again or fundamentalist Christians" (Pilmer, Oct. 14, 1996). State chair Brian Kennedy reports the number at 35 to 40 percent based on his sources of information (Kennedy 1996). In a relatively short time, the Christian Right had become a major force in GOP electoral politics in Iowa, its leaders and members were courted by the major presidential campaigns, and they defined the tone and social agenda of the Iowa caucus campaign.

The Dole campaign recognized very early the need to establish a strong relationship with the Christian Right. Dole pulled off a coup of sorts in late February 1995 when his office announced that Steve Scheffler, the field director for the Iowa Christian Coalition, would take a leave of absence to join the Dole campaign as "coalitions director." Scheffler had organized religious conservatives in Iowa for over ten years, had played a major role in the Robertson campaign in 1988, and had continued his organizational efforts for the movement as a paid staff member. He was also serving his second term on the Iowa GOP state central committee. The Gramm campaign had pursued Scheffler as well, and there were initial hard feelings about his decision to support Dole over Gramm in the 1996 caucus race (Scheffler 1996).

Scheffler monitored coalition activity in general and was the Dole campaign liaison with pro-life and pro-family groups, farmers, veterans, and most important, the Christian Right movement in Iowa. His assignment was to get endorsements and to win the support of as many of the faithful as possible. The protection of the right flank was not an easy assignment, as Dole was known for his ability to get things done, which meant frequent compromises. In the year of the conservative, compromise was a dirty word, and Scheffler had to persuade skeptics that Dole would not compromise on their social agenda. Scheffler's efforts eventually paid dividends, and in mid-November the Dole campaign released a list of leading religious conservatives who had endorsed Dole (Kearney Oct. 14, 1996).

But Dole was not the only candidate in Iowa courting the Christian Right. The Alexander, Buchanan, Gramm, and Keyes campaigns also sought their support, and with the exception of Specter, all the candidates made some effort to gain acceptance within the movement. Alexander professed his conservative credentials at every campaign stop and assumed the political positions of the Christian Right. But it was an uphill struggle from the start, as his earlier pronouncements on issues and actions taken in previous government positions made his commitment suspect (Scheffler 1996).

Keyes was the sentimental favorite of many of the Christian Right, and his fiery oratory drew good crowds whenever he spoke in the state.

His lack of organization and modest financial resources, as well as the nagging perception, fueled by the other candidates, that he could not win the nomination, limited Keyes's ability to expand his base of support in Iowa. Still, his core supporters stayed the course with their candidate.

Gramm, who had realized that his economic message alone did not attract support from the Christian Right, and Buchanan also competed with Dole for support from the Christian Right. Each espoused positions on social issues that were acceptable, and in public forums and appearances attempted to demonstrate that they were more pro-life, tougher on crime, and more fervently against illegal immigration than the others.

Buchanan, like Dole, had begun very early to build bridges to the Christian Right, which he saw as a natural constituency, and he enjoyed almost immediate success. Guy Rodgers, former national field director of the Christian Coalition, was hired in early 1995 as national campaign manager. Rodgers served in that capacity for about six months and during his tenure recruited other well-known members of the Christian Right into the Buchanan camp (Roepke 1996). In March, Drew Ivers was named cochair of Buchanan's Iowa effort. Ivers was a two-term member of the Republican state central committee and had served as Iowa chair of the Pat Robertson for President committee in 1987-88 (*Midday Record* Mar. 17, 1995). In late May, Rodgers recruited Marlene Elwell, another longtime Christian Right activist who had played a major role in Robertson's Michigan and Iowa efforts in 1986 and 1988, to serve as senior adviser to the Iowa campaign through the Ames straw poll (Roepke 1996).

In Iowa, Buchanan "was constantly on the lookout for ways to separate himself from the social conservative pack" (Tollerson 1995, 34). In a well-received speech to the Iowa Right-to-Life Convention in November, for example, Buchanan attempted to demonstrate that his right-to-life credentials were superior to those of the others by committing to a "right-to-life" vice-presidential running mate (author's notes from the event).

Gramm lacked Buchanan's rhetorical skills and ability to excite a crowd, but in spite of his early Democratic background was more of an establishment Republican than Buchanan. He billed himself as the conservative alternative to Dole and attempted to persuade members of the Christian Right that he was the more electable and would be true to their agenda. It was not an easy sell, however, as Gramm was "widely criticized by social conservatives for seeming reluctant to campaign on non-fiscal issues" (Greenblatt 1995, 1443). With time he became more comfortable speaking out on social issues, and at the Iowa Right-to-Life Convention, Gramm was his usual folksy, witty self and was well received by the membership (author's notes from the event).

The Right-to-Life Convention, however, may have also signaled that unlike 1988, when Pat Robertson had the support of the Christian Right to himself, the delegates to the convention seemed generally satisfied with Dole, Keyes, and Alexander on right-to-life issues as well as with Buchanan and Gramm. A Christian Right vote split among four or five candidates would limit its impact in Iowa, and according to Scheffler, that outcome was likely because the movement had matured and was now more pluralistic in outlook (Scheffler 1996).

Meanwhile, Steve Forbes was challenging the model of a traditional Iowa campaign. With only four months to campaign before the February caucuses, he had little time to build a grass-roots organization or to speak to dozens of service and professional clubs as the other candidates had been doing for months, or in some cases for years. Forbes visited Iowa infrequently in the late fall (seven days from September through December), and his campaign relied almost exclusively on radio and television advertising on a scale that was unprecedented in the history of the Iowa caucuses.

The early ads focused on Forbes's economic ideas and his "flat tax" proposal, which was simple, direct, and understandable. It was almost impossible to tune in a radio or TV program in Iowa during the fall months without hearing or seeing the Forbes tax message. It was not long before the biographical and issue ads gave way to negative ads (i.e., ads that include half-truths, distort or take facts out of context, raise doubts about the motives or the character of candidates, or employ a variety of techniques to portray candidates as nefarious beings), and, although Forbes attacked all the "Washington politicians" seeking the GOP nomination, Bob Dole was his favorite target. His ads sniped at Dole on a variety of issues, including his "record of legislative compromise" (Elving 1995, 3472), his postponement of a fall senate vote on term limits, and his reputed votes for sixteen tax increases in fourteen years (Cook 1995, 3676).

The Forbes ad campaign led to an "air war" in Iowa. The other campaigns responded with commercials of their own and before long, radio and television stations throughout Iowa were airing daily claims and counterclaims by the candidates that often stretched the truth. The other candidates proved they could make ads that were just as negative as Forbes's. A Dole ad, for example, asked, "Have you heard about Steve Forbes' risky ideas? Forbes supports welfare benefits for illegal aliens; Forbes opposes life sentences for three-time offenders; Forbes' flat tax would add 186 billion to the deficit; Forbes opposes a constitutional amendment to balance the budget. Untested leadership, risky ideas!"

A Gramm ad stated, "Of the three major candidates for president (Dole, Clinton, Gramm), two supported: a big government-run health care system; risking American lives in Bosnia; supported paying

Cartoon by Brian Duffy, © 1996, *Des Moines Register,* reprinted by permission

Steve Forbes was a late entrant in the 1996 Republican presidential race in Iowa. The flat tax was a major theme of his campaign, and his extensive TV ad campaign promoting the tax and denigrating his opponents altered the nature of the Iowa caucus campaign. Many of his negative ads were aimed at front-runner Bob Dole, hurting Dole's efforts in Iowa.

unwed mothers to have more children on welfare; abandoned their tax cut promises. I never will, won't!"

A Forbes ad supposedly drawing from the Congressional Record read "the official congressional record: Dole supported raising government pensions for himself and others in Congress."

President Clinton also got into the air war. One of his ads showed a picture of children while chronicling "drastic" GOP budget cuts. It then said that "President Clinton protects Medicare, Medicaid, education, and the environment," a line that would become a standard part of his presidential campaign (author's review of TV ads).

There are no comprehensive records of media spending in Iowa, but comparable data for 1988 and 1996 are available. Table 10.2 reports 1996 ad spending in Des Moines, the state's largest TV market, at WHO-TV and KCCI-TV, the NBC and CBS affiliates.

The contrast between the 1996 and 1988 caucus cycles is striking. Television advertising began earlier and was more extensive in 1996. Where late summer and fall commercials were the exception in 1987, they were the rule in 1995. Republican candidates spent about ten

Table 10.2.   1996 Republican spending at
WHO-TV and KCCI-TV

	WHO	KCCI
Forbes	$190,955	$252,745
Dole	119,165	145,720
Alexander	112,025	128,190
Lugar	109,740	103,960
Taylor	54,625	96,300
Gramm	47,405	67,540
Buchanan	41,045	59,885
Keyes, Dornan,		
Wilson, Specter	0	0
Total	674,960	854,340

Source: Created from records provided by Cheryl
Semerad, director of sales and marketing, WHO, and
Anne Marie Caudron, national sales manager, KCCI.

times as much on paid television in 1996 as they did eight years earlier (Table 8.4). Alexander, Dole, Forbes, and Lugar each exceeded the spending of the total GOP field in 1988, with Forbes, who was not constrained by Federal Election Commission (FEC) limits, leading the way by a wide margin.

Historically, and in accord with the grass-roots orientation of the traditional Iowa campaign, paid radio and television advertising were seldom used before 1988, and before 1996 paid ads tended to be the frosting on the cake in the final weeks of the campaign. Biographical profiles and issue ads designed to reinforce the messages personally delivered by the candidates during the months of campaigning began running after the Christmas holiday season in the 1988 cycle. The Gephardt ads in 1988, particularly the sixty-second Hyundai commercial focusing on barriers to trade, are believed to have advanced his standing in the caucuses, but there is little other evidence that paid radio and TV ads have had an impact on the outcome of the Iowa caucuses.

Forbes changed the nature of the Iowa campaign, and pundits wondered whether it was possible to "buy" the caucuses (Alter 1996). By December Forbes's media strategy appeared to be working. The press focused on him, and a strong showing in the December Iowa Poll further enhanced coverage. Dole led with 41 percent, followed by Forbes with 12 percent, Gramm 9, Buchanan 7, Alexander 6, Keyes 4, Lugar 3, and Taylor and Dornan 1 each, with 16 percent undecided. Forbes and Dole were the only candidates to achieve double figures in the poll. Although Dole's lead was unchanged from September, Gramm's percentage had been cut in half. Support for the remainder of the field was much the same as three months earlier. Wilson and Specter were no longer active candidates by the time of the December poll (Iowa Poll: 1995, poll no. 336).

The December poll results received national attention. The *Wall Street Journal* discussed the Forbes candidacy in light of the good poll news "rolling in" from Iowa, Arizona, and New Hampshire (Seib 1995d, A20). A *Boston Globe* story stated that "in a demonstration of the power of the dollar, Forbes leap-frogged a field of better known Republicans to wind up second in the latest Iowa Poll" (Wilke 1995, 4A).

Dole's Iowa campaign manager thought the outcome showed that "you can buy a position in public opinion polls." Gramm's campaign manager warned that "television may be becoming more important in Iowa, but you still need to have the ground game here. [Forbes] just doesn't have it" (Fogarty 1995b, 2A).

Forbes had changed the nature of the Iowa race, but only time would tell if Gramm's faith in the "traditional Iowa campaign" was well placed. Forbes's ad campaign had forced the others to spend more of their resources on radio and television, and that caused financial stress for some campaigns. Kearney asserts that Forbes's media strategy altered Dole's focus on Gramm, whom he had judged to be the principal opposition. Dole had planned to use direct mailings with much of the material anti-Gramm, but when Forbes entered the race and surged in the polls, they changed their game plan to include anti-Forbes ads on radio and TV. Dole spent much more money in the state than planned, primarily on media purchases, and was "forced" to "attack" after Forbes initiated negative ads against him. Kearney had hoped that Alexander and Gramm would go after Forbes and spare them some of the expense, which included both psychic and financial costs. Kearney reports that Dole partisans were upset by their candidate's negative ads, and he received many calls from supporters protesting the negative nature of the Dole campaign. He felt it was necessary, however, as their tracking poll data indicated that the Forbes ads were doing great damage to Dole (Kearney Mar. 8, 1996).

The late campaign in Iowa was dominated by the air war and intensive candidate activity in the state. Buchanan's initial television commercials aired after the first of the year, and candidate spending on ads at WHO and KCCI almost doubled from December to January. While the air war escalated, the candidates also campaigned in Iowa at a record pace. They shored up their campaign organizations for the final caucus push, spoke to groups around the state, participated in candidate forums, and in effect performed on the Iowa stage for the national media who were now following the race closely. The nine active candidates spent 141 days in Iowa from January 1 to February 12, 1996. Forbes, now a vigorous campaigner, spent fourteen days in the state, and Dole, whose November and December visits had been limited to two days by the ongoing budget struggle between the Congress and President Clinton, which tied him down in Washington, also campaigned fourteen days in Iowa.

As the front-runner, Dole continued to bear the brunt of the criticism from the other campaigns and particularly from Forbes's radio and TV ads. He did enjoy some good moments, however. Christian Right activist Marlene Elwell, who had left the Buchanan campaign after the Ames poll, joined the Dole campaign in December as a paid staff member "to help with pro-life groups and the Christian Coalition" (Kearney Oct. 14, 1996).

Dole also held one of the more novel events of the late campaign; on January 6 he staged a pep rally of sorts called the "Cavalcade of Governors" for his Iowa campaign workers. Senator Dole and nine governors (Terry Branstad of Iowa, Steve Merrill of New Hampshire, Arne Carlson of Minnesota, Jim Edgar of Illinois, Kirk Fordice of Mississippi, Bill Graves of Kansas, Ed Schafer of North Dakota, Tommy Thompson of Wisconsin, and George Voinovich of Ohio), one lieutenant governor (Mike Huckabee of Arkansas), and two former Iowa governors (Bob Ray [1969-83] and Norman Erbe [1961-63]) attended the noon rally at the Des Moines Convention Center.

The "Cavalcade of Governors" took some of the attention from the televised presidential debate in South Carolina that evening in which six of the GOP candidates participated. The Des Moines event received local, state, and national press coverage, including crews from CNN and NBC. Bob Schieffer included it on CBS's "Saturday Evening News," and there was a story on National Public Radio (NPR) on Monday morning. The six candidates in South Carolina, obviously annoyed that Dole had skipped the debate, sent many barbs his way. Dole's explanation for his presence in Iowa rather than South Carolina was that he had to return to Washington for early evening budget negotiations with President Clinton and Speaker Gingrich.

In each caucus cycle the candidates appear on a common stage at several forums. In addition to the Right to Life Convention previously discussed, the Iowa Farm Bureau and the Iowans for Tax Relief events involved the participation of six and eight candidates, respectively. The grand finale of the caucus season, however, is the presidential debate sponsored by the *Des Moines Register.* In the budget-cutting spirit of the times, the January 13 debate was held in the studio of Iowa Public Television, which seats about 340 people, rather than in the 2700-seat Des Moines Civic Center, the site of previous *Register* debates. Three months of planning went into the event, which ran smoothly (Riedel-King 1996).

Iowa politicians and some 175 local and national reporters were on hand for the debate. The unseasonably warm weather permitted outside interviews, which was fortunate for reporters who had to watch the debate on TV from a makeshift pressroom. CNN, C-Span, Iowa Public TV, WOI-radio for NPR, WHO-radio, and the Radio Iowa Network (which also provided on-line coverage) broadcast the debate live (the first *Register* debate CNN had televised live since 1984).

The moderator, *Register* editor Dennis Ryerson, was seated in the middle of a semicircle that included candidates Lugar, Dornan, Buchanan, Alexander, Keyes, Forbes, Gramm, Taylor, and Dole. The forum was interesting, informative, and at times entertaining even though the format did not lend itself to a real debate. There were occasional sidebars between the candidates, who gave minispeeches and repeated the campaign themes and messages they had been conveying to Iowa audiences for months, or in some cases for almost three years.

Only Gramm consistently attacked Dole, who fended him off well with humor and witty retorts. Most of the attention, however, went to Steve Forbes, now second in the Iowa Poll. The other candidates sniped at him with a certain degree of success. Alexander called Forbes's flat tax proposal "a truly nutty idea" and mocked it as a remedy for every ill afflicting America (Harwood 1996, B5). Forbes missed an opportunity to broaden his message to the American people during this forum by sticking so closely to his flat tax message.

Perhaps the best line of the day was one by Dole. Gramm, noting that President Clinton had praised the senator on the budget negotiations, asked, "Bob, is there some kind of secret deal you're cutting with Bill Clinton and can you share it with us while we're here?" Dole retorted, "Next time you're in town, look me up," referring to Gramm's frequent absences from Washington during the budget negotiations to campaign (author's notes from the event).

The Louisiana Republican state central committee upset top Iowa Republicans when they announced plans to switch from a March presidential primary to regional caucuses on February 6, six days before the Iowa caucuses. Iowans moved quickly to defend their "first-in-the-nation" status. Senator Charles Grassley asked the Justice Department "to investigate whether Louisiana's change in its election law violates the Federal Voting Rights Act," which requires Justice Department approval for changes in election procedures "that might dilute minority voting strength." Iowa GOP chair Brian Kennedy jawboned with Louisiana party officials and "asked all Presidential contenders not to campaign in Louisiana." Kennedy eventually sought written pledges from the presidential candidates that they would not participate in the Louisiana caucuses, and only Gramm, Buchanan, and Keyes failed to sign a pledge (Holmes 1995, A1).

Presidential candidate Morry Taylor added to the drama when he announced at a December 22 news conference in a joint appearance with Kennedy that he would file suit in federal district court to block the Louisiana change. Taylor said that in early January he would "sue the Louisiana Republican Party under the 1965 Voting Rights Act for switching the state's voting process from an open primary to a closed caucus" (Taylor press release Dec. 22, 1995). The court decision issued on January 26 rejected Taylor's attempt to block the change, and although he considered appealing the decision to the U.S. Supreme Court (Taylor press release Jan. 27, 1996), he did not pursue the case.

In the meantime, Gramm and Buchanan, and to a lesser extent Keyes, campaigned in Louisiana for the 21 delegates at stake in the caucuses. Gramm had won a straw vote at the state GOP convention a year earlier (Cook 1996a, 313), had "helped inspire and engineer the early caucus in his neighboring state," and had hoped to use Louisiana as "a springboard into Iowa." A month before the caucuses Gramm "had boasted that he would win all 21 delegates," and the day before the event said that "he would win most" (Cook 1996b, 363).

When the results were in, Buchanan had won 13 of the delegates, Gramm 8, and Keyes none. Because Gramm had set high expectations in essentially a two-person race with Buchanan, the defeat was very damaging to his campaign. *Congressional Quarterly* declared that the senator "finds himself on the brink of the abyss" after losing the "high-stakes" Louisiana caucuses. Apparently not learning from his previous mistake, Gramm put more pressure on himself by declaring the day after Louisiana that "he would have to finish in the top three in Iowa or face the end of his presidential campaign." (Gramm had frequently stated there would be "only three tickets out of Iowa," a reference to the fact that no fourth-place finisher in Iowa had ever gone on to win the nomination [Apple 1996].) Buchanan, on the other hand, was jubilant. He had won what Gramm had called "a sort of semifinal to decide who is the real conservative candidate" (Cook 1996b, 364), and although the press did not fully realize it at the time, he moved into the final week of the Iowa campaign with tremendous momentum, whereas Gramm was on the defensive in the final days of the Iowa campaign.

The *Register*'s final Iowa Poll, reported in Table 10.3, was published on February 10, two days before the caucuses. Among the top-tier candidates, Dole and Gramm lost ground, while Forbes, Buchanan, and Alexander gained. Although Dole's lead had narrowed substantially since December, his supporters were the least likely to "be persuaded to switch their loyalty at this late date." Dole also led Buchanan among "fundamentalist Christians," who according to the survey constituted about one-third of likely caucus attenders, and among "self-described conservatives" (Fogarty 1996, 1A).

Although he came in a solid second in the poll, Forbes also received a negative rating of 46 percent, up 20 percentage points since the December Iowa Poll. Buchanan had picked up some support among those surveyed after his victory in the Louisiana caucuses, perhaps indicating some momentum. The poll indicated that "the negative

Table 10.3.   1996 *Des Moines Register* Iowa Polls

	5-95	9-95	12-95	2-96
Dole	57	40	41	28
Forbes	—	—	12	16
Gramm	11	18	9	8
Buchanan	6	7	7	11
Alexander	2	7	6	10
Keyes	1	3	4	4
Lugar	1	2	3	2
Taylor	—	2	1	2
Dornan	1	1	1	0
None/other	21	20	16	19
Sample size (no.)	405	400	407	628
Margin of error (%) +/−	4.9	4.9	4.9	3.9

tone of the campaign" was hurting Dole and Gramm as well as Forbes. Finally, a very large minority (19%) of the likely caucus attenders were still undecided just two days before the caucuses (Iowa Poll: 1996, poll no. 337).

The Democratic Campaign

Iowa Democrats undertook a caucus campaign even though President Clinton was unchallenged in his bid for renomination. In previous caucuses, incumbent presidents without challengers (Reagan in 1984 and Bush in 1992) had been satisfied to let the opposing party's contest dominate the news from Iowa. The Clinton-Gore reelection team, however, conducted a vigorous caucus campaign in Iowa. President Clinton, Mrs. Clinton, Vice-President Gore, and other executive branch surrogates visited the state regularly, a Clinton-Gore campaign office was opened in Des Moines, and the Democratic National Committee (DNC) aired a large number of ads for the president on Iowa TV and radio stations.

The presidential visits to Iowa began with a highly publicized "non-political" trip to Des Moines and Davenport to view damage from the devastating floods in the summer of 1993. In November 1994, the president returned to Iowa to campaign for gubernatorial candidate Bonnie Campbell. During a two-day visit in April 1995, he met with staff of the *Register,* attended the White House Rural Summit at Iowa State University, and addressed the Iowa Legislature at the state capitol.

On a second two-day visit in October, Clinton delivered the keynote speech at the Iowa Democratic Party's annual Jefferson-Jackson Day dinner in Des Moines and attended an international summit of sorts in Cedar Rapids, where he and the Czech and Slovak presidents met and dedicated the new National Czech and Slovak Museum and Library. The president paid another two-day visit to the state on February 10 and 11, the final days before the precinct caucuses. He spoke to large and enthusiastic audiences in Iowa City and Mason City on Saturday and to an overflow crowd at the Knapp Center at Drake University on Sunday.

First Lady Hillary Rodham Clinton made two separate trips to Iowa, and Vice-President Al Gore made four well-publicized visits to maintain a Clinton-Gore presence in the state. Cabinet members and presidential advisers also visited periodically (author's records of Democratic visits to Iowa).

The president also developed a campaign organization in the state. On July 26, 1995, he announced that veteran Iowa political activist and former Democratic party executive director Mike Tramontina would lead the Clinton-Gore '96 reelection campaign in Iowa (*Midday Record* July 26, 1995). In mid-December a campaign office was opened in Des Moines across the street from the Iowa Democratic Party headquarters. Tramontina and a staff of eleven that eventually grew to sixteen worked to generate enthusiasm among the party faithful for the upcoming Democratic precinct caucuses and to build a Clinton-Gore infrastructure in the state, which Clinton had bypassed in 1992 due to Senator Harkin's favorite son campaign (Tramontina 1996). Table 10.4 reports Democratic spending for ads at WHO-TV and KCCI-TV in Des Moines.

President Clinton's commercials were sponsored by the DNC, but the tag accompanying the ads listed the Iowa Democratic Party (IDP).

The DNC-sponsored media reelection campaign in Iowa for President Clinton was unprecedented. The party in the White House had not previously purchased commercial time at WHO or KCCI for the caucuses. The DNC began purchasing TV advertising in August 1995 as part of their national reelection campaign and by the time of the caucuses had placed ads worth almost $180,000 at the two sta-

Table 10.4.   1996 Democratic National Committee spending for President Clinton at WHO-TV and KCCI-TV

WHO	KCCI
$89,125	$89,860

Source: Created from records provided by Cheryl Semerad, director of sales and marketing, WHO, and Anne Marie Caudron, national sales manager, KCCI.

tions, a sum that exceeded or approximated the spending of seven of the GOP candidates.

The Clinton-Gore campaign succeeded in sharing some of the media attention with the GOP campaign and in energizing Iowa Democrats. According to Tramontina, attendance at the Democratic caucuses was very good, particularly in urban areas.

The 1996 Caucuses

The caucuses arrived amidst a final blitz of charges and countercharges in the media ad war that had dominated the last weeks of the campaign. After a two-year campaign and months of speculation about the likely outcome, there would finally be some results. Republican candidates spent much more time in Iowa than their party's candidates in 1988 had (520 days, compared with 364), and even without data for Forbes, Taylor, Keyes, and Dornan, the money spent in Iowa was also a GOP record. Since Forbes and Taylor financed their own campaigns and did not accept federal funds, they were not bound by FEC spending limits in Iowa. Based on expenditures at the two central Iowa television stations, Forbes exceeded the million-dollar Iowa limit applicable to candidates accepting federal matching funds. Table 10.5 reports candidate spending and the number of candidate days in Iowa during the 1996 caucus cycle. It also documents the time spent in Iowa by the candidates in the last six weeks of the campaign.

Media Coverage

In the 1988 caucus cycle (as discussed in Chapter 8), full-time, on-site media coverage in Iowa began in August 1987 and grew steadily through the first of the year. In the 1996 cycle, no national news bureaus opened before the first of the year. Several factors contributed to the late start in media coverage of the Iowa race. First, the media had been preoccupied with the O. J. Simpson murder trial, the civil war in Bosnia, and the federal budget deadlock. Second, in the Midwest— perhaps nationally—there had been a systematic reordering of what newspapers cover. The economic squeeze brought about by declining circulation led to more local coverage, more feature stories, and less political coverage (Lambrecht 1996). Budgets had been tightened, and some reporters found it necessary to conduct interviews by phone rather than travel to Iowa to do their research (Seplow 1995), or to pay periodic visits to the state to cover candidates or special events in lieu of a permanent presence in the state. (In 1988 the *Chicago Tribune*, for example, had based two reporters in Des Moines from late November through the caucuses. In 1996, it was January 22 before they estab-

Table 10.5.   1996 Republican precaucus campaign
activity and spending

	Days in Iowa[a]		Spending in Iowa[b]
	Total	Jan. 1 to Feb. 12	
Alexander	79	20	$615,015
Buchanan	70	14	669,083
Dole	41	14	1,040,306
Dornan	6	3	
Forbes	21	14	
Gramm	69	20	958,778
Keyes	42	17	
Lugar	43	15	538,694
Specter	27	—	63,431
Taylor	92	24	
Wilson	10	—	21,962
Others	20	—	546
Total	520	141	3,907,815

[a] Specter and Wilson were no longer active candidates. The campaign activity covers the period from January 20, 1993, through February 12, 1996. The data were collected from the individual campaigns by the author.

[b] Spending data are from the Federal Election Commission based on 1996 year-end reports. The figures are preliminary, and Keyes had not yet completed a report. The Iowa limit was $1,046,984. As noted in previous chapters, spending data substantially understate actual campaign expenditures. The Clinton-Gore campaign, for example, reported total Iowa expenditures of $108,735 on their preliminary FEC filing. They did not have to report that the DNC spent an additional $180,000 for ads at WHO and KCCI alone.

lished a six-day-a-week presence in Iowa [Hardy 1996].)

The limited early coverage of the caucuses is reflected in Table 10.6, which compares television coverage of the Iowa precinct caucuses and the New Hampshire primary election by CBS's evening and weekend news for six election cycles. CBS coverage of the GOP race was extensive, but most of the stories (twenty-five of thirty-seven on Iowa, thirty-two of forty-three on New Hampshire) aired within one week of the date of the nominating event. CBS aired slightly more New Hampshire stories in 1996, reflecting their late start in covering the campaign. In the past, early CBS coverage of the campaign has centered on the Iowa caucuses.

When the Simpson trial finally ended, CNN and the news divisions of the national press were behind schedule in covering the presidential race. They picked up coverage substantially after the first of the year, and by the time of the caucuses an estimated 3000 journalists and technicians from 25 countries were in Iowa for a firsthand look at the process (Lickteig 1996, 9A).

Republican Caucus Results

The results of the Republican caucuses are shown in Table 10.7. Although only a straw poll, and unrelated to delegate selection, the results were "votes" to the media and they were reported nationally and internationally. The GOP caucuses had assumed the role of a pri-

Table 10.6.   CBS news stories on Iowa and New Hampshire, 1975–76 through 1995–96

	July 1 to June 30					
	1975–76	1979–80	1983–84	1987–88	1991–92	1995–96
Iowa	13	54	11	69	5	37
N.H.	44	40	22	38	31	43

Source: Data are from the *Television News Index and Abstracts,* produced by Vanderbilt University. The criteria for constructing the table are discussed in the source note for Table 6.2.

mary election, with the straw poll the principal order of business. The traditional functions of a precinct caucus—selection of county delegates and committee members and platform development—were irrelevant to many if not most who attended.

Bob Dole was the winner in Iowa, but his narrow margin of victory failed to meet the expectations of the pundits. The *Washington Post*

Table 10.7.   1996 Republican caucus straw-poll results

	Preferences	Percentage
Dole	25,378	26.3
Buchanan	22,512	23.3
Alexander	17,003	17.6
Forbes	9816	10.2
Gramm	9001	9.3
Keyes	7179	7.4
Lugar	3576	3.7
Taylor	1380	1.4
No preference	428	0
Dornan	131	0
Others/undecided	47	0
Total	96,451	99.2

Source: Voter News Service (VNS) from 2104 of 2142 precincts (98.2%). The turnout of 96,451 was 16.5 percent of the 583,641 Republicans registered on February 1, 1996. VNS replaced the News Election Service, the former vote-counting organization. It is a vote-counting and polling consortium composed of ABC, CBS, NBC, CNN, Fox, and AP. VNS tabulated the vote totals with the cooperation of the Republican Party of Iowa and used entrance poll data to predict the outcome accurately before the caucuses started. At 6:55 P.M., five minutes before the caucuses began, VNS sent the following message to its approximately 100 subscribers: "Dole is the winner. Among early voters in our entrance poll, Dole has a clear lead, followed by Buchanan, and Alexander" (Stout 1996).

described his victory as "pallid in comparison with 1988," when his percentage of the vote in Iowa was 11 points higher (Balz and Walsh 1996, A1). The *Wall Street Journal* thought that "Mr. Dole's relatively narrow victory in Iowa, which he captured with 37% of the vote in 1988, underscores the limits of the 72-year-old candidate's appeal at a time when the GOP's center of gravity has shifted to a new generation of conservatives" (Harwood and Davis 1996, A16). There were exceptions, however. The *New York Times* stated simply that "Senator Bob Dole won the Iowa Republican caucuses" and thus "preserved his position as front-runner in the nine-person field" (Berke 1996, A1).

As always there were surprises, and in 1996 they were the stronger-than-expected finishes of Pat Buchanan and Lamar Alexander and the relatively poor showings of Phil Gramm and Steve Forbes. Buchanan was the big winner in the expectations game. The *Times* thought he "established himself as a strong contender by surging to second place" in Iowa (Berke 1996, A1). The *Journal* concluded that "Mr. Buchanan rode a wave of support from conservative Christians to a strong second place finish" (Harwood and Davis 1996, A16). *Congressional Quarterly* said that with victories in Alaska, Louisiana, and Iowa, Buchanan had accomplished his strategy of supplanting Gramm "as the leading conservative alternative" to front-runner Bob Dole (Greenblatt 1996, 401). The Buchanan strategy was rewarded when Gramm dropped out of the nominating race two days after the Iowa caucuses.

Lamar Alexander's third-place finish was viewed as respectable by the press, but he did not enjoy the headlines that Buchanan earned. The *Times* noted that "after plodding anonymously along the campaign trail for more than a year, Mr. Alexander today found himself basking in a new glare." The interpretations were tempered, but Alexander had grabbed one of the three tickets out of Iowa and was elated with his showing. He declared a few hours after leaving Iowa "that the race will come down to Senator Dole and me" (Berke 1996, A1).

Table 10.8 shows that Dole's victory on a county basis was more pervasive than indicated by the statewide caucus poll. He won in seventy of Iowa's ninety-nine counties and came in second in twenty-six and third in the remaining three counties. Buchanan also did well on a statewide basis, but his strength was more localized; sixteen of the twenty-four counties he won were in the rural and very conservative

Fifth Congressional District in northwest Iowa.

Alexander won in five counties, was second in fifteen, and was third in sixty-three. The only other candidates to finish as high as second were Gramm in Fremont County and Keyes in Iowa, Lynn, and Mills counties. Forbes's multimillion-dollar TV and radio campaign netted him third-place finishes in three counties, one of which was a tie with Alexander.

Iowa had again started the winnowing process. Gramm was out of the race two days after the caucuses, although it was probably Louisiana that felled him. Darrell Kearney thought Gramm's decision to contest Louisiana and to miss a key senate farm vote hurt him with Iowans, and when he lost in Louisiana after predicting victory, "he went into free fall in Iowa and near the end, most of his supporters went over to Buchanan" (Kearney Mar. 8, 1996).

For all intents and purposes, the second-tier candidates had been written off even before the Iowa results were known. Keyes, Lugar, Taylor, and Dornan were rarely mentioned in the last days of the Iowa campaign or in postcaucus stories, and *USA Today* predicted their campaigns "will soon end" (Keen 1996, 3A).

Table 10.8.   1996 Republican caucus straw-poll results by county

	Counties won	Counties second	Counties third[a]
Dole	70	26	3
Buchanan	24	54	19
Alexander	5	15	63
Forbes	0	0	3
Gramm	0	1	7
Keyes	0	3	4
Lugar	0	0	1
Taylor	0	0	0
Dornan	0	0	0

Source: Constructed using county data compiled by the Associated Press and reported in the *Des Moines Register* on February 13, 1996, p. 8A.
[a]Alexander and Forbes tied for third in Crawford County.

The Forbes campaign was in limbo after Iowa. Iowa had signaled something about Forbes—his weaknesses as a candidate or the limits of his media campaign—but he was not winnowed out of the race. The combination of "slipping in the polls" and a fourth-place showing in Iowa would finish most candidates, but Forbes's financial resources guaranteed him another day in New Hampshire.

The national press corps left Iowa en masse the day after the caucuses on a plane chartered by the Republican Party of Iowa to fly them nonstop to New Hampshire. Their job of covering the "first-in-the-nation" primary election was made somewhat easier by Iowa, since they would now have to cover only the Dole, Buchanan, Alexander, and Forbes campaigns.

The press based their analyses of the Iowa results on the entrance poll of 2053 randomly selected caucus attenders at seventy caucus sites that was conducted by the Voter News Service (VNS), which replaced the News Election Service (all poll numbers are from VNS data printed with the *Register* article by Fogarty and Roos [1996, 8A]). Dole was the winner among older caucus attenders, garnering 41 percent of those age sixty or older, compared with 19 percent for Buchanan and 18 percent for Alexander. He led Alexander by a three-to-two margin among those whose annual earnings exceeded $75,000, and he edged out Alexander 29 to 28 percent among the "moderate" participants. Although 59 percent said that age made "no difference," a third of all respondents felt that "as president, Dole's age would hurt him," and only 11 percent of that subgroup supported Dole.

Alexander and Buchanan were the primary beneficiaries of votes from the 23 percent of caucus attenders who made their decisions in the final three days before the caucuses, winning 31 and 24 percent, respectively. Alexander outdistanced Dole's 33 percent by carrying 46 percent of the respondents for whom the "most important factor" in determining their support was the ability to "beat Bill Clinton," perhaps indicating that Alexander's oft-repeated message to "remember your ABCs—Alexander Beats Clinton"—registered with many caucus attenders.

The Christian Right constituted 35 percent of caucus attenders. Buchanan won 42 percent of their support and 37 percent of the one-third attending who described themselves as "very conservative." We can extrapolate from these figures that 63 percent of Buchanan's caucus support came from members of the Christian Right and 54 percent from the "very conservative" subgroup. He led the field among respondents with incomes under $30,000, with 30 percent of their support. He led by a wide margin among those for whom abortion was an important factor in their decision, with 51 percent of their support, but the abortion issue "mattered most" to only 8 percent of the caucus attenders, running well behind conservative values, electability, and Washington experience. Despite Buchanan's large lead among the Christian Right and social conservatives, Dole, Gramm, and Keyes collectively won about half of their support, thus denying Buchanan an outright victory in Iowa.

In summary, the VNS entrance poll data show that the typical 1996 GOP caucus attenders were middle-aged, middle-class conservatives who supported candidates they believed held conservative values, were electable, and had experience in Washington. Although they were a significant force and the major source of Buchanan's support, the Christian Right made up slightly more than one-third of the GOP caucus attenders and split their support among several candidates.

Contrary to the media hype and predictions by state chair Kennedy of record GOP attendance of 135,000 for the 1996 caucuses (Hartman 1996, 2A), a disappointing turnout of 96,451 citizens attended the precinct meetings, or 16.5 percent of the 583,641 registered Republicans in Iowa. Since independents and Democrats willing to register as Republicans are permitted to participate in the GOP meetings, the actual participation level was something less. Kennedy attributed the low turnout to "nine candidates failing to draw bright-line distinctions on how they varied from each other. And the tone and tenor of the campaign turned everyone off" (Cook 1996c, 402). The poll tally of 96,451 was the lowest recorded turnout in a contested GOP caucus by almost 10,000 people.

Others agreed that several months of negative ads had taken their toll. A *Register* editorial defended the right of candidates to criticize the records and ideas of their opponents but was critical of the negative nature of the campaign commercials. The writer concluded that a daily barrage of negative radio and TV commercials "sows contempt and mistrust for all politicians and corrodes democracy itself" (*DMR* Feb. 14, 1996, 10A).

Dole's campaign manager believed the negative ads altered the Iowa caucus race. In his opinion, the Forbes barrage seriously damaged Dole in Iowa, but he thought Forbes was brought down by his own ads because they led to apathy and cynicism on the part of potential caucus goers, and the resulting low turnout hurt both Dole and Forbes (Kearney Mar. 8, 1996). Dick Redman of the Alexander campaign was not surprised by the small turnout "because the interest just wasn't out there, and the negative ads and excessive phone calling turned people off in the end" (Redman 1996).

Perhaps the last word on the issue came from the candidate himself. Speaking to reporters in New Hampshire two days after the precinct caucuses, Forbes acknowledged "that his attack ad strategy had hurt him in Iowa. Forbes said that he had 'spent too much time discussing the records of his opponents'" and vowed to change the focus to his stands on the issues in New Hampshire (Minzesheimer 1996, 4A).

It will be some time before we know how much the Forbes media campaign changed the nature of the caucuses, but in 1996 Iowa was no longer an example of "retail" politics at its best. Rather, the campaign was a hybrid of "retail" and "wholesale" politics. It is likely that the traditional Iowa campaign will continue in some form since the successful Dole, Buchanan, and Alexander campaigns each built significant organizations in Iowa and invested heavy amounts of personal campaign time in the state. The late-starting Forbes campaign, which lacked the organizational component and relied on radio and television to reach the voters, was unsuccessful.

Part of the message from Iowa may be that candidates can overdo it with negative ads, but the 1996 caucuses seem to reaffirm the necessity for candidates to invest a significant amount of time in Iowa running for the nomination. It is also very likely that the trend started in 1988 to employ paid radio and television earlier and more extensively will become a regular part of the Iowa caucuses, and that will move the Iowa campaign closer to those conducted in primary election states. The Iowa caucus campaign is becoming less distinctive. Television may eventually alter the amount of time candidates spend in the state and the need for well-developed campaign organizations, but I doubt that will occur before the 2000 caucuses. The caucus meetings themselves also continue to change. The focus in 1996 was the caucus night poll. Many people, including quite a few Democrats in some areas, showed up to vote and then left without participating in the other business of the caucuses. Meetings were shorter and the focus was almost totally on the horse race.

The discussion of the 1996 caucuses would not be complete without some mention of the continuing saga of the defense of Iowa's first-in-the-nation status. Each presidential cycle, other states move their events closer to the "official" beginning dates in Iowa and New Hampshire, and a state or two (Alaska and Louisiana in 1996) attempt to grab some of the glory by moving their nominating event ahead of Iowa's. The national Republican party, unlike the Democrats, has never supported a fixed timetable for its caucus and primary events.

In January 1996 GOP national chair Haley Barbour appointed a Task Force on Primaries and Caucuses to study the party's nominating process. The task force held a hearing in Washington, D.C., in May to gather information on how to overcome the hectic nature of the front-loaded and highly compressed primary and caucus schedule. Iowa chair Brian Kennedy and New Hampshire Governor Steve Merrill offered their ideas on how to improve the schedule while preserving their states' early roles (Norman 1996, 6A). Kennedy proposed "special protections" for the first-in-the-nation status of Iowa and New Hampshire and a limit on the number of nominating events that might be held each month, but could not win support for either proposal. The committee issued a report in July, and its recommendations, as modified by the rules committee, were approved by the GOP National Convention in August as part of the rules governing the presidential nominating process in 2000 (Kennedy 1997).

The new Republican rules prohibit states from holding nominating events earlier than February 1, 2000, and require that they certify a date for their caucus or primary election by July 1, 1999. This requirement should put an end to states "leapfrogging" one another (late in the game) and moving their nominating events closer to the beginning of the schedule. To spread out the schedule and encourage states to hold their nominating events later, bonus delegates will be awarded. States who hold contests between March 15 and April 14 will receive a 5 percent increase in delegates, between April 15 and May 14, a 7.5 percent bonus, and after May 15, a bonus of 10 percent (CQ Aug. 17, 1996, 2299).

The rules do not preserve the early positions of Iowa and New Hampshire, and any state can schedule its nominating contest on February 1. Louisiana's partial success in stealing Iowa's limelight in 1996 probably means they will try again in 2000, and Louisiana's example will probably inspire more states to do the same. But the 2000 caucus campaign in Iowa is already under way. Richard Gephardt, Lamar Alexander, Jack Kemp, and Steve Forbes had all been in Iowa by mid-June of 1997.

The Impact of the 1996 Caucuses

The candidates and the media apparently accepted Iowa as the "official" starting point for the 1996 presidential campaign. In spite of the bad press about Iowa's predictive powers, or lack thereof, in 1988 and the gap in attention in 1992 due to Senator Harkin's candidacy, the Republican caucuses attracted more candidate attention than in previous GOP caucuses. Although it began later, media coverage in the final weeks also rivaled that of 1988.

The widespread use of paid TV continued to change the nature of the Iowa campaign. Retail politics was still very much in evidence, but in the final months of the 1996 campaign the reliance on radio and television advertising increased. Forbes's extensive use of negative ads led to an "air war" in Iowa and forced the other campaigns to expend a larger share of their budgets than planned on television advertising. To some degree, however, the Iowa campaign may simply have reflected a national trend toward increased reliance on paid TV and negative advertising. As noted in Chapter 8, Ed Rollins argues that the nature of political campaigns in America changed in 1988 with the widespread use of paid TV. The permanent effect on Iowa is not clear. If extensive use of paid TV continues in future caucus campaigns, Iowa will become prohibitively expensive for all but the most well-funded campaigns, and part of the rationale for accepting Iowa as a starting point in the presidential race will be lost.

The 1996 caucuses again illustrated how difficult it is for presidential aspirants, no matter how well known, to maintain interest in and enthusiasm for their candidacies over two presidential cycles. The Dole campaign experienced many of the same difficulties in Iowa that Bush had encountered in 1988—complacency and perhaps overconfidence, an aging organization, a lack of passion and excitement among supporters, a businesslike approach to the campaign, and the inability to articulate a vision for the future. Dole also had difficulty appealing to younger voters in Iowa. The crowds at his events were disproportionately made up of senior citizens. Dole's well-funded national organization enabled him to win the GOP nomination, but Iowa exposed weaknesses that Clinton exploited in the general election campaign.

Buchanan and Alexander were the "surprises" of the 1996 caucuses. The media chose to focus on Buchanan, whom they saw as a real threat to Dole after Iowa. The interpretation of the Iowa results gave Buchanan media momentum and put Dole on the defensive going into New Hampshire. When Buchanan edged Dole in the New Hampshire primary, he gained yet more media attention. But Buchanan was a minority, protest candidate and his level of support remained in the area of 25 percent throughout the national campaign. Although he made life uncomfortable for Dole, he never really threatened Dole for the nomination. Once again, as a result of the caucuses, the media highlighted a candidate who had little if any chance of winning the nomination. Dole—like Clinton, Bush, and Dukakis in recent elections—demonstrated that momentum from Iowa is no substitute for a large war chest and the ability to field a national campaign organization. Jimmy Carter is still the only dark-horse candidate to win his party's presidential nomination as a result of momentum gained in the Iowa caucuses!

Part of the reason for the Buchanan and Alexander surprises in 1996 was the failure of the polls in Iowa to discern their relatively high levels of support. In 1988, the Iowa Poll missed much of Robertson's support, and that was the case with Buchanan as well. The *Register* sampled Republicans likely to participate in the caucuses, but Buchanan drew many supporters from outside that population, and the poll consistently failed to detect this support. In fairness to those who conduct the Iowa Poll, the wide-open nature of the caucuses (anyone can participate) and the widespread use of paid TV and negative ads made the 1996 campaign more volatile than previous campaigns. In the final week, the number of "undecided" respondents was higher than usual, Gramm and Forbes were losing support, and Buchanan and Alexander were on the upswing.

The final Iowa Poll was conducted February 3 through 8, four to nine days before the caucuses, so it did not reflect most of the fluctuation in support that took place in the final week, as well as Buchanan's non-Republican support. Buchanan's 23.3 percent of the caucus vote was more than double his 11 percent share in the final Iowa Poll. The comparable figures for Alexander were 17.6 percent in the caucuses and 10 percent in the poll. Forbes's totals changed in the reverse direction—10.2 percent in the caucuses, compared with 16 percent in the final poll. Moreover, the Iowa Poll numbers for Buchanan and Alexander did not reach double digits until the final survey.

The expectations game relies very heavily on public opinion polls, so it is little wonder that the media were surprised by the 1996 Iowa caucus results. Those who play the expectations game may need to remind themselves of the limits of public opinion polling. The Iowa Poll uses current methods and technology to conduct its surveys, but polls were never intended to predict future events. They are subject to several limitations, most notably in the case of Iowa the difficulty of identifying likely caucus attenders.

The tendency for Iowans to support midwesterners in the caucuses continued in 1996, even though Dole's support was somewhat modest. Dole, like fellow midwestern candidates McGovern, Mondale, Gephardt, and Simon, benefited from his home state's proximity to Iowa.

Finally, the media appear to have adjusted their expectations of Iowa's role in the 1996 nominating process. Unlike 1988, when much was made of Iowa's failure to provide a boost for caucus winners Gephardt and Dole, the media played up the "surprises" from the caucuses and Iowa's role as a winnower.

References

Alter, Jonathan. 1996. "Can You Really Buy a Caucus?" *Newsweek*, January 22, p. 38.

Apple, R. W., Jr. 1996. "Victory Laced with Caution." *New York Times*, February 13, p. A1.

Balz, Dan, and Edward Walsh. 1996. "Dole Edges Buchanan in Iowa GOP Vote." *Washington Post*, February 13, p. A1.

Berke, Richard L. 1995. "Surprising Straw Poll Gives Dole a Glimpse of the Battles Ahead." *New York Times*, August 21, p. A1.

———. 1996. "Dole Tops Field in Iowa Caucuses." *New York Times*, February 13, p. A1.

Buell, Emmett H., Jr. 1996a. "The Invisible Primary." In *In Pursuit of the White House: How We Choose Our Presidential Nominees,* edited by William G. Mayer, 1-43. Chatham, N.J.: Chatham House.

———. 1996b. "The 'Invisible Primary' Revisited." Paper delivered at the annual meeting of the Southern Political Science Association, Atlanta, November 9.

Congressional Quarterly Weekly Review. 1995 and 1996.

Cook, Rhodes. 1995. "Forbes Candidacy Producing Eye-opening Poll Showings." *Congressional Quarterly,* December 2, pp. 3674-76.

———. 1996a. "Dole Suffers Bit of a Chill in Alaska Straw Vote." *Congressional Quarterly,* February 3, pp. 313-14.

———. 1996b. "Gramm's Candidacy Teeters after Loss in Louisiana." *Congressional Quarterly,* February 10, pp. 363-65.

———. 1996c. "Dole's Shaky Lead Faces Test in Volatile New Hampshire." *Congressional Quarterly,* February 17, pp. 399-403.

Day, Mike. 1995. Interview with author, July 25. Day and Jeanette Schmett were the managers of Lugar's Iowa campaign.

Des Moines Register. 1995 and 1996.

Elving, Ronald D. 1995. "Benefits from Powell Decision Spread among Candidates." *Congressional Quarterly,* November 11, pp. 3470-72.

Fineman, Howard. 1995. "Richie Rich on the Stump." *Newsweek,* July 24, p. 47.

Fogarty, Thomas A. 1995a. "Poll Shows Dole Ahead but Slipping." *Des Moines Register,* September 17, p. 1A.

———. 1995b. "Forbes Ads Flood Airwaves in Iowa." *Des Moines Register,* December 11, p. 2A.

———. 1996. "Dole Still Strong in Iowa." *Des Moines Register,* February 10, p. 1A.

Fogarty, Thomas A., and Jonathan Roos. 1996. "Procrastination Factor Weighs in for Alexander." *Des Moines Register,* February 13, p. 8A.

Frum, David. 1995. "The Elite Primary." *Atlantic Monthly,* November, pp. 22-36.

Gibbs, Steve. 1995. Telephone interview with author, June 16; interview with author, July 25. Gibbs was Dole's first campaign manager in Iowa.

Greenblatt, Alan. 1995. "Buchanan Hopes His Voice Will Give Him a Voice." *Congressional Quarterly,* May 20, pp. 1442-47.

———. 1996. "Buchanan's 'Long-Shot' Campaign." *Congressional Quarterly,* February 17, p. 401.

Hadley, Arthur T. 1976. *The Invisible Primary.* Englewood Cliffs, N.J.: Prentice Hall.

Hardy, Tom. 1996. Interview with author, January 22. Hardy is a reporter for the *Chicago Tribune.*

Hartman, Holly. 1996. "Is Caucus Now Up for Grabs?" *Des Moines Register,* February 9, p. 2A.

Harwood, John. 1995. "GOP Race Loses Air of Predictability after Gramm Ties Dole in Iowa Poll." *Wall Street Journal,* August 21, p. A10.

———. 1996. "Rivals' Attacks in Lively Iowa Debate Underscore Forbes' Growing Strength." *Wall Street Journal,* January 15, p. B5.

Harwood, John, and Bob Davis. 1996. "Dole Fends Off Late Surge by Buchanan to Win Crucial First Test in Iowa Caucuses." *Wall Street Journal,* February 13, p. A16.

Haus, Bob. 1995. Telephone interview with author, July 17; interview with author, July 25. Haus was Gramm's Iowa campaign manager.

Holmes, Steven A. 1995. "As Primary Season Approaches, States Vie for Position and Profit." *New York Times,* December 8, p. A 1.

Humeston, John. 1995. Interview with author, June 19; telephone interview with author, August 23. Humeston was operations manager of the Alexander campaign in Iowa.

Hurley, Chris. 1996. Telephone interview with author, February 21. Hurley was Keyes's Iowa campaign chair.

Iowa Poll. 1995 and 1996. Vols. for 1995 and 1996. Des Moines: Des Moines Register and Tribune Company.

Jackson, Andy. 1995. Telephone interview with author, November 21. Jackson was an employee of the Keyes campaign.

Kearney, Darrell. 1995. Telephone interview with author, October 24. Kearney was Dole's second Iowa campaign manager.

———. 1996. Telephone interviews with author, March 8 and October 14.

Keen, Judy. 1996. "Dole Looking over His Shoulder." *USA Today,* February 13, p. 3A.

Kennedy, Brian. 1995. Telephone interview with author, August 24. Kennedy was chair of the Republican Party of Iowa from 1995 to 1997.

———. 1996. Telephone interview with author, October 14.

———. 1997. Telephone interview with author, March 19.

Klein, Joe. 1995. "A Plausible Hothead?" *Newsweek,* May 29, p. 45.

Kramer, Michael. 1995. "Why Dole Hasn't Lost It." *Time,* September 4, p. 34.

Lambrecht, Bill. 1996. Telephone interview with author, January 5. Lambrecht is a reporter for the *St. Louis Post-Dispatch.*

Lickteig, Mary Ann. 1996. "The Media Menagerie Provides a Sideshow to the Caucus Circus." *Des Moines Register,* February 13, p. 9A.

Masteller, Kathleen. 1995. Telephone interview with author, July 26. Masteller was a finance assistant for the Republican Party of Iowa during the 1996 caucuses.

Midday Record. 1995.

Minzesheimer, Bob. 1996. "Forbes: Attack Ads Backfire in Iowa." *USA Today,* February 15, p. 4A.

Newsweek. 1995.

New York Times. 1995 and 1996.

Norman, Jane. 1996. "Spread Out the Primary Season, Iowa and New Hampshire Say." *Des Moines Register,* May 31, p. 6A.

Oldfield, Duane M. 1996. "The Christian Right in the Presidential Nominating Process." In *In Pursuit of the White House: How We Choose Our Presidential Nominees,* edited by William G. Mayer, 254-82. Chatham, N.J.: Chatham House.

Pilmer, Sharon. 1996. Telephone interviews with author, February 12 and October 14. Pilmer was the director of the Iowa Poll from 1992 through 1996.

Powell, Stewart M. 1995. "Candidate Forbes Vows a Tax Overhaul." *Des Moines Register*, September 23, p. 5A.

Redman, Dick. 1996. Telephone interview with author, February 21. Redman was Alexander's Iowa campaign chair.

Riedel-King, Chris. 1996. Telephone interview with author, January 16. Riedel-King was the *Register* employee responsible for debate arrangements.

Robinson, Kayne. 1995. Conversation with author, February 12.

Roepke, Mark. 1995. Interview with author, July 25. Roepke was Buchanan's Iowa campaign manager.

———. 1996. Interview with author, October 18.

Scheffler, Steve. 1996. Telephone interview with author, December 2. Scheffler is the field director of the Iowa Christian Coalition and was an employee of the Dole campaign in Iowa.

Schwieder, Dorothy. 1996. *Iowa: The Middle Land*. Ames, Iowa: Iowa State University Press.

Seib, Gerald. 1995a. "Quayle, in an Unexpected Move, Quits Presidential Race, Puts 'Family First.'" *Wall Street Journal*, February 10, p. A10.

———. 1995b. "Alexander Would Send Chunks of Government Back to the States." *Wall Street Journal*, February 24, A1.

———. 1995c. "Powell's Exit Sparks Debate over the Shape of Politics in America." *Wall Street Journal*, November 9, p. A1.

———. 1995d. "Forbes Boomlet: A Rogue Force Stalks the Field." *Wall Street Journal*, December 6, p. A20.

Seplow, Stephen. 1995. Telephone interview with author, November 9. Seplow is a reporter for the *Philadelphia Inquirer*.

Shillinger, Kurt. 1995. "Dole Takes Hit in 'Important' Early Iowa Poll." *Christian Science Monitor*, August 21, p. 1.

Stanhope, Phil. 1995. Telephone interviews with author, August 23 and December 12. Stanhope was Taylor's Iowa campaign manager.

Stout, David. 1996. "Calling Results of Caucuses Before They Even Begin." *New York Times*, February 13, p. A19.

Taylor, Maurice. 1995 and 1996. Campaign press releases, December 22 and January 27.

Taylor, Paul. 1995. "Money Not All in Gramm Surge." *Washington Post*, August 21, p. A10.

Tegeler, Gretchen. 1997. Telephone interview with author, April 22. Tegeler is the director of the Iowa Department of Management.

Television News Index and Abstracts. 1975-76, 1979-80, 1983-84, 1987-88, 1991-92, 1995-96. Nashville, Tenn.: Vanderbilt University.

Tollerson, Ernest. 1995. "In Iowa, Buchanan Tries to Convince Conservatives That He's Their Man." *New York Times*, December 3, p. 34.

Tramontina, Mike. 1996. Telephone interview with author, November 26. Tramontina was Clinton's Iowa campaign manager.

Wall Howard, Phoebe. 1994. "Specter Pushes for GOP Reforms." *Des Moines Register*, June 14, p. 5M.

Wall Street Journal. 1995.

Walsh, Edward. 1994. "In Iowa, GOP Debates a Fundamental Message." *Washington Post*, June 26, p. A 6.

Wilke, Curtis. 1995. "The Power of Deep Pockets." Reprinted from the *Boston Globe* in the *Des Moines Register*, December 6, p. 4A.

Chapter 11

The 2000 Caucuses: More Important than Ever

IOWA'S "FIRST-IN-THE-NATION" caucuses have played an important role in the presidential nominations of at least one of the major parties in nearly every nominating cycle since 1972. Over this time both parties in Iowa have adopted and refined their rules governing participation in the precinct caucuses, determining candidate commitments, and selecting delegates to subsequent conventions in their respective, multi-stage processes. Another part of the "institutionalization" of Iowa's Democratic and Republican caucuses is the inordinate coverage they nearly always receive, not only from local and national news media, but also from the news organizations of other nations. More often than not, however, changes in presidential nominating politics traceable to frontloading have jeopardized the priority of Iowa's precinct caucuses and forced state party leaders to operate in violation of national party rules. Such threats to Iowa's first-in-the-nation status cast doubt on the permanency of its settled procedures as well as on its role in an ever-evolving system of presidential selection.

Precaucus Activity

For the 2000 election, the Republican National Committee had put into place new rules governing the presidential nominating process. These rules prohibited states from holding nominating events earlier than February 1, and required state parties to certify a date for their caucuses or primary election by July 1, 1999. Early certification was supposed to put an end to states "leapfrogging" one another and moving their nominating events closer to the beginning of the window. To spread out the schedule and to encourage states to hold their nominating events later, bonus delegates were to be awarded. Unfortunately, the parties now had different rules: the Republican window began February 1, one month earlier than the March 1 Democratic starting date. Moreover, unlike the Democrats, Republican rules did not protect the early positions of Iowa and New Hampshire.

The promise of bonus delegates had little impact, and when California moved its primary date to March 7, other states also moved their nominating events closer to the front. Primary and caucus date changes led to the familiar Iowa-New Hampshire two-step as they adapted their dates to the ever-changing national calendar. Iowa's parties rescheduled the caucuses three times. The original date was February 21, but Louisiana Republicans prompted a move to February 7 when they picked an earlier date for their caucuses (Yepsen 1999a, 1M). The second change to January 31 was in anticipation of New Hampshire moving its primary to February 8 to fend off a likely move by South Carolina (Yepsen 1999d, 5M). But, when New Hampshire announced in late September that it would hold its primary election on February 1, the Iowa parties faced a dilemma. They could stay with the January 31 date and hold their caucuses two days before New Hampshire or change the date for a third time to comply with an Iowa law requiring an eight-day separation between New Hampshire and Iowa (Yepsen 1999e, 8M). The Iowa parties opted to move the caucuses to January 24 in spite of the logistical problems associated with another change and knowing they would be violating both parties' national rules.

The Republican Campaign

On June 12, 1998, the Republican Party of Iowa held a "First in the Nation Gala" in Cedar Rapids that coincided with their state convention. The purpose as stated on the tickets was to give those attending an early opportunity "to meet some of the top national Republicans who are considering a run for the White House in 2000," and to raise funds for the state party. The 1998 Gala was a replay of the "Star-Spangled Preview" held four years earlier in Des Moines. Ten individuals of varied national stature addressed the gathering in an order determined by draw—Steve Forbes, Alan Keyes, Lamar Alexander, Marilyn Quayle (for husband Dan), John Kasich, Bob Smith, Marc Racicot, John Ashcroft, Bob Barr, and Gary Bauer. Keyes opened his speech with "Bill Clinton is a liar," and that set the tone for the rest of the evening. There was a new wrinkle in 1998: all participants except Barr and Racicot held receptions that ranged from Alexander's

"Taste of Tennessee" dinner for 500 people to Ashcroft's ice cream social. C-Span aired the event live and press coverage was extensive with approximately 100 national and local reporters attending (Hugh Winebrenner's notes from the event).

Although billed as an early opportunity to meet top national Republicans, it is likely that most of those attending the Gala had already had some contact with the potential GOP presidential candidates. The Iowa exploratory visits began at about the same time in 1997 as in past caucus cycles, but the early campaign in this cycle was more intense. By the time of the Gala, fifteen Republican presidential "explorers" had spent 122 days in Iowa courting activists. As of that date in 1993-94, eight candidates had campaigned 39 days in Iowa and in 1985-86, six candidates campaigned 29 days (all data on "days in Iowa" were collected by Hugh Winebrenner). The increased activity was undoubtedly due to the lack of a clear front-runner. Although George W. Bush was already leading in the Gallup Poll (all Gallup polls cited are national surveys) at the time of the Gala, he had not yet visited Iowa.

GOP hopefuls visited frequently and helped raise funds for the state Republican Party and for Iowa candidates in the mid-term election (by the November 1998 election, presidential hopefuls had spent 190 days in Iowa). The "invisible primary" would eliminate several well-known Republicans between the GOP Gala and the Iowa precinct caucuses, but at one point or another in the precaucus campaign nineteen individuals explored their chances in Iowa.

In late March 1997, Lamar Alexander was the featured speaker at a Lincoln Club fundraiser in Des Moines. Alexander was embarking on his second bid for the Republican nomination and was the first GOP hopeful to visit Iowa in the 2000 cycle. By the time he announced an exploratory committee in early January 1999, Alexander had spent 36 days in Iowa and had gained the support of outgoing Governor Terry Branstad and many of his team. He ran TV ads in August 1998, among the earliest on record. Alexander opened a Des Moines office with a staff of five immediately after filing exploratory papers. The staff grew to 12 by the time Alexander came to Iowa in June to announce county chairs in all 99 counties (Kochel 1999).

Gary Bauer, a leading religious conservative and longtime President of the Family Research Council in Washington, D.C., made his first Iowa appearance in mid-April 1997. He spoke at a breakfast at the First Church of the Open Bible in Des Moines, and later in the day visited with Republican legislators at the Statehouse. He returned two days later and attended all five GOP district conventions. Not well known in Iowa, Bauer would campaign vigorously in the state targeting social and Christian conservatives (Yepsen 1997a, 5M). Bauer also ran early TV ads in September 1998 calling for President Clinton's resignation. After filing exploratory papers with the Federal Election Commission (FEC) in February 1999, he became a regular visitor. He hired full-time aides who opened an office in April with a staff of five that grew to 11 by the Iowa Straw Poll (Popma 1999). He attempted to distinguish his candidacy from the conservative field by describing himself as "the most consistent Reagan Republican," and by emphasizing his anti-abortion stance and his view that normalization of relations with China was appeasement.

Congressman John Kasich, chair of the House Budget Committee, spoke to a large crowd at the "Abe Lincoln Gala" in Des Moines in mid-May 1997 (Yepsen 1997b, 8B). By the time he filed exploratory committee papers with the FEC in January 1999, Kasich had spent 18 days in Iowa. On the same day he filed with FEC, Kasich hired Iowa political veteran Karen Slifka, who ran a one-person operation from her home until they opened a campaign office in Des Moines on April 1. The staff grew to seven in early June (Slifka 1999), but the campaign suffered a crushing blow when Kasich finished a distant tenth in the June Iowa Poll with the support of only 1 percent of the likely caucus participants (June 1999 Iowa Poll cited in McCormick 1999a). The June 25-27 Gallup Poll had Kasich's support at 3 percent (all Gallup Poll results are from Mayer 2004, 114-27). Two weeks later he dropped out of the race, citing fund-raising difficulties.

Steve Forbes began his second caucus campaign with speeches to Republican audiences in three Iowa cities in mid-June 1997. He had entered the 1996 race very late and relied on radio and TV advertising with limited success. Forbes indicated that he had not decided whether to enter the contest, but if he did it would be "a full-fledged early start" (Yepsen 1997c, 5M). In late May 1998 Forbes made Bob Haus the Midwest field director of his PAC, and Haus began laying the groundwork for an Iowa campaign. In March 1999 Forbes filed exploratory papers with the FEC (Haus March 22, 1999). By mid-April he had a Des Moines office up and running with 10 employees (Stineman 1999).

It was beginning to look like a rerun of the 1996 campaign when conservative talk-show host Alan Keyes spoke at a rally in Cedar Rapids on July 3, 1997. Like Alexander and Forbes he was a veteran of the caucus wars, but unlike the others Keyes had waged a low-budget campaign and would do the same in this caucus cycle. He was a frequent visitor in the early stages of the 2000 campaign employing a "rally strategy." Keyes spent two days a month in Iowa and held three "renewing America" rallies in public places, usually high schools. The meetings were advertised in local papers with the goal of attracting as many people as possible to hear Keyes' message of God and family (Granzow March 3, 1999).

Keyes opened a Des Moines campaign office on July 1, 1999, with three full-time employees (Granzow July 16, 1999). In the lead-up to the Iowa Straw Poll he spent more time in the state and by the August poll had logged 44 days in Iowa. This time around Keyes was competing with a large field of presidential hopefuls, each of whom claimed to be Christian and conservative.

Former vice president Dan Quayle made his initial visit to Iowa in mid-July 1997. The two-day trip included stops in Des Moines where he spoke at a Polk County GOP picnic, attended fundraisers for two state lawmakers, appeared on a radio show, and at a fundraiser in Council Bluffs (Mayes 1997, p. A1). Quayle had decided after a 1995 Iowa visit to forego a presidential run in 1996, but now he embarked on a vigorous effort. His Campaign America PAC opened a Midwest office in Cedar Rapids on January 15, 1998, a one-person operation in the home of Gary Geipel, his Midwest field director (Geipel 1998). Although well liked by the conservative wing of the party, Quayle still bore scars from his vice-presidential days. The image of "intellectual lightweight" had to be overcome, and he had to distinguish his candidacy from the very conservative field.

New Hampshire Senator Bob Smith was perhaps the least known of the 2000 presidential explorers. He attended a fundraiser for Senator Grassley in September 1997, and spent the next three days meeting with conservative activists. A strident social conservative, Smith let it be known that he would hold the other GOP candidates' feet to the fire on social issues. Smith came out of the chute running and by the Gala had campaigned 28 days in Iowa.

Elizabeth Dole, president of the American Red Cross, visited Des Moines in October 1997. Dole had an impressive record of public service and was the wife of Bob Dole, for whom she had campaigned in Iowa four years earlier. She announced on her third trip to Iowa, in

March 1998, the formation of an exploratory committee, but spent only five days in the state in 1997-98. Dole announced in January 1999 that she was leaving the Red Cross "to consider a White House candidacy" (Harwood 1999, A8). She opened an office in Des Moines in early May 1999 and by August employed a staff of nine that put all their efforts into identifying and turning out supporters for the Iowa Straw Poll (Shaw August 24, 1999). Dole declared her candidacy on July 1 and spent 19 of the next 45 days in Iowa working toward a strong showing in Ames.

Missouri Senator John Ashcroft spoke at a fundraiser in Des Moines in early November 1997. Like so many of the hopefuls, he stressed his fiscal and social conservatism. By the summer of 1998 Ashcroft had spent 17 days in the state courting religious and social conservatives. In August Ashcroft's PAC ran $26,500 worth of radio and newspaper ads in a dozen cities to promote a four-day cross-state tour (Sawyer 1998, A5). Less than two weeks later, he launched a $175,000 TV ad blitz in the four major viewing areas of the state touting his two-rate tax system (*DMR* Aug. 24, 1998, 3A). The vigorous early campaign and substantial media spending did not produce the desired results. Ashcroft was one of the first to exit the race on January 5, 1999.

Arizona Senator John McCain was in Iowa on February 18, 1998, to hold a Senate sub-committee hearing on high airline fares. He also did some fund-raising for Iowa candidates and met with the editorial board of the *Register* (Yepsen 1998a, 3A). McCain made two more trips to Iowa, but did not participate in the Iowa Straw Poll, and in November announced that he would bypass the Iowa caucuses (Yepsen 1999f, 1M). He did, however, participate in two Iowa debates in December and January.

Pat Buchanan visited Iowa in late April 1998 to promote his book, *The Great Betrayal: How American Sovereignty and Social Justice Are Being Sacrificed to the Gods of the Global Economy* (Yepsen 1998b, 2M). This was the third Iowa campaign for the well-known pit bull from the right. His surprise second place finish in the 1996 caucuses boosted him into New Hampshire, where he shocked the Republican establishment by winning the primary election and nipping at Bob Dole's heels in succeeding primaries. Buchanan returned to Iowa in March 1999 and announced his candidacy. Adept at using free media to run a low-budget campaign, he reiterated the message used in the 1996 caucus cycle that the North American Free Trade Agreement (NAFTA) was the cause of many of America's problems ranging from the loss of jobs to the flow of illegal drugs into the country. In the spring and summer Buchanan spent 35 days in Iowa pointing to the Iowa Straw Poll in August. He opened a campaign office in Des Moines in late May, and by mid-June employed three full-time staff (Erickson 1999).

While the other presidential hopefuls swarmed over Iowa, George W. Bush remained in Texas. He had been the front-runner in Gallup polls since September 1997. The Texas Governor wrote to Mary Kramer, President of the Iowa Senate, inviting her to bring a delegation of legislators to Austin for a visit. Kramer and a dozen of her colleagues flew to Texas on two small planes on February 8, 1999, and met with Bush for about two hours over breakfast at the Governor's mansion. He queried the delegation about Iowa and how he might be received in the state. Bush told the group he had not made up his mind about running and that he was committed to avoiding out-of-state politics until the end of the Texas legislative session in May. They in turn presented to him two letters of support signed by the vast majority of the GOP members of the Iowa legislature. According to Kramer, the primary mission of the group was to persuade Bush to campaign in Iowa if he chose to seek the nomination (Kramer May 2008).

In early March, Bush formed an exploratory committee. In short order he hired staff including one the most successful political operatives in Iowa, Luke Roth, as executive director. Roth had an office functioning by mid-May and on his first Iowa visit in June Bush announced that he was running for president.

The last candidate to visit Iowa was Utah Senator Orrin Hatch. He announced his candidacy on July 1, 1999, on CNN's "Larry King Live." Hatch made his first visit to Iowa in late July. Senator Grassley advised Hatch to skip the Iowa Straw Poll and plan a strong post-Ames campaign because he had only three weeks to generate a turnout for the event (Norman 1999, 1A). But Hatch pushed ahead, hired a staff person, and competed in Ames. His office was not really operational until November, and not surprisingly the Straw Poll did not go well for Hatch.

Several other individuals, including some very well-known political figures, visited Iowa in the precaucus period, tested the political waters, and decided not to enter the race. They included Jack Kemp, the 1996 vice-presidential nominee, House Speaker Newt Gingrich, Wisconsin Governor Tommy Thompson, Oklahoma Representative J.

C. Watts, New York City Mayor Rudy Giuliani, and Tennessee Senator Fred Thompson.

The late spring and summer of 1999 were very intense times as the candidates prepared for the Iowa Straw Poll. They spent 240 days in Iowa from April 1 to August 14, when the Straw Poll took place. They usually traveled the state by bus, gave speeches, and mixed with crowds wherever they could find them. A day in mid-July from the Bush campaign is typical. Bush arrived a little early for a pancake breakfast at Tower Park in Des Moines. He shook hands and flipped a few pancakes to the delight of the crowd of about a hundred people. WHO-TV interviewed him for their "drive time" show and he held a mini press conference. Bush stayed about 30 minutes, boarded his bus and, followed by a press bus, left for Ames, Marshalltown, and Newton for similar events (Hugh Winebrenner's notes from the event).

During the summer of 1999 two events had an impact on the campaign. The *Register* published the results of an Iowa Poll on June 27. Bush led the field even though he had been a declared candidate for only one day when the survey of likely GOP caucus goers began. The percentages of support for the candidates in the sample were: Bush 40, Dole 13, Forbes 10, Keyes 5, Buchanan 5, Alexander 4, McCain 3, Bauer 3, Quayle 3, Kasich 1, Smith less than 1, and undecided 13 (June 1999 Iowa Poll cited in McCormick 1999a). The publicity surrounding Bush's declaration of candidacy probably had some effect on the survey, but he was doing even better nationally. A June 25-27 Gallup Poll had his support at 59 percent, with everyone else in the single digits.

The second event was the release of national fund-raising totals for the first six months of 1999. Bush had raised $37.1 million, a sum that dwarfed his nearest Republican opponents: Steve Forbes, $9.4 million ($6.7 million self-financed), and John McCain, $6.3 ($2 million from his Senate campaign fund). The others lagged even farther behind (FEC June 30, 1999).

The primary purpose of the Iowa Straw Poll since its inception in 1979 has been to raise funds for the Republican Party of Iowa, but the event has taken on a life of its own. Bush's huge lead in fund-raising and in national and state public opinion polls put the other candidates' campaigns in tenuous positions. They all needed some good news to buck up supporters and bring in campaign dollars. Yet Bush's lead meant that he too needed a strong finish in the poll because of the "expectations game." He was the front-runner, the leader in fundraising and the public opinion polls, and now he was expected to win in Ames.

While the candidates put in long days on the campaign trail, their staffs worked even longer hours. Most of the campaigns purchased from the Republican Party of Iowa lists of individuals who had attended prior caucuses (Smith, Bauer, Forbes, Quayle, Alexander, Kasich, Bush, and Dole each paid $10,000 for the list of about 135,000 people who attended the 1988, 1992, and 1996 caucuses). McCain, Buchanan, Keyes, and Ashcroft did not purchase the list (Hall Cerwinske 1999). Hatch did not buy the list but obtained it from "another source" (Miller, A. 1999). Some of the campaigns provided transportation to Ames for the Iowa Straw Poll from several points around the state. According to the party a total of 37,183 tickets were sold although not all were used (Miller, S. 1999).

The 1999 Iowa Straw Poll can only be described as a "happening." The weather was good and the crowd was huge. Approximately 35,000 people filled the area around the Hilton Coliseum at Iowa State University for a grand carnival with very large tents (Forbes' was air conditioned), food and drink, entertainment, and celebrities signing autographs. The nine participating candidates visited with supporters at their tents. Voting was limited to Iowans 18 and older with a picture ID, and the lines at the voting stations were long and slow moving. Editorial writers called the event a throwback to nineteenth-century political gatherings with fun for the whole family (see, for example, the *Des Moines Register* [Aug. 16, 1999, 6A], the *New York Times* [Aug. 16, 1999, A18], and *Wall Street Journal* [August 16, 1999, A14]).

When the program began at 4 o'clock only about a third of the crowd could fit into the auditorium. The candidates were allotted 13 minutes each for speeches and the party turned off the public address system during the remarks by Keyes and Quayle after each exceeded the time limit. Buchanan brought down the house with his Clinton-baiting remarks, and Forbes paid the price for dropping several hundred balloons during his pre-speech demonstration when the other campaigns drowned out the first several minutes of his speech by loudly popping the balloons (Hugh Winebrenner's notes from the event). The results reported in Table 11.1 were announced at 9 o'clock to the reporters remaining in the hall (as of August 12, 650 press credentials had been issued) and the C-Span audience viewing the event (Hall Cerwinske 1999).

The fallout was immediate. On the Monday following the Iowa Straw Poll, Alexander ended his candidacy. Three more of the candidates left the GOP field within 10 weeks of the Straw Poll. Quayle (Aug. 27) and Dole (Oct. 20) dropped out. Buchanan withdrew (Oct. 25) from the GOP to pursue the Reform Party nomination. The Straw Poll reduced the field to Bush, Forbes, Bauer, Keyes, and Hatch (Smith had dropped out of the Republican Party on July 12 to run as an independent). Waiting in New Hampshire was John McCain.

The problem for candidates (other than Bush and Forbes) was money. As Bush raised millions of dollars, the other candidates found it increasingly difficult to raise funds. They desperately needed Bush to stumble. But when Bush won in Ames and emerged even stronger, the money dried up for most of the others. The Straw Poll had accelerated the winnowing process. The compression of the primary and caucus season had moved everything forward and put even more emphasis on fund-raising, poll standing, and success in early events like the Iowa Straw Poll.

Table 11.1.   1999 Iowa straw poll

Bush, G. W.	7,418	31.3%
Forbes	4,921	20.8
Dole, E.	3,410	14.4
Bauer	2,114	8.9
Buchanan	1,719	7.3
Alexander	1,428	6.0
Keyes	1,101	4.6
Quayle	916	3.9
Hatch	558	2.4
McCain	83	0.4
Kasich	9	0
Smith	8	0
Total	23,685	100.0

Source: Republican Party of Iowa.

The Iowa GOP emerged as a big winner for having raised nearly one million dollars through a variety of creative means. In 1999, for the first time, the party rented the parking lot as well as Hilton Coliseum (in 1995 the candidates had to rent space directly from Iowa State). The party then auctioned parking lot spaces to the candidates to erect tents and hold receptions. Bush ($43,500) outbid Forbes ($42,900) for 60,000 square feet of prime location adjacent to the Coliseum and the others paid from $1000 to $8000 for their spaces depending on proximity to the building. Thirty booths inside the hall were sold to organizations and vendors for $250 each (Miller, S. 1999).

The Republican campaign in Iowa slowed dramatically after the Ames event. GOP candidates spent only 33 days in the state between the Straw Poll and the end of October. During that period, the FEC released third quarter national fund-raising results and Bush's success was more bad news for the other campaigns. Bush raised $57.1 million, Forbes $20.6 ($16.4 self-financed), McCain $9.3 ($2.0 from his Senate campaign fund), Bauer $6.3 (includes a $1 million loan later repaid with public matching funds), Keyes $2.5, and Hatch $1.3 (FEC September 30, 1999).

In November the *Register* published a second Iowa Poll. Bush maintained his huge lead over the field and Forbes was now a solid second. The remainder of the field lagged far behind. The percentages of support for the candidates in the survey were: Bush 49, Forbes 20, McCain 8, Bauer 7, Keyes 5, Hatch 1, and undecided 10 (Nov. 1999 Iowa Poll cited in McCormick 1999b). A Nov. 4-7 Gallup Poll had Bush support at 68 percent, McCain 12 percent, and the remaining candidates in single digits. The Bush juggernaut was rolling over the field in Iowa.

Since Pat Robertson successfully organized the Christian Right in 1988 its members have been a force in Republican caucus politics and have successfully moved the party to the right on social issues. They typically constitute 35 percent to 40 percent of those attending GOP caucuses. They hold the candidates strictly accountable on the wedge issues of prayer in school, abortion, and gay rights. Robertson in 1988 and Buchanan in 1996 owed their second place finishes in Iowa to a well-organized, unified Christian Right. According to the June Iowa Poll, the top issue for Iowa Republicans was once again moral and family values, followed by education, and then the economy. The only candidate who did not fully endorse the positions of the Christian Right was John McCain, and he was bypassing Iowa. All the others vigorously pursued their support.

However, the Christian Right had become more pluralistic in outlook, and each of the campaigns had the support of evangelical activists. Ione Dilley, chair of the Christian Coalition in Iowa and a Bush supporter, observed that there were "Christian Coalition people working in each of the campaigns" (Buttry 2000, 1A). If evangelicals divided their support among several candidates, their impact on the race would be limited.

The use of radio and TV advertising in caucus campaigns initiated in 1988 became a big part of the precinct caucuses in the 1996 cycle. Iowa has succeeded in retaining its retail politics even though radio and TV spending has increased. Alexander, Ashcroft, and Bauer aired TV ads in the late summer and early fall 1998. Forbes also ran early TV ads beginning in June before the Iowa Straw Poll.

Unlike 1996 when he initiated an air war of negative advertising, Forbes now had a strong organization in place, and for the most part, used TV to introduce himself and his policy stands to Iowa viewers. Most of the TV advertising, however, is aired late in the campaign. There were of course some negative ads, but nothing like those in 1996. The Republican candidate spending at the NBC and CBS affiliates in Des Moines is presented in Table 11.2. The total spending at the two stations in 2000 was about the same as in 1996, although Forbes spent substantially more at each.

Debates or forums involving the presidential candidates are a regular part of Iowa campaigns. There were only two Republican debates in the 2000 cycle as compared to four in the 1996 campaign. The WHO presidential debate (The Iowa Debate) was held on December 13 before a nearly full house at the Civic Center in Des Moines. All of the Republicans still standing—Bauer, Bush, Forbes, Hatch, Keyes, and McCain—took part. WHO-TV news anchor John Bachman and Tom Brokaw of NBC moderated and asked most of the questions. The event was broadcast nationally. The Republican Party of Iowa assisted with tickets and press credentials and, according to Communications Director Ann Dougherty, 220 press credentials were issued.

Front-runner Bush took the stage with the most to lose, having appeared both mechanical and shallow to pundits in previous New Hampshire and Arizona debates. Only Forbes responded literally to

Table 11.2.   2000 Republican spending at WHO-TV and KCCI-TV

	WHO	KCCI
Forbes	$287,335	$461,325
Bush, G. W.	161,395	214,395
Bauer	112,490	121,575
Alexander	58,125	85,135
Ashcroft	0	33,400
Hatch	0	10,000
Keyes	3,845	7,075
Total	623,190	932,905

Source: Table created from records provided by Mary Hiatt, Traffic Manager, WHO, and Anne Marie Caudron, National Sales Manager, KCCI. The Alexander (We the Parents) and Bauer (American Renewal) figures include early ad purchases by their PACs. Ashcroft's PAC (American Values) purchased his ads.

Brokaw's question asking each candidate to name the political philosopher most influential in his thinking. First up, Forbes touted the natural rights argument of John Locke. Keyes sidestepped the philosophical dimension by embracing all of the delegates who showed up in Philadelphia for the 1787 Constitutional Convention. Bush drained whatever remained of the question's premise by answering "Jesus Christ because he changed my heart," and that put the rest of his rivals in a bind, obliging most of them with the notable exception of McCain to profess that they, too, revered Jesus (Hugh Winebrenner's notes from the forum).

The *Register* sponsored another debate on January 15 at the small Iowa Public Television studio in the Des Moines suburb of Johnston. Perhaps the most unusual thing about the event was the 51-degree temperature. The good weather allowed TV crews from CNN, Fox News, and C-Span to do their stories outside, but it also brought out a number of demonstrators who were peaceful but boisterous.

The debate, although only the second held in Iowa, was the seventh joint appearance in recent months. The question and answer format did not allow a real interchange, so candidates took turns giving speeches. The candidates returned repeatedly to their themes—e.g., Forbes (flat tax and anti-abortion), Keyes (the moral decline of America), and McCain (campaign finance reform)—and all six gave good synopses of the messages they had conveyed to Iowa audiences for months. On the lighter side, when Bauer attempted to establish his working-class roots by telling the audience that he was the son of a janitor, Hatch chimed in "I was a janitor" (Hugh Winebrenner's notes from the debate).

Money was in the news as the Republican campaign reached the end of the year. The year-end report for 1999 showed that Bush had raised $67.6 million, Forbes $33.9 ($28.7 self-financed), McCain $15.5 ($2.0 from his Senate campaign fund), Bauer $9.7 ($2.9 million in loans later repaid with public matching funds), Keyes $4.4 ($926,000 in loans later repaid with public matching funds), and Hatch $2.3 ($200,000 in loans) (FEC December 31, 1999). Bush's total was "more than three times his original goal of $20 million for the year" and more than double the fund-raising record in a pre-election year (Corrado 2001, 100).

Bush was continuing a fund-raising trend employed by successful candidates in recent pre-election years, namely raising large sums of money from $1,000 donors. His "Pioneers" (individuals who agreed to raise at least $100,000 for the candidate) brought in many new donors and Bush received "74 percent of his total 1999 receipts from $1,000 donors." A slight break in the trend toward the reliance on large donors occurred when John McCain received $1.4 million in donations via the Internet in the week following his New Hampshire primary victory. McCain's Internet donations reached $3.7 million by the end of February, largely in small contributions (Corrado and Gouvea 2004, 60-61).

In January the *Register* published in quick succession two more GOP Iowa polls, reported in Table 11.3. The final poll was published the day before the caucuses. There was little change in the horse race. Bush remained far ahead and Forbes retained his second place position. (A January 17-19 Gallup Poll had Bush at 63 percent, McCain 19 percent, and the others still in single digits.) Respondents were asked in the final poll how much they were influenced by endorsements from political leaders. Only 10 percent said they were influenced "a lot," 26 percent "a little," and 63 percent "not much" at all. We need only recall that Terry Branstad, one of Iowa's most popular governors, endorsed Lamar Alexander. The survey also found that 34 percent of

Table 11.3.   1999-2000 *Des Moines Register* Republican Iowa Polls

	6-99	11-99	1-8-00	1-23-00
Bush, G. W.	40%	49	45	43
Forbes	10	20	18	20
Keyes	5	5	9	8
McCain	3	8	8	8
Bauer	3	7	7	6
Hatch*	N/A	1	2	1
Others**	26			
Undecided	13	10	11	14
Sample size	397	500	500	600
Margin of error (%) is +/-	4.9	4.4	4.4	4.0

*Hatch entered the race after polling started in June.
**The "others" category includes the percentages for candidates who withdrew from the race between June and November 1999—Elizabeth Dole 13, Pat Buchanan 5, Lamar Alexander 4, Dan Quayle 3, John Kasich 1, and Bob Smith less than 1.

likely caucus-goers described themselves as "born again" Christians (Jan. 16-21, 2000, Iowa Poll cited in McCormick 2000b).

Bush was clearly the winner in the "invisible primary." Nationally, he won the "money primary," the Gallup polls by huge margins, and the contest for endorsements. He also placed first in all four of the Iowa polls and won the Straw Poll after only two months of campaigning in Iowa. One student of presidential nominations asserts that the winners in the invisible primary normally capture their party's presidential nomination (Mayer 2004, 83-132).

Republican Caucus Results

The results of the Republican caucuses are presented in Table 11.4. It is important to remember that the results are from a vote (Straw Poll) that is unrelated to delegate selection. That said, the caucuses are treated like a primary election and the Straw Poll is the only reason many attend the gatherings. Many call it a night after the vote results are announced.

Table 11.4.   2000 Republican precinct caucus results

	Preferences	Percentage (%)
Bush, G. W.	35,948	41.0
Forbes	26,744	30.5
Keyes	12,496	14.3
Bauer	7,487	8.5
McCain	4,093	4.7
Hatch	898	1.0
TOTAL	87,666	100

Source: Republican Party of Iowa from 2,114 of 2,131 precincts (99.2%). Bush was the winner in 80 of Iowa's 99 counties, Forbes was first in 16 counties, and Bauer won the other 3 counties. The turnout of 87,666 was 15 percent of the 582,510 Republicans registered on January 1.

Bush won convincingly. He exceeded two-time caucus winner Bob Dole's vote total of 37 percent in 1988, which he had set as a goal, and increased his share of the vote from the Straw Poll. The *Register* headline "Bush, Gore win easily: Forbes a strong No. 2" said it all. Bush met expectations and affirmed his front-runner status (Zeleny 2000, 1A). The *New York Times* called Bush "the clear victor" in the precinct caucuses, giving his front-runner status new legitimacy (Berke 2000, A1). The *Wall Street Journal* devalued the Bush victory somewhat by stating that he "triumphed in Iowa over a relatively weak field" (Davis and Calmes 2000, A20).

Weak field or not, Bush was the winner in almost every category measured by the Voter News Service (VNS) entrance poll. He won within every age group, carried both sexes, was the first choice among liberals, moderates, and conservatives, and perhaps surprisingly, was the leader among the "religious right," who comprised 36 percent of the GOP caucus-goers. In terms of issue stands he placed first on five of the seven posed, but finished second on "taxes" and near the bottom on "abortion" (VNS Jan. 24, 2000).

The three newspapers gave Forbes credit for his "strong" second place finish, noting that he combined his commitment to a flat tax with a strong opposition to abortion. The VNS survey supports that interpretation, as the only issue categories won by Forbes were "taxes" and "abortion." Forbes successfully redefined himself as a champion of the conservative wing of the Republican Party.

The Democratic Campaign

As he had been in the 1988 caucus cycle, Missouri Congressman Dick Gephardt was the first Democrat to make an exploratory trip to Iowa. The reason for the March 1997 visit, he asserted, was to encourage leading Democrats to run for Congress (Fogarty 1997, 5M). Although he visited periodically, Gephardt announced on February 3, 1999, that he would not seek the Democratic nomination. Senator Paul Wellstone of Minnesota made several exploratory trips to Iowa before announcing on January 9, 1999, that he would not be a candidate. Jesse Jackson, a well-known veteran of two caucuses, briefly tested the waters in Iowa before announcing on March 24, 1999, that he would not seek the Democratic nomination. Nebraska Senator Bob Kerrey ran for the nomination in 1992 and considered another presidential run in 2000. He first visited Iowa in March 1998, spent the better part of a year traveling the country, and although his political action committee had some success at fund-raising, Kerrey declared on December 13, 1998, that he would not be a candidate for the Democratic nomination. Another senator mentioned as a potential candidate, John Kerry of Massachusetts, never traveled to Iowa and announced his decision not to run in late February, leaving the field to Gore and Bradley.

Vice President Al Gore visited Iowa in late June 1997 and spoke to the American Federation of State, County and Municipal Employees state convention. He made several stops during the day including the taping of Iowa Public Television's "Iowa Press." This was Gore's second run for the Democratic nomination. He was the last of eight candidates to initiate an Iowa caucus campaign in 1987, and the late start hurt the then relatively unknown Gore. After his Iowa campaign failed to make progress he bypassed Iowa and New Hampshire and concentrated on the Super Tuesday states. On his way out the door Gore violated the eleventh commandment by speaking ill of the Iowa caucuses (see chapter 8). Ten years later, he ate a little crow and during the taping of the Iowa Press program said, "I love Iowa" (Yepsen 1997d, 1A). Name identification was no longer a problem for Gore. Moreover, he reflected "President Clinton's popular middle-of-the-road approach combining fiscal restraint with social progressiveness" (Means 1997, 9A). The vice president was now the leading candidate for the Democratic nomination and he had the support of 47 percent of those surveyed in a September 6-7, 1997 national Gallup Poll. The support for his nearest competitor, Bill Bradley, barely reached double digits.

Former New Jersey Senator Bill Bradley made his first trip to Iowa on October 1, 1998. The former New York Knicks basketball star and Rhodes scholar campaigned with gubernatorial candidate Tom Vilsack before making stops in Dubuque and Iowa City. Bradley had to decide whether to challenge Gore in Iowa or concentrate his efforts and resources closer to home in New Hampshire. He filed candidacy papers with the FEC in January 1999, and opted for an all out effort in Iowa. Bradley started the race well behind in the national polls. The January 8-10, 1999, Gallup Poll put Gore support at 47 percent and Bradley support at 12 percent.

Bradley and Gore began making regular campaign visits to Iowa in early 1999. Bradley spent the first four days of February campaigning in the state. His days included private meetings with supporters and potential supporters, speeches in a variety of venues (often colleges), meetings with the press, fundraisers, lunches and dinners, and an occasional basketball game. On a three-day campaign swing through eastern Iowa in late February, Bradley pledged not to accept PAC contributions (Yepsen 1999b, 8M). Most of his visits were for two to four days.

Gore tended to make one- or two-day trips to the state. On March 15 he traveled to Iowa and New Hampshire to announce his candidacy. A week later he returned to give speeches at Iowa State University and at a UAW meeting in Des Moines. On an early April two-day trip to Iowa, he and Mrs. Gore spent a night on the farm of Keith and Susan McKinney in Colo, a small town east of Ames. Gore was told about the plummeting farm economy and how the McKinneys had gotten out of the hog business. A major drawback for the vice president was obvious during that visit: a massive security detail arrived several days before Gore and literally took over the farm (Dukes-Lee 1999, 1A). In the coming months his staff would attempt to deal with the problem of "security isolation."

By April both candidates had hired staff. Soon thereafter, Gore had an office up and running with a limited staff. The number of aides grew rapidly and by early June six people were employed in the spacious office. Bradley did not have an office until later in June, but there were two field staff on board by June 1. In the interim Senator Wellstone dropped by and endorsed Bradley.

The campaign was just getting into full swing when the *Register* published the Democratic results of its first Iowa Poll on July 4, 1999. (The Democratic and Republican surveys were carried out over the same time period but the results were published one week apart.) Gore held a huge lead in the survey. Sixty-four percent of those polled favored Gore, 24 percent supported Bradley, and 12 percent were undecided (June 1999 Iowa Poll cited in Roos 1999a). The June 25-27 Gallup Poll had Gore at 64 percent, Bradley at 28 percent, and 8 percent undecided.

There was also evidence of early fund-raising differences. National fund-raising totals for the first six months of 1999 showed Gore well ahead in the "money primary." He had raised $17.5 million, considerably more than Bradley's $11.7. Bradley was raising sufficient funds to remain competitive in Iowa and New Hampshire but would have to do better to compete in the long run. Bush's second quarter total of $37.1 exceeded the combined total of Gore and Bradley (FEC June 30, 1999).

In the summer both candidates began receiving important endorsements. AFSCME, the Iowa UAW, and Christie Vilsack, the wife of the recently elected Iowa governor, endorsed Gore. Senator Bob Kerrey, like Wellstone, made a trip to Iowa to endorse Bradley (Yepsen 1999c, 6M). Endorsements are valued by the candidates and receive coverage by the media, but according to the findings of the January 16-21 Iowa Poll they mattered little to likely caucus participants. Perhaps the party activists were not thinking of the endorsements of labor unions and large commercial groups that provide money and manpower for the candidates.

During the summer the Republicans dominated the news with the Iowa Straw Poll. Nine Republican candidates logged 201 days in Iowa during the June-August period. Bradley (14 days) and Gore (7 days), on the other hand, visited infrequently. Their Iowa coordinators, however, were busy building campaign organizations, and with large budgets they put together huge bureaucracies.

Gore got the jump on Bradley, so that by late August his Iowa organization employed 21 full-time staffers. By mid-December, this figure had increased to 94 full-time staffers, 45 deployed in Des Moines and the remainder assigned to work the 14 most Democratic towns. Gore operatives paid particular attention to organizing precincts and had established a presence in 1450 out of the 2131 precincts (Hildebrand December 14, 1999). The staff had developed a strategy to deal with the "security isolation" of the vice president observed in his Colo farm visit. The strategy included three types of campaign venues that were more easily controlled for security purposes: bus tours with 20 or so people on a specially equipped bus that allowed Gore to visit with each of those on board; house parties of varied sizes depending on the capacity of the house, with Gore circulating among those present; and beer and brat parties of up to 450 people where Gore shook hands with everyone present (Hildebrand August 24, 1999).

The Bradley office was "officially" opened on July 1. They were behind in organizational development, but in the late summer and early fall they put together an impressive organization. By mid-December they had 58 employees, 42 in the field, organized by congressional district, county, and precinct. Chairs were in place in all 99 counties, and precinct captains in over half of their tier 1 and 2 precincts (covering about one-half of the Democrats in Iowa).

Bradley's organization forked over $12,500 to the Iowa Democratic Party for a list of previous caucus-attendees. His staff painstakingly identified 66,000 names of those likely to show up for the 2000 precinct caucuses. The second list consisted of 174,000 less dependable participants. These lists figured in the ranking of Iowa's counties according to the ratio of Democrats to Republicans, thus allowing Bradley to make the most effective use of his resources (Lucas 1999).

While the GOP campaign ebbed after the August Straw Poll, the Democratic campaign heated up. Between Labor Day and the caucuses, Bradley was in Iowa on 41 days and Gore 27 days. Both were now benefiting from their voter research and spent most of their time in heavily Democratic areas of the state.

On October 9 the Iowa Democratic Party held its annual Jefferson-Jackson Day dinner at the Polk County convention center in Des Moines. The dinner is the major fundraiser of the year, and it is timed perfectly for Democratic presidential candidates to appear and make their case before the partisans most likely to attend the precinct caucuses. The first joint appearance of Vice President Al Gore and former Senator Bill Bradley brought out 3,000 Iowans.

Bradley spoke first as a result of losing a coin flip. He portrayed himself as the underdog candidate attempting to keep the campaign on a high plane against a vice president who represented the entrenched power of the Washington establishment. Gore portrayed Bradley as a disloyal Democrat for voting for President Reagan's 1981 spending cuts and for leaving the Senate in 1996 after the Gingrich-engineered GOP takeover of the Congress. He also challenged Bradley to an immediate series of debates. Gore's decision to be aggressive may have been prompted by Bradley's recent "wave of positive publicity" and his good poll numbers in New Hampshire and New York (Berke and Seelye 1999, 30). Money may also have had something to do with Gore's posturing. Bradley made inroads in fund-raising during the third quarter. Although trailing Gore in total receipts, $19.1 million to $24.1 million, Bradley outraised him by roughly $800,000 in the third quarter of 1999 (FEC September 30, 1999).

Released in November 1999, the second Iowa poll showed that Gore still enjoyed a big lead over Bradley among Democrats, 54 percent to 32 percent, with 14 percent undecided. These figures indicated that Gore's initially gargantuan lead had been cut in half. The same poll showed that most Iowans likely to take part in the Democratic caucuses viewed Gore and Bradley favorably (Nov. 1999 Iowa Poll cited in Roos 1999b). The Nov. 4-7 Gallup Poll had Gore's support at 58 percent, Bradley 33 percent, and 9 percent undecided, and that was only a small improvement for Bradley.

The Democrats began running radio and TV ads in Iowa in the fall. Unlike the Republicans, there had been no summer advertising and no TV spending by the early dropouts. The ads were with rare exceptions positive. Most were biographical in nature or presented the candidates' policy stands (Hugh Winebrenner's tape of the ads).

The Democratic candidate spending at the NBC and CBS affiliates in Des Moines is presented in Table 11.5. The Bradley campaign spent about one-third more than the Gore campaign at the two TV stations, which is not surprising because Bradley had been playing catch-up from the day he entered the Iowa race.

The results of a third Iowa Poll published by the *Register* on January 8 mirrored the outcome of the second survey. Gore was again the choice of 54 percent of the respondents, Bradley's 33 percent was one point better, and the undecided were down a point to 13 percent. Gore, the political insider, had a hold on the majority of the likely caucus-goers and Bradley was not able to chip away at that support.

On the same day that the newspaper released the Iowa Poll the *Register* held a presidential debate for the two Democratic candidates. The debate took place one week before the Republican event described earlier. A January thaw and bright sunshine raised the temperature into the mid-40s. The media conducted their interviews outside but were denied their preferred introduction: "from freezing (or snowy) Iowa." The location and format of the debate were the same as those for the Republican debate.

There was a substantive discussion of the issues and a fair amount of give and take between the candidates. There was more agreement than disagreement—both supported campaign finance reform, major changes in the Freedom to Farm Act, equal pay for equal work to overcome the gender wage gap, greater control over handgun purchases, more money for education, tax breaks for ethanol production, and a drug program for seniors. Bradley favored universal health coverage; Gore wanted a more limited program. Gore would protect Medicaid; Bradley would replace it with a voucher program. Bradley called for registration and licensing of all handguns; Gore would require a photo license ID to purchase a handgun. Gore chastised Bradley for his vote against mandating ethanol use and his vote not to fund flood relief for Iowa in 1993. With only two candidates, the event proceeded like a real debate as opposed to the usual exchange of sound bites in a multi-candidate forum (Hugh Winebrenner's tape of the debate).

Table 11.5.   2000 Democratic spending at WHO-TV and KCCI-TV

	WHO	KCCI
Bradley	$151,460	$309,600
Gore	132,040	203,775
Total	283,500	513,375

Source: Table created from records provided by Mary Hiatt, Traffic Manager, WHO, and Anne Marie Caudron, National Sales Manager, KCCI.

The Iowa Brown and Black Coalition held a presidential forum in Des Moines between Gore and Bradley on January 17, the evening of Martin Luther King, Jr., Day. The audience included a large minority representation and the questions reflected concerns seldom heard at Democratic or Republican debates. Some of the topics included: displaying the confederate flag in South Carolina, racial profiling, inner city educational improvement, underrepresentation of minorities in medical schools, and felon voting rights. Medicaid was the one issue where there was some disagreement and the candidates had adequate time to make their positions clear. Mostly, the two candidates took like positions on the issues and pandered to the minority crowd (Hugh Winebrenner's tape of the debate).

Money and polls were in the news as the Democratic campaign entered the new year. The year-end report for 1999 showed the two candidates in a virtual tie in the "money primary." Gore had raised $27.8 million and Bradley $27.5 million, and the startling news was Bradley's fourth-quarter success. He erased Gore's fund-raising advantage by bringing in over twice as much in contributions as the vice president during the three-month period (FEC Dec. 31, 1999).

The final Iowa Poll released by the *Register* on the day before the caucuses showed that Gore's lead had increased. The results of the four Democratic Iowa polls are displayed in Table 11.6. It appears the campaign had limited impact on the race in Iowa.

Gore was better known at its onset and the June poll likely reflected his higher name recognition. The large shift in support between the first and second polls suggests that Bradley succeeded in creating a positive image among Iowa Democrats. By late summer, however, Gore had the traditional union components and the party establishment in his corner. Nationally, Gore continued to dominate. The January 17-19 Gallup Poll had Gore support at 60 percent, Bradley 27 percent, and undecided 13 percent. Gore was the winner in the "invisible primary," but he exceeded Bradley in fund-raising by only $300,000. He had been the front-runner from day one and now sought a big win in Iowa.

The final month of the caucus campaign was a great time to see and hear presidential candidates in Iowa. The six Republicans and two Democrats virtually lived in the state as they attempted to stimulate their supporters to attend the caucuses. The candidate days in Iowa of both parties are displayed in Table 11.7. The Republican total of 614

Table 11.6.   1999-2000 *Des Moines Register* Democratic Iowa Polls

	6-99	11-99	1-8-00	1-23-00
Gore, Al	64%	54	54	56
Bradley, Bill	24	32	33	28
Undecided	12	14	13	16
Sample size	403	500	501	600
Margin of error (%) is +/-	4.9	4.4	4.4	4.0

days exceeds their previous record of 520 days set in 1996.

When the candidates spend a great deal of time in Iowa, the press is not far behind. It is not possible to get a reliable estimate of the number of reporters that covered the caucuses at any given time. CNN coverage of the final week before the caucuses gives an indication of the scope of the media activity: the cable network had 200 staff members in Iowa working on eight separate shows and newscasts (Marks 2000, A20).

Democratic Caucus Results

The Democratic caucus results are shown in Table 11.8. The results are projections of support that each candidate would command if the state convention were held the next day. They are not votes and should not be confused with vote totals resulting from a primary election.

Gore came close to doubling Bradley's delegate numbers in the caucuses. His percentage of the delegate equivalents was the second largest ever recorded in a contested caucus race. Although Bradley ran a well-organized caucus campaign, Gore had the support of the "entrenched power" in Iowa—organized labor and the Iowa Democratic establishment.

The *Register* called Gore's win "decisive" and opined that he blunted the Bradley challenge (Roos 2000, 1A). The *New York Times* called the outcome a "setback" for Bradley because he had "campaigned aggressively in the state" (Berke 2000, A1). The *Wall Street Journal* thought Gore "handily defeated" Bradley (Davis and Calmes 2000, A20).

Table 11.7. 2000 Precaucus days in Iowa

Republican	Total	Jan. 1-Jan. 24
Alexander	79	*
Ashcroft	17	*
Bauer	66	12
Buchanan	36	*
Bush, G. W.	29	10
Dole, E.	36	*
Forbes	83	14
Hatch	45	13
Kasich	36	*
Keyes	64	13
McCain	5	1
Quayle	44	*
Smith	52	*
Others	22	*
Total	614	62

Democratic	Total	Jan. 1-Jan. 24
Bradley	79	17
Gephardt	10	*
Gore	48	13
Jackson	6	*
Kerrey	8	*
Wellstone	18	*
Total	169	30

*No longer active candidates.
The "others" category includes Gingrich 4, Giuliani 3, Kemp 9, F. Thompson 1, T. Thompson 2, Watts 3. The campaign activity covers the period from January 20, 1997 through January 24, 2000. Hugh Winebrenner collected the data from the individual campaigns.

The VNS entrance poll documented the completeness of the Gore victory. He was the choice of every age group, both sexes, and all income groups except those with an annual income over $75,000. He carried registered Democrats but lost among Independents by a small margin, and was the choice among liberals, moderates, and conservatives. He carried union members by a three-to-one margin and also won the support of non-union members. On issues, Gore's position was preferred on Social Security/Medicare, education, health care, taxes, jobs, and the economy (VNS, Jan. 24, 2000).

Participation was low at both parties' precinct caucuses. Only 87,666 citizens attended the Republican meetings, the lowest recorded turnout by almost 9000 in a contested GOP caucus. The Democratic turnout of 60,700 was less than 11 percent of those registered. Given the overwhelming leads by Bush and Gore in the polls, it is likely that many Iowans decided the costs of caucus attendance outweighed the benefits.

The failure of the Democratic Party to provide attendance figures for their caucuses in a timely manner produced a new controversy over accurate attendance figures, which is a variation of the old issue of which results from the Democratic caucuses should be tabulated and reported to the public. Eventually party leaders provided complete attendance figures, but it took several days to accomplish the task.

Just as the candidates attempt to put the best spin on what is likely to happen, or did happen in an electoral event, the parties hope to

Table 11.8.   2000 Democratic precinct caucus results

	State delegate equivalents (%)
Gore	63.44
Bradley	34.92
Uncommitted	1.6
Other	0.05
Total	100

Source: Iowa Democratic Party from 2131 of 2131 precincts.
The turnout of 60,760 was 10.8% of the 562,989 Democrats
registered on January 1.

generate interest in their caucuses. This leads to a tendency to exaggerate interest in and to predict record turnouts for the meetings. Occasionally the hype and spin of projected record turnout face the reality of low attendance figures. The 2000 caucuses were something of a replay of 1996 in that officials of both parties predicted high turnout levels that failed to materialize.

The Impact of the 2000 Caucuses

There were few surprises in the 2000 caucuses. George W. Bush and Al Gore, the front-runners, led in the polls from beginning to end. Bush had the benefit of a good name and a weak field and Gore enjoyed the advantages of a sitting vice president. Bush's unprecedented success at fund-raising made it very difficult for the other Republicans to compete. Gore was unable to outdistance Bradley in the "money primary," as both raised sufficient funds to contest beyond New Hampshire. Bush and Gore garnered the lion's share of endorsements and dominated the news. They won the "invisible primary" and affirmed their front-runner statuses by handily winning the caucuses.

The Republican campaign was one of the most intense seen in Iowa, but as candidates began running out of money the winnowing began. Ten competed in the Iowa Straw Poll, but only six survived that event. When John McCain decided to bypass Iowa, only five were around for the finale. If there was a surprise, it was Forbes's success. He was able to reinvent himself and finished stronger than expected. In the end Iowa did what it is best known for: winnowing the field.

The Democratic campaign began with Vice President Gore attempting to scare off potential challengers. He almost succeeded, but Senator Bradley stayed in and conducted a credible Iowa campaign even though in the end he had little to show for his efforts. Iowa might have knocked Bradley out of the race had not the next contest been in New Hampshire.

But Iowa not only winnowed the field, it also supported the eventual nominees. On March 9, two days after Bush and Gore swept Super Tuesday, McCain and Bradley withdrew from the race. Bush had a few anxious moments along the way, but the front-runners finished on top. For the first time since Carter in 1976 an Iowa caucus winner would be the next president.

Scholars have argued with few exceptions that the front-loaded, compressed nomination schedule favors the front-runners (Mayer 2001, 15). Raising money is perhaps the best way to become a front-runner. Bush and Gore, the 2000 front-runners, powered through Iowa and left with the financial resources and momentum to over-power their opposition by Super Tuesday.

Finally, paid television has become a big part of the Iowa campaign, but has not dramatically changed the nature of it. While the candidates spend thousands of dollars to make their way into living rooms via TV, they also traverse the state visiting with just plain Iowans at every stop. Some may question whether the Iowa campaign is good for the presidential nominating process, but the candidates, the press, and most Iowans seem to like starting in Iowa.

References

Berke, Richard L. 2000. "The 2000 Campaign: The Overview—Iowans Deliver Victory to Bush and Gore." *New York Times*, January 25, p. A1.

———, and Katharine Q. Seelye. 1999. "Gore Calls Bradley to More Debates." *New York Times*, October 10, p. 30.

Buttry, Stephen. 2000. "Evangelical Christians Retain Political Power." *Des Moines Register*, January 11, p. 1A.

Corrado, Anthony. 2001. "Financing the 2000 Elections." In *The Election of 2000*, edited by Gerald M. Pomper, 92-124. New York: Chatham House.

———, and Heitor Gouvea. 2004. "Financing Presidential Nominations under the BCRA." In *The Making of the Presidential Candidates 2004*, edited by William G. Mayer, 45-82. Lanham, MD: Rowman & Littlefield.

Davis, Bob, and Jackie Calmes. 2000. "Gore, Bush Headed Toward Victories in Iowa." *Wall Street Journal*, January 25, p. A20.

Des Moines Register. 1998, 1999.

Dukes Lee, Jennifer. 1999. "Farm Family Gears Up for The Gores." *Des Moines Register*, April 7, p. 1A.

Erickson, Steve. 1999. Telephone interview with Hugh Winebrenner, June 7. Erickson was a Buchanan campaign aide.

Federal Election Commission. 1999. *FEC Reports on Financial Activity: Receipts of Presidential Primary Campaigns 1999*. Washington, D.C.: Federal Election Commission.

Fogarty, Thomas A. 1997. "Gephardt Seeks House Candidates." *Des Moines Register*, March 26, p. 5M.

Geipel, Gary. 1998. Telephone interview with Hugh Winebrenner, January 15. Geipel was Midwest Field Director for the Quayle campaign.

Granzow, Ron. 1999. Telephone interviews with Hugh Winebrenner, March 3 and July 16. Granzow was Iowa Chair of the Keyes campaign.

Hall Cerwinske, Andrea. 1999. Telephone interview with Hugh Winebrenner, June 14. Hall Cerwinske was Organization Director, Republican Party of Iowa.

Harwood, John. 1999. "Elizabeth Dole Resigns Red Cross Post, Shows Interest in 2000 Presidential Bid." *Wall Street Journal*, January 5, p. A8.

Haus, Bob. 1999. Telephone interview with Hugh Winebrenner, March 22. Haus was a consultant for the Forbes campaign.

Hildebrand, Steve. 1999. Interviews with Hugh Winebrenner, August 24 and December 14. Hildebrand was Iowa State Director for Gore.

Iowa Poll. 1999 and 2000. Des Moines: Des Moines Register and Tribune Company.

Kochel, Dave. 1999. Telephone interview with Hugh Winebrenner, June 7. Kochel was Iowa Campaign Manager for Alexander.

Kramer, Mary. 2008. Telephone interview with Hugh Winebrenner, May 23. Kramer was President of the Iowa Senate.

Lucas, Dan. 1999. Interview with Hugh Winebrenner, December 16. Lucas was Iowa Campaign Director for Bradley.

Marks, Peter. 2000. "Iowa Teetering Under the Weight of Cameras and Ink." *New York Times*, January 24, p. A 20.

Mayer, William G. 2001. "The Presidential Nominations." In *The Election of 2000*, edited by Gerald M. Pomper, 12-45. New York: Chatham House.

———. 2004. "The Basic Dynamics of the Contemporary Nomination Process." In *The Making of the Presidential Candidates 2004*, edited by William G. Mayer, 83-132. Lanham, Md.: Rowman & Littlefield.

Mayes, Kris. 1997. "Quayle Visits Iowa with Eyes on 2000." *Arizona Republic*, July 14, p. A1.

McCormick, John. 1999a. "Bush Zooms to Big Lead in Iowa Race." *Des Moines Register*, June 27, p. 1A.

———. 1999b. "Bush Stays Far Ahead in Poll of Republicans." *Des Moines Register*, November 14, p. 1A.

———. 2000a. "Majority Feels Part of Strong Economy." *Des Moines Register*, January 8, p. 4A.

———. 2000b. "Caucusers Say Iowa Reflects U.S.-Poll." *Des Moines Register*, January 24, p. 4A.

———, and Jonathan Roos. 2000. "Poll: Endorsements Influence Few Voters." *Des Moines Register*, January 23, p. 5B.

Means, Marianne. 1997. "Bob Kerrey: Second Time Around?" *Des Moines Register*, July 29, p. 9A.

Miller, Andy. 1999. Telephone interview with Hugh Winebrenner, December 15. Miller was Iowa Campaign Director for Hatch.

Miller, Sarah. 1999. Telephone interviews with Hugh Winebrenner, August 31 and December 21. Miller was Finance Director, Republican Party of Iowa.

New York Times. 1999.

Norman, Jane. "Hatch Plans to Compete in Iowa GOP Straw Poll." *Des Moines Register*, June 24, p. 1A.

Popma, Marlys. 1999. Telephone interview with Hugh Winebrenner, April 22. Popma was Deputy National Political Director of the Bauer campaign.

Roos, Jonathan. 1999a. "Poll: Gore Leads Bradley." *Des Moines Register*, July 4, p. 1A.

——. 1999b. "Bradley Gains in Iowa Poll." *Des Moines Register*, November 14, p. 1A.

——. 2000. "Gore: 'We've Just Begun.'" *Des Moines Register*, January 25, p. 1A.

Sawyer, Jon. 1998. "Ashcroft Runs Ads in Iowa, with Eye on Presidential Race He Touts Unfinished Tax-cut Plan." *St. Louis Post-Dispatch*, August 11, p. A5.

Shaw, Monty. 1999. Telephone interview with Hugh Winebrenner, August 24. Shaw was Iowa Campaign Manager for Dole.

Slifka, Karen. 1999. Telephone interview with Hugh Winebrenner, July 16. Slifka was Iowa Campaign Manager for Kasich.

Stineman, John. 1999. Telephone interview with Hugh Winebrenner, May 28. Stineman was Iowa Campaign Manager for the Forbes campaign.

Voter News Service. January 24, 2000.

Wall Street Journal. 1999.

Yepsen, David. 1997a. "Resist Party Pressure and Stick With Values, Conservative Urges." *Des Moines Register*, April 17, p. 5M.

——. 1997b. "On Iowa Visit, Budget Panel Chief Kasich Lauds New Pact." *Des Moines Register*, May 18, p. 8B.

——. 1997c. "Forbes: Leaders Need to Set an Agenda." *Des Moines Register*, June 18, p. 5M.

——. 1997d. "Gore Sows Seed for 2000." *Des Moines Register*, June 29, p. 1A.

——. 1998a. "McCain: Town Hall Meet a 'Disaster.'" *Des Moines Register*, February 19, p. 3A.

——. 1998b. "Buchanan Prescribes a Return to Tariffs." *Des Moines Register*, April 30, p. 2M.

——. 1999a. "Vilsack: Democrats' Caucuses Will Move." *Des Moines Register*, February 4, p. 1M.

——. 1999b. "Bradley Campaign Vows: No PAC Contributions." *Des Moines Register*, February 23, p. 8M.

——. 1999c. "Bradley Gets Kerrey's Backing." *Des Moines Register*, July 6, p. 6M.

——. 1999d. "Republican Committee Changes Caucuses to Jan. 31." *Des Moines Register*, August 7, p. 5M.

——. 1999e. "Iowa, N.H. Dance Caucus 2-Step Again." *Des Moines Register*, September 29, p. 8M.

——. 1999f. "McCain Makes Decision to Skip Iowa Caucuses." *Des Moines Register*, November 17, p. 1M.

Zeleny, Jeff. 2000. "Keyes Third, Bauer Fourth." *Des Moines Register*, January 25, p. 1A.

Chapter 12 The 2004 Caucuses: Change and Continuity

DESPITE THE DIFFICULTIES in unseating an incumbent president in modern times, the elections of 1980 and 1992 proved that it was possible. When President Bush's approval ratings declined from their post-9/11 peak, a number of Democrats considered entering the presidential race in 2004.

The 2004 cycle saw the decline of the expected front-runner, Representative Dick Gephardt; the sudden ascent and even more sudden collapse of a new front-runner, Governor Howard Dean; the autumn stall and then ultimate success of Senator John Kerry; and the emergence of Senator John Edwards on the basis of a strong second-place finish in the Iowa caucuses. The 2004 caucuses revealed unexpected strengths and weaknesses in the Democratic candidates, and failing to meet or exceed expectations in Iowa shapes the analyses of the campaigns and reporters as they move on to New Hampshire.

This is precisely the continuity we found in the 2004 Democratic caucuses, before which journalistic and popular opinion had all but conceded the nomination to Dean. The change in the 2004 caucuses was the combination of increased numbers of new participants and Dean's extensive use of the Internet for fundraising and organizing, presaging the caucus strategy of Senator Barack Obama in 2008.

The National and Iowa Contexts

Despite continuing issue concerns such as health care, tax policy, and education, the 2004 political cycle dawned in an era completely different from that of 2000. While the 1990s had been a period of relative peace and prosperity, by 2004 the country was marked by the lingering effects of recession and, more dramatically, by the events of 9/11. As the presidential campaign started, "national security dominated

283

the debate, intertwined with the war in Iraq and often overshadowing the economy and other domestic issues" (Brower 2005, 2). By the beginning of 2004, in fact, two-thirds of Democrats nationwide opposed the war (Ceaser and Busch 2005, 87). Moreover, many Democrats still questioned the legitimacy of the Bush presidency after the disputed election and Supreme Court decision of 2000. Democrats wanted to take back what they considered should have rightfully been a Democratic presidency, and they believed that the 2004 election would provide a good opportunity to do so.

While the events of 9/11 and their aftermath were of concern to Iowans, domestic issues also mattered. Survey response percentages to the question of the single most important issue facing the nation were: the economy and jobs 24, homeland security 20, taxes and federal spending 19, education 12, and health care 10, with the remainder of the responses in single digits (Research Polls 2000).

Iowa was a politically divided state in 2004. Democrats had been very successful in statewide elections: Vice President Al Gore carried the state in 2000, and in 2002 Governor Tom Vilsack and Senator Tom Harkin both won reelection comfortably. On the other hand, Iowa remained substantially Republican territory below the state level, despite voting Democratic for president in every election since 1988. After the 2002 mid-term election Republicans controlled the Iowa House (54-46), the Iowa Senate (29-21), and four of the five Iowa Congressional seats. Finally, Republicans had a 51,000 margin over the Democrats in voter registration, though both trailed "no party" registrants substantially.

The Campaign

Iowa Democrats entered the 2004 election cycle determined to select a presidential nominee who could defeat President Bush, and there would be no shortage of hopefuls. Providing that former Vice President Al Gore chose not to run, the race for the Democratic nomination was wide open. President Bush faced no caucus challenge, leaving the political action to the Democrats.

Democratic hopefuls begin to visit the state shortly after President Bush's inauguration. John Edwards, freshman senator from North Carolina, was the first to appear in Iowa, delivering a speech at Drake

University on March 3, 2001. He emphasized his common-man roots, telling audiences that he was the son of a textile worker and the first in his family to attend college. Edwards voted in favor of granting President Bush the authority to prosecute the war in Iraq, though he later would apologize for that "mistake" ("From Courtroom to Campaign Trail" 2004). Generally known as a moderate, he returned to Iowa twice in 2001, but picked up the pace in 2002 and visited the state nine times, including attending the Iowa State Fair in August and the party's annual Jefferson-Jackson Day dinner in October (all "days in Iowa" data are from Appleman 2004).

The second Democrat to visit Iowa was John Kerry of Massachusetts, a Vietnam War veteran first elected to the Senate in 1984. His poignant question at a 1971 appearance before the Senate Foreign Relations Committee, "How do you ask a man to be the last man to die for a mistake?" was popular with Iowa Democrats if less so elsewhere ("Vietnam Vet Kerry Moved from Senate Witness to Senate" 2004). Though a "Massachusetts Democrat," a phrase popularized by Republicans over the years to signify a liberalism out of touch with the rest of the country, Kerry offered Democrats a war record they hoped could counter decades-old Republican charges that the Democrats were soft on defense. He was the guest of honor at a reelection fundraiser for Governor Vilsack in Mount Pleasant in June 2001 attended by about 400 people (Dukes 2001, 2B). Kerry returned in late June 2002 to campaign for Iowa candidates and speak at the October Jefferson-Jackson Day dinner also attended by Edwards. He voted in favor of the 2002 Congressional authorization to use force against Iraq. Kerry tended to have a ponderous, upper-class speaking style that would cause him difficulties in everyday Iowa.

The third Democratic hopeful to visit Iowa in 2001 was a familiar face, Congressman Dick Gephardt of Missouri, the 1988 caucuses winner. He campaigned for Congressman Leonard Boswell in July (Bolten 2001, 2B). Reflecting his district in St. Louis, which made him a 14-term Congressman, he enjoyed substantial support among labor unions and more moderate to conservative blue-collar, urban, ethnic, and Catholic Democrats. Gephardt returned in April 2002 to campaign for Iowa candidates and attend an ice-cream social and a United Auto Workers pancake breakfast.

The last hopeful to visit Iowa in 2001 was Joe Lieberman of Connecticut, who had been Al Gore's vice-presidential running mate in 2000. Lieberman, a moderate Democrat, was first elected to the Senate in 1988 after a term as Connecticut Attorney General. The first Jewish candidate for national office, Lieberman attended a fundraiser for Senator Harkin and then a Hanukkah party at Beth El Jacob synagogue in Des Moines in December ("Lieberman Aims for the Democratic Center" 2004). Although he enjoyed high name recognition, Lieberman was unable to become competitive in Iowa.

Three more possible Democratic candidates made their first visits during 2002. In February Howard Dean of Vermont attended a fundraiser for second district Congressional candidate Julie Thomas. Trained as a physician, Dean had an extensive political career in Vermont, moving from the Vermont House of Representatives to the Lieutenant Governor's office, and upon the death in 1991 of Governor Richard Snelling, he became governor and served in that capacity until January 2003.

As governor, Dean had moved the state budget into surplus, cut taxes, established health-care coverage for children under the age of 18, and signed the nation's first civil-union law for gays and lesbians. He was an outspoken critic of the Bush administration's decision to attack Iraq in 2003 ("The Up and Down Candidacy of Howard Dean" 2004). Largely due to Dean, "The Iraq War was regularly invoked as the 'test' of a Democrat's fitness to be president" (Ceaser and Busch 2005, 73). Dean argued that Democrats were too quick to compromise and go along with Bush policies instead of standing up for Democratic principles (interview with Howard Dean 2003).

Just days after Dean's visit, the Reverend Al Sharpton spoke at the Des Moines Area Community College and then preached at Union Baptist Church. An African American who appeared to be trying to assume the Jesse Jackson role of self-appointed spokesman for Black America, Sharpton appeared infrequently in Iowa and had little impact on the caucuses.

Dennis Kucinich of Ohio was the last potential candidate to visit in 2002. A Cleveland politician, Kucinich was elected to the U.S. House of Representatives in 1996. A self-styled Roosevelt Democrat, his base of political support was organized labor. He opposed such measures as NAFTA and GATT while supporting a national health-insurance program and social security. Kucinich's position as a traditional New

Deal liberal was in sharp contrast to the more centrist Democratic Leadership Council (DLC) politicians like President Clinton and Vice President Gore. A strong opponent of the Iraq war, he unsuccessfully challenged President Bush's authority to launch the attack ("Kucinich-old-school Democrat, FDR-style" 2004). Kucinich was the keynote speaker at the Iowa AFL-CIO state convention on August 14.

By the end of 2002 seven possible candidates had visited Iowa to explore their caucus potential. When Gore finally announced that he would not be a presidential candidate in 2004, the race was wide open (Gore's 60 Minutes interview December 15, 2002). Three lesser-known politicians visited Iowa in 2003. In February former Ambassador to New Zealand Carol Moseley Braun of Illinois spoke at a series of President's Day events in Iowa, New Hampshire, and South Carolina sponsored by the American Women Presidents Organization. Only one person, plus reporters, showed up at the Iowa event. Like Sharpton, she visited infrequently and had little impact on the caucuses ("Back on, Then off the Campaign Trail" 2004).

Bob Graham of Florida visited Iowa in late April. A former Florida state representative, state senator, and governor, Graham was elected to the Senate in 1986. A moderate in the DLC mold, Graham chaired the Senate Intelligence Committee when the Democrats briefly controlled the body in 2001-02, and became a strong critic of President Bush's use of intelligence and homeland security policy ("Despite Impressive Background, Florida Senator Quits Race" 2004). Finally, in September, retired four-star general Wesley Clark gave a paid speech to a large audience at the University of Iowa, telling them that he never would have voted for war in Iraq (Beaumont 2003b). Clark decided to bypass the Iowa caucuses and spent only three days in the state ("Ex-general Ends Bid for Nation's Top Office" 2004). Other prominent Democrats who showed interest in the 2004 race but did not take the plunge included Senators Evan Bayh of Indiana, Joe Biden of Delaware, Bill Bradley of New Jersey, Tom Daschle of South Dakota, Christopher Dodd of Connecticut, Russell Feingold of Wisconsin, and Dianne Feinstein of California.

The candidates began to enter the race officially either by formal announcement or by filing papers with the Federal Election Commission to establish a presidential exploratory committee. Dean and Kerry entered in 2002. The other eight entered in 2003. The Iraq War, again, was central among the Democrats. Dean, Graham, and Clark "entered the race on the basis of their opposition to the war" (Ceaser and Busch 2005, 74).

The candidates worked hard in the early months of the campaign for political support in general and to establish in-person contact with party activists. To facilitate its efforts the Iowa Democratic Party made available to the candidates, as it had in the past, a list of previous caucus-attendees. Seven candidates (Dean, Edwards, Gephardt, Graham, Kerry, Kucinich, and Lieberman) paid the substantial sum of $65,000 for the list (Sterzenbach 2009).

Despite Dean's early entry into the race and extensive campaign time in Iowa, he had not demonstrated great fund-raising ability. Kerry, Edwards, and Gephardt led the field (national fund-raising totals by quarter are displayed in Table 12.1) in the first quarter of 2003. Almost 41 percent of Gephardt's total and 26 percent of Kerry's total came from transfers from previous campaigns. Without those transfers, Kerry still would have led the field, though only narrowly over Edwards, and Gephardt would have remained in third place, though only narrowly over Lieberman (FEC March 31, 2003).

Nevertheless, the candidates' standings in the national money race did not translate into equivalent poll standings. The *Register* published the first Iowa Poll of likely Democratic caucus participants on August 3, 2003. Dean led with 23 percent, followed by Gephardt with 21, Kerry 14, Lieberman 10, Edwards 5, Kucinich 4, and Graham, Moseley Braun, and Sharpton 1 each, with 20 percent undecided. Dean had campaigned strongly against the Iraq War and the poll revealed that 39 percent of the respondents believed that the only candidate who could defeat President Bush in 2004 was one who opposed the war from the beginning. At that point in the precaucus period, Dean was well positioned. The poll found that his support was fairly broad-based (Aug. 2003 Iowa Poll cited in Roos 2003a). Indeed, by the end of the third quarter of 2003, Dean had begun to lead in the invisible primary. According to Brook Brower, "during late summer and early fall, Dean raised roughly $15 million, and in November he received the endorsements of the American Federation of State, County, and Municipal Employees (AFSCME), the Service Employers International Union (SEIU), and the International Union of Painters and Allied Trades (IUPAT)" (Brower 2005, 4). By all measures of the invisible primary, particularly money and poll standing, "Dean appeared to lead the pack in late 2003" (Day, Hadley, and Stanley 2005, 76).

The candidates made frequent personal appearances in Iowa before small and large groups of people, introduced themselves, and spread their messages in a variety of ways. Senator Harkin sponsored "Hear It from the Heartland" forums that started in the early spring and lasted into the early fall 2003 (Appleman 2004). These took place around the state and featured a single candidate at each site. The featured candidate delivered brief opening remarks, engaged in a 45-minute question-and-answer session with a pre-selected audience of 100-150 people, and then had five minutes for closing remarks. Also on an individual basis, candidates appeared on "Iowa Press," the public-affairs program aired statewide on Iowa Public Television where they were questioned by a panel of Iowa journalists. Dean was featured on three shows, Kerry on two, and Gephardt, Kucinich, Graham, and Edwards on one each. Clark, Lieberman, Moseley Braun, and Sharpton did not appear on the program (Iowa Press 2003).

They also appeared with other candidates in forums, whether in a formal debate or in an informal setting. The ten announced candidates appeared jointly 14 times with candidate attendance varying from event to event. Two such forums were held in the spring and summer of 2003. The first aired by C-SPAN was an AFSCME event in May in Des Moines, and an America's Hometown Forum in Newton followed in June.

The intense forum period began in mid-August and extended into January 2004. Three forums took place in three days in August, not coincidentally during the August 7-17 run of the Iowa State Fair. The fair attracts approximately a million visitors during its 10-day run and offers candidates the atmosphere of a small-town corner café on a huge scale, enabling them to meet and greet a large number of Iowans and often deliver brief remarks.

Senator Harkin's annual fund-raising steak fry on September 13 near Indianola drew over 5000 people in spite of bad weather. Seven candidates and former President Bill Clinton attended, with Clinton the center of attention (Beaumont 2003a). A month later, the American Association of Retired Persons (AARP) held a forum in Des Moines, with six candidates participating. This was a key constituency for the candidates due to Iowa's aging population, and historically most caucus-goers tend to be in their middle years and beyond. Indeed, 68 percent of Democratic participants in the 2004 caucuses were 45 years older or older (Entrance Polls: Iowa 2004).

With the January 19 caucus date approaching, the event schedule accelerated in November with four major forums in the space of 10 days. The field had shrunk somewhat: Graham withdrew from the race on October 6, and in mid-October Lieberman announced that he would no longer campaign in Iowa. On November 15, six candidates took part in an afternoon forum at the National Summit of Agriculture & Rural Life in Des Moines. The main event, however, was held that evening: the Iowa Democratic Party's Jefferson-Jackson Day Dinner, the largest annual party-sponsored event. Over 7500 Democrats attended the 2003 dinner that attracted 250 reporters and raised over $300,000 for the party. Hillary Clinton was the master of ceremonies and was greeted very warmly by the crowd (Beaumont 2003c). There were enthusiastically staged entrances, particularly by Dean, whose supporters arrived in 43 buses (Pearson and Zeleny 2003, 11). Dean, Edwards, Gephardt, Kerry, Kucinich, and Moseley Braun spoke at the dinner. They criticized the record of the Bush administration when addressing such issues as the Iraq War, the economy, health care, and the environment.

A final forum in November 2003 was a debate sponsored and broadcast by MSNBC, and simulcast on WHO-TV, the local NBC affiliate in Des Moines. Tom Brokaw of NBC News moderated the debate, thus signaling its importance. Dean, Clark, Gephardt, Kucinich, Moseley Braun, and Sharpton were present in Des Moines, while Edwards and Kerry took part from Washington. As the front-runner, Dean was the target of his fellow candidates as everyone staked out positions on domestic issues. President Bush's Iraq War policy came in for criticism as well, with Clark in particular attempting to establish the national-security focus of his candidacy (Henderson 2003).

The MSNBC debate was the last major caucus event in 2003. All fall the race had seemed to be between Dean and Gephardt, with Dean ahead in July, and now according to the *Register's* November poll, Gephardt had pulled ahead. Despite the intensive campaigning since August, the proportion of undecided likely caucus participants remained high at 19 percent. The percentages of support for each candidate were: Gephardt 27, Dean 20, Kerry 15, Edwards and Lieberman

5 each, Clark 4, Kucinich 3, and Moseley Braun and Sharpton 1 each (Nov. 2003 Iowa Poll cited in Roos 2003b).

Three-fourths of those who supported a particular candidate said they could still be persuaded to support someone else, while only one-fourth said they were firm in their choice. On November 3, the same day the Iowa Poll was published, the New Hampshire Union Leader ran an article titled, "Kerry Is Collapsing; Can he Save His Campaign?" The story began: "Sen. John Kerry's campaign is falling apart at the seams. His poll numbers continue to look bleak, and undecided Democrats both in early primary states and nationwide are not responding to his overtures" (*New Hampshire Union Leader* 2003). Apparently, few expected a Kerry surge.

Nevertheless, in the money chase, Kerry was competitive, although Dean had opened a large lead over the field. Edwards and Gephardt had raised almost exactly the same amounts but lagged well behind Dean. Both Dean and Kerry decided to forego federal matching funds. FEC data reported in Table 12.1 reveal the candidates' quarterly progress and total receipts as of December 31, 2003.

Figures for spending in Iowa are not readily available. Iowa economist Harvey Siegelman estimated that the economic impact of the

Table 12.1.   2003 National fund raising

	3-31-03	6-31-03	9-31-03	12-31-03
Kerry	$10,155,867	$15,962,991	$19,889,641	$25,057,443
Edwards	7,398,836	11,896,045	14,401,615	16,235,550
Gephardt	5,929,925	9,750,802	13,580,663	16,488,049
Lieberman	3,012,623	8,118,313	11,690,561	13,823,407
Dean	2,944,362	10,527,822	25,301,214	40,959,621
Graham	1,119,161	3,136,326	no report	withdrew
Kucinich	172,695	1,708,356	3,373,176	6,227,898
Clark			3,491,109	13,699,256
Sharpton	107, 456	159,615	280,930	408,342
Moseley Braun	72,451	217,109	342,302	492,069

Source: Federal Election Commission, 2003. FEC Reports on Financial Activity: Receipts of Presidential Primary Campaigns 2003. Washington, D.C.: Federal Election Commission.

2004 Iowa Caucuses "was approximately $50 to $60 million," although that includes all spending (e.g., the visiting media) and not just spending by the campaigns (Iowa Caucus 2008). Data from the two top-rated stations in Des Moines, KCCI-TV, the CBS affiliate, and WHO-TV, the NBC affiliate, reveal that Dean was the first to purchase ad time at KCCI, with a buy of $44,000 in June 2003 and $9,000 in July. Edwards spent $81,000 in August, and then Kerry and Gephardt joined Dean and Edwards buying ads every month from September to caucus day in January. Of the KCCI total, $559,000 was spent in December 2003 alone. Table 12.2 reports ad spending at WHO and KCCI. The Democrats' 2004 advertising spending at the two stations was approximately 50 percent greater than the total spending by both Democrats and Republicans in the 2000 caucus campaign.

Drake University political scientist Arthur Sanders examined FCC filings for the four major Des Moines commercial stations (KCCI-TV, WHO-TV, WOI-TV, and KDSM-TV), and found that Dean, Gephardt, Edwards, and Kerry ran a total of 9019 ads (computed from Sanders 2005, 93). Table 12.3 includes cable stations and Kucinich's spending. The difference in cost between network and cable is striking: in raw-average terms, the cable ads cost $12.96 apiece, while the network ads cost $398.85 apiece. (For a more complete discussion of TV advertising during the primary and caucus season, see Ridout 2008.)

Table 12.2. 2004 Democratic spending at
WHO-TV and KCCI-TV

	WHO	KCCI
Dean	$422,875	$572,000
Edwards	412,950	506,000
Kerry	353,950	414,000
Gephardt	339,145	388,000
Kucinich	2,560	40,000
Total	1,573,480	1,920,000

Table created from records provided by Zoe Goedicke,
Traffic Manager, WHO-TV, and Anne Marie Caudron,
National Sales Manager, KCCI-TV. Ten independent
groups spent another $556,000 at KCCI.

Table 12.3.   2004 Television ads in the Des Moines viewing area

| | Network Television | | Cable Television | |
	number	cost	number	cost
Dean	2,969	1,037,100	3,475	40,170
Edwards	2,008	968,575	0	0
Gephardt	2,065	783,590	11,519	102,076
Kerry	1,977	848,700	3,689	91,856
Kucinich	240	54,975	1,020	21,152
Totals	9,259	3,692,940	19,703	255,254

Source: Sanders 2005, 93.

The summer and fall were very busy in terms of candidate activity in the state. The large number of events clustered around the Iowa State Fair led to an impressive number of candidate days (53) in August. The four leading Democrats concentrated their attention on Iowa in the final quarter with candidate visits averaging over 40 per month.

The Endgame

In Iowa Kerry's campaign seemed to be on life support by mid-December. He was seen as "a floundering candidate with an unclear message and a campaign that many Democrats, Beltway pundits, and primary voters viewed as dead on arrival" (Brower 2005, 2-3). Then two events altered the political dynamic. Some Iowa Democrats began to worry about Dean's suitability and viability as a candidate: did he have the temperament to be a successful candidate, and did he really have the capacity to beat President Bush? Democrats who had such worries started to look for an acceptable alternative. Many liked Edwards, but they saw him as too young and inexperienced. Others thought Clark a possible alternative to Dean and "by the late summer of 2003, the Clark option was . . . backed by a shadowy contingent in the Democratic Party establishment that included many advisers of former President Bill Clinton (if not Bill Clinton himself)." They "saw Clark as the only candidate who could stop Howard Dean" (Ceaser and Busch

2005, 90). But Clark was bypassing the caucuses, and thus the only other viable alternative in Iowa was Kerry. One writer thought Clark's decision to skip the caucuses and focus on New Hampshire was an overlooked but critical decision in terms of opening the door for Kerry in Iowa (Todd 2005, 31).

Then in late December Kerry came out with his best TV ad of the campaign. It showed him dressed in denim and standing at a fence with a barn in the background (it was Iowa, after all—or at least the Iowa in the minds of those not from Iowa), and it had him talking directly to the camera and thus to the TV viewer. Kerry spoke in a down-to-earth, straightforward manner, in sharp contrast to his usual tendency to talk at people instead of talking to and with them. In the ad, Kerry seemed to be approachable, a major consideration in Iowa, and he became the safe place for those looking for an alternative to the more mercurial Dean (Dennis Goldford's notes).

In the space of eight days in January 2004, three major events were held. On January 4, the *Register* held its highly publicized presidential debate, broadcast statewide by Iowa Public Television. Seven candidates participated, with Clark and Sharpton not present. Though Lieberman by that point had decided not to contest the caucuses, he used the debate to attack Dean's views on the Iraq War. Kerry, too, went after Dean, while Gephardt attacked Edwards on trade issues. Other issues discussed at length included NAFTA and taxes (Beaumont 2004a, A1).

Two days later six of the candidates participated in a two-hour, audio-only debate at the State Historical Museum in Des Moines sponsored by National Public Radio. Without a studio audience, the candidates were prompted by moderators to engage in discussions with each other in a more relaxed format.

On January 11, eight candidates (Clark was not present) took part in the Iowa Brown and Black Presidential Forum carried live by MSNBC and by tape delay on C-SPAN and Iowa Public Television. The forum focused on African American and Latino issues. In view of the concerns some Iowa Democrats had about Dean, his campaign was not helped by Sharpton's allegation that as governor he had a poor record of appointing minorities to his cabinet (Beaumont 2004b, 1A).

After that final forum, the candidates continued the hectic pace of visits to the state through the caucuses on January 19. Table 12.4 reports the January visits as well as the total candidate days in Iowa.

Table 12.4.   2004 Precaucus days in Iowa

Democratic	Total	Jan. 1-Jan. 19
Clark	3	0
Dean	110	14
Edwards	77	14
Gephardt	75	17
Graham	31	0
Kerry	82	15
Kucinich	67	10
Lieberman	20	2
Moseley Braun	12	3
Sharpton	8	1
	—	—
Total	485	76

Source: Appleman 2004

The final Iowa Poll conducted in mid-January suggested that Dean had reached a plateau, that Gephardt was not surging as he had hoped, and that Kerry and Edwards had gained some momentum (Jan. 2004 Iowa Poll cited in Roos 2004). The poll results are shown comparatively in Table 12.5.

A comparison of lead changes in the three Iowa Polls shows the importance of timing. Dean fell from first place in July to third place in January, while Gephardt dropped from second to fourth place. Moving in the opposite direction, Kerry went from third in July to first and Edwards came from a distant fifth place to second place. The MSNBC/ Reuters/Zogby tracking poll over the course of the last ten days of the caucus campaign showed similar results (Curry 2004). Nevertheless, all the major polls missed the Kerry and Edwards momentum even if some (including the Iowa Poll) correctly predicted the order of finish (Blumenthal 2007). So what happened?

The Democrats' 2004 caucus turnout was 124,331, double the Democratic turnout of 60,700 in 2000, and was almost a quarter of the registered Democrats. The results of the 2004 Democratic caucuses are shown in Table 12.6. Kerry won the most votes in five of the six most urbanized counties in the state (Dubuque, Blackhawk, Linn, Johnson,

Table 12.5.   2003-04 *Des Moines Register* Democratic Iowa Polls

	8-03	11-03	1-18-04
Dean	23	20	20
Gephardt	21	27	18
Kerry	14	15	26
Lieberman	10	5	1
Edwards	5	5	23
Kucinich	4	3	3
Clark	*	4	2
Graham	1	**	**
Moseley Braun	1	1	1
Sharpton	1	1	1
Not sure/Uncommitted	20	19	5
Sample size	402	501	600
Margin of error (%) is +/-	4.9	4.4	4.0

*Clark entered the race after the August poll.
**Graham withdrew from the race before the November poll.

and Scott, all in eastern Iowa), while Edwards won only Polk County (*Des Moines Register* 2004, 12S).

   Judging by the entrance poll taken as people arrived at their caucus sites, Dean failed to win the support of those constituencies on whom he had based his candidacy: new voters, particularly young voters, and those who vehemently opposed the Iraq War. Nearly half of those participating in the caucuses did so for the first time, but the Kerry-Edwards-Dean-Gephardt order of finish held with first-time caucus-goers as well. Among younger caucus participants (17-29 years old), Dean finished ahead of Edwards but still behind Kerry. Even those who used the Internet for election information preferred Kerry to the Internet-savvy Dean. As to the issue of the Iraq War, Dean did relatively well among those who strongly disapproved of the war, but he still trailed Kerry ("Entrance Polls: Iowa" 2004). Despite his endorsement by former Vice President Al Gore in December, Dean's "short temper that reared its head after hostile questions from voters as well as a ten-

Table 12.6.   2004 Democratic precinct caucus results

	State delegate equivalents (%)
Kerry	37.09
Edwards	32.57
Dean	17.36
Gephardt	11.17
Kucinich	1.03
Other	0.48
Uncommitted	0.18
Clark	0.11
Total	99.9

Source: Iowa Democratic Party from 1993
of 1993 precincts. The turnout of 124,331 was
23.3% of the 533,107 Democrats registered
on January 1, 2004.

dency to shoot from the hip" (Marx 2005, 42) led to concerns among Iowa Democrats about his temperament.

The entrance poll showed that while caucus participants valued Dean's strong stands and Edwards' caring for others, they valued most what they took to be Kerry's experience and ability to beat Bush. As to when caucus-goers made up their minds, Dean suffered from the truth of the old maxim that timing is everything in politics. His strongest support came from caucusgoers who made up their minds more than a month prior to caucus night. Both Dean and Gephardt peaked too soon, and their attacks on each other in TV ads late in the campaign were dubbed a "murder suicide" (Ceaser and Busch 2005, 102), leaving an opening for Edwards to move into second place.

Kerry and Edwards benefited from caucus-goers' concerns about the viability of the Dean and Gephardt candidacies. Yet Kerry was in a position to reap that benefit only because of his major staff shakeup in November, the infusion of his and his wife's personal funds into the campaign in December, and the unexpected support from a former Vietnam crewmate (Brower

2005, 5-6, 9). Kerry was also aided by support "from veterans and fire-fighters," groups that "are conveniently spread across the state." Dean, on the other hand, relied heavily on "out-of-state volunteers, who were not especially credible when talking with locals on their door-steps" (Burden 2005, 29). Indeed, the surge of "Deaniacs" into Iowa proved counterproductive. Though many Iowa Democrats "shared Dean's anti-war sentiment and liberal economic views, they bitterly re-sented being approached en masse by out-of-staters" (Marx 2005, 45).

The Impact of the 2004 Iowa Caucuses

The Iowa caucuses do not pick the presidential nominees so much as they provide candidates with the opportunity to test-drive their cam-paign organizations, and to get reactions from real people concerning their personal appeal and their campaign themes. The primary role of the caucus is to winnow the field and the 2004 caucuses accomplished the task. Even before caucus night on January 19, Clark and Lieber-man had decided to compete in later primaries after not gaining any traction in Iowa, while Graham dropped out on October 6, 2003, and Moseley Braun, endorsing Dean, withdrew on January 15, 2004. After his poor fourth-place finish in the caucuses, Gephardt pulled out the next day ("Second Try, Same Result for Gephardt" 2004). Kucinich and Sharpton continued their campaigns even though their caucus perfor-mances indicated they had no realistic chance of winning the nomi-nation. The caucus campaign provided the opportunity for the previ-ously unknown Dean to soar unexpectedly to front-runner status, and yet it exposed his equally unexpected weaknesses in temperament and ability to accommodate the various Democratic constituencies.

A surprise in 2004 was the mixed results of the invisible primary. As Barry Burden has noted, "In contrast to previous elections, money and momentum turned out to be imperfect predictors of who would win the Democratic nomination for president in 2004" (Burden 2005, 18). Dean was the winner of the "money primary," led in early national and Iowa polls, and was the recipient of many endorsements, yet he did not win his party's nomination. National polls showed Dean ris-ing steadily from the summer throughout the fall, but he peaked too soon, declining precipitously in December just before a sharp spike for both Kerry and Edwards (Franklin 2007). Despite his success in the invisible primary, many Iowa Democrats who favored Dean early began to grow uncomfortable about his limitations as November and December wore on into January. Searching for a viable alternative, they settled on Kerry. Dean's failure to meet expectations and Kerry's and Edwards' success in exceeding expectations set the campaign narrative as the process moved to New Hampshire. The caucuses allowed both Kerry and Edwards to break through to national prominence even as they illustrated Kerry's remoteness and difficulty in speaking plainly to ordinary voters, and Edwards' lack of national experience. This was the continuity of the 2004 caucuses.

The change came in the form of technology and demographics. As to technology, the Dean campaign was the first to make extensive use of the Internet as an organizational and fundraising tool. An article in *Wired Magazine* described how Dean used the Internet to raise money and to organize thousands of volunteers. By mid-November 2003 Dean had more than 140,000 members in his group on the web site meetup.com, one of the early social networks (Wolf 2004). The usefulness of the Internet and the possible impact of younger voters would not go unnoticed in the 2008 Iowa caucus cycle. (For a discussion of the growth and use of the Internet in electoral politics, see Hull 2008, chapter 4.)

Finally, despite the belief that frontloading the nomination calendar would decrease the importance of Iowa and New Hampshire, "the opposite turned out to be true and the frontloading made Iowa and New Hampshire more important than they had ever been" (Todd 2005, 31).

References

Appleman, Eric. "Democracy in Action." 2004. www.gwu.edu/~action/P2004.html.

"Back on, Then off the Campaign Trail." 2004. www.cnn.com/Election/2004/special/president/candidates/braun.html.

Beaumont, Thomas. 2003a. "Democrats Bask in Glow of Clinton." *Des Moines Register*, September 14, p. 1A.

———. 2003b. "Clark Says He Wouldn't Have Voted for War." *Des Moines Register*, September 20, p. 1A.

———. 2003c. "Clinton, Democrats Fire Up Crowd." *Des Moines Register*, November 16, p. 1A.

———. 2004a. "Rivals Sling Darts at Dean." *Des Moines Register*, January 5, p. A1.

———. 2004b. "Dean Defends His Record on Race." *Des Moines Register*, January 12, p. 1A.

Blumenthal, Mark. 2007. "How Accurate Were the Iowa Polls in 2004 and 2000?" December 29. www.pollster.com/blogs/how_accurate_were_the_iowa_pol .php.

Bolten, Kathy A. 2001. "Tax Increase Possible, Gephardt Says." *Des Moines Register*, July 22, p. 2B.

Brower, Brook. 2005. "Nominations and Conventions." In *Divided States of America: The Slash and Burn Politics of the 2004 Presidential Election*, edited by Larry J. Sabato, 1-23. New York: Pearson-Longman.

Burden, Barry C. 2005. "The Nominations: Technology, Money, and Transferable Momentum." In *The Elections of 2004*, edited by Michael Nelson, 18-41. Washington, D.C.: CQ Press.

"Caucus Results." 2004. *Des Moines Register*, January 20, p. 12S.

Ceaser, James W., and Andrew E. Busch. 2005. *Red over Blue: The 2004 Elections and American Politics*. Lanham, Md.: Rowman & Littlefield Publishers.

Curry, Tom. 2004. "Kerry, Dean, Gephardt in Statistical Tie." January 15. www .msnbc.msn.com/id/3965938.

Day, Christine L., Charles D. Hadley, and Harold W. Stanley. 2005. "The Inevitable Unanticipated Consequences of Political Reform: The 2004 Presidential Nomination Process." In *A Defining Moment: The Presidential Election of 2004*, edited by William Crotty, 74-107. Armonk, NY: M. E. Sharpe.

"Despite Impressive Background, Florida Senator Quits Race." 2004. www.cnn .com/ELECTION/2004/special/president/candidates/graham.html.

Dukes, Jennifer. 2001. "Kerry Contrasts His Views to Bush's." *Des Moines Register*, June 25, p. 2B.

"Entrance Polls: Iowa." January 19, 2004. http://www.cnn.com/ELECTION/2004/ primaries/pages/epolls/IA/index.html.

"Ex-general Ends Bid for Nation's Top Office." 2004. www.cnn.com/ELEC TION/2004/special/president/candidates/clark.html.

Federal Election Commission. 2003. Receipts of Presidential Primary Campaigns 2003. Washington, D.C.: Federal Election Commission.

———. Presidential Pre-Nomination Campaign Receipts through December 31, 2003. Washington, D.C.: Federal Election Commission.

Franklin, Charles. 2007. "Primaries Past." July 30. http://www.pollster.com/blogs/ primaries_past.php.

"From Courtroom to Campaign Trail, Edwards Displays Ambition." 2004. www .cnn.com/ELECTION/2004/special/president/candidates/edwards.html.

Fukiyama, Francis. 2006. *The End of History and the Last Man*. New York: Free Press.

Gore's *60 Minutes* Interview. December 15, 2002. http://www.cbsnews.com/ stories/2002/12/15/60minutes/main533091.shtml.

Henderson, O. Kay. 2003. "Democrats Cover a Variety of Issues in Des Moines." Radio Iowa, November 25. http://www.radioiowa.com/gestalt/go.cfm?object id=45B1949D-32A5-4940-81A0136DDBE4CFB4.

Hull, Christopher C. 2008. *Grassroots Rules: How the Iowa Caucus Helps Elect American Presidents*. Stanford, CA: Stanford University Press.

Interview with Howard Dean. July 2, 2003. National Public Radio, Morning Edition. http://www.npr.org/programs/specials/democrats2004/transcripts/dean_trans.html.

Iowa Caucus 2008. www.iowacaucus.org/iacaucus.html.

Iowa Press—2003 transcripts. 2003. www.iptv.org/iowapress.

"Kerry Is Collapsing; Can He Save His Campaign?" 2003. *New Hampshire Union Leader*. November 3, p. A12.

Krauthammer, Charles. 2003. "Bracing for the Apocalypse." February 13. Townhall.com.

"Kucinich-old-school Democrat, FDR-style." 2004. www.cnn.com/ELECTION/2004/special/president/candidates/kucinich.html.

"Lieberman Aims for the Democratic Center." 2004. www.cnn.com/ELECTION/2004/special/president/candidates/lieberman.html.

Marx, Claude R. 2005. "The Rise and Fall of Howard Dean." In *Divided States of America: The Slash and Burn Politics of the 2004 Presidential Election*, edited by Larry J. Sabato, 37-49. New York: Pearson-Longman.

Pearson, Rick, and Jeff Zeleny. 2003. "Democratic Rivals Target Dean at Iowa Bash-Hillary Clinton Urges Party Unity to Defeat Bush." *Chicago Tribune*, November 16, p.11.

"Preacher Ends Another Electoral Event." 2004. www.cnn.com/ELECTION/2004/special/president/candidates/sharpton.html.

"Research Polls 2000." KCCI-TV. December 2006.

Ridout, Travis N. 2008. "Television Advertising during the Presidential Nomination Season." In *The Making of the Presidential Candidates 2008*, edited by William G. Mayer, 99-118. Lanham, MD: Rowman & Littlefield.

Roos, Jonathan. 2003a. "Dean Leads Democrats, But Many Undecided." *Des Moines Register*, August 3, p. 1A.

———. 2003b. "Gephardt Inches Ahead in Iowa." *Des Moines Register*, November 9, p. 1A.

———. 2004. "Kerry, Edwards Surge." *Des Moines Register*, January 18, p. 1A.

Sanders, Arthur. 2005. "The Impact of BCRA on the Presidential Nomination Process: The Iowa Caucuses." In *Dancing without Partners: How Candidates, Parties and Interest Groups Interact in the New Campaign Finance Environment*, edited by David B. Magleby, J. Quin Monson, and Kelly D. Patterson, 83-97. Provo, Utah: Center for the Study of Elections and Democracy, Brigham Young University.

"Second Try, Same Result for Gephardt." 2004. www.cnn.com/ELECTION/2004/special/president/candidates/gephardt.html.

Sterzenbach, Norm. 2009. E-mail to Dennis Goldford, August 31. Sterzenbach was the executive director of the Iowa Democratic Party.

Todd, Chuck. 2005. "Campaign 2004: The Hidden Story." In *Divided States of America: The Slash and Burn Politics of the 2004 Presidential Election*, edited by Larry J. Sabato, 25-35. New York: Pearson-Longman.

"The Up and Down Candidacy of Howard Dean." 2004. www.cnn.com/ELEC TION/2004/special/president/candidates/dean.html.

"Vietnam Vet Kerry Moved from Senate Witness to Senate." 2004. www.cnn.com/ ELECTION/2004/special/president/candidates/kerry.html.

Wolf, Gary. 2004. "How the Internet Invented Howard Dean." December 1. www .wired.com/wired/archive/12.01/dean.html.

Chapter 13 The 2008 Caucuses: From Iowa to the White House

THE IOWA CAUCUSES allow little-known and/or under-funded candidates to compete relatively inexpensively and become contenders by exceeding the expectations set by political pundits. That opportunity was attractive in 2008 because of declining Republican fortunes and the wide-open race for the presidential nomination in both parties. Despite early media focus on Republicans Rudy Giuliani and John McCain and on Democrats Hillary Clinton and John Edwards, the caucuses revealed weaknesses in their candidacies as well as in those of Mitt Romney and Fred Thompson, and strengths in the candidacies of Republican Mike Huckabee and Democrat Barack Obama. At the same time, the now usual challenges to Iowa's early position in the nomination process led to the caucuses being held at their earliest date ever.

Precaucus Activity

The national and state political context of the 2008 caucus cycle found Democrats enthusiastic and Republicans pessimistic about their chances in the presidential and congressional elections. In contrast to what appeared to be increasing Republican strength in 2004, the Democrats won control of Congress in 2006 for the first time since 1994. Under the impact of what appeared to be a stalemate in the Iraq War and the botched federal response to hurricane Katrina, President Bush's approval ratings declined from just over 50 percent in early 2005 to a low of 34 percent during 2007 (computed from ABC News/ *Washington Post* polls at www.pollingreport.com/Bushjob 2007). Likewise, the Republican Party saw its average unfavorable rating rise to about 55 percent, in contrast to the Democrats' favorable rating of 52 percent during 2006-07 (computed from data at www.gallup.com).

The political environment in Iowa also was difficult for Republicans during the 2008 cycle. President Bush's ratings declined after the attacks of 9/11 and the subsequent invasion of Iraq. His combined excellent/good and fair/poor rating went from 60 to 39 percent in June 2003, to an average of 32.8 to 65.4 percent in five Research 2000 polls in 2006 (Research Polls 2000). By November 2007, his approval/disapproval numbers in Iowa were 26 to 72 percent, and even among Republicans they were only 55 to 43 percent (www.kcrg.com).

Although Bush carried the state in 2004 and Senator Charles Grassley easily won reelection, the remainder of the GOP ticket fared poorly in the 2006 mid-term elections. The state's U. S. House delegation went from 4-1 Republican to 3-2 Democratic; Democratic Secretary of State Chet Culver succeeded retiring Democratic Governor Tom Vilsack; and Democrats regained control of both houses of the general assembly for the first time since 1996. Finally, Democrats gained an edge over Republicans in active registered voters for the first time since 1994, going from a 51,000 deficit in January 2004 to a 29,978 advantage in January 2007 (Iowa Secretary of State 2008).

As the 2008 caucuses approached, there was a general similarity between Iowa Democrats and Democrats nationwide, and between Iowa Republicans and Republicans nationwide, regarding issues of concern. For both national Democrats and Iowa Democrats the three most important issues were Iraq, the economy, and health care. For Republicans nationally, the three most important issues were terrorism, Iraq, and illegal immigration; for Iowa Republicans, they were the economy, illegal immigration, and abortion, with terrorism right behind (Opinion Research: "Iowa Poll" 2007). The major distinction in the precaucus survey is that Iowa Republicans ranked abortion as their third-most important issue, reflecting the fact that upwards of 40 percent of likely Republican caucus participants are conservative, evangelical Christians. By contrast, Republicans nationwide ranked abortion and social issues sixth. Consequently, while Iowa continued to be racially and ethnically unrepresentative of the nation as a whole, in 2008 there appeared to be few differences between Iowans and Americans generally regarding the issues of greatest concern.

Republican Precaucus Activity

The 2008 presidential election marked the first contest since 1952 without a sitting president or vice president running for the nomination. For the prospective 2008 Republican candidates, Iowa offered an opportunity for them to emerge as alternatives to the early favorites, Arizona Senator John McCain and former New York Mayor Rudy Giuliani. Over the course of five national polls from February 2005 to June 2006, McCain led all Republicans with an average of 30.4 percent to Giuliani's 25.6 percent (CNN/USA Today Gallup Polls 2005 and 2006; Gallup Poll 2006), and among Iowa Republicans in December 2006 McCain led with 27 percent, followed by Giuliani with 26 percent and everyone else in single digits (Research 2000 Polls KCCI 2006). McCain had chosen not to contest the caucuses in 2000, due largely to his longstanding opposition to ethanol subsidies and his rocky relationships with religious conservatives that led him to refer to their leaders as agents of intolerance (Barstow 2000). Giuliani supported abortion rights, a position that compromised his standing among Iowa's religious conservatives. Both early leaders, therefore, had at best soft support among the social and religious conservatives who are a substantial portion of the Republican base in Iowa. This left an opening on the right that many prospective candidates could attempt to exploit.

Republican candidates sought to reestablish the Reagan coalition, though no one candidate embraced its three principal strands: "compassionate conservatives" (including evangelicals), "conventional conservatives," and "national security hawks" (Ceaser, Busch, and Pitney 2009, 54). In terms of viability, the wide range of Republican candidates in 2008 could be divided into three categories: prospective candidates who visited Iowa but decided to forego the race; declared caucus candidates who never constituted a serious challenge and remained in the second tier; and major, first-tier candidates, some of whom were presumptively first-tier and others who used the precaucus season to establish themselves as such.

Five prospective candidates visited Iowa but ultimately did not enter the race. Former House Speaker Newt Gingrich visited for two days in May 2005 on a book tour, following a busy schedule that included book signings, fundraisers for the state Republican Party, appearances on Iowa Public Television's "Iowa Press" and WHO-TV's "The Insiders," meetings with the *Register*'s and *Sioux City Journal*'s editorial boards, and several events at Cornell College in Mt. Vernon. Governor George Pataki of New York attended the annual meeting of the National Governors Association (NGA) held in Des Moines on July 16-17, 2005, and participated in various activities. On October 22 and 23 Tennessee Senator (and medical doctor) Bill Frist attended a physicians' roundtable and was a guest at the Party's fifth annual Ronald Reagan dinner in Des Moines. A week later, Nebraska Senator Chuck Hagel delivered the Manatt-Phelps Lecture in Political Science at Iowa State University. Frist and Hagel had contributed generously to Iowa Republican candidates, $34,500 from Frist and approximately $7000 from Hagel (Mooney 2005). The last individual in this group was Virginia Senator George Allen. A seemingly attractive southern conservative long considered a possible Republican presidential nominee, Allen had lost his 2006 reelection bid to Democrat Jim Webb in one of the closest senate races in the country, despite Allen's two-to-one money advantage (Barone and Cohen 2007, 1666-67).

Six individuals declared their candidacies but were never able to break out of the second tier. In early July 2005, four-term Colorado Congressman Tom Tancredo spent two days in the state, attending house parties in the eastern Iowa cities of Davenport, Cedar Rapids, Cedar Falls, and Dubuque as a special guest of the Iowa Christian Coalition. Tancredo was known as a strong conservative and supporter of the National Rifle Association who also opposed President Bush's prescription-drug bill. He became best known, however, for his hardline position on immigration, calling for tougher enforcement against illegal immigrants and increased border security (Barone and Cohen 2007, 325-27). On January 16, 2006, former Virginia governor Jim Gilmore spoke at a Polk County Republican organizational meeting. Gilmore had been elected in 1997 and served one term, but was almost unknown outside of Virginia.

Another second-tier prospect was Tommy Thompson, who left his long-time position of governor of Wisconsin to join the Bush administration as Secretary of Health and Human Services in January 2001, serving in that capacity until January 2005. He made a relatively low-key visit to Sioux City on September 9. The little-known Duncan Hunter, a 14-term Republican Congressman from southern California, held a hunting event for military veterans on December 16 in Baxter, just east of Des Moines. A strong conservative, Hunter had chaired the House Armed Services Committee and now concentrated on military issues (Barone and Cohen 2007, 295-98). Hunter and Chicago businessman John Cox announced their candidacies before the 2006 mid-term elections in November (Appleman 2008). And, after establishing an exploratory committee in January 2007, Congressman Ron Paul, a nine-term congressman from the Gulf coast of Texas visited Iowa in April. A former Libertarian Party presidential candidate in 1988, Paul opposed the Iraq War, supported returning to the gold standard, ending all government funding of education, and cutting the defense budget (Barone and Cohen 2007, 1575-77).

Finally, the presumptively or soon-to-be major caucus candidates included McCain, Giuliani, Kansas Senator Sam Brownback, Massachusetts Governor Mitt Romney, Arkansas Governor Mike Huckabee, and, eventually, former Tennessee Senator Fred Thompson. McCain had bypassed Iowa in 2000 and was repeatedly asked whether he intended to contest the caucuses in 2008. On April 13, 2006, he made his first visit to the state in the new cycle and attended fundraisers for Iowa legislative, gubernatorial, and Congressional candidates. McCain also met with Marlys Popma, a long-time evangelical and political activist who later in the year joined the McCain campaign as deputy state director. The Arizona Republican appeared at this point to be the "establishment" candidate among the Republican field, despite the fact that his traditional political brand was that of a maverick. McCain's main competition in early 2006 was Giuliani, who visited on May 1 and met with various Republican leaders and spoke at events in Des Moines and Davenport in support of Iowa candidates.

The soft support for both McCain and Giuliani among the social and religious conservatives left, as noted earlier, an opening on the right that other candidates would attempt to exploit. That was the strategy Senator Sam Brownback of Kansas followed, the first potential candidate to visit Iowa after the inauguration of President Bush on January 20, 2005. In an earlier visit in December 2004, Brownback had focused his attention on social and religious conservatives. On May 3, 2005, he focused on business and economic matters, traveling to Iowa to meet with reporters, business leaders, state legislators, and the president of the Iowa Farm Bureau. Elected to the U.S. House of Representatives as part of the Republican surge of 1994, Brownback won a special election in 1996 to serve the final two years of Bob

Dole's term after Dole resigned to pursue a presidential bid (Barone and Cohen 2007, 656-59). He was reelected to a full term in 2004.

Romney and Huckabee came to the 2005 NGA meeting in Des Moines in mid-July and attended a fund-raising luncheon for the Iowa Republican Party and also participated in other activities over the course of their stay. Elected in 2002 after a highly successful investment career and an unsuccessful Senate challenge to Edward Kennedy in 1994, Mitt Romney was a Mormon and a graduate of Brigham Young University with an MBA from Harvard. He made a national name for himself when he took over the floundering Salt Lake City Winter Olympics Organizing Committee in February 1999, and saved the 2002 winter games (Barone and Cohen 2003, 771-73). At the NGA conference Romney met with Republican leaders in the Iowa General Assembly and had dinner with former GOP governor Terry Branstad. Romney's Commonwealth PAC followed the tradition of sharing resources with Iowa candidates for elective office. He provided over $75,000 to candidates and to the state party for the mid-term elections (Mooney 2005). Romney's generosity reflected the fact that the Republican and Democratic parties of Iowa are very good at convincing prospective presidential candidates that state politicians remember the financial help they receive.

Mike Huckabee, like Bill Clinton, was a native of Hope, Arkansas. Huckabee had been educated in Baptist colleges and had served as a Baptist minister in Pine Bluff and Texarkana, where he started a 24-hour television station, and in 1989 became president of the Arkansas Baptist Convention (Barone and Cohen 2003, 130-32). After losing a 1992 senate race to incumbent Democrat Dale Bumpers, Huckabee was elected Lieutenant Governor in 1993, and assumed the governorship when Jim Guy Tucker resigned in 1996. He was reelected in 1998 and again in 2002, but did not seek reelection in 2006. He followed Republican orthodoxy and cut income taxes, but raised the state sales and gas taxes and, in populist fashion, passed a program to provide health insurance to parents above the Medicaid income limits. Huckabee was a witty and engaging speaker who played the guitar in a rock band and published a book about his significant weight loss.

Huckabee was well positioned to benefit from an Iowa campaign. After Pat Robertson's Christian Coalition experienced difficulties in the early 2000s, Iowa supporters decided to break from that organization and establish the Iowa Christian Alliance ("About Iowa Christian

Alliance" 2006). President Steve Scheffler announced the new organization at an event on March 6, 2006, with Huckabee as the keynote speaker. He emphasized the necessary and legitimate role of people of faith in the political process and public policy.

Despite the large field, one more contender would join the race in 2007. Many Republicans yearned for someone who might become the next Ronald Reagan, and they hoped to find him in actor and former Tennessee Senator Fred Thompson. He had won the remainder of Al Gore's senate term in 1994 and was reelected in 1996. Thompson did not seek reelection in 2002 and returned to acting (Barone and Cohen 2003, 1482). In March 2007 he announced on Fox News Sunday that he was considering a presidential bid (Barone and Cohen 2007, 1496-99). Thompson visited Iowa during the state fair in August, and like other candidates spoke at the *Register's* Soap Box venue at the fair. After announcing on the Tonight Show on September 5 that he was running, he returned to Iowa on September 6-8 for a number of appearances before traveling to New Hampshire.

The Republicans, then, had a wide range of candidates; by the end of 2006, 14 possible GOP candidates had visited Iowa for 119 days. The problem that became apparent during the caucus campaign, however, was that each of them "was grounded in one of the three prominent wings of the Republican Party: national security conservatives (Giuliani, Hunter, and McCain), fiscal conservatives (Romney, Fred Thompson, and Paul), or social issues conservatives (Brownback, Huckabee, and Tancredo)" (Burden 2010, 27). There was no unifying candidate.

Democratic Precaucus Activity

During 2005 and 2006, nationwide Gallup polls indicated the Democratic race was between Hillary Clinton and everyone else. In five national polls from February 2005 to June 2006, Clinton led the pack with an average of 39.6 percent, followed by John Kerry at 16.2 percent, John Edwards at 14.2 percent, and the others in single digits (CNN/USA Today Gallup Polls 2005 and 2006; Gallup Polls 2005 and 2006). Iowa Republicans thought Clinton would be the nominee. At a Romney appearance in August 2007 in suburban Des Moines, one person asked, "What I want to know more than anything else is, can you beat Hillary Clinton?" The questioner did not ask about anyone else (Dennis Goldford's notes, August 2, 2007). For the Democrats, the Iowa caucuses offered the opportunity for someone to emerge as the main alternative to Clinton.

Like the Republicans, the wide range of Democratic candidates divide into three categories: prospective candidates who visited Iowa but decided to forego the race; caucus candidates who never constituted a serious challenge and remained in the second tier; and major, first-tier candidates, some of whom were presumptively first-tier and others who used the precaucus season to establish themselves as such.

Six prospective candidates visited Iowa but ultimately did not enter the race. John Kerry visited on December 10, 2004, ostensibly to thank his Iowa supporters for their support in the 2004 presidential race. Former Virginia governor Mark Warner, who had won an impressive victory in 2001 that included rural support, visited on June 6-7, 2005. He dined with Governor Tom Vilsack, and the following day they hosted a town-hall meeting on the American high school. Warner returned to the state and spoke to an Iowa Democratic Party luncheon during the NGA conference. In the summer and fall of 2005, three more Democrats made their first stops in Iowa. Indiana Senator Evan Bayh visited the state on August 2-4. The son of former Senator Birch Bayh and a "moderate," Evan Bayh was an attractive candidate to many Democrats because he had won election to the governor's office and the U.S. Senate in one of the most Republican states in the union (Barone and Cohen 2007, 601-03). Bayh spoke at a Des Moines luncheon honoring Congressman Boswell, held a press conference, and stopped at Democratic Party headquarters. The next day he traveled to Waterloo for Democratic functions, and finally he attended business and education events in the Des Moines area. A year later, Bayh also attended the 2006 Iowa State Fair before deciding not to run.

Four weeks after Bayh's first visit, retired General Wesley Clark spent two days in the state on August 31 and September 1. Clark had opted out of the Iowa caucuses to concentrate on New Hampshire in his unsuccessful 2004 bid for the Democratic nomination, a move he later conceded was a mistake. The last potential candidate to visit Iowa in 2005 was former Senate Majority and Minority Leader Tom Daschle of South Dakota. After eight years as the state's only U.S. House representative, Daschle was elected to the Senate in 1986. He was reelected twice before being targeted by Republicans and defeated by former Congressman John Thune in 2004. He came to the state on November 5 to keynote the Party's annual Jefferson-Jackson dinner. Finally, on April 28-29, 2006, Wisconsin Senator Russ Feingold attended a number of events in eastern and central Iowa, including several Congressional district conventions and campaign fundraisers. A third-term senator first elected in 1992, Feingold was best known as a principal sponsor of the McCain-Feingold campaign-finance reform legislation. Generally a reliable liberal, Feingold went his own way at times, including casting the only vote against the Patriot Act (Barone and Cohen 2007, 1765-69).

Six individuals—New Mexico governor Bill Richardson, Senators Christopher Dodd (Connecticut) and Joe Biden (Delaware), Ohio Representative Dennis Kucinich, former Alaska Senator Mike Gravel, and former Iowa Governor Tom Vilsack—became caucus candidates but never constituted a serious challenge and remained in the second tier. Richardson also attended the 2005 NGA meeting and spoke at a fundraiser for the Iowa Trial Lawyers Association. He had an impressive resume that included service as a Congressman, U.S. Ambassador to the United Nations, Secretary of the Department of Energy, and was elected governor of New Mexico in 2002 and 2006 (Barone and Cohen 2007, 1092-95). Nevertheless, he never scored higher than 11 percent support among Iowa Democrats (Research Polls 2000).

Biden attended the 2006 Iowa State Fair on his first visit to the state August 10-13. A six-term senator from Delaware, he held powerful seats on the Senate Judiciary committee and Senate Foreign Relations committee (Barone and Cohen 2007, 363-67). Biden had run for the presidency in 1988, but that bid was derailed by a combination of alleged plagiarism in a speech and serious health problems. During his first visit in 2006 he attended several fundraisers for Iowa candidates and met with Democratic activists at various events. A month later, Dodd was in Iowa on September 9-10 to campaign with Congressman Boswell, gubernatorial candidate Chet Culver, and other state candidates. He also participated in a roundtable discussion with education leaders. From a political family, Dodd was a five-term senator first elected in 1980. Like Biden, his long seniority earned him seats on the key committees of Banking, Housing and Urban Affairs, and Foreign Relations (Barone and Cohen 2007, 336-39).

Like Biden and Dodd, neither Kucinich nor Gravel ever reached double-digit support in Iowa (Research Polls 2000). Mike Gravel had served in the Senate from 1969 to 1981, and was best known for releasing the Pentagon Papers in 1971 (Mike Gravel 2007). He visited Iowa in June 2006 and conducted a series of media interviews in Des Moines, Ames, Cedar Rapids, and Davenport. Kucinich did not show up in Iowa until April 2007, when he met with activists, and spoke with Democratic state legislators and the *Des Moines Register's* editorial board, among other activities.

Finally, another dark horse, former Iowa governor Tom Vilsack, announced his candidacy on November 30, 2006. He had been elected governor in 1998 after 30 years of Republican control of the office and was reelected in 2002. Perhaps fortunately for Iowa—so it did not risk a repeat of the events of 1992 when Senator Harkin's candidacy effectively ended national interest in the Democratic caucuses—Vilsack's candidacy was short. He announced on February 23, 2007, that he was withdrawing from the race due to lack of funds (Beaumont 2007a).

Against the background of the six prospective candidates who opted out and the six who never got out of the second tier, the 2008 Iowa caucuses became a contest among three first-tier candidates. The first of these was former Senator John Edwards of North Carolina, discussed in chapter 11, who had built a strong base of support in Iowa in the 2004 campaign. His first 2005 visit to the state, on March 31 and April 1, included a keynote speech honoring Iowa Representative Leonard Boswell, taping "Iowa Press," joining striking truck drivers on a picket line, meeting with inner-city groups, and attending John Edwards's thank-you reception.

The second major candidate was a relative newcomer, Senator Barack Obama of Illinois, not initially seen as a first-tier competitor. Elected to the Senate in 2004, 44-year-old Obama had been a community organizer, a lecturer at the University of Chicago Law School, and a state senator (Barone and Cohen 2007, 538-43). He achieved national recognition with his speech that electrified the delegates to the 2004 Democratic National Convention. Obama created his Hopefund PAC in January 2005, and began traveling extensively to support Democratic candidates and to discuss topics of the day, particularly criticizing Bush's handling of the Iraq War. Though he publicly downplayed running for president, Obama quietly hired experienced campaign staff (Barone and Cohen 2007, 542). The last of the potential candidates making their first visit to Iowa in 2006, he traveled to Iowa on September 17 as a special guest at Senator Harkin's annual fund-raising steak fry. Two weeks later he returned to support Democratic Congressional candidate Bruce Braley in Davenport.

Finally, the last of the major candidates to visit Iowa was Hillary Clinton, making her first visit in the 2008 cycle on January 26-28, 2007. The former First Lady and Senator from New York had not re-turned to the state since her enthusiastic reception at the 2003 Jef-ferson-Jackson Day dinner. She made the rounds: an interview with *Register* political columnist David Yepsen, a private meeting with labor leaders, two town-hall-style "Conversation with Iowans" events, and a brief stop at an African American festival. One "Conversation with Iowans" event was at the Dale and Lois Bright Community Center at East High School Community Center in Des Moines, and the other was at the home of Dan and Marcia Rogers in Cedar Rapids.

Despite the affection she enjoyed among Iowa Democrats, the cau-cuses presented potential difficulties for Clinton. She faced a thematic problem that would trouble her in Iowa and beyond. On the one hand, she argued that she had her own political identity independent of her husband's presidency; on the other, whenever she made a claim to the nomination on the basis of experience, that claim tied her right back to the Clinton presidency. Second, unlike Edwards, who had built an organization for the 2004 caucuses that could be resurrected for 2008, Clinton had no such organization. Bill Clinton had not contested the caucuses when Iowa Senator Harkin ran in 1992, and there was no intra-party challenge to him in 1996. The question for the Clinton campaign was whether the caucuses could be an early demonstration of political strength or a possible threat to the implicit argument of inevitability. Moreover, with the frontloading of the primary season that included a Super Tuesday of 23 Democratic primaries and cau-cuses, one could question how worthwhile the Iowa caucuses might be when campaign resources—especially the candidate's time and money—might better be used elsewhere. Such considerations led to a Clinton campaign memo dated May 21, 2007, which was leaked to reporters as the campaign was announcing details of her weekend trip to Iowa. The writer, deputy campaign manager Mike Henry, argued that Iowa was a weak state for Clinton and the caucuses should be bypassed (Beaumont 2007c).

In response to the controversy created by the leaked memo, Clinton immediately disavowed it, continued her Iowa tour, and announced plans to visit Iowa with Bill Clinton July 2-5 ("Ex-president to Join Sen. Clinton in Iowa" 2007). The evening of July 2, they attended a huge rally at the state fairgrounds in Des Moines. The crowd was excited and enthusiastic, but many people said they had come mostly to see Bill Clinton and remained undecided as to whether to support Senator Clinton in 2008. Bill Clinton spoke briefly and encouraged the crowd to think well of the other candidates but to see that Hillary would be the strongest possible nominee. Senator Clinton then gave a speech devoid of specifics and perhaps better suited for the general election (Dennis Goldford's notes July 2, 2007).

With Senator Clinton the Democratic field was set. By the end of 2006, eleven potential Democratic candidates (12 counting Kerry's December 2004 "thank you" trip) had spent 111 days in Iowa (Appleman 2008). After Edwards, Kucinich, and Gravel announced their candidacies in 2006, Kerry decided not to run. Dodd (January), Biden (January), Clinton (January), Obama (February), and Richardson (May) formally joined the race by announcing their candidacies and exploratory committees in 2007. The 2008 Iowa Democratic caucus campaign was then in full swing.

2007: Full Speed Ahead

The Iowa campaign was intense and candidates of both parties traversed the state at record or near record levels in 2007 and 2008, but it was not due just to the media focus on the process. Frontloading was also having an impact on the caucus campaign. Frontloading occurs in part because of the ongoing argument that "unrepresentative" Iowa plays a disproportionate role in the nomination process. Democrats in particular believed that Iowa favors liberal candidates who may not be the strongest possible nominees in the general election. The pressure of other states wanting to have more—and earlier—influence on the nomination process and to diminish the influence of Iowa has led to more states holding their primaries or caucuses earlier in the election year. The contrast between the 2004 and 2008 primary calendars is striking: whereas 37.1 percent of the Democratic primaries and caucuses were held by the end of February 2004 (there was no meaningful Republican challenge to President Bush), 69.1 percent of the Democratic contests and 68.6 percent of the Republican contests would be held by the end of February 2008 ("Presidential Primary and Caucus Dates" 2008).

Since the beginning of the modern period of the Iowa precinct caucuses in 1972 and through 2004, the caucuses have been held between January 19 and February 20. On August 19, 2006, the Democratic National Committee (DNC) adopted its delegate-selection rules for the 2008 national convention. As a compromise of sorts but cloaked in political rhetoric, the DNC added the Nevada caucuses and the South Carolina primary to the early 2008 calendar to balance the perceived regional biases of Iowa and New Hampshire (Highlights of the Rules 2006). The Iowa caucuses were scheduled for January 14, 2008, the Nevada caucuses January 19, the New Hampshire primary January 22, and the South Carolina primary January 29. The other states would be free to hold their primaries or caucuses after February 5. This arrangement preserved Iowa's first-in-the-nation caucus and New Hampshire's first-in-the-nation primary.

Despite the DNC's schedule, the candidates faced the possibility of shifting terrain because some states unilaterally moved their primaries to dates earlier than February 5. Florida moved its primary from March 11 to January 29, and then Michigan moved its primary to January 15 (Shapiro 2007). Because New Hampshire law required that its primary be held at least seven days before the next primary event, Michigan's action meant that New Hampshire would change its date. That in turn would force Iowa to set an even earlier date due to an Iowa law requiring that its caucuses be held at least eight days before any other nominating event. Under this scenario the latest the New Hampshire primary could be held was January 8, and that would have forced Iowa to move to December 31, 2007. Because no one in Iowa wanted to hold the caucuses on New Year's Eve, the date would have had to be before Christmas or between Christmas and New Year's Eve.

Apart from the question of penalties for states violating DNC and RNC rules and the disparate impact on the candidates, events seemed to be spinning out of control. It was nearly Thanksgiving before the political calendar was finally set. According to Craig Robinson, political director of the Republican Party of Iowa at the time, the RNC was kept informed by the Iowa GOP, allowing them to opt for January 3. The "big drama," Robinson said, was what the Democrats would do in light of that Republican decision (Robinson 2010). Norm Sterzenbach, the executive director of the Iowa Democratic Party (IDP), said the Iowa party viewed the DNC rather than the state statute as the controlling authority. The IDP was worried about the possibility that the DNC would demand that the caucus date be moved to December 2007, but when they talked in advance to the DNC about the eight-day issue, the DNC "strongly, strongly suggested that Iowa remain in 2008" (Sterzenbach 2010).

Iowa's parties thus agreed on a January 3 caucus date, and New Hampshire settled on a primary date of January 8, only five days after Iowa. Both the RNC and DNC acquiesced to the January 3 date. As for the Iowa statute that required the eight days between the caucuses and the New Hampshire primary, both the Iowa Republican and Iowa Democratic parties viewed it as unenforceable and gave little thought to it (Robinson 2010, Sterzenbach 2010). Indeed, despite the assumption by most caucus actors of the continuing validity of a law on the books, the Iowa Attorney General's office considers it unenforceable because it is unconstitutional (Miller 2010).

The Republican Campaign

The new January 3 date shortened the campaign time before the caucuses by almost two weeks, making it even more hectic. As in past caucus cycles, candidates of both parties introduced themselves and spread their messages in a variety of ways. There were appearances before small groups in varied venues, larger rallies, and town-hall meetings. Candidates appeared with state and local politicians, met with almost every conceivable type of group and organization, rode in parades, and delivered countless speeches.

Candidates also liked to meet with the editorial boards of Iowa newspapers and appear on local television to broaden their reach. Iowa Public Television's *Iowa Press*, with its statewide audience, was a favorite. Twelve candidates—six Democrats and six Republicans (Biden, Edwards, Huckabee, Richardson, and Romney had two appearances each; Brownback, Clinton, Dodd, McCain, Obama, Tancredo, and Tommy Thompson had one each)—appeared 17 times on *Iowa Press* during 2007 (*Iowa Press* 2007). Presidential candidates popped up everywhere, on TV, at grocery stores, at baseball games, and at the state fair.

Most prominently, candidates appeared together in debates or party events that lent themselves to intense press coverage. During 2007 the Republicans held six multi-candidate events and the Democrats a mind-boggling 15. The first of the major Republican events was the Lincoln Day Unity Dinner on April 14 in Des Moines. This was the opening event because Iowa Republicans did not hold their traditional joint candidate event in conjunction with the mid-term state convention in 2006. The Lincoln Day Unity Dinner almost did not get off the ground either. McCain, Romney, and Giuliani did not plan to attend, but party officials persuaded Giuliani to participate by moving the starting time back an hour and letting him speak first so that he might make another engagement in Topeka. When Giuliani agreed to attend, McCain and Romney followed suit and the event was saved (Kearney 2008). Brownback, Gilmore, Huckabee, Tancredo, Tommy Thompson, and Cox (travel problems kept Hunter away) also attended and spoke to about a thousand party activists. Implicitly criticizing Giuliani's pro-choice history, they competed for the title of "most conservative" on such issues as abortion and illegal immigration. Gilmore drew a few murmurs from the crowd when he said "Rudy McRomney is not a conservative" (Beaumont 2007b).

The next multi-candidate event was the Presidential Candidates Forum held jointly by Iowans for Tax Relief and the Iowa Christian Alliance in Des Moines on June 30. Tommy Thompson, Huckabee, Brownback, Romney, Tancredo, and Hunter attended and spoke; Gilmore, McCain, Giuliani, and Fred Thompson were invited but did not attend, and Ron Paul was not invited, stirring a mini-tempest. Nearly a thousand people attended, and while many had positive things to say about the candidates, Huckabee drew an "enthusiastic ovation," both for his Christian credentials and for his support of a fair tax (Yepsen 2007a).

In May between the two events the *Register* published its first Iowa Poll of the caucus season. The survey of likely caucus-goers showed Romney with a strong early lead. The results were Romney 30 percent, McCain 18, Giuliani 17, Tommy Thompson 7, Brownback 5, Huckabee 4, Tancredo 4, and Hunter, Gilmore, and Cox 1 each, with 12 percent undecided. Romney had performed well in the two national debates, was building a solid campaign organization in Iowa, and had been successful in fund-raising (May 2007 Iowa Poll cited in Roos 2007a). Giuliani led in the national polls for most of 2007 ("White

House 2008: Republican Nomination" 2008). But it was early and the summer events schedule was heavy.

The next two joint events received national media attention. A debate held at Drake University in Des Moines on Sunday, August 5, was aired live by the ABC News program, *This Week*. Brownback, Giuliani, Huckabee, Hunter, McCain, Paul, Romney, Tancredo, and Tommy Thompson participated. The candidates engaged in the standard recitation of Republican policy positions and attacks on the Democrats in general and Clinton and Obama in particular. Brownback sharply attacked Romney as he and Huckabee vied to emerge as the religious-conservative alternative to the former Massachusetts governor. Many Republicans liked what Brownback and Huckabee had to say, but leaned to Romney at this point because they saw him as a potential general-election winner and were not convinced that Brownback or Huckabee could win. Neither Giuliani nor McCain made much of an impact that morning (Dennis Goldford's notes August 5, 2007). Indeed, McCain's campaign nationwide appeared to be stumbling: "In the second quarter of 2007 he raised $11 million, whereas Romney pulled in $20 million (including $6 million of his own funds) and Giuliani raised $17 million" (Burden 2010, 28).

The second major Republican multi-candidate event in August was the Iowa Straw Poll held on the 11th at Iowa State University in Ames. Most of the campaigning during the spring and summer of 2007 was aimed at this key event. To facilitate identifying potential supporters, the party made available for a substantial fee a list of 125,000 names of previous caucus-goers. The price was 25 cents per name or $32,000 for the complete list; seven candidates (Romney, McCain, Giuliani, Brownback, Tancredo, Fred Thompson, and Paul) purchased the entire list (Kearney 2009). Principally a fundraiser, the Straw Poll raised $1.2 million, $800,000 of which went to the Iowa Republican Party. The campaigns purchased most of the $35 tickets to distribute to supporters, provided free food and entertainment on the grounds of Hilton Coliseum, and some provided free transportation to the event from many locations around the state (Robinson 2008).

The 2007 Iowa Straw Poll featured the dominant and centrally located tents of Romney and Brownback, with the other tents scattered around the periphery. The party had held an auction for the tent locations, raising over $120,000 (Romney paid $25,000 for his site, Brownback $20,000, Tancredo $16,000, Tommy Thompson $15,800,

Huckabee $15,000, Cox $15,000, and Hunter $15,000). Candidates gave speeches during the course of the early afternoon, and attendees had until 6 P.M. to cast a vote for their preferred nominee. The event drew a huge media presence, with 453 credentialed people representing 176 media outlets, including 38 journalists representing 28 international media outlets (Robinson 2008).

The results of the straw poll shown in Table 13.1 were a victory for Romney, but one diminished by the absence of his first-tier opponents. Tommy Thompson dropped out the next day, but the big story, eclipsing the Romney victory, was the emergence of Mike Huckabee. From an out-of-the-way tent behind Hilton Coliseum, he bested Brownback despite being outmatched by the latter's huge financial investment in the straw poll. His speech to the crowd as political rhetoric was masterful. The straw poll established Huckabee as the principal social-conservative alternative to Romney. The Romney presence at the straw poll was massive, as evidenced by money, organization, and attention to detail. His supporters wore yellow shirts provided by the campaign and the sea of yellow shirts seemed to engulf everyone else. Nevertheless, there was no first-tier opposition, and the 14,302 vote total was considerably less than the 23,685 votes in the 1999 Iowa Straw Poll (Dennis Goldford's notes and Republican Party of Iowa).

Table 13.1.   2007 Iowa straw poll

Romney	4,516	31.6
Huckabee	2,587	18.1
Brownback	2,192	15.3
Tancredo	1,961	13.7
Paul	1,305	9.1
Thompson, T.	1,039	7.3
Thompson, F.*	203	1.4
Giuliani*	183	1.3
Hunter	174	1.2
McCain*	101	0.7
Cox	41	0.3
Total	14,302	100

*Did not compete in or attend the event.
Source: Republican Party of Iowa.

Heading into the fall, Romney and Huckabee gained some momentum while Iowa Republicans attempted to gauge the impact of Fred Thompson's entrance into the race. McCain and Giuliani were spending little time in Iowa, as the former vacillated about the importance of the caucuses and the latter opted to concentrate on Florida. The *Register* published its second Iowa Poll of likely caucus-goers on October 7, and there were big changes from the May poll. Romney maintained his large lead, but Fred Thompson was now in second place, and Huckabee in third, with McCain and Giuliani fading. The results were Romney 29 percent, Fred Thompson 18, Huckabee 12, Giuliani 11, McCain 7, Tancredo 5, Paul 4, Brownback 2, Keyes 2, and Hunter 1, with 9 percent undecided. Fred Thompson had been in the race for only a month at the time of the survey and had made only two trips to Iowa (October Iowa Poll cited in Roos 2007b). Brownback withdrew from the race on October 19, after his disappointing showing in Ames and registering near the bottom in the October Iowa Poll.

The Reagan Dinner on October 27 was another GOP multi-candidate event, and about 600 activists attended to see and hear Huckabee, Hunter, Paul, Tancredo, Fred Thompson, and Cox. With the top three candidates absent (Romney, Giuliani, and McCain), Huckabee and Thompson received top billing. Most touted their conservative credentials, and Thompson in particular attempted to establish his (Beaumont 2007d). Thompson's speech, however, disappointed many of those present (Kearney 2008).

A third Iowa Poll carried out in late November and published in the *Register* on December 2 suggested that Huckabee, not Fred Thompson, would be the conservative alternative to Romney in Iowa. Huckabee led the field while Fred Thompson was now a distant fourth in the survey. Romney had lost a little ground but was still in second place. The poll results were Huckabee 29 percent, Romney 24, Giuliani 13, Fred Thompson 9, McCain and Paul 7 each, Tancredo 6, and Hunter 1, with 4 percent undecided. Huckabee enjoyed a large lead over Romney among those who said they were born-again Christians. The race was still very fluid, however, as 60 percent of those surveyed said they could be persuaded to change their mind. (December 2 Iowa Poll cited in Roos 2007c). Huckabee's emergence as the religious-conservative alternative to Romney and his increased success in his fund-raising gained attention, but front-runner status brings on new problems.

Some conservative groups did not think him conservative enough, and he was called a populist, a fiscal liberal, and inexperienced (Shear and Eilperin 2007).

The final multi-candidate event of 2007 was the *Register*'s Republican Debate on December 12, just three weeks before the January 3 caucuses. Nine candidates participated in the debate held at the studios of Iowa Public Television in Johnston (Romney, Huckabee, Paul, Hunter, Tancredo, Fred Thompson, McCain, Giuliani, and Alan Keyes, a favorite of social conservatives who was allowed to participate and at times dominated the event). Despite his increasing strength, Huckabee managed to stay somewhat in the background, but he did apologize to Romney for questioning his Mormon faith in a *New York Times Magazine* interview set to appear that weekend (Barabak 2007). The *Times* called the debate a "sleepy affair" and noted that most sparks flew between the candidates and the moderator, *Register* editor Carolyn Washburn, over the rigid format of the debate that prevented direct interchanges between the candidates (Cooper and Luo 2007, 34). A week after the debate, citing low poll numbers, Tancredo ended his candidacy and endorsed Romney (Olinger 2007).

The final Iowa Poll was conducted just days before the caucuses and published in the *Register* on January 1. The results are reported comparatively in Table 13.2. Here the gradual decline of Romney's support is evident, as he was unable to connect with Iowa Republicans, in contrast to the remarkable surge in support for Huckabee following his breakout after the Ames Straw Poll as the populist-conservative alternative to Romney. Survey respondents who described themselves as "born-again" or "fundamentalist Christians" comprised almost 50 percent of the sample and about half of them (47 percent) supported Huckabee, whose lead had grown. Romney held on to second place in the poll but gained little. McCain, in third place, was the only other candidate reaching double figures in the poll, while Giuliani's support simply collapsed after he decided not to campaign actively in what his campaign leaders saw as unpromising territory. It looked as if the Christian Right would again have a major influence in the GOP caucuses.

Table 13.2.   2007 *Des Moines Register* Republican Iowa Polls

	5-07	10-07	12-07	1-08
Romney	30	29	24	26
McCain	18	7	7	13
Giuliani	17	11	13	5
Thompson, T.	7	*	*	*
Brownback	5	2	*	*
Huckabee	4	12	29	32
Tancredo	4	5	6	*
Hunter	1	1	1	1
Gilmore	1	*	*	*
Cox	1	0	0	0
Paul	0	4	7	9
Thompson, F.	#	18	9	9
Keyes	#	2	0	1
Undecided	12	9	4	4
Sample size	401	405	500	800
Margin of error (%) is +/–	4.9	4.9	4.4	3.5

\# Not declared candidates.

*Dropped out.

The Democratic Campaign

While Republicans looked for the next Ronald Reagan, Iowa Democrats—hungry after eight years of Republican control of the presidency—turned out in large numbers for their events. As in past caucuses most of the candidates (Biden, Clinton, Dodd, Edwards, Obama, Richardson, and Vilsack) purchased from the Iowa Democratic Party a list of previous caucus attendees. The $65,000 the candidates paid for the list in 2003 became a very steep $100,000 in 2007—Warner paid half before deciding not to run (Sterzenbach August 31, 2009).

The first three multi-candidate events in 2007 got off to modest starts due to mixed participation by the candidates. Before the candi-

date forums picked up in August, the *Register* published its first Democratic Iowa Poll of the season on May 20. The Democratic candidates
had spent 175 days in Iowa by the time of the first survey and were
well known throughout the state. The survey of likely caucus participants found a close three-person race between Edwards, Obama, and
Clinton. The poll results were Edwards 29 percent, Obama 23, Clinton
21, Richardson 10, Biden 3, Kucinich 2, Gravel 1, and Dodd 0, with
11 percent undecided. Eighty percent of the sample expressed favorable feelings about Edwards, reflecting the good will he had built in
Iowa over the course of two caucus campaigns. Clinton, the leader in
all the national polls ("White House 2008: Democratic Nomination"
2008), was a more controversial figure but was viewed favorably by
two-thirds of those polled (May 2007 Iowa Poll cited in Roos 2007d).

August was a very busy month in Iowa for the Democratic candidates. There were three multi-candidate events and the state fair,
which always draws candidate attention. The main event of the
month was the debate at Drake University broadcast nationally by
ABC's *This Week* on Sunday morning, August 19 (two weeks after Republicans appeared on the same program). All eight candidates participated. There were no gaffes and no big gains, but Clinton looked
more poised and confident than she had in earlier events. Edwards
exhibited the harder edge he had assumed since he announced his
focus on poverty, and Obama struggled somewhat with the format
that inhibited the soaring rhetoric he liked to use. Richardson turned
in a competent, enthusiastic performance, but, despite having run a
large number of TV ads in Iowa, his numbers were not moving much
(Dennis Goldford's notes August 19, 2007).

Two more joint events were held in September. Six of the eight candidates attended Senator Harkin's 30th annual fund-raising steak fry
in Indianola on Sunday, September 16, and spoke to a huge audience
(15,000 tickets were sold). Obama talked about health care reform,
and he and Edwards took a few shots at Clinton, who did not respond
in kind (Yepsen 2007b). Biden, Dodd, and Richardson spoke as well,
but the big three received the bulk of the attention. A second forum
sponsored by AARP and Iowa Public Television was held in Davenport
on September 20.

October was a relatively quiet month in terms of joint appearances,
but the candidates spent 61 days in the state, and the *Register* published a new Iowa Poll on October 7. The second survey of the year

found that Clinton had moved into the lead (she also led in all the national polls), with Edwards dropping to second, closely followed by Obama in third. The results were Clinton 29 percent, Edwards 23, Obama 22, Richardson 9, Biden 6, Kucinich and Dodd 1 each, Gravel 0, with 11 percent undecided. Apparently Clinton's summer campaign in Iowa that included husband Bill on two trips and policy speeches about Iraq and health care gave her a boost (October 2007 Iowa Poll cited in Beaumont and Roos 2007).

There were three more joint Democratic events in November, and the candidates by this time probably could anticipate what the others would say in response to the usual questions. The main event was the Jefferson-Jackson Dinner in Des Moines on November 10, with six candidates attending. Kucinich and Gravel, who did not have active campaigns in the state, were not invited. The party fundraiser drew a crowd of 9000. The candidates all spoke and the crowd was enthusiastic and boisterous. Edwards and Obama spoke last and took a few shots at Clinton, with Edwards alleging that Clinton was too closely associated with special interests and Obama chiding her for supporting the Iraq War resolution in the senate (Beaumont 2007e).

The six active candidates spent 83 days campaigning in Iowa in November, and now it was time for another Iowa Poll. The third survey was released by the *Register* on December 2 and had a surprise—Obama was now leading in Iowa (although the differences were within the margin of error) even though Clinton maintained her lead in national polls. Obama and Clinton had switched places, with Edwards a close third. It began to look as if the race might go to the wire. The results were Obama 28 percent, Clinton 25, Edwards 23, Richardson 9, Biden 6, Dodd and Kucinich 1 each, and Gravel 0, with 7 percent undecided. Obama was seen as the inspirational candidate and had the support of the youngest of the likely caucus-goers (December 2007 Iowa Poll cited in Beaumont 2007f). Going into the final weeks of the campaign, the Democratic caucus contest was a three-person race, with Edwards fading. Edwards had hoped that Iowa would establish him as the alternative to Clinton, but the unexpected emergence of Obama undermined that strategy.

December was the last chance for Edwards to regroup while Clinton and Obama vied for the lead. Their opportunities lay in four multi-candidate events in December. The Heartland Presidential Forum, organized by three non-profit groups concerned with farming, immigration, and urban poverty, took place during the day on December 1. Dodd, Edwards, Kucinich, and Obama were there in person, and Clinton, unable to get there in time due to an ice storm in Des Moines and a hostage situation at one of her offices in New Hampshire, participated by phone. A large crowd of over 3000 people attended the event, and Clinton was booed following her response to a question by an immigrant rights organizer (Jacobs 2007). Later that evening the candidates participated in the Iowa Brown and Black Presidential Forum to discuss issues of importance to African Americans and Hispanics in Iowa, such as licensing unauthorized immigrants and relations with Cuba. Clinton arrived in time to join the other six candidates in the two-hour program (Beaumont 2007g).

On December 4, all the candidates but Richardson (who attended a funeral) participated in a two-hour debate held by NPR News and Iowa Public Radio in Des Moines. The forum dealt with China trade policy, immigration, and Iran ("Debate Check" 2007). Capping off a very long year of debates, Biden, Clinton, Dodd, Edwards, Obama, and Richardson took part in the *Register's* Debate on December 13 (one day after the GOP *Register* debate) at Iowa Public Television in Johnston. The debate was low-key, and there were no defining moments or major mistakes. The theme of the debate was "change" and the six argued over who might be the better agent of change in Washington (Beaumont 2007h).

The Final Countdown

The candidates in both parties now had the organizational task of mobilizing and insuring the turnout of the supporters they identified during the long caucus campaign. Voter turnout is the essential element of electoral politics, but it is especially so for caucuses, where much more time and effort are required to participate. Organizing turnout was also important because of the fluid nature of caucus support. The *Register* polls, including the final survey completed in late December, are summarized in Table 13.3. Obama increased his lead in the final poll as first-time participants and independents indicated their support. Clinton and Edwards held their levels of support, while Richardson and Biden lost ground (January 2008 Iowa Poll cited in

Beaumont 2008). Nationally, Clinton maintained her lead in the polls over Obama until February 2008 ("White House 2008: Democratic Nomination" 2008).

The ad wars were intense in December. The advertising expenditures by the candidates at CBS affiliate KCCI-TV and NBC affiliate WHO-TV in Des Moines are displayed in Table 13.4. Obama and Romney were the big spenders at the two top-rated Des Moines stations. The ad spending has grown dramatically at KCCI and WHO from caucus to caucus. The 2000 Democratic total was $796,875 (two candidates), $3,493,480 (five candidates) in 2004, and $4,998,760 (five candidates) in 2008. The Republican total for 2000 was $1,556,095 (seven candidates) and $3,598,375 (eight candidates) in 2008. When combined, the total 2008 spending for candidates of both parties was $8,597,135. Add to that total the $805,200 spent at the ABC affiliate, WOI-TV (Shelton 2008), and the grand total reaches $9,402,335. The Iowa campaign was getting more and more expensive.

Overall spending is always difficult to determine. Using calculations based on information from CNN, the Wisconsin Ad Project, FEC

Table 13.3.   2007 *Des Moines Register* Democratic Iowa Polls

	5-07	10-07	12-07	1-08
Edwards	29	23	23	24
Obama	23	22	28	32
Clinton	21	29	25	25
Richardson	10	8	9	6
Biden	3	5	6	4
Kucinich	2	1	1	1
Gravel	1	0	0	0
Dodd	0	1	1	2
Undecided	11	11	7	6
Sample size	400	399	500	800
Margin of error (%) is +/ –	4.9	4.9	4.4	3

Table 13.4.   2008 Democratic and Republican spending
at KCCI-TV and WHO-TV

	KCCI	WHO
Democrats		
Obama	$1,076,000	$899,995
Clinton	732,000	556,090
Edwards	424,000	334,660
Dodd	286,000	295,355
Biden	223,000	171,660
Richardson	706,000	523,760
Total	3,447,000	2,781,520
Republicans		
Romney	980,000	422,475
Huckabee	192,000	142,040
Thompson, F.	184,000	122,090
Paul	132,000	125,110
Hunter	12,000	9,900
Giuliani (KCCI website)	3,000	0
Tancredo	0	44,000
Total	1,503,000	865,615
Grand Total	4,950,000	3,647,135

Source: Table created from records provided by Zoe Goedicke,
Traffic Manager, WHO, and Anne Marie Caudron, National Sales
Manager, KCCI.

Presidential Reports, and others, one source estimated that candidates spent $51,593,849 on the 2008 Iowa Caucuses. The figure includes TV, radio, and newspaper ads, campaign headquarter rentals, hotels, food, car rentals, and other transportation costs such as buses and flights ("What Was the Financial Outcome of the 2008 Financial Caucuses?").

The Caucuses

After all the hard work and a nearly three-year campaign, January 3 finally arrived. The candidates had virtually lived in Iowa for the final five weeks of the campaign. GOP candidates campaigned 70 days in the state in December and January and the Democrats 143 days. The total candidate days in Iowa during the three-year campaign are shown in Table 13.5.

The combined total of 1194 Iowa campaign days for the candidates of both parties in 2008 far exceeded the previous high of 999 days in the 1988 campaign cycle. Although media spending continued to grow, the candidates saw Iowa as a retail politics state that required a great deal of personal attention. There was also a huge local, regional, national, and international media presence. The executive director of the Iowa Democratic Party estimates that the two parties issued at least 2500 press credentials. Media came from Australia, Belgium, Canada, France, Germany, Great Britain, Ireland, Japan, Poland, Scandinavia, Slovak Republic, South Korea, and Spain, among others, including al-Jazeera and al-Hurra from the Arab world (Sterzenbach July 29, 2009). The caucus results are displayed in Tables 13.6 and 13.7.

In each caucus, a relatively unknown candidate overtook and defeated the initial front-runner. Why? The 2008 Iowa caucuses experienced a massive increase in turnout driven mostly by general Democratic enthusiasm and a narrow but enthusiastic slice of Republicans participating, despite the dispirited mood in the party. The 2008 Democratic turnout of 239,872 nearly doubled the previous record turnout of 124,000 in 2004. Somewhat of a surprise, the 119,188 Republicans who voted in the 2008 caucus straw poll exceeded the previous record of 108,806 in 1988. According to CNN entrance polls, 57 percent of the Democratic participants had never attended a caucus before. More than Democrats showed up for their meetings: 76 percent of the participants in the Democratic caucuses self-identified as Democrats, 20 percent as independents, 3 percent as Republicans, and 2 percent as "other." Obama won 32 percent of the Democrats, Clinton 31, and Edwards 23. Obama brought in many of these new participants, winning 41 percent of the independents to 17 percent for Clinton and 23 percent for Edwards. More impressive was the increase in participation by younger voters. Although 60 percent of the

Table 13.5.   2008 Precaucus days in Iowa

Republican	Total
Brownback	59
Gilmore	9
Gingrich	18
Giuliani	22
Huckabee	75
Hunter	25
McCain	43
Pataki	21
Paul	20
Romney	77
Tancredo	71
Thompson, F.	31
Thompson, T.	65
Others	15
Total	551

Democratic	Total
Biden	120
Clinton, H.	74
Dodd	105
Edwards	110
Kucinich	9
Obama	89
Richardson	77
Others	59
Total	643

Source: Eric Appleman, Democracy in Action, collected the data from the individual campaigns. The Republican "others" category includes Allen 3, Frist 10, and Hagel 2. The Democratic "others" category includes Bayh 21, Clark 7, Daschle 3, Feingold 6, Kerry 9, and Warner 13. Iowa Governor Vilsack was not included in the count. The campaign activity covers the period from January 20, 2005 through January 3, 2008.

Table 13.6.   2008 Republican precinct caucus results

	Preferences	Percentage
Huckabee	40,841	34.4
Romney	29,949	25.2
Thompson, F.	15,904	13.3
McCain	15,559	13.1
Paul	11,817	10.0
Giuliani	4,097	3.5
Hunter	524	0.4
Tancredo	5	0
Total	118,696	100

Source: Republican Party of Iowa from 1,781 of 1,781 precincts. Huckabee was the winner in 74 of Iowa's 99 counties, Romney was first in 24 counties, and Paul won in Jefferson County. The turnout of 118,696 was 20.6 percent of the 576,231 Republicans registered on January 1.

Table 13.7.   2008 Democratic precinct caucus results

	State Delegate Equivalents (%)
Obama	37.58
Edwards	29.75
Clinton, H.	29.47
Richardson	2.11
Biden	0.93
Uncommitted	0.14
Dodd	0.02
Total	100

Source: Iowa Democratic Party from 1,781 of 1,781 precincts. The record turnout of 239,872 was 39.6 percent of the 606,209 Democrats registered on January 1.

Democrats and 73 percent of the Republicans were 45 years of age and older, 22 percent of the Democrats and 11 percent of the Republicans were ages 17-29 (Entrance Polls: Iowa. 2008). The comparable percentages for Democrats less than 30 years of age in 2004 and 2000 were 17 and 9 percent (Entrance Polls: Iowa. 2004). With his message of "change," Obama "sought to expand the universe of caucus-goers to include nontraditional targets such as young people, Republicans, and independents" (Ceaser, Busch, and Pitney 2009, 114). He did so.

Females dominated the Democratic caucuses (57 percent to 43 percent) while males commanded the Republican meetings (56 percent to 44 percent). The Democratic participants were 54 percent liberals, 40 percent moderates, and 6 percent conservatives. Republicans were more homogeneously conservative, with 88 percent self-identifying as very or somewhat conservative and only 11 percent claiming to be moderates. The increase in Republican turnout probably resulted from Huckabee's attraction to born-again or evangelical Christians, who increased their proportion of the participants by half to 60 percent in 2008 ("Entrance Polls: Iowa" 2008).

About 359,000 of Iowa's registered voters (18.7 percent) took part in the 2008 caucuses. This was a large increase in caucus participation from past years but still an admittedly small proportion even if not significantly unrepresentative in terms of issue concerns.

The 2008 caucuses continued the winnowing process that began in the months leading up to the actual date. On the Democratic side, Biden and Dodd dropped out of the race within hours of the caucus results, having been shown, along with Kucinich and Gravel, not to have any realistic chance of contending for the nomination.

On the Republican side, the caucus process showed that Hunter, Tancredo, Brownback, and Paul (despite the fervor of his supporters) had developed no significant support. Second, it showed that Fred Thompson would likely fail to justify the hopes of his supporters as they sought another Ronald Reagan. Third, the ultimate failure of the Giuliani campaign suggests that a candidate needs to participate in at least one of the first two major events—Iowa or New Hampshire—as McCain would do in New Hampshire even as his campaign almost melted down in the summer of 2007. Giuliani had taken "the unprecedented step of skipping the first six primaries and caucuses to focus on Florida" (Burden 2010, 29; Ceaser, Busch, and Pitney 2009, 62), and, despite having raised $58.5 million in 2007 to Romney's $53 million and McCain's $37 million (Currinder 2010, 170), it did not work.

Fourth, the process showed a fundamental flaw in the Romney campaign strategy. On the assumption that McCain would be the establishment candidate, Romney attempted to run to his right by targeting social and religious conservatives, so influential in Iowa Republican circles. The irony of his strategy is that Romney appealed for support from a constituency that considers religious beliefs and values to be extremely important in both private and public life but was suspicious of Romney's own religion. His nationally televised speech on religion, politics, and the presidency on December 6, 2007, was of no avail. Romney was hurt by the fact that Huckabee, more so than Obama or Clinton, was the identity-politics candidate in the 2008 Iowa caucuses and the nomination contest in general. Obama attempted not to run as the black candidate, and Clinton, while occasionally moving in the identity direction, did not run as the female candidate. Huckabee, by contrast, ran as the Christian candidate. In his second TV ad in Iowa, the first written words on the screen were "Christian leader," and his first spoken word was "faith" (Dennis Goldford's notes). McCain's decline "and the inability of Giuliani or Romney to capitalize decisively led to a vacuum that invited the entrance of new candidates" (Ceaser, Busch, and Pitney 2009, 63). With the withdrawal of Brownback in October 2007, Huckabee became the religious-conservative alternative.

As they had in the past, the caucuses revealed unexpected strengths and unexpected weaknesses in the candidates and campaigns. They provided a relative assessment of the candidates, leaving the rest of the country to decide what to do with that assessment. The winners' "bounce" is sometimes limited, as shown by New Hampshire's preference for Clinton and McCain days later.

The 2008 Iowa caucuses revealed weaknesses in the Clinton and Romney campaigns. They made Huckabee (under-funded) and Obama (not well known) real players, because Iowa provided a relatively inexpensive place and accessible range of local individuals and groups with whom the candidates could interact. Indeed, Huckabee had raised only $9 million in 2007, $8 million of which came after June (Currinder 2010, 170). It is difficult to believe that Huckabee, and less certainly Obama, could have broken through and captured media attention in a wholesale politics state. Obama showed that he could attract the white vote. Iowa also showed that the Edwards campaign was not going anywhere. And, for only the third time (Carter 1976, Bush 2000), the winner of a contested Iowa caucus would go on to win the presidency.

The invisible primary discussed in earlier chapters produced mixed results in 2008. On the Republican side, "no one emerged as the front-runner" (Burden 2010, 28). Among Democrats, Clinton held strong leads in the national public opinion polls throughout 2007 and into early 2008. She also received her share of endorsements, but money dominated the campaign. The clear winner in the "money primary" was Obama. One writer called his fund-raising organization the "Amazing Money Machine." In February 2007 alone the Obama campaign raised $55 million ($45 million over the Internet with most in donations of $200 or less [Green 2008]), and that was a third more than Howard Dean raised in all of 2003 and only $2.6 million less than the Bush campaign raised in all of 1999. Although Clinton led the Democratic candidates in early fund-raising, Obama soon surged ahead. Clinton raised $36.1 million in the first quarter of 2007 and $21 million in the second, whereas Obama raised $25.8 million in the first and $32 million in the second. He established a larger donor list than any other Democrat, and one-third of his contributions came over the Internet, 90 percent of which were less than $100. Using proven fund-raising techniques, "Clinton collected 75 percent of her contributions from individuals who gave $1,000 or more, whereas Obama raised 54 percent of his money from such donors" (Currinder 2010, 168-69). Obama revolutionized fund-raising and, in politics, money trumps all.

Whatever the future holds for the Iowa caucuses, by December of 2009 Republicans Mike Huckabee, Louisiana Governor Bobby Jindal, Mississippi Governor Haley Barbour, Nevada Senator John Ensign (prior to his marital troubles), Indiana Congressman Mike Pence, and Minnesota Governor Tim Pawlenty, former New York Governor George Pataki, and former vice-presidential candidate Sarah Palin had all made post-election visits to Iowa. Presidential candidates will consider the Iowa caucuses important as long as the media does, and the media will consider them important as long as the candidates do.

References

"About Iowa Christian Alliance." 2006. www.iowachristian.com.

Appleman, Eric. 2008. "Democracy in Action." www.gwu.edu/~action/P2008.html.

Barabak, Mark Z. 2007. "Controversy Dwarfs Debate—Religion Again Moves to the Fore after Huckabee Apologizes for Raising Questions about the Mormon Faith." December 13. http://articles.latimes.com/2007/dec/13/nation/na -campaign 13.

Barone, Michael, and Richard E. Cohen. 2003. *The 2004 Almanac of American Politics*. Washington, D.C.: National Journal Group.

———. 2007. *The 2008 Almanac of American Politics*. Washington, D.C.: National Journal Group.

Barstow, David. 2000. "McCain's Holy War Targets Religious Right." February 29. www.newyorktimes.com.

Beaumont, Thomas. 2007a. "Farewell, '08." *Des Moines Register*, February 24, p. 1A.

———. 2007b. "Republican Candidates Make Case to Iowans." *Des Moines Register*, April 15, p. 1A.

———. 2007c. "Aide Advises Clinton: Skip Iowa." *Des Moines Register*, May 24, p. 1B.

———. 2007d. "Republicans Talk Up Conservative Credentials." *Des Moines Register*, October 28, p. 1B.

———. 2007e. "Democrats Tussle into Home Stretch." *Des Moines Register*, November 11, p. 1B.

———. 2007f. "Obama, Huckabee Leap into the Lead." *Des Moines Register*, December 2, p. 1A.

———. 2007g. "Democrats Soften Tone at Minority Forum." *Des Moines Register*, December 2, pp. 1, 4B.

———. 2007h. "Democrats Trumpet Need for Change." *Des Moines Register*, December 14, p. 1A.

———. 2008. "Poll: Obama, Huckabee Lead in Final Stretch." *Des Moines Register*, January 1, p. 1A.

———, and Jonathan Roos. 2007. "Clinton, Romney Lead in Iowa." *Des Moines Register*, October 7, p. 1A.

Burden, Barry C. 2010. "The Nomination: Rules, Strategies, and Uncertainty." In *The Elections of 2008*, edited by Michael Nelson, 22-44. Washington, D.C.: CQ Press.

Ceaser, James W., Andrew E. Busch, and John J. Pitney, Jr. 2009. *Epic Journey: The 2008 Elections and American Politics*. Lanham, MD: Rowman & Littlefield.

CNN/USA Today Gallup Poll. February 4-6, 2005; August 5-7, 2005; December 9-11, 2005; February 9-12, 2006; Gallup Poll June 1-4, 2006. http://pollin greport.com/wh08dem2.htm.

Cooper, Michael, and Michael Luo. 2007. "Final Debate before Iowa Caucuses Shows Uncertainty at Top of Republican Field." *New York Times*, December 13, p. 34.

From Iowa to the White House

Currinder, Marian. 2010. "Campaign Finance: Fundraising and Spending in the 2008 Election." In *The Elections of 2008*, edited by Michael Nelson, 163-86. Washington, D.C.: CQ Press.

"Debate Check: Behind Democratic Responses." December 4, 2007. http://www .npr.org/templates/story/story.php?storyid=16876030.

"Entrance Polls: Iowa." January 19, 2004. http://www.cnn.com/ELECTION/2004/ primaries/pages/epolls/IA/index.html.

"Entrance Polls: Iowa." January 2, 2008. http://www.cnn.com/ELECTION/2008/ primaries/results/epolls/#IADEM.

"Ex-president to Join Sen. Clinton in Iowa." June 19, 2007. www.msnbc.msn.com/ id/19307112/.

Green, Joshua. 2008. "The Amazing Money Machine." *Atlantic Monthly*, June, pp. 52-63.

"Highlights of the 2008 Rules." August 21, 2006. www.democrats.org/a/2006/08/ highlights-of-t.php.

Iowa Code 43.4. Political party precinct caucuses. http://www.legis.state.ia.us/ IACODE/2001SUPPLEMENT/43/4.html.

Iowa Press transcripts. 2007. www.iptv.org/iowapress.

Iowa Secretary of State web site. 2008. www.sos.state.ia.us/elections.

Jacobs, Jennifer. 2007. "Democrats Hear Stories of Injustice." *Des Moines Register*, December 2, p. 1B.

"KCRG-TV9 Iowa Poll Results." November 15, 2007. http://www.kcrg.com/explore politics/11385156.html.

Kearney, Darrell, finance director of the Republican Party of Iowa. 2008. Interview with Hugh Winebrenner and Dennis Goldford, July 14.

Kearney, Darrell. 2009. Telephone interview with Dennis Goldford, August 18.

"Mike Gravel." 2007. http://en.wikipedia.org/wiki/mike_gravel.

Miller, Tom. 2010. Telephone interview with Dennis Goldford, March 17.

Mooney, Brian C. 2005. "Romney Ready to 'Test Waters' on Iowa Swing." *Boston Globe*, July 15. http://www.boston.com/news/local/massachusetts/ar ticles/2005/07/15/romney_ready_to_test_waters_on_iowa_swing/.

Olinger, David. 2007. "Immigration Issue Sped to the Top without Him: Tancredo Considers a Run against Salazar in 2010." *Denver Post*, December 21, p. A4.

Opinion Research: "Iowa Poll." December 14-18, 2007. http://i.a.cnn.net/ cnn/2007/images/12/20/topia1.pdf.

"President Bush: Job Ratings." January 13-16, 2009. www.pollingreport.com/Bush Job1.htm.

"Presidential Primary and Caucus Dates." May 6, 2008. http://archive.stateline .org/flash-data/Primary/2008_presidential_primaries.pdf.

Research Polls 2000. http://www.kcrg.com/internal?st=print&id=11385156&path=/ explorepolitics.

"Research Polls 2000." KCCI-TV. December 2006.

Robinson, Craig, political director of the Republican Party of Iowa during the 2007 Iowa Straw Poll. 2008. Telephone interview with the Dennis Goldford, July 16.

———. 2010. Telephone interview with Dennis Goldford, March 17.

Roos, Jonathan. 2007a. "Republicans: McCain, Giuliani in Tight Race for Second Place." *Des Moines Register*, May 20, p. 1A.

———. 2007b. "Clinton, Romney Lead in Iowa." *Des Moines Register*, October 7, p. 1A.

———. 2007c. "Romney Slips to Second, Giuliani Overcomes Thompson; 6 in 10 Open to Switching Support." *Des Moines Register*, December 2, p. 1A.

———. 2007d. "Edwards, Romney Lead Early." *Des Moines Register*, May 20, p. 1A.

Shapiro, Walter. 2007. "Florida Election Mayhem for 2008." July 2. www.salon.com/news/feature/2007/07/02/primaries/index.html.

Shear, Michael D., and Juliet Eilperin. 2007. "Suddenly, Huckabee Is in Romney's Rearview Mirror: Polls Show That the Two Are in Virtual Tie in Iowa." *Washington Post*, November 25, p. A6.

Shelton, Randy, operations manager of WOI-TV. 2008. E-mail to Dennis Goldford, July 28.

Sterzenbach, Norm, executive director of the Iowa Democratic Party. 2009. Telephone interview with Dennis Goldford, July 29 and e-mail to Dennis Goldford, August 31.

———. 2010. Telephone interview with and e-mail communication to Dennis Goldford, March 15.

Thomas, Helen. 2005. "Newt Gingrich Hopes We Remember only the Good Times." *Seattle Post-Intellingencer*, April 22. www.seattlepi.com/opinion/221114_thomas22.html.

"What Was the Financial Outcome of the 2008 Iowa Caucuses?" 2008. www.iowacaucus.biz.

"White House 2008: Democratic Nomination." August 23-24, 2008. www.pollingreport.com/wh08dem.htm.

"White House 2008: Republican Nomination." August 23-24, 2008. www.pollingreport.com/wh08rep.htm.

Yepsen, David. 2007a. "Conservatives at GOP Forum Seek Specifics." *Des Moines Register*, July 1, p. 2B.

———. 2007b. "Candidates Serve Meaty Performance to Voters." *Des Moines Register*, September 18, p. 11A.

Chapter 14 Media Event or Local Event? The Caucuses in Perspective

OFFICIALS OF BOTH STATE PARTIES, correspondents for the national media, and candidates for the presidency have all cooperated in making the Iowa precinct caucuses a weather vane for the presidential nominating process. The 1972 decision by the Iowa Democratic Party to move its caucus date up to implement party reforms had an immediate impact on the presidential nominating process. The earlier date made Iowa the first round of selecting Democratic convention delegates. Reporters and presidential candidates noticed Iowa's new first-in-the-nation status. Further changes in state caucus procedures by the Democrats in 1972 and 1976 and by the Republicans in 1976 and 1980 made possible the creation of a media event by instituting a common date for the meetings and providing "results" or "outcomes" from the process.

The news media, faced with the problem of covering a number of candidates in the initial stages of presidential campaigns, recognized Iowa as a source of early evidence about the progress of the race. The news trendsetters—the *New York Times* and the *Washington Post*—were among those who "discovered" the precinct caucuses, and they pointed the way to Iowa in 1976 for political reporters embarrassed by their errors of judgment in the 1972 Muskie-McGovern race. R. W. Apple, Jr., of the *New York Times* focused media attention on the local meetings. His stories about the 1972 outcomes and the surprisingly strong McGovern finish, and his stories about the 1975 Jefferson-Jackson Day preference poll, in which he alerted the nation to the strong Carter campaign in Iowa, focused attention on the precinct caucuses as a source of hard news for the news media.

Two presidential candidates, George McGovern and Jimmy Carter, used the caucuses effectively in order to gain media attention for their campaigns, and in the process they contributed to Iowa's growth as a media event. McGovern, realizing that the early date for the 1972 precinct caucuses could attract media attention, quietly organized a grass-roots Iowa campaign that brought coverage from national news organizations. After an exploratory trip to the state in 1975, Carter decided to launch an all-out effort in the precinct caucuses. When it began to appear that his organizational effort might pay dividends, it was in Carter's interest to turn the caucuses into a media event to maximize the surprise of an Iowa victory, should one occur. Apple was very helpful in that regard.

Working behind the scenes to make the Democratic caucuses a media event was the state Democratic Party, and particularly the state chair, Tom Whitney. He and party staffers cooperated with the presidential hopefuls to gain press exposure for the candidates' 1976 campaigns in Iowa. The party made every effort to accommodate the media demand for evidence of the progress of the presidential campaign, including holding preference polls and providing timely statewide results of the caucus process. Whitney's efforts proved mutually beneficial to the party, the media, and the candidates, because each gained something from the increased visibility of the precinct caucuses.

The multiple efforts of party, press, and presidential candidates were so successful in turning the Iowa caucuses into a media event that by 1980 Iowa rivaled New Hampshire for prominence as a nominating event. But along the way the promoters lost sight of the fact that caucus and convention systems do not produce outcomes in the way that primary elections do. The caucuses are not elections in any ordinary sense of the term (though delegates to county conventions are elected), but rather party business meetings on whose shoulders the country—the press in particular—places more weight than they were designed to bear. All that the caucus represents, boiled down to its simplest form, is an answer to the question, "By the way—while you're here conducting party business, whom do you, the party activists, prefer as the party's candidate for the presidency?" However, because Iowa selects delegates in its caucus and convention process, the media attribute more meaning to its results than to those in states that hold isolated presidential polls or "beauty contests."

Finally, the Democrats use of preference groups, designed for the purpose of instituting proportional voting, complicate and confuse the democratic will because individual votes are not counted and reported directly, but rather appear in the form of "state delegate equivalents" that reporters and the public never seem to understand. Despite repeated requests by the press for individual votes, Democratic leaders have consistently asserted that the delegate equivalents best represent what takes place at their caucuses, namely the selection of delegates to the county conventions.

The lack of independent controls over the tabulation and release of caucus outcomes is perhaps even more serious than are the misleading results. In Iowa, unlike states holding primary elections where state officials administer the electoral process, the political parties conduct the caucuses and collect and process their own caucus results with no independent checks. Iowa parties could actually report what they pleased before 1988, the year a new Iowa law made it illegal for those reporting caucus results to "willfully" omit or falsify results or fail to perform their duties. That law did not change the fact that the parties themselves administer the electoral processes in their caucuses.

The Iowa precinct caucuses have been turned into a mediality in every sense of Robinson's use of the term. The basically local functions of the caucuses are obscured by the practice of featuring the meetings as an early test in the horse race for the nomination. Fueled by the interdependent relationship that has developed among Iowa's parties, the press, and the presidential candidates, the contrived nature of the event and the lack of meaningful results are glossed over. One could argue that no rational person would design the existing American presidential-nominating system deliberately, but the role of the Iowa caucuses is ultimately a historical accident ("It's all Jimmy Carter's fault," so to speak) that grew organically into the institution it is today.

Regardless, the popularity and the influence of the precinct caucuses continue, largely because their transformation into a national event has benefited those who helped create it. Iowa has benefited from the national publicity surrounding the caucuses, particularly the numerous in-depth stories about the state and its people. The caucuses have generated funds for both political parties and large sums of money for the state's businesses, and the national attention has helped both parties by stimulating interest and participation in the caucus process. State officials of both parties are pleased to identify sources of citizen support nine or ten months before the November election.

The media have benefited from the fact that the caucuses provide them with early "evidence" of the progress of the various presidential campaigns. The early indicator helps the media define and label the status of presidential contenders and affords the presidential candidates themselves a testing ground for their candidacies. In Iowa, they can demonstrate their ability to organize and pull off a presidential campaign and, if successful, gain extensive national exposure.

Iowa is a small, homogeneous, midwestern farm state composed largely of small cities and rural areas. The political culture and demography of the state may be typical of the American heartland, but an aging population, the absence of big cities, and the small number of nonwhites make it a poor mirror of the national political culture, and its political activists are not ideologically representative of primary election participants or the national electorate. Although no one state can legitimately claim to mirror the national electorate, larger states complain that Iowa influences the candidate selection process far more than it should, given its lack of demographic and political representativeness.

Although many observers and practicing political people argue that the Iowa caucuses should not play the role they have come to play in determining our presidential nominees, the caucuses will retain that role as long as no one can agree on what should replace them. In any serial nomination process, some state is going to be a gatekeeper and thus exert significant influence. Iowa is not first because it is important; it is important because it is first. Indeed, as other states have compressed the primary schedule in an attempt to lessen Iowa's influence and increase their own, they have unwittingly increased the significance of the caucuses. Nevertheless, as a media event, the Iowa caucuses reaffirm the truth of Machiavelli's dictum, "the great majority of mankind are satisfied with appearances, as though they were realities, and are often even more influenced by the things that seem than by those that are."

In presidential nomination, the name of the game is *perception*, and the reality of the Iowa precinct caucuses has long been replaced by the media perception of them. It is not so much the caucus event per se but the media report of that event that shapes the presidential selection process. Iowa is first. The precinct caucuses provide early evidence—hard news—on the progress of the presidential race. This is the perception of Iowa's role, and it is therefore the reality of the precinct caucuses.

Extensive media coverage changes the nature of the political process, and nowhere more conspicuously than in the presidential selection process. As described by Patterson, the modern presidential race is a media campaign. The media have become the principal linkage between candidates and voters in national campaigns, and voters have grown to rely on the media for an interpretation of, as well as information about, the political campaigns. In the process, the media have become not only reporters of the news but also important actors in the electoral process. They identify the candidates for the American public; by emphasis or neglect they decide which issues are important; they are instrumental in establishing a set of expectations about the candidates' likelihood of success; they evaluate the progress of the race according to the expectations they help to create; and finally, they determine the "winners" and "losers," again according to their own expectations.

The evaluation of caucus and primary outcomes is a complex process based on the perceptions of journalists who seldom report in a straightforward way that, for example, candidate A received 49 percent of the vote and candidate B 17 percent. The candidate who receives the most delegates or votes is not always declared the winner, and candidates who do not do well in an absolute sense are not always called losers. Rather, those labels are assigned according to how well candidates meet or fail to meet expectations. The Bush (2000), Gore (2000), and Mondale (1984) victories were significant because they met the very high expectations of their front-runner roles; the strong finishes of Carter (1976), Bush (1980), Obama (2008), and Huckabee (2008) were "surprises" because the candidates were perceived to have fared much better than expected. Likewise, the second-place finishes of Robertson (1988) and Buchanan (1996) were "surprises" because expectations for them were low. The perception of losing is equally important. The media may dismiss candidates who fail to meet the expectations of their roles. The handicappers were certain that Ted Kennedy posed a real threat to Carter in 1980 and thought John Glenn (1984), Phil Gramm and Steve Forbes (1996), and Howard Dean (2004) would be serious challengers. When their shares of the delegate equivalents or votes were much less than expected in Iowa, they were virtually dismissed as viable candidates. When front-runners Bush (1988), Dole (1996), and Clinton (2008) failed to meet the high expectations of their roles, the media questioned their viability as candidates and subjected them to a great deal of bad press.

After a long dry spell, recent winners in Iowa (Obama, Kerry, Gore, George W. Bush, and Dole) have gone on to win their parties' nomination. The frontloading of the primary season and the heavy reliance on paid TV changed the dynamics of the presidential race. Bush and Dukakis (1988), Dole (1996), and McCain (2008) demonstrated that well-bankrolled candidates are able to rebound after setbacks in the first-in-the-nation caucuses. Although the myth of Iowa as a kingmaker may live on in some circles, only three Iowa caucus winners (Carter, George W. Bush, and Obama) have won the presidency. Moreover, it has been more than 30 years since the last little-known candidate, Jimmy Carter, rode the momentum from Iowa to the White House.

The Iowa caucuses do not reliably pick the president or even the party nominees. Instead, they produce the first "official" measure of party activists' opinions of their potential presidential nominees. To be sure, since 1972 no candidate failing to finish among the top three places in caucus results has gone on to win the presidency, and some caucus results, like the second-place finish of Pat Robertson in 1988, herald the entrance of an important new voting bloc in American politics. Yet this shows that caucuses can be influential without being determinative.

The caucuses provide candidates with the opportunity to test-drive the campaign organizations they have assembled, such as getting reactions from Iowans to their personal appeal and their campaign themes. In the retail-politics context of the caucuses, candidates have to treat ordinary citizens as real people, with questions and concerns they can voice to the candidates, rather than, as is so often the case in "wholesale" politics, as campaign props at media events. Past caucuses have allowed relatively unknown and under-funded candidates to campaign on a retail basis in a relatively inexpensive state in order to exceed the expectations set by professional caucus observers in the press and academe. Recently, however, the big spenders (Obama, Kerry, George W. Bush, Gore) have prevailed in Iowa. Huckabee, with solid support from the Christian Right, has been the only relatively unknown, under-funded candidate to win in recent caucuses. Yet, several big spenders (H. Clinton, Romney, Dean, and Forbes) did not win in the caucuses. Adequate funding has become a prerequisite for, but not a guarantee of, caucus success.

Although the Iowa caucuses may no longer be able to "make" dark-horse presidential candidacies in the present environment, they still "break" them. In each cycle several dark-horse candidates, usually under-funded, enter the presidential race, and most are no longer viable after Iowa. Typically, Iowa and New Hampshire eliminate half the field or more. This is the role that Iowa is best known for: winnowing the field. Without an alternative nomination system acceptable to everyone interested and involved in the process, Iowa's traditional role will continue.

Index

ABC-TV: coverage of 1976 Democratic precinct caucuses, 69; coverage of 1984 Democratic precinct caucuses by, 122-124; coverage of 1992 Democratic precinct caucuses by, 196-197; coverage of 2008 Republican debate at Drake University, 318; coverage of 2008 Democratic debate at Drake University, 323
abortion issue, 14, 209, 212
Abramowitz, Alan, 21-22
advertising (paid): effects of, 177-179; and Malcolm (Steve) Forbes, Jr., campaign, 227-228; negativism and, 242-243. *See also* media coverage
age of eligibility for caucus participation, 29. *See also* demographics of population, 20-21, 41
agribusiness. *See* farm issues
Alexander, Lamar: 1996 Caucus Kickoff, 215-218; 1996 *Des Moines Register* Iowa Poll results and, 215, 219, 227, 232, 247; 1996 GOP "Star-Spangled Preview" and, 205; 1996 precaucus campaign activity and spending, 236; 1996 Republican precaucus activity, 207-208; 1996 Republican precinct caucus results, 238-239, 241; 1996 Republican spending at WHO-TV and KCCI-TV, 226-227; 1998 GOP "First in the Nation Gala" and, 254-255; 1999 Iowa straw poll and, 262; 2000 Republican radio and TV advertising of, 264-265
Allen, George: 2008 Republican precaucus activity, 306
Anderson, John, 83, 94
anti-nuclear groups, 23
anti-war groups, 23; 1968 Democratic

National Convention and, 40-41; 1968 Democratic precinct caucuses and, 37; representativeness of Iowa and, 23
Apple, R. W.: 1976 Democratic precinct caucuses, 68, 70; 1988 interpretations, 171, 174; Jefferson-Jackson Day poll and, 62-63, 65; media influence of, 337-338
arms control. *See* nuclear disarmament
Ashbrook, John, 53
Ashcroft, John: 1998 GOP "First in the Nation Gala" and, 254-255; 2000 Republican precaucus campaign activity of, 258; 2000 Republican radio and TV advertising, 264-265
Askew, Reubin: 1984 Democratic precaucus activity, 113, 115-116; 1984 Democratic precinct caucuses, 126; 1984 precaucus campaign spending, 120-121; 1984 *Des Moines Register* debate and, 118-119; STAR*PAC of 1983 and, 116; withdrawal for presidential candidacy of, 130
Avenson, Don, 188

Babbitt, Bruce: 1988 Democratic campaign spending of, 149-151; 1988 Democratic precaucus activity, 140, 143, 146, 148-149; 1988 Democratic precinct caucus results, 169, 172; 1988 *Des Moines Register* Democratic poll results, 152; 1988 precaucus spending, 165; strategy of, 141
Bailey, Douglas, 166
Baker, Howard: 1979 Republican precaucus campaigning, 86; 1980 Republican precaucus activity, 82-84; 1980 Republican precinct caucuses,

90, 94; 1988 Republican precaucus
activity, 154
Baker, Russell, 111
balloting (secret), 29
Barbour, Haley, 244
Bauer, Gary L.: 1999 Iowa straw poll,
262; 1999-2000 *Des Moines Register*
Republican Iowa Poll results, 267;
2000 Republican radio and TV advertising, 264-265; 2000 Republican
precinct caucus results, 267-269
Bayh, Birch, 65; 1976 Democratic
precinct caucus results, 68-70; 1976
media projections for, 65-66; 1976
straw poll and, 60
Bayh, Evan: 2008 Democratic precaucus activity, 310
Beardsley, Harry, 40
Bedell, Berkley, 116
Belgian endive suggestion, 142
Bennett, William, 204
Bentsen, Lloyd: 1976 Democratic
presidential nomination and, 61;
1976 media projections for, 65-66;
1992 presidential nominations and,
186
Biden, Joe: 1988 Democratic precaucus activity and, 138-139; 1988
Democratic precaucus polling
results, 143, 146, 148-149; 1988
precaucus spending of, 165; 2008
Democratic precaucus activity, 311;
2008 Democratic *Des Moines Register* debate, 325; 2008 *Des Moines
Register* Iowa Poll results, 325-326;
2008 Democratic radio and TV
advertising, 326-327; 2008 precinct
caucus results, 328-331
bonus delegates, 244
Bork, Robert, 135, 147
Bradley, Bill, 186; 2000 Democratic
campaign, 270-279; 1999 *Des
Moines Register* Democratic Iowa
Poll results, 271; 2000 Democratic
campaign organization, 271-272;
1999 Jefferson-Jackson Day dinner,
272-273; 2000 Democratic radio
and TV advertising expenditures,
273-274; 2000 *Des Moines Register*

debate, 274-275; 2000 Iowa Brown
and Black Coalition debate, 275;
1999-2000 *Des Moines Register*
Democratic Iowa Poll results, 276;
2000 Democratic precinct caucus
results, 276-279
Branstad, Terry, 18; 1987 "Jobs,
Growth and Competitiveness" task
force, 142; 1994 Iowa elections and,
201; 1996 Caucus Kickoff, 216;
"Cavalcade of Governors," 229;
reorganization plan of, 15
broadcast media. *See* media
broadcast media coverage, 4, 6; 1976
Democratic precinct caucuses,
69-70; 1980 Democratic precinct
caucuses, 98-99; 1980 Republican
precinct caucuses, 91-96; 1984
Democratic precinct caucuses,
122-126; 1984 *Des Moines Register*
debate, 118-120; 1988 comparison before and after Iowa events,
176; 1988 Democratic precaucus
debates, 144, 146; 1988 Democratic precinct caucuses, 149; 1988
premature declaration of winners,
170; 1988 Republican precaucus
activity, 161-162; 1988 Republican
precinct caucuses, 166-168; 1992
Democratic precinct caucuses, 196-
197; 1996 Democratic precaucus
activity, 233-234; 1996 Republican
precaucus activity, 215; 2000 *Des
Moines Register* Democratic debate,
274-275; 2000 *Des Moines Register*
Republican debate, 265-266; 2000
WHO presidential debate, 264-265;
2004 *Des Moines Register* presidential debate, 294; 2007 *Des Moines
Register* Democratic debate, 325;
2007 *Des Moines Register* Republican
debate, 321; and Bruce Babbitt, 141;
"Cavalcade of Governors," 229; effect of Super Tuesday on, 136-137;
and Malcolm (Steve) Forbes, Jr.,
224-226; and Pat Buchanan, 209.
See also media coverage
Brown, Jerry: 1979 Democratic precaucus campaigning and, 88; 1992

Democratic precaucus activity and, 190-191, 195; 1992 Democratic precinct caucuses results, 195

Brown, Ron, 21

Brownback, Sam: 2007 *Des Moines Register* Republican Iowa Poll results, 321-322; 2007 Iowa straw poll results, 319; 2008 Republican debate at Drake University, 318; 2008 Republican Lincoln Day Unity Dinner, 317; 2008 Republican precaucus activity, 307; 2008 precinct caucus results, 328-332; 2008 Republican Presidential Candidates Forum, 317

Buchanan, Pat, 22; 1992 Republican precaucus activity and, 194; 1992 Republican precinct caucuses and, 197-198; 1996 Caucus Kickoff, 215-218; 1996 *Des Moines Register* Iowa Poll and, 215, 219, 227, 232, 247; 1996 GOP "Star-Spangled Preview" and, 204-205; 1996 Iowa Right-to-Life Convention and, 223-224; 1996 precaucus campaign activity and spending, 236; 1996 Republican precaucus activity and, 208-209, 231; 1996 Republican precinct caucus results, 238-242; 1996 Republican spending at WHO-TV and KCCI-TV, 226-227; 1999 Iowa straw poll, 262; 2000 Republican precaucus campaign activity, 258-259

budgets. *See* campaign spending

Buell, Emmett, Jr., 204

Bumpers, Dale, 141

Bush, George, 22; 1980 Republican precaucus activity, 82-84; 1980 Republican precinct caucuses and, 90, 93-97; 1988 caucus difficulties, 245-246; 1988 postcaucus coverage, 175-176; 1988 precaucus activities, 153-154, 157; 1988 precaucus spending, 165; 1988 Republican caucus straw-poll results, 173-174; 1988 Republican "Cavalcade of Stars" and, 160; 1988 Republican spending for TV ads and, 162; 1992

Republican precaucus activity and, 185-186, 194; on significance of Iowa caucuses, 81

Bush, George W., 303-304; 1999 Iowa straw poll, 262; 1999-2000 *Des Moines Register* Republican Iowa Poll results, 267; 2000 Republican precaucus campaign activity, 259-260; 2000 Republican precinct caucus results, 267-269; 2000 Republican radio and TV advertising, 264-265

California scheduling rules, 187

campaign spending: 1980 precaucus, 90-91; 1984 precaucus, 120-121; 2008 precaucus, 326-327; impact upon Iowa's economics, 101; limits, 235

Campbell, Bonnie: 1988 criticism of NES by, 170; 1994 Iowa elections and, 201; 1996 Democratic precaucus activity, 233

Campbell, Edward, 105

candidate preference group: Democrats use of, 338-339. *See also* presidential preference polls

Carlson, Arne, 229

Carter, Jimmy: 1976 Democratic precaucus activities, 58, 60; 1976 Democratic precinct caucus results, 68-70; 1976 media projections for, 65-66; 1980 "Cess Poll," 98-99; 1980 Democratic precinct caucuses, 87-90; benefits from media coverage, 76; impact on precinct caucuses, 337-338; Iranian hostage crisis and, 86-87; Jefferson-Jackson Day and, 62-63; national delegate equivalents and, 73; presidential campaign strategy of, 137-138

caucus and convention systems: historical aspects, 25-27; modern aspects, 27-28

caucuses, 71; abuses of, 25; eligibility, 29; historical aspects, 25-27; locations, 62; regulations of, 28-29, 131-132, 186-187; return headquarters of, 43; validity of results, 70-73

Caucus Kickoff '96, 206, 215-218. *See*

also precinct caucuses *for specific dates*
caucus reform. *See* reform decisions; regulations
"Cavalcade of Governors," 229
"Cavalcade of Stars," 160, 215
CBS: 1976 coverage of Democratic precinct caucuses, 69-70; 1980 coverage of precinct caucuses, 91-93; 1984 reduced coverage of precinct caucuses, 122-123; 1988 coverage of Iowa and New Hampshire, 167-168; 1992 coverage of Democratic precinct caucuses, 196; 1996 coverage of Iowa and New Hampshire, 237
census data, 19-21, 41
"Cess Poll" of 1980, 98-99
Cheney, Dick, 204-205
Chisholm, Shirley, 49
Christian Broadcasting Network (CBN), 154-155
Christian Right: 1988 Republican precaucus activity and, 154-155; 1992 Republican precaucus activity and, 194; 1996 Republican precaucus activity and, 209, 221-223; 1996 Republican precinct caucuses and, 241-242; 2000 Republican precaucus activity, 263-264; Alan Keyes and, 212; representativeness of Iowa and, 23, 194. *See also* Robertson, Pat
civil rights issues, 117
Clark, Wesley: 2008 Democratic precaucus activity, 310
Clarke, George W., 27
Clinton, Bill: 1988 Democratic precaucus activity and, 142; 1992 Democratic precaucus activity and, 190, 195; 1992 Democratic precinct caucuses results, 195, 197; 1996 Democratic precaucus activity and, 233-235
Clinton, Hillary Rodham, 233; 2008 Democratic debate at Drake University, 323; 2008 Democratic precaucus activity, 313-314; 2008 *Des Moines Register* Democratic debate,

325; 2008 *Des Moines Register* Democratic Iowa Poll results, 325-326; 2008 Democratic radio and TV advertising, 326-327; 2008 Heartland Presidential Forum, 324-325; 2008 Iowa Brown and Black Presidential Forum, 325; 2008 Jefferson-Jackson Day dinner and, 324; 2008 precinct caucus results, 328-333
CMF&Z, 203
CNN: 1984 coverage of precinct caucuses, 122; 1996 coverage of Republican precaucus activity, 210; coverage of O. J. Simpson trial, 220-221
Code of Iowa, 28-29
Commission on Presidential Nominations, 103-106
Committee on House Administration, 131-132
computers, 96-97. *See also* tabulation systems
Connally, John: 1980 precinct caucuses and, 90; 1980 Republican precaucus activity, 82-84, 86; 1980 Republican precinct caucuses, 94
Conservatism: 1996 Republican party and, 221-224, 241-242; Alan Keyes and, 212; Pat Buchanan and, 209. *See also* Christian Right
Contract with America, 201
county conventions: 1968 delegate selection controversy and, 37-38; 1972 Democratic results, 51; county delegates selection, 27-28; Democratic selection of delegates to, 42-44; Republican selection of delegates to, 44. *See also* delegate selection
Cox, John: 2007 *Des Moines Register* Republican Iowa Poll results, 321-322; 2007 GOP Reagan Dinner; 2007 Iowa straw poll results, 319; 2008 Republican Lincoln Day Unity Dinner, 317; 2008 Republican precaucus activity, 307
Crane, Phillip, 82-84, 90, 94
Cranston, Alan: 1984 Democratic precaucus activity, 112; 1984

Democratic precaucus campaign
spending, 120-121; 1984 Democratic precinct caucuses, 126; 1984
Des Moines Register debate and, 118-
119; 1984 retention of early caucus
dates and, 105; 1988 Democratic
campaign spending, 149-150; questionable fund-raising techniques of,
114-116; STAR*PAC of 1983 and,
116-117; withdrawal for presidential candidacy of, 130
Craver, Roger, 166
Cuomo, Mario, 186

Daley, Richard J., 40-41
dark-horse candidacy, 76; Iowa caucuses and, 343; Tom Vilsack and,
312
Daschle, Tom: 2008 Democratic precaucus activity, 310-311
Day, Mike, 210-211
Dean, Howard: 2004 Democratic
campaign fund-raising, 291; 2004
Democratic platform, 286; 2004
Democratic precinct caucus results,
295-298; 2004 Democratic radio
and TV advertising, 291-293
death penalty issues, 14
debates: 1979 impact of cancellation,
90; 1984 *Des Moines Register,* 118-
120; 1988 Democratic precaucus
activity and, 144; 1988 *Des Moines
Register* Republican presidential,
163; 1996 Republican precaucus
activity and, 229-230; 2004 *Des
Moines Register* presidential, 294;
2008 *Des Moines Register* Republican
presidential, 321
DeConcini, Dennis, 131
delegate equivalents: 1972 Democratic
precinct caucuses, 48; 1976 Carter
campaign and, 70; 1988 Democratic precinct caucus and, 169; 1992
Democratic precinct caucuses and,
195-196; proportional representation and, 43; state, 69, 72, 245. *See
also* state delegate equivalents
delegate selection: 1980 Democratic
precinct caucuses and, 100-101;

1984 precinct caucuses and, 109; to
county conventions, 41-42; Democratic, 42-44; Democratic party
rules changes and, 4; effects of
large citizen participation upon, 93;
fifteen percent rule and, 71; media
projections of, 50-51; Republican,
44; residency requirement for counties, 37-38
delegates: bonus, 244; county, 27-28;
uncommitted, 49-51
Democratic caucuses: 1968, 37-38;
1972, 45-46, 48-53; 1976, 67-70;
1980, 98-101; 1984, 123-127; 1988,
168-172; 1992, 195-197; 2000, 269-
279; 2008, 328-333
Democratic National Committee
(DNC): 1996 Democratic precaucus
activity and, 233-234; 2008 caucuses and, 315-316; development
of 1992 schedules, 186-187; Hunt
Commission proposals and, 109;
nominating process regulations
and, 103-106
Democratic party: 1968 national convention, 41; 1976 national convention, 73; 1976 validity of precinct
results, 71-73; delegate selection
and, 30; effect of activists, 22; fifteen percent rule of, 71; growth in
Iowa, 18-19; News Election Service
and, 124; precinct caucuses and,
28-29; reforms, 4, 30, 32, 40-41
Democratic precaucus activities: 1976,
58, 60-63, 65-66; 1980, 87-90;
1984, 110-120; 1988, 137-144,
146-152; 1992, 191, 193-194; 1996,
233-235; 2000, 253-267; 2004, 283-
293; 2008, 303-314
demographics: 1996 GOP citizens,
241-242; candidate accessibility due
to, 101-102; grass-roots organization and, 81; Iowa profile, 19-23,
340
Des Moines, Iowa: role in caucus support, 101, 129
Des Moines Register debate: 1984, 118-
120; 1988, 144, 146, 163; 1996,
219, 229-230; 2000, 265-266, 274-

275; 2004, 294; 2008, 325
Des Moines Register Democratic Iowa
Polls: results, 14-15, 151-152, 214-
215, 276, 325-326; validity of, 246-
247. *See also* Jefferson-Jackson Day
DNC. *See* Democratic National Committee (DNC)
Dodd, Christopher: 2008 Democratic *Des Moines Register* debate,
325; 2008 Democratic precaucus
activity, 311; 2008 Democratic
radio and TV advertising, 326-327;
2008 *Des Moines Register* Iowa Poll
results, 325-326; 2008 Heartland
Presidential Forum, 324-325; 2008
Iowa Brown and Black Presidential
Forum, 325; 2008 precinct caucus
results, 328-331
Dole, Bob: 1980 Republican precaucus
activity, 82-84; 1980 Republican
precinct caucuses, 90, 94; 1988 Republican caucus straw-poll results,
173-174; 1988 Republican "Cavalcade of Stars" poll results, 160;
1988 Republican precaucus activity,
154; 1988 spending, 162, 165; 1996
Caucus Kickoff, 215-218; 1996
"Cavalcade of Governors," 229;
1996 *Des Moines Register* Iowa Poll
results, 215; 1996 Republican campaign activity and spending, 236;
1996 Republican precaucus activity,
205-206, 228; 1996 Republican
precinct caucus results, 238-239,
242; 1996 Republican spending at
WHO-TV and KCCI-TV, 226-227;
caucus outcome of, 22
Dole, Elizabeth: 1999 Iowa straw poll,
262; 2000 Republican precaucus
campaign activity, 257-258; *Des
Moines Register* Iowa Poll and, 219,
227, 232; difficulties in 1996 caucuses, 245-246
Dornan, Bob: 1996 Caucus Kickoff,
215-216, 218; 1996 *Des Moines Register* Iowa Poll, 215, 219, 227, 232;
1996 Republican precaucus activity,
212, 236; 1996 Republican precinct
caucus results, 238, 240; 1996 Republican spending at WHO-TV and

KCCI-TV, 226-227
Dukakis, Michael: 1988 Democratic
campaign spending, 149-151,
165; 1988 Democratic precaucus
activity, 142-144, 146-152; 1988
Democratic precinct caucus results,
169, 171-172; 1988 *Des Moines Register* Iowa Poll results, 152; caucus
outcome, 22
duPont, Pete: 1988 precaucus spending, 165; 1988 Republican caucus
straw-poll results, 173-174; 1988
Republican "Cavalcade of Stars"
poll results, 160; 1988 Republican
precaucus activity, 155; 1988 Republican spending for TV ads, 162

economic effects: from media coverage, 76; of Tom Harkin, 192
economics, 144, 146; 1996 precinct
caucuses and, 203; populism and,
138-139; state revenue of 1996, 201
Edgar, Jim, 229
Edwards, John: 2004 Democratic
campaign fund-raising, 291; 2004
Democratic platform, 284-285;
2004 Democratic precinct caucus
results, 295-298; 2004 Democratic
radio and TV advertising, 291-293;
2008 Democratic debate at Drake
University, 323; 2008 *Des Moines
Register* Democratic debate, 325;
2008 *Des Moines Register* Democratic Iowa Poll results, 325-326; 2008
Democratic precaucus activity, 312;
2008 Democratic radio and TV advertising, 326-327; 2008 Heartland
Presidential Forum, 324-325; 2008
Iowa Brown and Black Presidential
Forum, 325; 2008 Jefferson-Jackson
Day dinner and, 324; 2008 precinct
caucus results, 328-333
education, 15-16
election laws: Iowa General Assembly
and, 26-27. *See also* regulations
election projections. *See* media projections
Elwell, Marlene, 223, 229. *See also*
Christian Right
Emmetsburg, Iowa, 98-99

English, Emory, 25-26
Environmental Protection Agency (EPA), 212
Erbe, Norman, 229
ethnic groups: 1972 Democratic caucuses and, 53; inclusion in state delegations, 41; Iowa demographics and, 20
expenditures. *See* campaign spending

Farm Bureau, 23; 1984 precaucus activities, 117-118; farming issues, 136, 139, 201; Michael Dukakis and, 142
Feingold, Russ: 2008 Democratic precaucus activity, 311
Fernandez, Ben: 1980 Republican precaucus fundraising, 84; 1988 Republican "Cavalcade of Stars" poll results, 160; 1988 Republican precaucus activity, 158
fifteen percent viability rule, 71
Flansberg, James, 60
Forbes, Malcolm (Steve), Jr.: 1996 *Des Moines Register* Iowa Poll and, 227-228, 232; 1996 Republican precaucus campaign activity and spending, 213-214, 221, 236; 1996 Republican precinct caucus results, 238-239, 241; 1996 Republican spending at WHO-TV and KCCI-TV, 226-227; 1998 GOP "First in the Nation Gala," 254-255; 1999 Iowa straw poll, 262; 1999-2000 *Des Moines Register* Republican Iowa Poll results, 267; 2000 Republican precaucus campaign activity, 256; 2000 Republican precinct caucus results, 267-269; 2000 Republican radio and TV advertising, 264-265; on negative campaign, 243; paid advertising and, 224-226
Ford, Gerald: 1976 Republican precaucus activity, 66-67; 1976 Republican precinct caucuses, 73-74; media portrayal of, 6
Fordice, Kirk, 229
foreign policy issues, 135
forum: 2004 Democratic campaign forum period, 289-294

Freedom Council. *See* Robertson, Pat
Frist, Bill: 2008 Republican precaucus activity, 306
frontloading: 2008 caucuses and, 314-315, 342
Frum, David, 204
fund-raising: 1976 Democratic precinct caucuses, 60-62; 1976 Jefferson-Jackson Day dinner, 60-62; 1980 Jefferson-Jackson Day dinner, 89; 1980 precaucus expenditures and, 90-91; 1980 Republican precinct caucuses, 84-86; 1984 Democratic precinct caucuses and, 127; 1984 Jefferson-Jackson Day dinner, 114-116; 1988 Jefferson-Jackson Day dinner, 138-140; 1988 Republican "Cavalcade of Stars," 158-160; 1992 Jefferson-Jackson Day dinner, 191; 1996 Caucus Kickoff, 215-218; 1996 Democratic precinct caucuses, 233; 1996 GOP "Star-Spangled Preview," 204-205; 1996 Jefferson-Jackson Day dinner, 233; 1999 Jefferson-Jackson Day dinner, 272-273; 2000 Democratic campaign, 271, 275; 2000 Republican campaign, 266; 2003 Democratic National fund raising, 291; 2003 Jefferson-Jackson Day dinner, 290; 2004 Democratic campaign, 288; 2007 Iowa Straw Poll; 2008 Jefferson-Jackson Day dinner, 324; Malcolm Forbes's 1996 self-financing, 213-214

gambling issues, 202
gender groups: 1972 Democratic caucuses and, 53; inclusion in state delegations, 41; Iowa demographics and, 20
general assembly. *See* Iowa General Assembly
Gephardt, Richard: 1988 Democratic campaign spending, 149-151; 1988 Democratic precaucus activity, 137-138; 1988 Democratic precaucus polling results, 143, 146, 148-149; 1988 Democratic precinct caucus results, 169, 171-172; 1988 *Des*

Moines Register Democratic Iowa
Poll results, 152; 1988 precaucus
spending of, 165; 1992 presidential
nominations and, 186; 2004 Democratic campaign fund-raising, 291;
2004 Democratic platform, 285;
2004 Democratic precinct caucus
results, 295-298; 2004 Democratic
radio and TV advertising, 291-293;
Hyundai TV commercial of, 150-
151
Gifford, Charles, 105
Gilmore, Jim: 2007 *Des Moines Register*
Republican Iowa Poll results, 321-
322; 2008 Republican Lincoln Day
Unity Dinner, 317; 2008 Republican precaucus activity, 306; 2008
Republican Presidential Candidates
Forum, 317
Gingrich, Newt: 2008 Republican
precaucus activity, 305-306
Giuliani, Rudy: 2007 *Des Moines Register* Republican Iowa Poll results,
321-322; 2007 Iowa straw poll
results, 319; 2008 *Des Moines Register* Republican presidential debate,
321; 2008 Republican debate at
Drake University, 318; 2008 Republican Lincoln Day Unity Dinner,
317; 2008 Republican precaucus
activity, 307; 2008 Republican precinct caucus results, 328-331; 2008
Republican Presidential Candidates
Forum, 317; 2008 Republican radio
and TV advertising, 326-327
Glenn, John: 1984 Democratic precaucus activity, 112-113, 115-116; 1984
Democratic precaucus campaign
spending, 120-121; 1984 Democratic precinct caucuses, 126-127; 1984
Des Moines Register debate and, 118-
120; 1984 retention of early caucus
dates and, 105; STAR*PAC of 1983
and, 116; withdrawal for presidential candidacy of, 130
GOP (Grand Old Party), 18; 1996 use
of media coverage, 203. *See also*
Republican Party
Gore, Albert, Jr.: 1988 Democratic pre-

caucus activity, 143; 1988 Democratic precaucus polling results,
143, 146, 148-149; 1988 Democratic precinct caucus results, 169; 1988
Des Moines Register Democratic Iowa
Poll results, 152; 1988 precaucus
spending of, 165; 1992 presidential nominations and, 186; 1996
Democratic precaucus activity,
233-235; 1999 *Des Moines Register*
Democratic Iowa Poll results, 271;
1999 Jefferson-Jackson Day dinner,
272-273; 1999-2000 *Des Moines
Register* Democratic Iowa Polls,
276; 2000 Democratic campaign,
269-279; 2000 Democratic precinct
caucus results, 276-279; 2000
Democratic spending for TV and
radio ads, 273-274; 2000 *Des Moines
Register* debate, 274-275; 2000 Iowa
Brown and Black Coalition debate,
275; views on STAR*PAC, 147
governors of Iowa, 18
Gramm, Phil: 1996 Caucus Kickoff,
215-218; 1996 *Des Moines Register*
Iowa Poll results, 215, 219, 227,
232; 1996 GOP "Star-Spangled
Preview" and, 205; 1996 Republican precaucus campaign activity,
206-207, 222-224, 230-231; 1996
Republican precaucus spending,
226-227, 236; 1996 Republican pre-
cinct caucus results, 238-240, 242
Grassley, Charles, 230-231
grass-roots politics, 81-82
Gravel, Mike: 2008 Democratic precaucus activity, 311-312; 2008 *Des
Moines Register* Democratic Iowa
Poll Results, 325-326; 2008 precinct
caucus results, 328-331
Graves, Bill, 229
Gulf War. *See* Persian Gulf War

Hagel, Chuck: 2008 Republican precaucus activity, 306
Haig, Alexander: 1988 Republican
caucus straw-poll results, 173-174;
1988 Republican "Cavalcade of
Stars" poll results, 160; 1988 Repub-

lican precaucus activity, 154, 156; 1988 Republican precaucus spending, 162, 165

Harding, William L., 27

Harkin, Tom: 1992 Democratic precaucus activity, 188-191, 193-194; 1992 Democratic precinct caucus results, 195, 197

Harris, Fred: 1976 Democratic precinct caucus results, 68-70; 1976 media projections for, 65-66; 1976 straw poll and, 60-61

Hart, Gary: 1972 Democratic caucuses, 46, 50; 1984 Democratic precaucus activity and spending, 112, 115, 120-121; 1984 Democratic precinct caucuses, 126-127; 1984 Des Moines Register debate results, 118-119; 1988 Democratic campaign spending of, 150, 165; 1988 Democratic precaucus activity and, 138-139; 1988 Democratic precaucus polling results, 143, 148-149; 1988 Democratic precinct caucus results, 169, 172; 1988 departure from presidential race, 143; 1988 Des Moines Register Democratic Iowa Poll results, 152; funding benefit from media coverage, 127; STAR*PAC of 1983 and, 116

Hatch, Orrin: 1999 Iowa straw poll, 262; 1999-2000 Des Moines Register Republican Iowa Polls, 267; 2000 Republican precaucus campaign activity, 259; 2000 Republican precinct caucus results, 267-269; 2000 Republican radio and TV advertising, 264-265

Haughland, Jean, 105

Haus, Bob, 207

Heslop, Kate, 158-160

Hollings, Ernest: 1984 Democratic precaucus activity, 113, 115-116; 1984 Democratic precinct caucuses, 126; 1984 Des Moines Register debate and, 118-120; 1984 precaucus campaign spending, 120-121; STAR*PAC of 1983 and, 116; withdrawal for presidential candidacy of, 130

homosexuality issues, 14

House Subcommittee on Telecommunication, Consumer Protection, and Finance, 125

Huckabee, Mike, 229; 2007 Des Moines Register Republican Iowa Poll results, 321-322; 2007 GOP Reagan Dinner, 320; 2007 Iowa straw poll results, 319; 2008 Des Moines Register Republican presidential debate, 321; 2008 precinct caucus results, 328-332; 2008 Republican debate at Drake University, 318; 2008 Republican Lincoln Day Unity Dinner, 317; 2008 Republican precaucus activity, 307-309; 2008 Republican Presidential Candidates Forum, 317; 2008 Republican radio and TV advertising, 326-327

Hughes, Harold: 1968 Democratic caucuses, 53; 1968 Democratic precinct caucuses, 38; endorsement by Edmund Muskie, 46

Humphrey, Hubert: 1968 Democratic National Convention, 41; 1972 Democratic caucuses, 46, 49; 1976 media projections for, 65-66; 1976 straw poll and, 60

Hunt Commission: 1984 precinct caucuses and, 109; Democratic National Committee and, 43. See also Commission on Presidential Nominations

Hunter, Duncan: 2007 Des Moines Register Republican Iowa Poll results, 321-322; 2007 GOP Reagan Dinner, 320; 2007 Iowa straw poll results, 319; 2008 Des Moines Register Republican presidential debate, 321; 2008 precinct caucus results, 328-331; 2008 Republican debate at Drake University, 318; 2008 Republican precaucus activity, 306-307; 2008 Republican Presidential Candidates Forum, 317; 2008 Republican radio and TV spending, 326-327

Hyde, Tim, 28

invisible primary, 204
Iowa Brown and Black Coalition presidential forum, 117, 275, 294, 325
Iowa Carter for President Steering Committee, 60
Iowa Christian Alliance: 2008 Republican Presidential Candidates Forum and, 317; creation of, 308-309
Iowa Christian Coalition, 194. *See also* Iowa Christian Alliance
Iowa Code. *See* Code of Iowa
Iowa Democratic Party: compliance with national party rules, 104-106; *Iowa Democratic Party Data Book,* 129
Iowa General Assembly, 28, 30; date of caucuses and, 30, 32; legislation for reporting caucus results, 168, 339; reform bills and, 26-27; regarding 1978 schedule of primaries, 77; reorganization plan of, 15
Iowa Political Handbook 1992, 194
Iowa Polls: 1996 Republican precaucus activity, 227; results of, 14-15. *See also Des Moines Register* Democratic Iowa Poll
Iowa State Education Association: endorsement of Howard Baker, 83; Jimmy Carter and, 88; support for Walter Mondale by, 111
Iowa: The Middle Land (Dorothy Schwieder), 11
Iran-Contra affair: and 1988 precaucus activity of George Bush, 153, 163
Iranian hostage crisis, 86, 90
issues: in 2004 political cycle, 283-284; in 2008 political cycle, 303-304; abortion, 14, 209, 212; civil rights, 117; death penalty, 14; economic populism, 138-139; family values, 202; farming, 117-118, 136, 139, 142, 201; foreign policy, 135; gambling, 202; gender, 14; nuclear disarmament, 112, 116-117, 143; welfare, 16. *See also* Right-to-Life Convention; special interest groups
Ivers, Drew, 223

Jackson, Henry: 1976 Democratic caucus results and, 68-69; 1976 media projections for, 65-66; 1976 straw poll and, 60-61
Jackson, Jesse: 1972 Democratic precinct caucuses, 49; 1984 Democratic precaucus activity, 113, 116; 1984 Democratic precaucus campaign spending, 120-121; 1984 Democratic precinct caucuses, 126; 1984 *Des Moines Register* debate and, 118-119; 1988 Democratic campaign spending, 150; 1988 Democratic precaucus activity, 139; 1988 Democratic precaucus polling results, 143, 146, 148-149; 1988 Democratic precinct caucus results, 169, 172; 1988 *Des Moines Register* Democratic Iowa Poll results, 152; 1988 precaucus spending, 165; 1992 presidential nominations and, 186; caucus outcome of, 22
Jacksonian democracy, 25
Jahn, Marie, 58, 60
Jefferson-Jackson Day: 1976 Democratic fund-raising and, 60-63, 65; 1980 Democratic fund-raising and, 89-90; 1984 Democratic fund-raising and, 114-116; 1988 Democratic fund-raising and, 138-140; 1992 Democratic fund-raising and, 191, 193; 1996 Democratic fund-raising and, 233; 2000 Democratic fund-raising and, 272-273; 2004 Democractic fund-raising and, 285; 2008 Democratic fund-raising and, 324
Johnson, Lyndon, 37-38
JS/Day and Associates publicity firm, 210-211
judgeships, 26
Junior Tuesday, 1990

Kasich, John R., 262
KCCI-TV (Des Moines): 1988 campaign advertising records at, 149-151; 1988 Republican spending at, 161-162; 1996 Democratic spending at, 234; 1996; 1996 Republican precaucus campaign spending at,

226-228; 2000 Republican spending at, 265; 2008 Republican and Democratic spending at, 326-327
Kean, Thomas, 205
Kefauver, Estes, 4
KEMB-FM radio (Emmetsburg, Iowa), 98-99
Kemp, Jack: 1988 precaucus spending, 165; 1988 Republican caucus straw-poll results, 173-174; 1988 Republican "Cavalcade of Stars" poll results, 160; 1988 Republican precaucus activity, 154-155; 1988 Republican spending for TV ads, 162; effect of 1996 "invisible primary" on, 204
Kennedy, John F., 6
Kennedy, Robert, 37-38
Kennedy, Ted: 1980 campaign and effect on media, 100; 1980 "Cess Poll" and, 98-99; 1980 Democratic precinct caucuses, 87-90; 1980 precinct caucuses, 90, 102
Kenyon, Bill, 211
Kerrey, Bob: 1992 Democratic precaucus activity, 189-190, 195; 1992 Democratic precinct caucuses results, 195; 1992 presidential nominations and, 186
Kerry, John: 2004 Democratic campaign fund-raising, 291; 2004 Democratic platform, 285; 2004 Democratic precinct caucus results, 295-298; 2004 Democratic radio and TV advertising, 291-293; 2008 Democratic precaucus activity, 310
Keyes, Alan: 1996 Caucus Kickoff, 215-218; 1996 Des Moines Register Iowa Poll and, 215, 219, 227, 232; 1996 Republican precaucus campaign activity and spending, 212, 236; 1996 Republican precinct caucus results, 238, 240, 242; 1996 Republican spending at WHO-TV and KCCI-TV, 226-227; 1998 GOP "First in the Nation Gala," 254-255; 1999 Iowa straw poll, 262; 1999-2000 Des Moines Register Republican Iowa Polls, 267; 2000 Republican pre-

caucus campaign activity, 256-257; 2000 Republican precinct caucus results, 267-269; 2000 Republican radio and TV advertising, 264-265; 2007 Des Moines Register Republican Iowa Poll results, 321-322; 2008 Des Moines Register Republican presidential debate, 321
Kinnock, Neil, 146
Kissinger, Henry, 83-84
Kraft, Tim, 60, 62
Kucinich, Dennis: 2004 Democratic campaign fund-raising, 291; 2004 Democratic platform, 286-287; 2004 Democratic precinct caucus results, 295-298; 2004 Democratic radio and TV advertising, 291-293; 2008 Democratic precaucus activity, 311-312; 2008 Des Moines Register Democratic Iowa Poll results, 325-326; 2008 Heartland Presidential Forum, 324-325; 2008 Iowa Brown and Black Presidential Forum, 325; 2008 precinct caucus results, 328-331

Langley, Monica, 175
LaRouche, Lyndon, 165
Laxalt, Paul: 1988 precaucus spending of, 165; 1988 Republican precaucus activity of, 154, 156-157
Lieberman, Joe: 2004 Democratic campaign fund-raising, 291; 2004 Democratic platform, 285-286
Lincoln Day Unity Dinner: 2008 Republican campaign, 317
lottery in Iowa, 202
Louisiana Republicans, 230
Lugar, Richard: 1996 Caucus Kickoff, 215-218; 1996 Des Moines Register Iowa Poll results, 215, 219, 227, 232; 1996 precaucus campaign activity and spending, 236; 1996 Republican precaucus activity, 210-211; 1996 Republican precinct caucus results, 238, 240; 1996 Republican spending at WHO-TV and KCCI-TV, 226-227

Martin, Lynn, 205
Massachusetts Miracle, 142
Masteller, Kathleen, 215-216
Matthews, Donald R., 57
Mayer, William G., 21-22
McCain, John: 1999 Iowa straw poll, 262; 1999-2000 *Des Moines Register* Republican Iowa Polls, 267; 2000 Republican precaucus campaign activity, 258; 2000 Republican precinct caucus results, 267-269; 2007 *Des Moines Register* Republican Iowa Poll results, 321-322; 2007 Iowa straw poll results, 319; 2008 *Des Moines Register* Republican presidential debate, 321; 2008 precinct caucus results, 328-332; 2008 Republican debate at Drake University, 318; 2008 Republican Lincoln Day Unity Dinner, 317; 2008 Republican precaucus activity, 307; 2008 Republican Presidential Candidates Forum, 317
McCarthy, Eugene: 1968 Democratic precinct caucuses and, 37-38, 40; 1972 Democratic caucuses and, 46, 49
McClosky, Herbert, 22
McCurdy, Dave, 186
McGovern, George: 1972 Democratic precinct caucuses, 48-49, 51-53; 1984 Democratic precaucus activity, 113-116; 1984 Democratic precaucus campaign spending, 120-121; 1984 *Des Moines Register* debate and, 118-119; 1992 presidential nominations and, 186; grass-roots campaign of, 57; impact on precinct caucuses, 337-338; withdrawal for presidential candidacy of, 130
McGovern-Fraser Commission, 41
media: bias, 7, 9; as candidates' liaison, 5, 7; contrivance of, 72; coverage of precinct caucuses, 340-341; emphasis on dark-horse candidate by, 246; exploitation of Iowa caucuses, 7; future implications of, 243-244; historical role in elections, 3

media coverage: 1968 Democratic National Convention, 41; 1968 Democratic precinct caucuses, 38; 1968 Republican precinct caucuses, 36; 1972 Democratic precinct caucuses, 45-46; 1972 Republican precinct caucuses, 53; 1976 Carter campaign, 60; 1976 Democratic precinct caucuses, 69-70; 1976 Jefferson-Jackson Day, 62-63; 1976 precinct caucuses, 66-70; 1976 Republican precinct caucuses, 73-74; 1976 straw poll, 60-61; 1980 Republican precinct caucuses, 91-98; 1984 Democratic precinct caucuses, 121-127; 1984 *Des Moines Register* debate, 118-120; 1984 Jefferson-Jackson Day, 114-116; 1984 Republican precinct caucuses, 129; 1987 Presidential Campaign Hotline, 166; 1988 Democratic precaucus debates, 144; 1988 impact on Gary Hart, 143, 148; 1988 Republican "Cavalcade of Stars" and, 158; 1988 Republican precaucus activity and, 161-162; 1992 Democratic precaucus activities, 193; 1992 Democratic precinct caucuses, 196-197; 1996 Caucus Kickoff, 217-218; 1996 Republican precaucus campaign spending for, 226-227; 2000 *Des Moines Register* debate, 274; 2004 *Des Moines Register* debate, 294; 2008 *Des Moines Register* debate, 325; control of, 131-132; county delegate selection, 42; demand for outcomes, 43; economic benefits from, 76; effects of paid advertising, 177-179, 242-243; emphasis of early electoral events by, 76-77; exposure of Joe Biden's plagiarism due to, 147; and grass-roots politics, 82; of Jimmy Carter and Iran, 86; political power of, 101-103; pressure to retain early caucus dates and, 104-106; pros and cons of front-runner status, 111; RAGBRAI (*Register* Annual Great Bicycle Ride Across Iowa) and, 140; STAR*PAC of 1983 and, 116-117 media projections: 1972 Democratic caucuses, 48-50; 1976 precaucus activity, 65-66; 1984 Democratic precinct caucuses, 124-125; national delegate equivalents and, 73; validity of, 50

mediality: Iowa precinct caucuses and, 7, 9

Merrill, Steve, 216, 229

Mills, George, 40

minority groups. See ethnic groups

Mondale, Walter: 1984 Democratic precaucus activity, 110-112, 114; 1984 Democratic precinct caucuses, 126-127; 1984 Des Moines Register debate, 118-120; 1984 diminished media coverage, 123; 1984 precaucus campaign spending, 120-121; 1988 Democratic campaign spending, 149-150; questionable fundraising techniques of, 114-116; STAR*PAC of 1983 and, 116

Muskie, Edmond: 1972 Democratic precinct caucuses, 45-46, 48-49, 51-53; media manipulation of campaign, 57

National Czech and Slovak Museum (Cedar Rapids, Iowa), 233

national delegate equivalents, 43, 48, 52. See also delegate equivalents; delegate selection

national delegates: and 1976 precinct caucuses, 69, 72

NBC: coverage of 1976 Democratic precinct caucuses, 69; coverage of 1980 precinct caucuses, 91; coverage of 1984 precinct caucuses, 122; coverage of 1992 Democratic precinct caucus, 196

New Hampshire: 1972 impact of caucuses and, 55; 1984 precinct caucuses in, 122-123; 1988 Bush campaign and, 176; 1988 CBS coverage of, 167-168; 1992 ranking of Tom Harkin in, 197-198; 1992 scheduling rules and, 186-187; CBS news stories on, 237; media coverage comparison with Iowa, 92-93; media coverage of Gart Hart

in, 131; scheduling dispute with Vermont, 103-104

News Election Service (NES), 98; 1988 Democratic precinct caucuses and, 168, 170; Democratic party and, 124

newspaper coverage: 1976 precinct caucuses, 66-70, 74; Jefferson-Jackson Day poll and, 62-63. See also print media coverage

New York Times coverage. See Apple, R. W.

Nixon, Richard, 36, 41

nominating process: impact of 1976 media coverage in Iowa on, 76-77; impact of 1980 precinct caucuses upon, 101-103; national party rules concerning, 77

nonpartisan viewpoints, 17

nuclear disarmament: 1984 precaucus activities, 112, 116-117; Albert Gore Jr., and, 143

Nunn, Sam, 186

Obama, Barack: 2008 Democratic debate at Drake University, 323; 2008 Democratic precaucus activity, 312-313; 2008 Democratic radio and TV advertising, 326-327; 2008 Des Moines Register Democratic debate, 325; 2008 Des Moines Register Democratic Iowa Poll results, 325-326; 2008 Heartland Presidential Forum, 324-325; 2008 Iowa Brown and Black Presidential Forum, 325; 2008 Jefferson-Jackson Day dinner and, 324; 2008 precinct caucus results, 328-333

party organization, 18; characteristics of caucus participants and, 21-22; delegate selection and, 30; precinct caucuses and, 28; of third-party candidates, 22-23

Pataki, George: 2008 Republican precaucus activity, 306

patriotism, 13-14

Patterson, Samuel C., 11

Patterson, Thomas, 7, 9

Paul, Ron: 2007 Des Moines Register Re-

publican Iowa Poll results, 321-322;
2007 GOP Reagan Dinner, 320;
2007 Iowa straw poll results, 319;
2008 *Des Moines Register* Republican presidential debate, 321; 2008
precinct caucus results, 328-331;
2008 Republican debate at Drake
University, 318; 2008 Republican precaucus activity, 307; 2008
Republican Presidential Candidates
Forum, 317; 2008 Republican radio
and TV spending, 326-327
People Encouraging Arms Control Efforts (PEACE), 116
Persian Gulf War: Bill Clinton and,
190; effect on 1992 caucuses, 185-186; George Bush and, 194
plagiarism, 146-147
Plissner, Martin. *See* CBS
political culture, 13; hierarchy of party
business, 17-18; of Iowa, 13-15;
moralistic influences upon, 19; of
third-party candidates, 22-23
political parties: minor, 17; New
Deal realignment and, 18. *See also*
Democratic party; Republican party
political process disruption, 7
political profiles of caucus participants, 21-22
polls: 1976 Jefferson-Jackson Day,
60-63; 1980 Jefferson-Jackson Day,
89-90; 1984 Jefferson-Jackson Day,
114-116; 1984 public opinion, 116;
1988 Democratic precaucus activity
and, 138-140, 143, 146, 148-149;
1988 *Des Moines Register* Iowa
Democratic results, 151-152; 1988
Jefferson-Jackson Day, 138-140;
1988 Republican precaucus activity and, 157-158, 161, 164; 1992
Jefferson-Jackson Day, 191, 193;
1992 lack of, 192; 1992 presidential
preference, 193; 1996 *Des Moines
Register* Iowa Poll, 214-215; 1996
Jefferson-Jackson Day, 233; Christian Right and, 221-222; early election projections and, 125; validity
of, 246-247. *See also* straw polls
Pomper, Gerald, 135

Powell, Colin, 220-221
Powell, Jody, 58
prayer in schools, 14
precaucus activities (1976): Democratic party, 58, 60-63, 64-66, 67-73;
Gerald Ford and, 66-67; impact of,
75-77; location regulation, 67; media projections, 65-66; Republican
party, 66-67, 73-75; Ronald Reagan
and, 66-67; validity of results, 70-73
precaucus activities (1980), 90;
Democratic party, 98-101; Democratic precaucus activity, 81, 87-90;
impact upon presidential nominating process, 101-103; Jimmy Carter
and, 87-90; Republican party, 93-96; Republican precaucus activity,
81-87; Ted Kennedy and, 87-90;
validity of results, 96-98
precaucus activities (1984): civil rights
issues, 117; *Des Moines Register* debate, 118-120; farm issues, 117-118;
nuclear disarmament, 112, 116-117; Republican precaucus activity,
120; STAR*PAC of 1983, 116-117
precaucus activities (1988): debates,
144; Democratic and Republican
precaucus spending, 165; Democratic party, 137-144, 146-152;
Republican party, 153-163; Seven
Dwarfs and, 144, 146; validity of
results, 168
precaucus activities (1992): Democratic party, 191, 193-194; Republican
party, 194
precaucus activities (2000), 253-267,
269-276; bonus delegates, 253-254;
caucus date changes, 254; early
certification, 253
precaucus activities (2004), 284-298
precaucus activities (2008): Democratic party, 309-314, 322-325; *Des
Moines Register* Democratic debate,
325; *Des Moines Register* Republican
debate, 321; frontloading, 314-316;
Republican party, 305-309, 316-322
precinct caucuses: function and
regulations of, 28-29, 41-42. *See also*
caucuses

precinct caucuses (1968): impact of, 39-40; Republican party and, 35, 53
precinct caucuses (1976): results, 68-69
precinct caucuses (1984): Democratic precaucus activity, 110-120; Hunt Commission proposals and, 109; impact of, 129-131; results, 126
precinct caucuses (1988): impact of, 177-180; media coverage and, 166; presidential preference poll and, 172-173; Republican party, 172-177
precinct caucuses (1992): Democratic party, 195-197; impact of, 198; Republican party, 197-198
precinct caucuses (1996): impact of, 245-247; results, 238
precinct caucuses (2000): impact of, 279-280; results, 276-279
precinct caucuses (2004): impact of, 298-299; results, 295-298
preference polls. *See* presidential preference polls
Presidential Campaign Hotline, 166
presidential nominating process: 1984 Republican precinct caucuses and, 128; impact of 1980 precinct caucuses upon, 101-103; importance of television and, 5-6; regulations, 103-106; results of 1984 Democratic precinct caucuses, 126-127. *See also* regulations
presidential preference polls, 27; 1984 News Election Service and, 124; 1988 Republican precinct caucuses and, 172-173; 1992 Democratic precaucus activities and, 193-194; Republican party and, 44
presidential primaries. *See* primary elections
Pressler, Larry, 84
primary elections: control of season length and, 131-132, 136; importance of, 4-5; Iowa General Assembly and, 26-27; New Hampshire/Vermont dispute, 103-104. *See also* regulations
print media coverage: 1976 Demo-
cratic precinct caucus, 69; 1976 Republican precinct caucus, 74; 1980 Democratic precinct caucuses, 88, 99-100; 1980 Republican precinct caucuses, 93-94; 1984 Democratic precinct caucuses, 123-127, 125-127; 1984 *Des Moines Register* debate, 118-120; 1984 Jefferson-Jackson Day, 115-116; 1988 Democratic delegate equivalents, 170; 1988 Democratic precaucus debates, 144; 1988 Republican precinct caucuses, 166, 170; 1992 Democratic precaucus activity, 189-190; 1992 Democratic precinct caucuses, 197; 1996 Democratic precaucus activity, 233-234; 1996 Republican precaucus activity, 227, 229; 1996 Republican precinct caucus results, 239. *See also* media coverage
pro-choice. *See* abortion issue
public relations firms, 203, 210-211
publican opinion polls. *See* straw polls

Quayle, Dan, 204, 216; 1998 GOP "First in the Nation Gala," 254-255; 1999 Iowa straw poll, 262; 2000 Republican precaucus campaign activity, 257

RAGBRAI *(Register* Annual Great Bicycle Ride Across Iowa), 140
Rainbow Coalition, 139
Ranney, Austin, 18
Rapoport, Ronald, 21-22
Rasmussen, Clark, 38-39
Ray, Robert, 18, 74, 229
Reagan, Ronald: 1968 Republican precinct caucuses, 36; 1976 Republican precaucus activity, 66-67; 1976 Republican precinct caucuses, 73-74; 1980 Republican precaucus activity, 82; 1980 Republican precinct caucuses, 90, 93-97; 1984 Republican precaucus campaign activity and spending, 120-121; 1984 Republican precinct caucuses and, 128; effect upon GOP and politics, 135; impact of limited Iowa precaucus

appearances, 82, 84-87, 96, 102
reform decisions: 1972 Democratic
caucuses and, 53; of Democratic
party, 40-41; Iowa General Assembly and, 26-27; resulting in Iowa's
prominence, 30, 32
regulations: 1984 media projection
infractions, 124-125; 1992 primary
and caucus scheduling, 186-187;
1996 Caucus Kickoff results, 218-
219; Code of Iowa and, 28-29;
disinterest by Republican party
regarding length of caucus season,
31; governing caucus conduct,
71; Iowa General Assembly and,
26-27, 30, 32, 77, 168; of length of
primaries and caucuses, 131-132;
of presidential nominating process,
103-106; regarding reporting of
caucus results, 168; Task Force on
Primaries and Caucuses and, 244
reliability: of 1980 tabulation system,
96-97; media disregard for, 169; of
media projections, 51-52
reporting and analysis systems, 43. *See
also* tabulation system
representativeness: at 1972 Democratic caucuses, 53; importance at
grass-roots level, 41; of Iowa, 21-23;
third-party candidates and, 22-23
Republican caucuses: 1968, 35-37;
1972, 53; 1976, 73-75; 1980, 93-96;
1984, 129; 1988, 172-177; 1992,
197-198; 1996, 237-245; 2000, 254-
269; 2008, 328-333
Republican Council, 154
Republican Party: 1988 "Cavalcade
of Stars" fundraiser, 158-160; 1996
"Cavalcade of Governors," 229;
1996 control of Congress, 201; 1998
GOP "First in the Nation Gala,"
254-255; delegate selection and, 30;
dominance in Iowa, 18-19; effect of
activists, 22; effect of Ronald Reagan upon, 135; limited role in media coverage, 131; precinct caucuses
and, 28-29; presidential preference
poll and, 44; regulations concerning
scheduling of events, 230, 244

Republican precaucus activities: 1976,
66-67; 1980, 81-87; 1984, 120;
1988, 153-163; 1992, 194; 1996,
204-233; 2000, 254-267; 2008,
305-309
research on caucuses, 21-22
residency requirements, 37-38
Richardson, Bill: 2008 Democratic precaucus activity, 311; 2008 Democratic radio and TV advertising,
326-327; 2008 *Des Moines Register*
Democratic debate, 325; 2008 *Des
Moines Register* Democratic Iowa
Poll results, 325-326
Right-to-Life Convention (1996),
223-224
Right-to-Life groups, 23. *See also* Conservatism
Robertson, Pat, 221; 1988 disproportionate support of, 179-180;
1988 impact on GOP, 22, 176-177;
1988 Republican caucus straw-poll
results, 173-174; 1988 Republican
"Cavalcade of Stars" poll results,
160; 1988 Republican precaucus
activity of, 154-155, 158-159; 1988
Republican precaucus spending,
162, 165
Robinson, Michael J., 7, 70
Rockefeller, Jay, 186
Rockefeller, Nelson, 36
Rodgers, Guy, 223
Roehrick, John, 193, 195
Rollins, Ed, 151
Romney, Mitt: 2007 *Des Moines Register* Republican Iowa Poll results,
321-322; 2007 Iowa straw poll
results, 319; 2008 *Des Moines Register* Republican presidential debate,
321; 2008 precinct caucus results,
328-332; 2008 Republican debate at
Drake University, 318; 2008 Republican Lincoln Day Unity Dinner,
317; 2008 Republican precaucus
activity, 307-308; 2008 Republican
Presidential Candidates Forum,
317; 2008 Republican radio and TV
advertising, 326-327
Rumsfeld, Donald, 154, 156, 165

rural populations, 20. *See also* demographics

salaries of politicians, 16
same-sex marriage, 14
Sanford, Terry, 61, 65-66
Schafer, Ed, 229
Scheffler, Steve, 222
Schmett, Jeanette, 210-211
Schneider, William, 136
Schreurs & Associates, 203
Schroeder, Patricia, 186
Schwarm, Richard, 211
Schwieder, Dorothy, 11
Sears, John, 102-103
secret ballotting, 29
Seven-Hundred (700) Club. *See* Robertson, Pat
Shapp, Milton, 61, 65-66
Shogan, Robert, 174
Shriver, Sargent, 60-61, 65-66, 68-70
Simon, Paul: 1988 Democratic campaign spending, 149-151, 165; 1988 Democratic polling results, 143, 146, 148-149; 1988 Democratic precaucus activity, 141; 1988 Democratic precinct caucus results, 169, 171-172; 1988 *Des Moines Register* Democratic Iowa poll results, 152
Smith, Bob: 1998 GOP "First in the Nation Gala," 254-255; 1999 Iowa straw poll, 262; 2000 Republican precaucus campaign activity, 257
social welfare, 16
special interest groups, 23
Specter, Arlen: 1996 Caucus Kickoff, 215-218; 1996 *Des Moines Register* Iowa Poll results, 215, 219, 227; 1996 GOP "Star-Spangled Preview," 204-205; 1996 Republican precaucus campaign activity and spending, 209-210, 214, 226-227, 236
STAR*PAC (Stop the Arms Race Political Action Committee of Iowa), 116, 147
Stassen, Harold, 4, 84
state delegate equivalents, 43, 69, 72; 1972 Democratic precinct caucuses and, 48; 1976 Carter campaign and, 70; 1988 Democratic precinct caucus and, 169
Stedman, Murray S., Jr., 18
Stone, Walter, 21-22
straw polls: 1972 Democratic caucuses and, 53; 1976 Carter campaign and, 60; 1976 Republican precinct caucuses and, 73-75; 1980 Republican precinct caucuses and, 83-85, 93-95; 1984 delegate equivalents, 124; 1984 Democratic precaucus activities and, 114, 116; 1988 Republican caucuses and, 172-173; 1988 Republican "Cavalcade of Stars," 158-160; 1992 lack of, 192, 197-198; 1996 Caucus Kickoff, 206, 215-218; 1996 GOP "Star-Spangled Preview," 205; 1996 impact of GOP results, 237-238; 1996 Republican caucus results by county, 240; 1999 Iowa straw poll, 260-263; 2008 Republican Iowa straw poll, 318-319; New Hampshire/Vermont scheduling dispute and, 103-104; Republican party's delegate selection and, 44. *See also* polls
Super Tuesday, 21; 1988 addition of, 136; 1992, 190; 1996, 202; 2000 Gore campaign, 269
Swift, Al, 125

tabulation systems: 1992 Democratic precinct caucuses and, 195; fallibility of, 96-98, 123-124
Tancredo, Tom: 2007 *Des Moines Register* Republican Iowa Poll results, 321-322; 2007 GOP Reagan Dinner, 320; 2007 Iowa straw poll results, 319; 2008 *Des Moines Register* Republican presidential debate, 321; 2008 precinct caucus results, 328-331; 2008 Republican debate at Drake University, 318; 2008 Republican Lincoln Day Unity Dinner, 317; 2008 Republican precaucus activity, 306; 2008 Republican Presidential Candidates Forum, 317; 2008 Republican radio and TV advertising, 326-327

Task Force on Elections, 131-132
Task Force on Primaries and Caucuses, 244
taxes, 15
Taylor, Maurice (Morry): 1996 Caucus Kickoff, 215-216, 218; 1996 *Des Moines Register* Iowa Poll results, 219, 227, 232; 1996 Republican precaucus activity, 211, 216, 231, 236; 1996 Republican precinct caucus results, 238, 240; 1996 Republican spending at WHO-TV and KCCI-TV, 226-227
third-party candidates, 22
Thomas, William M., 125
Thompson, Fred: 2007 *Des Moines Register* Republican Iowa Poll results, 321-322; 2007 GOP Reagan Dinner, 320; 2007 Iowa straw poll results, 319; 2008 *Des Moines Register* Republican presidential debate, 321; 2008 precinct caucus results, 328-331; 2008 Republican precaucus activity, 307-309; 2008 Republican Presidential Candidates Forum, 317; 2008 Republican radio and TV advertising, 326-327
Thompson, Tommy, 215, 219; 2007 *Des Moines Register* Republican Iowa Poll results, 321-322; 2007 Iowa straw poll results, 319; 2008 Republican debate at Drake University, 318; 2008 Republican Lincoln Day Unity Dinner, 317; 2008 Republican precaucus activity, 306; 2008 Republican Presidential Candidates Forum, 317
Titan Tire Co. (Des Moines), 211
Tramontina, Mike, 234
Tsongas, Paul: 1992 Democratic precaucus activity, 188, 195; 1992 Democratic precinct caucuses results, 195, 197

Udall, Morris, 76-77; 1976 Democratic precinct caucus results, 68-70; 1976 media projections for, 65-66; 1976 straw poll and, 60-61; national delegate equivalents and, 73; regu-lation of length of primaries and caucuses, 131-132
uncommitted groups, 42-43, 49-51
United Auto Workers, 111
urbanization's influence on politics, 18-20

validity: of 1976 caucus attendance figures, 70-73; of 1980 Jefferson-Jackson Day poll, 89; of 1980 Republican caucus results, 96-98; of 1984 Democratic precinct caucuses, 123-124; of 1984 Jefferson-Jackson Day poll, 114-115; of 1984 News Election Service, 124; of 1988 Democratic precinct caucuses, 168; of 1996 broadcast media, 224-226; of 1996 Republican caucus attendance, 242; of Iowa as 1996 predictor, 203; of media projections and polls, 50, 246-247
Vermont scheduling dispute with New Hampshire, 103-104
Vietnam War, 37-38, 40-41
Vilsack, Tom: 2008 Democratic precaucus activity, 311-312
Voinovich, George, 229
vote counting services. *See* News Election Service (NES); tabulation systems
Voter News Service (VNS), 241-242
voting procedures, 19, 29

Wallace, George, 61, 65-66
Warner, Mark: 2008 Democratic precaucus activity, 310
Washington Post. See Witcover, Jules
Watergate, 57, 67
weighting of delegate equivalents, 43-44
welfare, 16
"Where's the beef?" slogan, 138-139
Whitney, Tom, 3; 1976 Republican precinct caucuses, 58, 67-68, 70-71, 75; impact on Democratic caucuses, 338; Jefferson-Jackson Day dinner and, 62
WHO radio (Des Moines): and Ronald Reagan, 82

WHO-TV (Des Moines): 1988 campaign advertising records at, 149-151; 1988 Republican spending at, 161-162; 1996 Democratic spending at, 234; 1996 Republican precaucus campaign spending at, 226-228; 2000 Republican spending at, 265; 2004 Democratic spending at, 292; 2008 Democratic and Republican spending at, 326-327

Wilder, L. Douglas, 188-189, 195

Wills, Garry, 177

Wilson, Pete: 1996 Caucus Kickoff, 215-218; 1996 *Des Moines Register* Iowa Poll, 215, 219, 227; 1996 precaucus campaign activity and spending, 236; 1996 Republican precaucus activity, 213-214; 1996 Republican spending at WHO-TV and KCCI-TV, 226-227

Wirth, Tim, 125

Witcover, Jules: 1976 Democratic precinct caucus results and, 68-69; 1976 Jefferson-Jackson Day poll and, 63; Muskie campaign and, 57-58